T0336035

A Selection of Image Analysis Techniques

This book focuses on seven commonly used image analysis techniques. It covers aspects from basic principles and practical methods, to new advancement of each selected technique to help readers solve image-processing related problems in real-life situations.

The selected techniques include image segmentation, segmentation evaluation and comparison, saliency object detection, motion analysis, mathematical morphology methods, face recognition and expression classification. The author offers readers a three-step strategy toward problem-solving: first, essential principles; then, a detailed explanation; and finally, a discussion on practical and working techniques for specific tasks. He also encourages readers to make full use of available materials from the latest developments and trends.

This is an excellent book for those who do not have a complete foundation in image technology but need to use image analysis techniques to perform specific tasks in particular applications.

Yu-Jin Zhang is a tenured professor of image engineering at Tsinghua University, Beijing, China. He earned his PhD in Applied Science from the State University of Liège, Belgium. He was a post-doc fellow of Delft University of Technology, Delft, the Netherlands. He is also a CSIG and SPIE fellow. Dr. Zhang has published 50 books and more than 500 research papers.

A Selection of Image Analysis Techniques

Techniques

From Fundamental to Research Front

Yu-Jin Zhang

CRC Press
Taylor & Francis Group
Boca Raton London New York

CRC Press is an imprint of the
Taylor & Francis Group, an **informa** business

First edition published 2023
by CRC Press
6000 Broken Sound Parkway NW, Suite 300, Boca Raton, FL 33487-2742

and by CRC Press
4 Park Square, Milton Park, Abingdon, Oxon, OX14 4RN

CRC Press is an imprint of Taylor & Francis Group, LLC

© 2023 Yu-jin Zhang

Library of Congress Cataloguing-in-Publication Data
Names: Zhang, Yu-Jin, 1954-author.
Title: A selection of image analysis techniques : from fundamental to research front / Yu-Jin Zhang.
Description: First edition. | Boca Raton : CRC Press, 2023. | Includes bibliographical references and index. |
Identifiers: LCCN 2022016652 (print) |
LCCN 2022016653 (ebook) | ISBN 9781032351094 (hardback) |
ISBN 9781032351162 (paperback) | ISBN 9781003325369 (ebook)
Subjects: LCSH: Image analysis.
Classification: LCC TA1637 .Z5278 2023 (print) |
LCC TA1637 (ebook) | DDC 621.36/7--dc23/eng/20220712
LC record available at https://lccn.loc.gov/2022016652
LC ebook record available at https://lccn.loc.gov/2022016653

ISBN: 978-1-032-35109-4 (hbk)
ISBN: 978-1-032-35116-2 (pbk)
ISBN: 978-1-003-32536-9 (ebk)

DOI: 10.1201/b23131

Typeset in Minion
by MPS Limited, Dehradun

Contents

Preface

I MAGE ANALYSIS IS A DISCIPLINE THAT HAS ATTRACTED A LOT OF attention in the information community. Image analysis technology has been widely used in many applications in our society. This book takes a new direction, combining the contents, characteristics and styles of both textbook and monography, to introduce image analysis technology.

This book is different from pure textbooks on image processing; it is also not a theoretical monograph on image analysis technology. The introduction is focused on several commonly used image analysis techniques. For each of these selected techniques, comprehensive coverage is provided. The book begins with essential concepts and basic principles, passes through the typical specific methods and practical techniques, and arrives at research frontier trends and latest developments.

This book is suitable for readers who do not have a complete foundation of image analysis, yet need to use image analysis techniques to perform specific tasks. From this book, readers can quickly grasp elementary knowledge from further study without the prerequisite for the relevant basis information; readers can find a suitable technique for solving practical problems, and they can learn about the latest developments in specific application domains.

The seven selected image analysis techniques are: image segmentation, segmentation evaluation and comparison, saliency object detection, motion analysis, mathematical morphology methods, face recognition and expression classification. This book does not attempt to cover all branches of image analysis technology; rather, it tries to give a profound discussion on those selected techniques. The presentations and discussions on each of these techniques are self-contained.

The materials in this book are arranged in eight chapters with 52 sections, 118 subsections, with 192 figures, 33 tables, and 308 numbered equations. Moreover, more than 300 key references are introduced and provided at the end of the book for further study.

Special thanks go to Taylor & Francis Group and their staff members. Their kind and professional assistance is truly appreciated.

Last but not least, I am deeply indebted to my wife and my daughter for their encouragement, patience, support, tolerance, and understanding during the writing of this book.

Yu-Jin Zhang
Department of Electronic Engineering
Tsinghua University, Beijing, The People's Republic of China

CHAPTER 1

Introduction

Images are entities obtained by observing the objective world in different forms and methods with various observation systems, which can directly or indirectly act on the human eye and then produce visual perception (Zhang 1996). The concept of image here is relatively broad, including photos, drawings, animations, videos, and even documents, etc. The image contains rich description information of the objects and scenes it represents, and is our main source of information.

To use the image, one needs to obtain the information that the image brings. People who pay attention to images often focus on the *objects* in the image (objects of interest in the objective scene), and the *image analysis technology* is mainly the processing technology for these objects, including how to extract them from the image, how to represent them, and how to obtain their description, how to identify and classify them, etc. Using the information and results obtained in this way, people can use images more objectively and effectively.

This book attempts to select some basic categories of the very commonly used image analysis technology and gives an introduction from shallow to deep (including basic principles, practical technologies, and development trends).

The contents of each section of this chapter are arranged as follows.

Section 1.1 gives a general introduction to image analysis, including the overview of various image technologies, their classification, as well as the definition of image analysis and the connection and difference with related technologies. In addition, it also summarizes the history and building blocks of the image analysis system.

Section 1.2 introduces a series of digital concepts commonly used in image analysis, including discrete distances, connected components, several digital models, and digital arcs and digital strings in discrete situations.

Section 1.3 introduces the widely used distance transform in image analysis. The definition and properties of distance transform are given first, and then the principle of using local distance to calculate global distance step by step is introduced. Finally, the serial realization method and parallel realization method of discrete distance transform are discussed separately.

DOI: 10.1201/b23131-1

Section 1.4 discusses the characteristics of this book. It elaborates and analyzes the three aspects of writing motivation, material selection, and structure arrangement. It not only gives the overall content and structural characteristics of the book, but also helps how to learn the material presented in this book.

1.1 INTRODUCTION TO IMAGE ANALYSIS

After years of research and development, many technologies have been developed for processing, analyzing, and interpreting digital images with computers. *Image technology* is a general term for various image-related technologies in a broad sense. At present, people mainly study digital images, and mainly apply computer image technology. This includes the use of computers and other electronic equipment to carry out and complete a series of tasks, such as image collection, acquisition, (compression) coding, watermark protection, storage and transmission, image synthesis, rendering and generation, image display and output, image transformation, enhancement, restoration and reconstruction of images, image segmentation, object detection, representation and description of images, feature extraction and measurement, correction and registration of multiple images or sequence images, 3-D scenery reconstruction and restoration, image database establishment, indexing and extraction, image classification, representation and re-cognition, image model establishment and matching, image and scene interpretation and understanding, and decision-making and behavior planning based on them. In addition, the image technology can also include the hardware design and production technology for accomplishing the above-mentioned functions.

1.1.1 Image Engineering

The above-mentioned technologies can be unified together and called *Image Engineering* (IE) technology. IE is a new interdisciplinary subject that systematically studies various image theories, technologies, and applications (Zhang 1996). From the perspective of its research methods, it can learn from many disciplines, such as mathematics, physics, physiology, psychology, electronics, and computer science. From the perspective of its research scope, it is related to and overlaps with many disciplines, such as pattern re-cognition, computer vision, and computer graphics. In addition, the research progress of IE is closely related to theories and technologies such as artificial intelligence, neural networks, genetic algorithms, fuzzy logic, and machine learning. Its development and application are related to and indivisible with medicine, remote sensing, communication, document processing, industrial automation, intelligent transportation, and so on.

If considering the characteristics of various IE technologies, they can be divided into three levels that are both connected and differentiated (as shown in Figure 1.1): *Image Processing* (IP) technology (Zhang 2017a), *Image Analysis* (IA) technology (Zhang 2017b), and *Image Understanding* (IU) technology (Zhang 2017c).

IP emphasizes the transformation between images. Although people often use IP to refer to various image technologies, the more narrowly defined IP mainly refers to various processing of images to improve the visual effect of the image and lay the foundation for automatic recognition or to compress and encode the image to reduce the

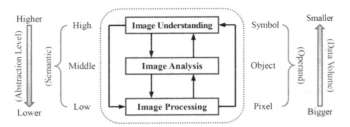

FIGURE 1.1 Schematic diagram of three levels of image engineering.

storage required space or transmission time to meet the requirements of a given transmission path.

IA is mainly used to detect and measure objects of interest in the image to obtain their objective information to establish a description of the image. If IP is a process from image to image, then IA is a process from image to data. Here, the data can be the result of the measurement of the object feature, or a symbolic representation based on the measurement. They describe the characteristics and properties of the object in the image.

IU is focused on further studying the nature of the objects in the image and their interrelationships based on IA and obtaining an understanding of the meaning of the image content and the interpretation of the original objective scene. If IA is mainly based on the observer-centered study of the objective world (mainly studying observable things), then IU is to a certain extent centered on the objective world, and with the help of knowledge, experience, etc., to grasp and interpret the whole objective world (including things that are not directly observed).

In summary, IP, IA, and IU have their own characteristics in terms of abstraction and data volume, and their operation objects and semantic levels are different. See Figure 1.1 for their interrelationships. IP is a relatively low-level operation, which is mainly processed at the pixel level of the image, and the amount of processed data is very large. IA enters the middle level. Segmentation and feature extraction transform the original image described by pixels into a more concise description of the object. IU is mainly a high-level operation. The object of the operation is basically the symbols abstracted from the description, and its treating processes and methods have many similarities with human thinking and reasoning. In addition, it can be seen from Figure 1.1 that the amount of data gradually decreases as the degree of abstraction increases. In particular, the original image data is gradually transformed into a more organized and more abstract representation through a series of operating procedures. In this process, semantics are continuously introduced, the objects of operation are changed, and the amount of data is compressed. On the other hand, high-level operations have a guiding effect on low-level operations and can improve the efficiency of low-level operations.

1.1.2 Classification of Image Technology

Beginning in 1996, the author carried out year-by-year statistics on the IE literature (more than 16,000 articles in total) for 15 important domestic academic journals and has analyzed

TABLE 1.1   The current image technology in the three levels of image processing, analysis, and understanding

Three Layers	Image Technology Categories and Names
Image Processing	Image acquisition (including various imaging methods, image capturing, representation and storage, camera calibration, etc.)
	Image reconstruction (including image reconstruction from projection, indirect imaging, etc.)
	Image enhancement/image restoration (including transformation, filtering, restoration, repair, replacement, correction, visual quality evaluation, etc.)
	Image/video coding and compression (including algorithm research, implementation and improvement of related international standards, etc.)
	Image information security (including digital watermarking, information hiding, image authentication and forensics, etc.)
	Image multi-resolution processing (including super-resolution reconstruction, image decomposition and interpolation, resolution conversion, etc.)
Image Analysis	Image segmentation and primitive detection (including edges, corners, control points, points of interest, etc.)
	Object representation, object description, feature measurement (including binary image morphology analysis, etc.)
	Object feature extraction and analysis (including color, texture, shape, space, structure, motion, saliency, attributes, etc.)
	Object detection and object recognition (including object 2-D positioning, tracking, extraction, identification and classification, etc.)
	Human body biological feature extraction and verification (including detection, positioning and recognition of human body, face and organs, etc.)
Image Understanding	Image matching and fusion (including registration of sequence and stereo image, mosaic, etc.)
	Scene restoration (including 3-D scene representation, modeling, reconstruction, etc.)
	Image perception and interpretation (including semantic description, scene model, machine learning, cognitive reasoning, etc.)
	Content-based image/video retrieval (including corresponding labeling, classification, etc.)
	Spatial-temporal techniques (including high-dimensional motion analysis, object 3-D posture detection, spatial-temporal tracking, behavior judgment and behavior understanding, etc.)

and reviewed its development. This survey task has been conducted for 27 consecutive years. The review series formed by yearly overview reflects the evolution of IE to a certain extent and shows the development trends of IE. Some summary references can be found in (Zhang 1996, 2002, 2009, 2015, 2018a,b).

The review series also carried out *image technology classification* (currently includes 23 sub-categories). Image technology in IP has six subcategories, IA has five subcategories, and IU has five subcategories. Other subcategories belong to technology applications. The classification of the three levels is shown in Table 1.1.

1.1.3 Image Analysis Definition and Research Content

As shown in Figure 1.1, image analysis is at the middle layer of image engineering. It not only needs to rely on the results of image processing but also lays the foundation for image understanding, which plays a role of connecting the past and the next. The definition of image analysis and its research content are all affected by the upper and lower layers of image engineering.

1.1.3.1 Definition of Image Analysis

There are different opinions on the definition and description of *image analysis*. Here are a few examples:

1. The purpose of image analysis is to construct a description of the scene based on the information extracted from the image (Rosenfeld 1984).

2. Image analysis often refers to the use of computers to process images to find out which objects are in the image (Pavlidis 1988).

3. Image analysis quantifies and classifies images and objects in images (Mahdavieh and Gonzalez 1992).

4. Image analysis considers how to extract meaningful measurement data from multidimensional signals (Young 1993).

5. The central problem of image analysis is to simplify grayscale images or color images with several megabytes into only a few meaningful and useful numbers (Russ 2006).

In this book, image analysis is seen as a process and technology that starts from the image and detects, extracts, represents, describes, and measures the objects of interest in order to obtain objective information and output data results.

1.1.3.2 The Difference and Connection between Image Analysis and Pattern Recognition

The main functional modules of image analysis are shown in Figure 1.2.

It can be seen from Figure 1.2 that image analysis mainly includes image segmentation, object representation and description, as well as characteristic analysis of measurement data (the object characteristics obtained can be used for judgment and decision-making). In order to accomplish these tasks, many corresponding theories, tools, and techniques need to be used and aided. The work of image analysis revolves around its operating object. *Image segmentation* is to separate the object from the image, the *object representation* and *object description* are to effectively represent and describe the object, and the characteristic analysis is to obtain the characteristics of the object. Since the object is a collection of pixels, image analysis pays more attention to the connections and relationships between pixels (such as neighborhoods, connectivity, path, distance, etc.).

FIGURE 1.2 Main content units of image analysis.

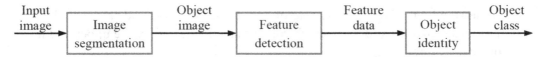

FIGURE 1.3   Image pattern recognition process.

Image analysis and pattern recognition are closely related. The purpose of *pattern recognition* (PR) is to classify different patterns, and image pattern recognition is to classify different image objects. A summary process for pattern recognition of images can be seen in Figure 1.3. Segment the input image to separate the object from the background, detect the object's features (parameters describing the characteristics), and perform measurement calculations for object identity. The object can be classified into a pre-defined category according to the obtained object feature quantity.

Comparing the two, the input of image analysis and image pattern recognition are the same, and their working steps are basically the same. The purpose of image analysis is to obtain the characteristics of the object in the image, in order to judge the object or lay a foundation for further understanding of the scene. The purpose of image pattern recognition is to identify and classify objects based on their characteristic data. Although the direct outputs of them are different, they can be converted to each other.

1.1.3.3 The Difference and Connection between Image Analysis and Image Processing
Image processing and image analysis have their own characteristics, which have been described separately in Sub-section 1.1.1. There are some differences between image processing and image analysis. Some people think that image processing (like word processing, food processing) is a reorganized science (Russ 2006). For a pixel, its attribute value may change according to the value of its neighboring pixels, or it may be moved to other places in the image, but the absolute number of pixels in the entire image does not change. For example, in word processing, one can cut or copy paragraphs, change fonts without reducing the number of words. Another example is in food processing, it is necessary to reorganize various ingredients to produce a better combination, rather than extract the essence of various ingredients. But image analysis is different. Its goal is to try to extract the descriptive coefficients from the image that concisely express the important information of the image, and to quantitatively express the content of the image.

Image processing and image analysis are connected. In many processes from collecting images to analyzing the results, various image processing techniques are used. In other words, the work of image analysis is often based on the results of image (pre)processing (see below).

1.1.3.4 Image Analysis System
Image analysis has a long history, and image analysis systems built using various image equipment and technologies have also been used for a long time. Here are a few events in the early history of the image analysis system (Joyce 1985):

1. The first system that used TV cameras to scan images for analysis was developed by a metal research institute, and its earliest model system was born in 1963.

2. The electronic era really began in 1969, when a company in the United States (Bausch and Lomb) produced an image analyzer that could store a complete black-and-white image in a small computer for analysis.

3. In 1977, Joyce Loebl, a British company, proposed a third-generation image analysis system that replaced hardware with software. The analysis function is separated from the image acquisition and is more versatile.

The image analysis system got in-depth research, rapid development and extensive application in the 1980s and 1990s. During the period, people proposed many typical system structures and established many practical application systems, for example, see (Zhang 1991; Zhang et al. 2001; Russ 2006).

The *image analysis system* must be based on hardware. Various analysis of images can generally be described in the form of algorithms, and most of the algorithms can be implemented in software, so now there are many image analysis systems that only need to use ordinary general-purpose computers. In order to increase the computing speed or overcome the limitations of general-purpose computers, special hardware can be used. After the 1990s, people designed a variety of image cards compatible with industry standard buses that can be inserted into a computer or workstation. These image cards include frame grabbers for image digitization and temporary storage, arithmetic logic units for arithmetic and logic operations at video speed, and memory such as frame buffers. After entering the 21st century, the integration of the system has further improved, and both the system on chip (SOC) and the graphics processing unit (GPU) have developed rapidly. These hardware advances not only reduce costs, but also promote the development of dedicated software for image processing. Many image analysis systems and image analysis software packages are now commercialized.

The composition of a basic image analysis system can be shown in Figure 1.4. It is very similar to the framework of the image processing system (where the original processing module is replaced by the analysis module), and it also has modules for collecting, communicating, storing, and outputting specific functions (many images are often processed by image technology for preprocessing before being analyzed). The final output of the analysis is either data (data measured on the object, result data of the analysis) or symbolic expression for further understanding, which is different from an image processing system.

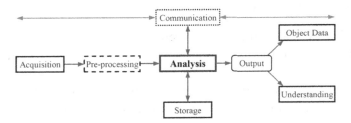

FIGURE 1.4   Schematic diagram of the structure of the image processing system.

The following two sections give a brief introduction to some basic knowledge about image analysis.

1.2 DIGITALIZATION IN IMAGE ANALYSIS

Image analysis needs to obtain measurement data of objects of interest in the image, and these objects of interest are obtained by discretizing continuous scenes in the scene. The *object* is an important concept and operand in image analysis, which is composed of connected pixels. The location and attributes of these connected pixels in space are closely related, and generally they constitute connected components in the image. To analyze the relationship between pixels in space, it is necessary to consider the spatial relationship between pixels, among which discrete distance plays an important role. For connectivity, the attribute relationship of pixels must also be considered in the distance relationship. In order to obtain accurate measurement data for the object, it is necessary to understand the digitization process and its characteristics in the analysis.

1.2.1 Discrete Distance

In digital images, pixels are discrete, and the spatial relationship between them can be described by discrete distance.

1.2.1.1 Distance and Neighborhood

If p, q, and r represent three pixels, respectively, and their coordinates are (x_p, y_p), (x_q, y_q), and (x_r, y_r), the *distance metric function d* shall meet the following three conditions:

1. $d(p, q) \geq 0$ (if and only if $p = q$, there is $d(p, q) = 0$);

2. $d(p, q) = d(q, p)$;

3. $d(p, r) \leq d(p, q) + d(q, r)$.

In digital images, it is often necessary to round the distance value (convert the real value to integer value). The commonly used rounding functions include:

1. Round-up function: also called the top function, denoted as $\lceil \cdot \rceil$. If x is a real number, then $\lceil x \rceil$ is an integer and $x \leq \lceil x \rceil < x + 1$.

2. Round-down function: also called the bottom function, denoted as $\lfloor \cdot \rfloor$. If x is a real number, then $\lfloor x \rfloor$ is an integer and $x - 1 < \lfloor x \rfloor \leq x$.

3. Rounding function: a commonly used rounding function, denoted as round ($\bullet$). If x is a real number, then round (x) is an integer and $(x - 1/2) < $ round $(x) \leq (x + 1/2)$.

With the help of distance, various neighborhoods of pixels can be defined. The *4-neighborhood $N_4(p)$* of a pixel $p(x_p, y_p)$ is defined as (see the pixel (x_r, y_r) marked with r in Figure 1.5(a)):

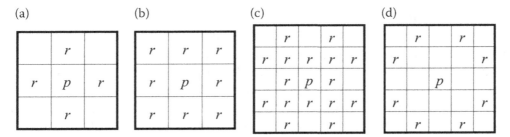

FIGURE 1.5 Schematic diagram of various neighborhoods.

$$N_4(p) = \{r \mid d_4(p, r) = 1\} \qquad (1.1)$$

where the *city-block distance* $d_4(p, r) = |x_p - x_r| + |y_p - y_r|$.

The *8-neighborhood* $N_8(p)$ of a pixel $p(x_p, y_p)$ is defined as (see the pixel (x_r, y_r) marked with r in Figure 1.5(b)):

$$N_8(p) = \{r \mid d_8(p, r) = 1\} \qquad (1.2)$$

where the *chessboard distance* $d_8(p, r) = \max(|x_p - x_r|, |y_p - y_r|)$.

The definition of neighborhood can also be extended. Above 4-neighborhood and 8-neighborhood is 16-neighborhood. The *16-neighborhood* $N_{16}(p)$ of a pixel $p(x_p, y_p)$ is defined as (see the pixel (x_r, y_r) marked with r in Figure 1.5(c)):

$$N_{16}(p) = N_8(p) \cup N_k(p) \qquad (1.3)$$

where the *knight neighborhood* $N_k(p)$ is defined as (see the pixel (x_r, y_r) marked with r in Figure 1.5(d)):

$$N_k(p) = \{r \mid d_k(p, r) = 1\} \qquad (1.4)$$

Here, the *knight distance* is calculated according to the number of steps required for the horse on the chessboard to move from one grid to another, which is also the length of the shortest k-path between two points on the image grid (Das and Chatterji 1988).

The knight distance can be defined with the help of the round-up function (only the first quadrant is considered):

$$
\begin{aligned}
&d_k(p, r) \\
&= \begin{cases} \max\left[\left\lceil\frac{s}{2}\right\rceil, \left\lceil\frac{s+t}{3}\right\rceil\right] + \left\{(s+t) - \max\left[\left\lceil\frac{s}{2}\right\rceil, \left\lceil\frac{s+t}{3}\right\rceil\right]\right\} \bmod 2 & \begin{matrix}(s, t) \neq (1, 0) \\ (s, t) \neq (2, 2)\end{matrix} \\ 3 & (s, t) = (1, 0) \\ 4 & (s, t) = (2, 2) \end{cases}
\end{aligned}
$$

$$(1.5)$$

where $s = \max[|x_p - x_r|, |y_p - y_r|]$; $t = \min[|x_p - x_r|, |y_p - y_r|]$.

1.2.1.2 Equidistant Disc

Given a discrete distance metric d_D, a disc with a radius of R ($R \geq 0$) centered on the pixel p is a point set that satisfies $\Delta_D(p, R) = \{q | d_D(p, q) \leq R\}$. When the position of the central pixel p is not considered, the disc with radius R can also be abbreviated as $\Delta_D(R)$.

Let $\Delta_i(R)$, $i = 4, 8$ represent an *equidistant disc* whose radius (distance) d_i from the central pixel is less than or equal to R, and $\#[\Delta_i(R)]$ represents the location of $\Delta_i(R)$ except for the central pixel, then the number of pixels increases proportionally with distance. For the city block distance disc, it has

$$\#[\Delta_4(R)] = 4 \sum_{j=1}^{R} j = 4(1 + 2 + 3 + \cdots + R) = 2R(R + 1) \tag{1.6}$$

Similarly, for the chessboard distance disc, it has

$$\#[\Delta_8(R)] = 8 \sum_{j=1}^{R} j = 8(1 + 2 + 3 + \cdots + R) = 4R(R + 1) \tag{1.7}$$

In addition, the chessboard distance disc is actually a square, so the following formula can also be used to calculate the number of pixels in the chessboard distance disc except the center pixel:

$$\#[\Delta_8(R)] = (2R + 1)^2 - 1 \tag{1.8}$$

Here are several different example values of $\Delta_i(R)$: $\#[\Delta_4(5)] = 60$, $\#[\Delta_4(6)] = 84$, $\#[\Delta_8(3)] = 48$, $\#[\Delta_8(4)] = 80$.

1.2.1.3 Chamfer Distance

The *chamfer distance* is an integer approximation to the Euclidean distance in the pixel neighborhood. From pixel p to its 4-neighbor pixels, it is only needed to move horizontally or to move vertically (called a-move). Because all movements are equal in terms of symmetry or rotation, the only possible definition of discrete distance is the d_4 distance, where $a = 1$. From the pixel p to its 8-neighbor pixels, except the horizontal movement or vertical movement, the diagonal movement (called b-move) to the diagonal pixel is also required. Considering these two kinds of movement at the same time, the chamfer distance can be recorded as $d_{a,b}$. The most natural b value is $2^{1/2}a$, but in order to simplify the calculation and reduce the storage capacity, both the a value and b value are taken as integers. The most commonly used set of values is $a = 3$ and $b = 4$. This set of values can be obtained as follows. Consider that the number of pixels that differ in the horizontal direction between pixel p and pixel q is n_x, and the number of pixels that differ in the vertical direction is n_y (without loss of generality, set $n_x > n_y$), then the chamfer distance between pixel p and pixel q for

$$D(p, q) = (n_x - n_y)a + n_y b \tag{1.9}$$

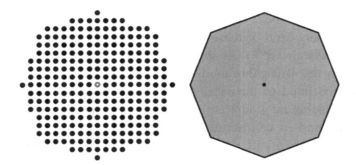

FIGURE 1.6 Example of chamfer distance disc.

The difference between it and the Euclidean distance is

$$\Delta D(p, q) = \sqrt{n_x^2 + n_y^2} - [(n_x - n_y)a + n_y b] \tag{1.10}$$

If let $a = 1$, $b = \sqrt{2}$, take the derivative of $\Delta D(p, q)$ with respect to n_y, then

$$\Delta D'(p, q) = \frac{n_y}{\sqrt{n_x^2 + n_y^2}} - (\sqrt{2} - 1) \tag{1.11}$$

Let the derivative be zero, and calculate the extreme value of $\Delta D(p, q)$ to get

$$n_y = \sqrt{(\sqrt{2} - 1)/2}\, n_x \tag{1.12}$$

That is, the distance between the Euclidean distance and chamfer distance of two pixels $\Delta D(p, q)$ takes the maximum value $(\sqrt{2\sqrt{2} - 2}) - 1)n_x \approx -0.09 n_x$ when the above formula is satisfied (the angle between the straight line and the horizontal axis is about 24.5°). It can be further proved that when $b = 1/2^{\frac{1}{2}} + (2^{\frac{1}{2}} - 1)^{\frac{1}{2}} = 1.351$, the maximum value of $\Delta D(p, q)$ would reach the minimum. Because $4/3 \approx 1.33$, so $a = 3$ and $b = 4$ are used in the chamfer distance.

Figure 1.6 shows two examples of equidistant discs based on the chamfer distance, where the left picture shows $\Delta_{3,4}(27)$, and the right picture shows $\Delta_{a,b}$.

1.2.2 Connected Components

The object in the image is a *connected component* composed of pixels. A connected component is a collection of connected pixels. Connectedness needs to be defined in terms of connectivity. *Connectivity* is a relationship between two pixels, in which both their mutual positional relationship and their mutual amplitude relationship must be considered. Two connected pixels are *adjacent* in space (that is, one pixel is in the neighborhood of another pixel) and meet a certain similarity criterion in amplitude (for grayscale images, their grayscale values should be equal, or more generally their grayscale values should be both in the same grayscale set *V*).

It can be seen from the above that the adjacency of two pixels is one of the necessary conditions for the connection of these two pixels (the other condition is that they are both in the same grayscale set V). As shown in Figure 1.5, two pixels can be *4-adjacent* (one pixel is within the 4-neighborhood of the other pixel) or *8-adjacent* (one pixel is within the 8-neighborhood of the other pixel). Correspondingly, two pixels can be *4-connected* (the two pixels are 4-adjacent) or *8-connected* (the two pixels are 8-adjacent).

In fact, another kind of connection can be defined, namely *m-connection* (*hybrid connection*). If two pixels p and r take values in a value set V and meet one of the following conditions, they are m-connected: (i) Pixel r is in $N_4(p)$; (ii) Pixel r is in $N_D(p)$ and $N_4(p) \cap N_4(r)$ does not include the pixels of the value of V. For further explanation of condition (ii) in hybrid connection, see Figure 1.7. Figure 1.7(a) shows that the pixel r is in $N_D(p)$, $N_4(p)$ includes four pixels labeled a, b, c, d, and $N_4(r)$ includes four pixels labeled c, d, e, f, $N_4(p) \cap N_4(r)$ includes two pixels labeled c and d. Suppose $V = \{1\}$, then Figure 1.7(b) and Figure 1.7(c), respectively, give an example of satisfying and dis-satisfying condition (ii). In the two images, the two shaded pixels are each other's di-agonal pixels, but the two pixels in Figure 1.7(b) do not have the same neighboring pixel with a common value of 1, while the two pixels in Figure 1.7(c) do have the same neighboring pixels with a common value of 1. In this way, the pixel p and pixel r in Figure 1.7(b) are m-connected but the m-connection between the pixel p and pixel r in Figure 1.7(c) is not established (they are connected through the pixel c).

It can be seen from the above, when 4-connection and 8-connection are possible between two pixels at the same time, the essential meaning of hybrid connection has the priority to use 4-connection, and to shield the 8-connection between the two pixels with 4-connection with the same pixel. Hybrid connection can be considered as a variation of 8-connection. It was introduced to eliminate the multi-path problem that often occurs when 8-connection is used. Figure 1.8 shows an example. In Figure 1.8(a), the pixel

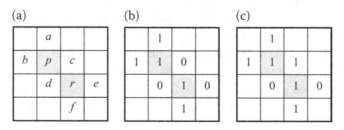

FIGURE 1.7 Further explanation of condition (ii) in hybrid connection.

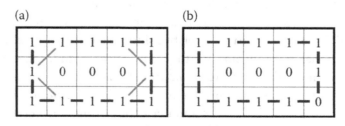

FIGURE 1.8 Hybrid connection for eliminating multi-path ambiguity.

marked 1 constitutes the boundary of the region composed of three pixels marked 0 at the center. Regarding this boundary as a path, there are two paths among the three pixels of the four corners, which is the ambiguity produced by the use of 8-connection. This ambiguity can be eliminated by m-connection, and the result is shown in Figure 1.8(b). Because the direct m-connection between the diagonal pixels cannot be established (Conditions (i) and (ii) in the hybrid connection are not satisfied), there is only one path left, and there is no ambiguity problem.

With 4-neighborhood, *4-adjacency* and *4-connection* can be defined. With 8-neighborhood, *8-adjacency* and *8-connection* can be defined. Likewise, with 16-neighborhood, *16-adjacency* and *16-connection* can be defined. Similar to the previous ambiguity problem when using 8-connection in 8-neighborhood, the use of 16-connection in 16-neighborhood will also cause ambiguity. As shown in Figure 1.9(a), there is an ambiguity connection problem from the central pixel to the pixels where the shadowed knight movement (as shown by the thin lines in the figure) are located. To solve this problem, the following *M-connection* can be defined in parallel to the definition of m-connection (Zhang 2000): If two pixels p and r take values in the same value set and meet one of the following conditions, they are M-connected: (i) Pixel r is in $N_4(p)$; (ii) Pixel r is in $N_D(p)$ and $N_4(p) \cap N_4(r)$ is the empty set; (iii) Pixel r is in $N_k(p)$ and $N_8(p) \cap N_8(r)$ is the empty set.

According to the above definition, M-connection can be regarded as a variant of 16-connection. The introduction of it can eliminate the connection ambiguity problem when using 16-connection. As shown in Figure 1.9(b), according to the definition of M-connection, there is only one path from the central pixel to the pixels of several horse steps. Pay attention to the path between the center pixel and the pixel at the bottom left of the horse step. Here, the connection between the pixel on the left of the center pixel and the pixel of the horse step does not exist because condition (ii) is not satisfied. In the same way, the connection between the right pixel and the center pixel of the knight movement does not exist, so there is only one path, as shown in the figure (Zhang 1999).

Connectedness can be seen as an extension of connectivity. It is a relationship established between two pixels with the help of some other pixels. Consider a series of pixels $\{p_i(x_i, y_i), i = 0, 1, \ldots, n\}$, when all $p_i(x_i, y_i)$ and $p_{i-1}(x_{i-1}, y_{i-1})$ are connected, then the two

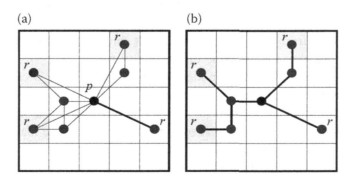

FIGURE 1.9   Sixteen-connection and M-connection.

pixels $p_0(x_0, y_0)$ and $p_n(x_n, y_n)$ have connectedness through some other pixels $p_i(x_i, y_i)$. If $p_i(x_i, y_i)$ and $p_{i-1}(x_{i-1}, y_{i-1})$ are 4-connected, then $p_0(x_0, y_0)$ and $p_n(x_n, y_n)$ have *4-connectedness*. If $p_i(x_i, y_i)$ and $p_{i-1}(x_{i-1}, y_{i-1})$ are 8-connected, then $p_0(x_0, y_0)$ and $p_n(x_n, y_n)$ have *8-connectedness*. If $p_i(x_i, y_i)$ and $p_{i-1}(x_{i-1}, y_{i-1})$ are 16-connected, then $p_0(x_0, y_0)$ and $p_n(x_n, y_n)$ have *16-connectedness*. If $p_i(x_i, y_i)$ and $p_{i-1}(x_{i-1}, y_{i-1})$ are m-connected, then $p_0(x_0, y_0)$ and $p_n(x_n, y_n)$ have *m-connectedness*. Furthermore, if $p_i(x_i, y_i)$ and $p_{i-1}(x_{i-1}, y_{i-1})$ are M-connected, then $p_0(x_0, y_0)$ and $p_n(x_n, y_n)$ have *M-connectedness*.

A series of pixels connected as above constitute a *connected component*, or a subset of the image, or a region in the image. In the connected component, any two pixels have connectedness through the connection of other pixels inside the component. For two connected components, if one or some pixels in one of the connected components are adjacent to one or some pixels in the other connected component, then these two connected components are adjacent; if one or some pixels in one of the connected components are connected to one or some pixels in another connected component, then these two connected components are connected, and these two connected components can be combined into one connected component.

1.2.3 Digitizing Model

The *digitizing model* to be discussed here is used to transform a spatially continuous scene into a discrete digital image, so it is a spatially quantified model.

1.2.3.1 Basic Knowledge

Here is some basic knowledge of digitizing models (Marchand-Maillet and Sharaiha 2000).

First, define the pre-image and domain of the digital set P:

1. Given a discrete point set P, a continuous point set S whose digitization is P is called a *pre-image* of P;

2. The region defined by the union of all possible pre-images S is called the *domain* of P.

There are many digitizing models, in which the quantization is always many-to-one mapping, so they are all irreversible processes. Therefore, the same quantization result image can be mapped from different pre-images. It can also be said that objects of different sizes or shapes may get the same discretization result.

Now consider a simple digitizing model. A square image grid is covered on a continuous object S, and a pixel is represented by an intersection point p on a square grid. This pixel belongs to the digitization result of S if and only when $p \in S$. Figure 1.10 gives an example. S is represented by the shaded part in the figure. The black dots represent pixel p belonging to S, and all p forms a set P.

Here, the distance between image grids is also called the sampling step, which can be represented by h. In the case of a square grid, the sampling step is by definition a real

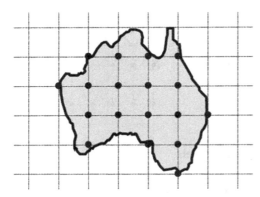

FIGURE 1.10   A simple digitizing model example.

(a)   (b)   (c)

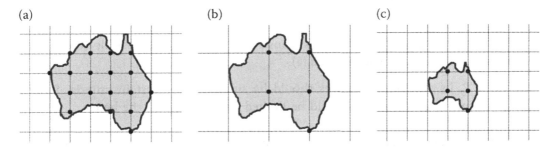

FIGURE 1.11   The effect of digitizing continuous collections with different sampling steps.

value, and $h > 0$, which defines the distance between two 4-neighboring pixels. The effect of different sampling steps is shown in Figure 1.11. In Figure 1.11(a), a given sampling step h is used to digitize the continuous set S. Figure 1.11(b) shows the result of digitizing the same set S with another sampling step $h' = 2h$. Obviously, this effect is equivalent to changing the size of the continuous set S with the scale h/h' and then digitizing it with the original sampling step h, as shown in Figure 1.11(c).

Analysis of this digitizing model shows that it may cause some inconsistencies:

1. A non-empty set S may be mapped to an empty digitized set. Figure 1.12(a) shows several examples, where each non-empty set (including two thin objects) does not contain any integer points.

2. The digital model is not translation invariant. Figure 1.12(b) gives several examples. The same set S may be mapped to an empty, disconnected, or connected digitizing set according to its position in the grid (the numbers of points in each set are 0, 2, 3, 6, respectively). In the terminology of image technology, the change of P under S translation is called *aliasing*.

3. Given a digitized set P, it is not guaranteed to accurately describe its pre-image S. Figure 1.12(c) shows several examples, where three consecutive objects with very different shapes all give the same digitized result (points in a row).

(a)   (b)   (c)

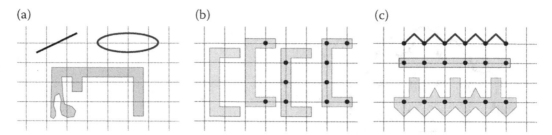

FIGURE 1.12   Examples of inconsistencies in the digitizing model.

It can be seen from above, a suitable digitizing model should have the following characteristics:

1. The digitized result of a non-empty continuous set should be non-empty.

2. The digitizing model should be as translational invariant as possible (that is, the aliasing effect is as small as possible).

3. Given P, its various pre-images should be similar under certain criteria. Strictly speaking, the domain of P should be limited and the smaller the better.

The commonly used digitizing models mainly include square box quantization, grid intersection quantization, and object contour quantization (Zhang 2017b). The following only introduces the digitizing model of square box quantization and grid intersection quantization.

1.2.3.2 Square Box Quantization

In *square box quantization* (SBQ), for any pixel $p_i = (x_i, y_i)$, there is a corresponding digitized box $B_i = [x_i - 1/2, x_i + 1/2) \times [y_i - 1/2, y_i + 1/2)$. To ensure that they completely cover the plane, a half-open box is defined here. A pixel p_i is in the digitized set P of S if and only when $B_i \cap S \neq \varnothing$ (that is, its corresponding digitized box B_i intersects with S). Figure 1.13 shows the digitized set (square box with a dot in the center) obtained by quantizing the continuous point set S in Figure 1.9 with a square box. The dotted line

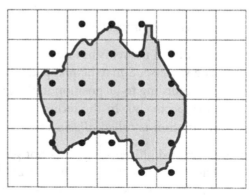

FIGURE 1.13   Digitizing example based on square box quantization.

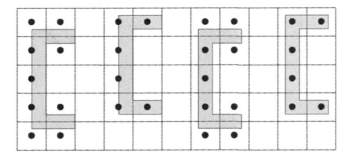

FIGURE 1.14 Using square box quantization can reduce aliasing.

represents the square division, which is dual to the square sampling grid. It can be seen from the figure that the square corresponding to a pixel intersects with S, and it will appear in the digitized set of its square box quantization. That is, the digitized set P obtained from a continuous point set S is the pixel set $\{p_i \mid B_i \cap S \neq \emptyset\}$.

The result of square box quantization of a continuous straight-line segment is a four-digit arc. The definition of square box quantization ensures that the non-empty set S will be mapped to the non-empty discrete set P, because it can be guaranteed that each real point can be uniquely mapped to a discrete point. However, this does not guarantee complete translation invariance, but can only greatly reduce aliasing. Figure 1.14 gives several examples, where the continuous set is the same as in Figure 1.12(b). The points in each discrete set are 9, 6, 9, and 6, which are closer to each other than the point sets in Figure 1.12(b).

1.2.3.3 Grid Intersection Quantization

Grid intersection quantization (GIQ) can be defined as follows. Given a thin object C, composed of continuous points, the intersection point between it and the grid line is a real point $t = (x_t, y_t)$, which depends on whether the target C intersects the vertical grid line or the horizontal grid line, and satisfies, respectively, $x_t \in I$ or $y_t \in I$ (where I represents the set of 1-D integers). This point $t \in C$ will be mapped to a grid point $p_i = (x_i, y_i)$, where $t \in (x_i - 1/2, x_i + 1/2) \times (y_i - 1/2, y_i + 1/2)$. In special cases (such as $x_t = x_i + 1/2$ or $y_t = y_i + 1/2$), the point p_i that falls on the left or above belongs to the discrete set P.

Figure 1.15 shows the results obtained for a curve C using grid intersection quantification. In this example, C is facing clockwise (as shown by the arrow in the figure). Any short, continuous line segment between C and the pixel marked with a dot is mapped to the corresponding pixel.

It can be proved that the quantified result of grid intersection of a continuous straight-line segment $[\alpha, \beta]$ is an 8-digit arc. Further, it can be defined by the intersection of $[\alpha, \beta]$ and horizontal or vertical (depending on the slope of $[\alpha, \beta]$) line.

Grid intersection quantization is often used as a theoretical model of image acquisition process. The aliasing effect of grid intersection quantization is shown in Figure 1.16. If the sampling step h is properly selected relative to the digitization of C, the aliasing effect is similar to that generated by square box quantization.

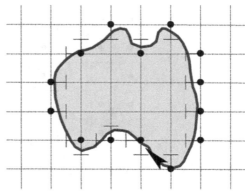

FIGURE 1.15 Grid intersection quantification example of continuous curve C.

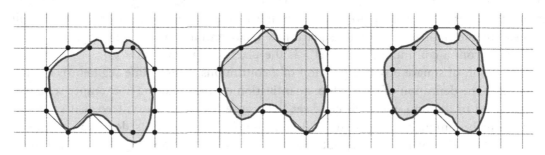

FIGURE 1.16 Aliasing effect caused by grid intersection quantization.

1.2.4 Digital Arc and Digital Chord

In Euclidean geometry, an arc is the part between two points on a curve, and a chord is a straight line connecting any two points on a conic. Continuous straight-line segments can often be regarded as special cases of arcs.

Digitizing set is a discrete set obtained by digitizing a continuous set using a digitizing model. When studying discrete objects, it can be regarded as the result of digitizing continuous objects, and the properties of continuous objects proved in Euclidean geometry can be mapped to discrete sets. Digital arcs and digital chords as well as some of their properties are discussed below (Marchand-Maillet and Sharaiha 2000).

1.2.4.1 Digital Arc

Given a neighborhood and the corresponding moving length, the chamfer distance between two pixels p and q relative to this neighborhood is the length of the shortest digital arc from p to q. Here, the *digital arc* can be defined as follows. Given a set of discrete points and the adjacent relationship between them, the digital arc P_{pq} from point p to point q is defined as the arc $P_{pq} = \{p_i, i = 0, 1, \ldots, n\}$:

1. $p_0 = p$, $p_n = q$;

2. $\forall i = 1, \ldots, n-1$, point p_i has exactly two adjacent points in arc P_{pq}: p_{i-1} and p_{i+1};

3. The endpoint p_0 (or p_n) has exactly one adjacent point in the arc P_{pq}: p_1 (or p_{n-1}).

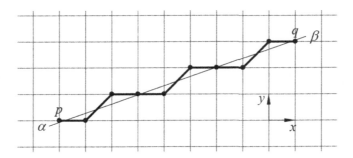

FIGURE 1.17 Digitizing results of grid intersection quantization for straight-line segments.

According to different adjacency relationships (such as 4-adjacency or 8-adjacency), different digital arcs (*4-digital arc* or *8-digital arc*) can be given respectively according to the above definition.

Consider the continuous straight-line segment $[\alpha, \beta]$ in the square grid given in Figure 1.17 (the segment is from α to β). Grid intersection quantization is adopted, and the points intersecting with grid lines between $[\alpha, \beta]$ are mapped to their nearest integer points. When there are two closest points with equal distance, the discrete point on the left of $[\alpha, \beta]$ can be selected first. The discrete point set $\{p_i\}_{i = 0, \ldots, n}$ obtained in this way is called the digitized set of $[\alpha, \beta]$.

1.2.4.2 Digital Chord

The following discusses *discrete linearity* and judges whether a digital arc is a digital chord.

The judgment of *digital chord* is based on the following principle: Given a digital arc from $p = p_0$ to $q = p_n$, $P_{pq} = \{p_i\}_{i = 0, \ldots, n}$, the distance between continuous line segment $[p_i, p_j]$ and the sum of each segment $U_i[p_i, p_{i+1}]$ can be measured with a discrete distance function, and it should not exceed a certain threshold. Figure 1.18 shows two examples, where the shaded region represents the distance between P_{pq} and the continuous line segment $[p_i, p_j]$.

It can be proved that if and only if for an 8-digit arc $P_{pq} = \{p_i\}_{i = 0, \ldots, n}$, any two discrete points p_i and p_j as well as the real point, ρ, in any continuous line segment $[p_i, p_j]$, there is a point $p_k \in P_{pq}$ such that $d_8(\rho, p_k) < 1$, then P_{pq} satisfies the properties of a chord.

To determine the properties of the chord, one can define a polygon around the digital arc, and all the continuous line segments between the discrete points on the digital arc are included in the polygon (as shown by the shaded polygon in Figure 1.19). This polygon will be called a visible polygon, because any point can be seen from any point in this polygon

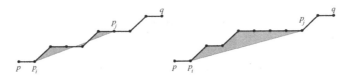

FIGURE 1.18 Examples of judging chord properties.

(a)   (b)

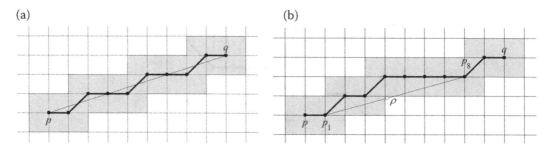

FIGURE 1.19   Examples of verifying that the chord properties are satisfied and not satisfied.

(that is, two points can be connected by a straight line all in the polygon). Figure 1.19 shows an example of verifying that the chord properties are satisfied and not satisfied.

In Figure 1.19(a), for all points $\rho \in R^2$ in the shaded polygon of the digital arc P_{pq}, there is always a point $p_k \in P_{pq}$ such that $d_8(\rho, p_k) < 1$. In Figure 1.19(b), $\rho \in [p_1, p_8]$ can make $d_8(\rho, p_k) \geq 1$ for any $k = 0, \dots, n$. In other words, ρ is outside the visible polygon, or p_8 cannot be seen from p_1 inside the visible polygon (and vice versa). This example of no-valid for chord properties shows that P_{pq} is not the result of digitizing a straight-line segment.

It can be proved that in the 8-digital space, the result of the digitization of a straight line is a digital arc, which satisfies the properties of the chord. Conversely, if a digital arc satisfies the properties of a chord, it is the result of the digitization of a straight-line segment.

1.3 DISTANCE TRANSFORM

Distance transform (DT) is a special transform that converts a binary image into a grayscale image, in which each object pixel is given a value indicating the distance between it and the object contour. The distance transform itself is a global concept, but it can be obtained with the help of the calculation of the local distance.

1.3.1 Definition and Property

Given an object in an image, the operation performed by the distance transform is to calculate the distance between each point in the object region and its closest point outside the region, and assign the distance value to the point. In other words, for a point in the object, the distance transform is defined as the closest distance between the point and the object boundary. More strictly, the distance transform can be defined as follows: Given a point set P, a subset B of P, and a distance function $d(.,.)$ that satisfies the metric conditions (as in Sub-section 1.2.1), the distance transform of P is assigned a point $p \in P$ the value:

$$DT(p) = \min_{q \in B}\{d(p, q)\} \tag{1.13}$$

In images, the commonly used distance metrics are mostly distance functions using integer arithmetic operations. For example, the d_4 distance and d_8 distance described in the previous section are both such metrics. The image with the same size as the original image and the value of DT(p) at each point $p \in P$ is called the distance map of the point set P, which can be represented by the matrix [DT(p)].

Given a set P and its boundary B, the above distance transform to P satisfies the following properties (Marchand-Maillet and Sharaiha 2000):

1. According to the definition, DT(p) is the radius of the largest disc centered on p and completely contained in P;

2. If there is exactly a point $q \in B$ such that DT(p) = $d(p, q)$, then there is a point $r \in P$ such that the disc with the center at r and the radius of DT(r) completely contains the disc with the center at p and the radius of DT(p);

3. Conversely, if there are at least two points q and q' in B such that DT(p) = $d(p, q)$ = $d(p, q')$, then there is no such a disc that it is completely included in P and it can include the disc with the center at p and the radius of DT(p). At this time, p is called the center of the largest disc.

The distance map can generally be represented by a grayscale image, where the grayscale value at each position is proportional to the distance transform value. For example, Figure 1.20(a) is a binary image. If the border of the image is regarded as the contour of the object region, Figure 1.20(b) is the grayscale image obtained after distance transform of Figure 1.20(a). The center value is relatively bigger; the surrounding values are relatively smaller. If the two white pixels in the center of the image are regarded as subset B, then Figure 1.20(c) is the grayscale image obtained by distance transform of Figure 1.20(a), the center value is the smallest, and the surrounding values change with the distances from the center.

1.3.2 Calculation of Local Distance

The above calculation of distance is a global operation, so the amount of calculation will be very large. To solve this problem, only local neighborhood information may be used. Consider the following properties: given a set P and its subset B, d is used to calculate the

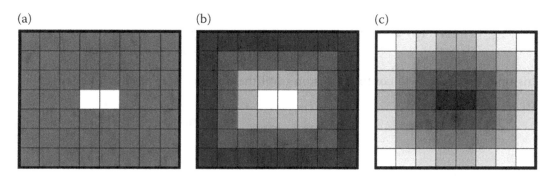

FIGURE 1.20 Binary image and its distance map represented by grayscale image.

distance function of the distance map. Then, for any point $p \in P°$ (i.e., $p \in P - B$), there is a neighborhood point q of p (i.e., $q \in N(p)$), so that the distance transform value $DT(p)$ of P satisfies $DT(p) = DT(q) + d(p, q)$. Further, because p and q are adjacent to each other, the moving length from p to q is $l(p, q) = d(p, q)$. Thus, for any point $p \notin B$, q can be characterized by $DT(q) = \min\{DT(p) + l(p, q), q \in N(p)\}$.

According to the above properties, when actually calculating the distance transformation, the mask containing the local distance can be defined, and the distance map can be calculated by expanding the local distance.

A mask for calculating distance transform with size $n \times n$ can be represented by a matrix $M(k, l)$ of $n \times n$, where the value of each element represents the local distance between pixel $p = (x_p, y_p)$ and its adjacent pixel $q = (x_p + k, y_p + l)$. Generally, the mask is centered on pixel p, so the size n is odd, and the subscripts k and l are included in $\{-\lfloor n/2 \rfloor, \ldots, \lfloor n/2 \rfloor\}$.

Figure 1.21 shows two masks for local distance extension. The mask on the left is based on the 4-neighborhood definition and is used to extend the d_4 distance. The mask on the right is based on an 8-neighborhood and is used to extend the d_8 distance or $d_{a,\,b}$ distance ($a = 1$, $b = 1$). The center pixel p is represented by a shaded region and represents the center of the mask ($k = 0$, $l = 0$). The size of the mask is determined by the type of neighborhood considered. The pixel value in the neighborhood of p has a corresponding length value moved from p. The value of the center pixel is 0, and infinity represents a large number.

The method of calculating distance map with mask can be summarized as follows. Given a binary image of $W \times H$, let its boundary set B be known. The distance map is a matrix with dimension $W \times H$ and value $[DT(p)]$. The matrix can be updated iteratively until a steady state. First, initialize the distance map (iteration index $t = 0$) as follows:

$$DT^{(0)}(p) = \begin{cases} 0 & \text{if} \quad p \in B \\ \infty & \text{if} \quad p \notin B \end{cases} \tag{1.14}$$

Then, when $t > 0$, place the center of the mask $M(k, l)$ at the pixel $p = (x_p, y_p)$, and use the following rules to propagate the distance from the pixel $q = (x_p + k, y_p + l)$ to p

$$DT^{(t)}(p) = \min_{k,j}\{DT^{(t-1)}(q) + M(k, l); q = (x_p + k, y_p + l)\} \tag{1.15}$$

This update process will continue to stop until the distance map no longer changes.

FIGURE 1.21   Masks for calculating distance transform.

1.3.3 The Realization of Distance Transform

In order to realize the distance transform, serial realization and parallel realization can be adopted, respectively, according to the characteristics of computing equipment. Both methods can give the same distance map.

1.3.3.1 Serial Implementation

The serial algorithm needs to scan the image twice, once from the upper-left corner to the lower-right corner (*forward scan*), and another time from the lower-right corner to the upper-left corner (*reverse scan*). In actual operation, the mask is first decomposed into two symmetrical sub-masks; then, these two sub-masks are used respectively to forward and backward scan, pixel by pixel, through the initial distance map defined by Equation (1.14), and adopt a method of calculation similar to convolution. When a certain pixel is scanned, the mask coefficient values and the corresponding values of the image are added together, and the minimum value of the obtained sum is assigned to the pixel corresponding to the center value of the mask. The following example can be used to introduce this process.

Consider the image shown in Figure 1.20(a). Let all the pixels form a set P, and the two white pixels in the center form a set B (this is done for the convenience of explanation). Now use the 3×3 mask shown in Figure 1.22(a) (with $a = 3$ and $b = 4$) to calculate the distance map. This mask can be decomposed into two symmetrical sub-masks, called the upper sub-mask and the lower sub-mask, respectively, as shown in Figure 1.22(b) and Figure 1.22(c).

1. Forward scan

Figure 1.23(a) shows the initial distance map $[DT(p)]^{(0)}$. Take the upper sub-mask along the sequence marked in Figure 1.23(b) to scan and update the values of each position of

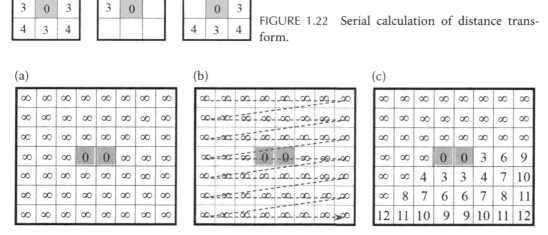

FIGURE 1.22 Serial calculation of distance transform.

FIGURE 1.23 Forward scan and results.

(a)

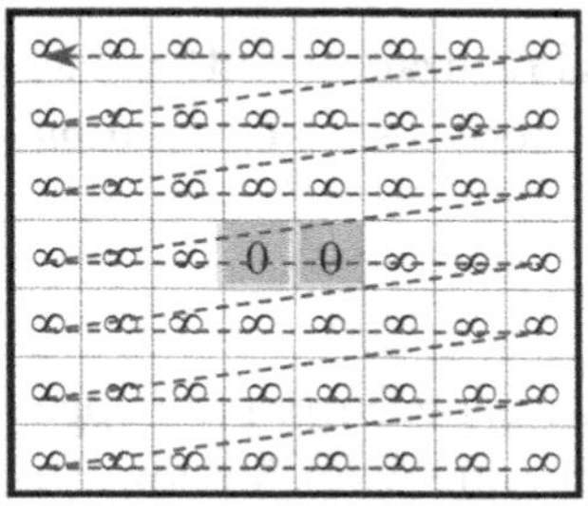

(b)

12	11	10	9	9	10	11	12
11	8	7	6	6	7	8	11
10	7	4	3	3	4	7	10
9	6	3	0	0	3	6	9
10	7	4	3	3	4	7	10
11	8	7	6	6	7	8	11
12	11	10	9	9	10	11	12

FIGURE 1.24   Reverse scan and results.

the initial distance map according to Equation (1.15). When the mask is at the image boundary, only the mask coefficients in the distance map are considered. The result of this scan is the distance map $[\mathrm{DT}(p)]^{(t')}$, as shown in Figure 1.23(c).

2. Reverse scan

In a similar way, take the lower sub-mask along the sequence marked in Figure 1.24(a) to scan and update the values of each position of the distance map $[\mathrm{DT}(p)]^{(t')}$ according to Equation (1.15). The result of this scan is the distance map shown in Figure 1.24(b). Figure 1.20(c) is the grayscale representation of the final distance map.

Obviously, the computational complexity of this algorithm is $O(W \times H)$, because the update rule in Equation (1.15) can be calculated in constant time.

1.3.3.2 Parallel Implementation

In the parallel computing structure, each pixel corresponds to a processor. First, obtain the initial distance map according to Equation (1.14), and then iteratively use the update rule of Equation (1.15) for calculating all pixels. This update process will continue until the distance map no longer changes and stops. The parallel algorithm can be represented as

$$\mathrm{DT}^{(t)}(x_p, y_p) = \min_{k,j}\{\mathrm{DT}^{(t-1)}(x_p + k, y_p + l) + M(k, l)\} \tag{1.16}$$

where $\mathrm{DT}^{(t)}(x_p, y_p)$ is the value at iteration t at (x_p, y_p), k and l are position values relative to the mask center $(0, 0)$, and $M(k, l)$ is the mask value of the corresponding position. The specific steps can be introduced with the following examples.

Still considering the image shown in Figure 1.20(a), still let all pixels form the set P and the two white pixels in the center form the set B. Now consider directly using the entire 3×3 mask shown in Figure 1.22(a) to calculate the distance map. The initial distance map is still as shown in Figure 1.23(a). Figure 1.25 shows the distance map obtained at each step of the parallel computing process. Figure 1.25(a) is the result of one calculation, and Figure 1.25(b) is the result of two calculations. After Figure 1.25(c), the distance map will not change, which is the final distance map.

(a)

∞	∞	∞	∞	∞	∞	∞	∞
∞	∞	∞	∞	∞	∞	∞	∞
∞	∞	4	3	3	4	∞	∞
∞	∞	3	0	0	3	∞	∞
∞	∞	4	3	3	4	∞	∞
∞	∞	∞	∞	∞	∞	∞	∞
∞	∞	∞	∞	∞	∞	∞	∞

(b)

∞	∞	∞	∞	∞	∞	∞	∞
∞	8	7	6	6	7	8	∞
∞	7	4	3	3	4	7	∞
∞	6	3	0	0	3	6	∞
∞	7	4	3	3	4	7	∞
∞	8	7	6	6	7	8	∞
∞	∞	∞	∞	∞	∞	∞	∞

(c)

12	11	10	9	9	10	11	12
11	8	7	6	6	7	8	11
10	7	4	3	3	4	7	10
9	6	3	0	0	3	6	9
10	7	4	3	3	4	7	10
11	8	7	6	6	7	8	11
12	11	10	9	9	10	11	12

FIGURE 1.25 Steps and results in parallel computing.

Unlike a serial algorithm, the number of scans required is always two; for a parallel algorithm, the number of scans required is equal to half of the maximum width of the widest object in the image and is the maximum value of the distance function.

Assuming that an ordinary serial computer is used for calculation, for an image of $N \times N$, the time required for the parallel algorithm is approximately $N^2 \times N/2 \times 8 = 4N^3$; while the time required for the serial algorithm is approximately $N^2 \times 2 \times (5 \times 2) = 20N^2$.

1.4 CHARACTERISTICS OF THIS BOOK

There are many books about image technology, so what are the special characteristics of this book? Let's have the discussion from the three aspects of writing motivation, material selection and contents, as well as structure and arrangement.

1.4.1 Writing Motivation

IE covers a wide range of fields and contains many technologies. It is a huge project to fully understand and master image technology step by step. However, in many image applications and related scientific research and development work, it is often necessary to use specific and specialized image technology to complete the task as soon as possible. Many textbooks introduce a lot of image technology little by little from shallow to deep, but it takes a long time for readers to reach a certain height and depth through learning one after another. Although some monographs have in-depth introduction to specific image technology, they require readers to have a better foundation at the beginning, so they are not suitable for readers who are initially exposed to image technology and have a special task to perform.

Refer to the schematic diagram in Figure 1.26. A complete introduction to IE should include three parts (similar to any discipline and field), or three layers (corresponding to the three parts from bottom to top in the figure): (i) first layer: essential concepts and basic principles; (ii) second layer: specific methods and practical techniques; (iii) third layer: research frontiers and latest development. In general, various textbooks mainly focus on the first layer (as shown by the lower-middle triangle in Figure 1.26) and cover mostly essential concepts and basic principles. If one starts with the essential concepts and learns basic principles little by little, the foundation will be relatively solid, but it will

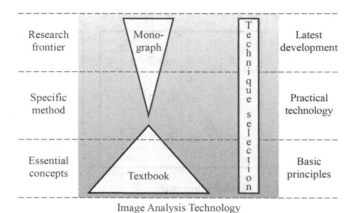

FIGURE 1.26 A complete introduction to the three layers of image analysis.

take a long time to reach the second layer. It will be difficult for people in different working fields who only need certain skills, and many other concepts and principles are not used. The monographs mainly focus on the third layer (as shown by the upper-middle triangle in Figure 1.26) and mainly focus on the research frontiers and latest development, which can be used as a reference for the cutting-edge innovative scientific research, but they have higher requirements for the reader's relevant foundation and need to have a more professional foreshadowing, and some technologies and methods may not be mature enough to solve the current real-world problems in practical applications.

This book attempts to combine the strengths of the textbook and monograph, and fill the gap between them, to meet the needs of readers who do not have the foundation of comprehensive image technology but need to use image techniques to solve specific tasks. To this end, according to the classification of image technology, we first select some of the more recently applied techniques to meet the needs of readers with specific applications; and then provide the introduction of each type of technology step by step, starting with the basic principles, so that readers with less fundamental knowledge can learn. We call it a selection of techniques, and for these selected techniques, three layers are penetrated, as shown in the rectangle on the right of Figure 1.14. When introducing these techniques, it not only starts overviewing the essential concepts and basic principles, providing enough introduction and explanation of current specific methods and practical techniques, but also involves some discussion on research frontier trends and latest results in conjunction with the development of technical methods.

1.4.2 Material Selection and Contents

This book focuses on (narrowly) IA (refer to Zhang 2017b) and selects seven types of technical fields and directions that are currently receiving widespread attention and are commonly used in many applications for introduction. They are as follows: (i) image segmentation, (ii) segmentation evaluation and comparison, (iii) saliency object detection, (iv) motion analysis, (v) mathematical morphology methods, (vi) face recognition, and (vii) expression classification. The definitions and explanations for the related terms appearing in the book can be found in Zhang (2021).

Each chapter focuses on one type of technology. The following summarizes the contents of these seven chapters separately.

Chapter 2 introduces image segmentation technology. First, a more formal definition of segmentation is given and existing methods are classified; then some typical techniques in the four categories of methods are introduced; then some practical techniques in two segmentation applications that have received widespread attentions: Color image segmentations and medical image segmentations are analyzed. Finally, some recent developments and further research are included.

Chapter 3 introduces the image segmentation evaluation technology. First, a layered method for segmentation and evaluation technology is proposed, and then a segmentation evaluation framework and its three important modules, performance evaluation, image synthesis, and algorithm testing, are introduced. Next, the characteristics of various segmentation evaluation criteria are analyzed in detail and some evaluation examples are presented; the comparison of evaluation methods and criteria is also discussed, and an example of system improving the segmentation performance with the aid of evaluation technology is given. Finally, some recent developments and further research are included.

Chapter 4 introduces salient object detection technology. First, the origin of the saliency name is explained, and then the basic principles and technical characteristics of using saliency for object detection are introduced. Next, several actual saliency region extraction techniques based on contrast, background prior, and the most stable region are respectively introduced, analyzed, and discussed. Finally, some recent developments and further research are included.

Chapter 5 introduces motion analysis technology. First, the research contents of motion analysis are summarized, and then some common techniques of moving object detection are introduced. Then, it focuses on a variety of typical methods of moving object segmentation, including methods based on optical flow field and model; also, the time information is combined to analyze the moving object tracking technology. Finally, some recent developments and further research are included.

Chapter 6 introduces mathematical morphology technology. Mathematical morphology includes binary mathematical morphology and grayscale mathematical morphology. The introduction of their mathematical foundation is provided. Next, starting from their respective basic operations, how to construct corresponding combined operations to achieve meaningful image analysis operations are first presented, and then some workable algorithms to solve practical problems in image analysis are further discussed. Finally, some recent developments and further research are included.

Chapter 7 introduces face recognition technology. First, it gives an overview of the research and application of face recognition, as well as the process and modules of face recognition; and then it focuses on the types and characteristics of commonly used subspace technologies. Next, some detailed introductions to the principles of face recognition modules and their technical directions are given, and some experimental results are given. Finally, some recent developments and further research are included.

Chapter 8 introduces facial expression classification technology. The principle and process of facial expression classification, as well as the existing facial expression classification standards and system performance are introduced. Then, the specific facial organ detection, typical facial expression feature extraction, and distinctive facial expression classification methods are separately discussed, and the experimental results are also provided and analyzed. Finally, some recent developments and further research are included.

This book assumes that the reader has a certain background in science and engineering, and has some understanding of linear algebra, matrices, signal processing, statistics, and probability. It would be better if there was certain knowledge of some basic image concepts, such as pixels, image representation, image display, image transformation, image filtering, and so on. It will be helpful to have some basic elementary information of signal processing, because a 2-D image can be seen as an augmentation of a 1-D signal, and IA is an extension of signal processing. This book is dominated by image technology to solve practical problems.

This book does not give too much consideration to the content from a comprehensive and systematic view, and the work experience and basic skills of practitioners in related industries are also a very useful point of view; rather, it only focuses on several specific technologies and provides information from the shallower to the deeper. Although it is not written as a pure textbook, it can be used as a supplement to the textbook, especially for in-depth introductions to specific directions. This book is not a monograph in the traditional sense. It does not only emphasize advanced and real-time features but mainly introduces some of the more mature technology methods in the near future (and also considers some of the latest scientific research results). This book attempts to cover the vertical range from introductory textbooks to research monographs in selected technical directions to meet the specific needs of readers (Figure 1.26).

1.4.3 Structure and Arrangement

The styles of the following chapters of this book are relatively consistent. At the beginning of each chapter, in addition to the introduction of the basic concepts and overall content, some application fields and occasions of the corresponding technologies are listed, which are reflected in the idea of application services; there is also an overview of each section to grasp the context of the whole chapter. There are some similarities in the arrangement and structure of the body content of each chapter. Each chapter has multiple sections, which can be divided into the following three parts from beginning to end (corresponding to the three levels in Figure 1.26).

1. Principle and technology overview

The first section at the beginning of each chapter has the contents as in typical textbooks. It introduces the principle, history, use, method overview, and development of the image technology. The goal is to give more comprehensive and basic information (a lot of examples and demonstrations can be found in Zhang, most of which come from professional textbooks (refer to (Zhang 2017b)).

TABLE 1.2   The classification table of the corresponding sections of the text of each chapter in this book

Sl. No.	Technology	Principles	Typical Techniques	Progress/Trends
Chapter 2	Image segmentation	Section 2.1	Sections 2.2–2.4	Section 2.5
Chapter 3	Segmentation evaluation	Sections 3.1–3.2	Sections 3.3–3.5	Section 3.6
Chapter 4	Significant object detection	Sections 4.1–4.2	Sections 4.3–4.5	Section 4.6
Chapter 5	Motion analysis	Section 5.1	Sections 5.2–5.4	Section 5.5
Chapter 6	Mathematical morphology	Section 6.1	Sections 6.2–6.4	Section 6.5
Chapter 7	Face recognition	Sections 7.1–7.2	Sections 7.3–7.6	Section 7.7
Chapter 8	Expression classification	Section 8.1	Sections 8.2–8.4	Section 8.5

2. Description of specific technical methods

The next few sections in the middle of each chapter have the contents combined from textbooks and monographs. They introduce several related typical technologies, which are described in detail in terms of methods. The goal is to give some ideas that can effectively and efficiently solve the problems faced by this type of image technology and provide solutions for practical applications. These sections can have a certain progressive relationship or a relatively independent parallel relationship. Most contents are mainly extracted from the literature in journals or conference papers. Most of them are followed up and researched, but they have not been written into professional textbooks or books.

3. Introduction to recent developments and directions

The last section of each chapter is more research-oriented. It is based on the analysis and review of relevant new documents in some important journals or conference proceedings in recent years. The goal is to provide some of the latest relevant information on focusing techniques and to help understand the progress and trends in the corresponding technology.

The arrangement of the main text in sections of each chapter is shown in Table 1.2.

From the perspective of understanding the technical overview, one can only look at the sections of the principle introduction. If one wants to solve practical problems, one needs to learn some typical techniques. To master the technology more deeply, one can also refer to the recent progress/trends and look at more references.

REFERENCES

Das, P.P., and B.N. Chatterji. 1988. Knight's distances in digital geometry. *Pattern Recognition Letters*, 7: 215–226.

Joyce, L. 1985. *Image Analysis: Principles and Practice*. USA: Joyce Loebl, Ltd.

Mahdavieh, Y., and R.C. Gonzalez. 1992. *Advances in Image Analysis*. USA: DPIE Optical Engineering Press.

Marchand-Maillet, S., and Y.M. Sharaiha. 2000. *Binary Digital Image Processing—A Discrete Approach*. USA: Academic Press.

Pavlidis, T. 1988. Image analysis. *Annual Review of Computer Science*, 3: 121–146.

Rosenfeld, A. 1984. Image analysis: Problems, progress and prospects. *Pattern Recognition*, 17: 3–12.

Russ, J.C. 2006. *The Image Processing Handbook*, 5th Ed. UK: CRC Press.

Young, I.T. 1993. Three-dimensional image analysis. *Proceedings of the VIP'93*, 35–38.

Zhang, Y.-J. 1991. 3-D image analysis system and megakaryocyte quantitation. *Cytometry*, 12: 308–315.

Zhang, Y.-J. 1996. Image engineering and bibliography in China. In *Technical Digest of International Symposium on Information Science and Technology*, 158–160.

Zhang, Y.-J. 1999. Two new concepts for N_{16} space. *IEEE Signal Processing Letters*, 6(9): 221–223.

Zhang, Y.-J. 2000. Mixed connectivity in 16-neighborhood. *Pattern Recognition and Artificial Intelligent*, 13(1): 90–93.

Zhang, Y.-J. 2002. Image engineering and related publications. *International Journal of Image and Graphics*, 2(3): 441–452.

Zhang, Y.-J. 2009. A study of image engineering. In: Khosrow-Pour, M., Ed. *Encyclopedia of Information Science and Technology*, 2nd Ed., VII: Chapter 575 (pp. 3608–3615). Hershey PA, USA: Information Science Reference.

Zhang, Y.-J. 2015. Statistics on image engineering literatures. In: Khosrow-Pour, M., Ed. *Encyclopedia of Information Science and Technology*, 3rd Ed., Chapter 595 (pp. 6030–6040). Hershey PA, USA: Information Science Reference.

Zhang, Y.-J. 2017a. *Image Engineering, Vol. 1: Image Processing*. Germany: De Gruyter.

Zhang, Y.-J. 2017b. *Image Engineering, Vol. 2: Image Analysis*. Germany: De Gruyter.

Zhang, Y.-J. 2017c. *Image Engineering, Vol. 3: Image Understanding*. Germany: De Gruyter.

Zhang, Y.-J. 2018a. Development of image engineering in the last 20 years. In: Khosrow-Pour, M., Ed. *Encyclopedia of Information Science and Technology*, 4th Ed., Chapter 113 (pp. 1319–1330).Hershey PA, USA: Information Science Reference.

Zhang, Y.-J. 2018b. An overview of image engineering in recent years. *Proceedings of the 21st IEEE International Conference on Computational Science and Engineering*, pp. 119–122.

Zhang, Y.-J. 2021. *Handbook of Image Engineering*. Singapore: Springer Nature.

Zhang, Y.-J., X.Y. Huang, and R. Li. 2001. A preliminary scheme for automatic detection of fine presswork defect. *Chinese Journal of Stereology and Image Analysis*, 6(2): 109–112.

CHAPTER 2

Image Segmentation

I mage segmentation is a key step in image analysis, and it is also a basic computer vision technology. *Image segmentation* refers to the technology and process of dividing an image into regions with characteristics and extracting objects of interest. The object here can correspond to a single region or multiple regions. For example, a car on the street in an image, or all the windows on the wall of a building in a photo. In image applications, image segmentation technology involves a wide range of fields.

Only after the image is segmented can it be counted as from image processing into image analysis. Image segmentation, object separation, feature extraction, and parameter measurement transform the original image into a more abstract and compact form, making higher-level analysis and understanding possible.

After about 60 years of research, image segmentation technology has made considerable progress, and thousands of methods have been proposed (Zhang 2014, 2015, 2018). In the following, it gives first the formal definition of image segmentation and various segmentation algorithms are classified; some typical algorithms from each category are selected and briefly introduced; then the color image segmentation and medical image segmentation are taken as examples for some specific discussions.

The contents of each section of this chapter are arranged as follows.

Section 2.1 first gives a stricter definition of image segmentation. Then it introduces a scheme for classifying image segmentation algorithms, and also gives a general discussion on the basic principles and characteristics of the algorithms in each category.

In Section 2.2, according to the proposed algorithm classification scheme, in view of the characteristics of the four categories of image segmentation algorithms, some representative algorithms are selected for a specific and detailed introduction. Not only the principal ideas are analyzed, but also the more detailed implementation methods are discussed.

Section 2.3 focuses on the segmentation of color images. Color images provide richer information, and it also requires the extension of the original gray-scale image segmentation technology. The characteristics of several types of typical technologies are analyzed here, and a distinctive color segmentation algorithm is also introduced in detail.

DOI: 10.1201/b23131-2

Section 2.4 mainly discusses the segmentation of medical images. In medical images, not only segmented objects with different shapes and complex structures are presented, but also many imaging interference factors appear, which bring many challenges. The algorithms of each generation are compared and analyzed, and a method for segmentation of high-dimensional images in time and space is also introduced.

Section 2.5 provides a brief introduction to some technique developments and promising research directions in the last year.

2.1 DEFINITION OF SEGMENTATION AND CLASSIFICATION OF METHODS

In the research and application of images, people are often only interested in certain parts of the image (interest here has a certain subjective meaning). These parts are often called *objects* or *foreground* (other parts are called *background*), and they generally correspond to specific regions of the image with unique and uniform properties. In order to identify and analyze the object, it is necessary to separate these relevant regions and extract the object region from them.

The following first gives a more formal definition of image segmentation, and then classifies image segmentation algorithms and briefly discusses the basic principles and characteristics of various algorithms.

2.1.1 Definition of Image Segmentation

The goal of *image segmentation* is to determine the attribution region of each pixel, so one can use the concept that an image is a set of pixels and use the following more formal methods to define:

Let the set R represent the entire image region, the segmentation of R can be regarded as dividing R into several non-empty subsets (sub-regions) $R_1, R_2, \ldots, R_n$ that meet the following five conditions:

1. $\cup_{i=1}^{n} R_i = R$.

2. For all i and j, $i \neq j$, there is $R_i \cap R_j = \emptyset$;

3. For $i = 1, 2, \ldots, n$, $P(R_i) = \text{TRUE}$;

4. For $i \neq j$, $P(R_i \cup R_j) = \text{FALSE}$;

5. For $i = 1, 2, \ldots, n$, R_i is a connected region.

where $P(R_i)$ represents a certain property of all elements in the set R_i, and $\emptyset$ is the empty set.

The above condition (1) indicates that the sum (union) of all sub-regions obtained by segmentation should be able to include all pixels in the image, or the segmentation should divide each pixel in the image into a certain sub-region. Condition (2) indicates that the sub-regions do not overlap each other, or that one pixel cannot belong to two regions at the same time. Condition (3) indicates that the pixels belonging to the same region obtained after segmentation should have some identical characteristics. Condition (4) indicates that the pixels belonging to the different regions obtained after segmentation should have some different characteristics. Condition (5) requires that the pixels in the same sub-region should be connected. The image segmentation is always carried out according to some segmentation criteria. Conditions (1) and (2) indicate that the segmentation criteria should be applicable to all regions and all pixels, while conditions (3) and (4) indicate that the segmentation criteria should help determine the representative characteristics of pixels in each region.

2.1.2 Classification of Image Segmentation Algorithms

After years of research and application of image segmentation, thousands of algorithms have been proposed. There are also many ways to classify them according to their technical characteristics. Generally speaking, image segmentation should be performed according to the characteristics of each region, where the characteristics can be grayscale, color, texture, and so on. Considering the previous definition of image segmentation, two aspects can be considered when classifying algorithms.

First, the segmentation of an image can often be based on two properties between pixel attribute values: discontinuity and similarity. Taking the segmentation of a grayscale image as an example, the pixels inside the regions generally have grayscale similarity, and the pixels on the boundaries between regions generally have grayscale discontinuities. Therefore, the segmentation algorithm can be divided into a *boundary-based algorithm* that uses the grayscale discontinuity between regions and a *region-based algorithm* that uses the grayscale similarity within a region. The region-based algorithm uses the region attribute and directly determines the region to which the pixel belongs, while the boundary-based algorithm first determines the boundary between the regions to determine the attribution of the pixel. Since the boundary and the region are complementary, the region enclosed by the boundary can be determined by detecting the boundary.

Secondly, according to the different processing strategies in the segmentation process, the segmentation algorithms can be divided into parallel algorithms and sequential algorithms. In *parallel algorithms*, all judgments and decisions can be made independently and simultaneously, while in *sequential algorithms*, the results of early processing can be used in subsequent processing. Generally, the calculation time required for sequential algorithms is often longer than that of parallel algorithms, but the robustness against noise is often stronger.

The above two classification criteria do not overlap and complement each other, so the segmentation algorithm can be divided into four categories according to these two criteria (see Table 2.1): (i) parallel boundary category; (ii) sequential boundary category;

TABLE 2.1 Segmentation algorithm classification table

Classification	Boundary (discontinuity)	Region (similarity)
Parallel processing	(i) Parallel boundary class	(iii) Parallel region class
Sequential processing	(ii) Sequential boundary class	(iv) Sequential region class

(iii) parallel region category; (iv) sequential region category. This classification method can not only meet the five conditions of the above segmentation definition, but also include all the various algorithms that have been proposed for image segmentation.

2.2 VARIOUS SEGMENTATION ALGORITHMS

According to the previous classification results, several typical and basic methods in each category are selected to introduce in the following.

2.2.1 Parallel Boundary Class Algorithms

The parallel boundary algorithms use a parallel mode to detect the object edge.

Edge detection is the key step of all boundary-based segmentation algorithms (including parallel boundary category and sequential boundary category). An edge generally exists between two adjacent regions with different gray values, and the gray value at the edge has accelerated changes, resulting in discontinuous gray values on both sides of the region boundary in the digital image. This discontinuity can often be easily detected by differentiation or derivative. Generally, first-order and second-order derivatives are commonly used to detect edges. When using the first-order derivative, the boundary position corresponds to the maximum value of the first-order derivative. When using the second-order derivative, the boundary position corresponds to the zero-crossing point of the second-order derivative.

The detection of the edges in the image can be done through convolution with the help of spatial differential operators. In fact, the derivative in the digital image is obtained by using the difference approximate differentiation. Here are some simple spatial differential operators.

2.2.1.1 Gradient Operator

The gradient corresponds to the first-order derivative, and the *gradient operator* is the first-order derivative operator. For a continuous function $f(x, y)$, its gradient at position (x, y) can be expressed as a vector:

$$\nabla f(x, y) = [G_x \quad G_y]^{\mathrm{T}} = \left[\frac{\partial f}{\partial x} \quad \frac{\partial f}{\partial y} \right]^{\mathrm{T}} \tag{2.1}$$

The magnitude (often abbreviated as gradient) and direction angle of this vector are, respectively:

$$\mathrm{mag}(\nabla f) = [G_x^2 + G_y^2]^{1/2} \tag{2.2}$$

$$\phi(x, y) = \arctan(G_y/G_x) \tag{2.3}$$

In practice, a small region mask convolution is commonly used to approximate the partial derivative in the above three equations. One mask each is used for G_x and G_y, so two masks are required to be combined to form a gradient operator. According to the size of the mask and the different values of the elements (coefficients) in the mask, many

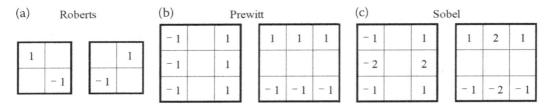

FIGURE 2.1   The masks of several commonly used gradient operators.

different operators have been proposed. The simplest gradient operator is the *Robert crossover operator*, and its two 2 × 2 masks are shown in Figure 2.1(a). The *Prewitt operator* and *Sobel operator* are more commonly used. They both use two 3 × 3 masks, as shown in Figure 2.1(b) and Figure 2.1(c), respectively. Among them, the Sobel operator often has a better effect.

The operator uses a similar convolution method, moves each mask on the image, and calculates the gradient value of the corresponding center pixel at each position, and then combines the gradient values of the two masks with different norms to obtain the final gradient value. When the edge gray value transition is sharp and the noise in the image is relatively small, the gradient operator will work better.

2.2.1.2 Laplacian Operator

Laplacian operator is a kind of second-order derivative operator. For image $f(x, y)$, its Laplacian value at position (x, y) is defined as follows:

$$\nabla^2 f = \frac{\partial^2 f}{\partial x^2} + \frac{\partial^2 f}{\partial y^2} \tag{2.4}$$

In digital images, the calculation of the Laplacian value can also be realized with the help of various masks. The basic requirement for the mask here is that the coefficient corresponding to the center pixel should be positive, and the coefficient corresponding to the neighboring pixels of the center pixel should be negative, and the sum of all these coefficients should be zero. The three typical masks are shown in Figure 2.2, and they all meet the above requirements. The Laplacian operator is a second-order derivative operator, so it is quite sensitive to the noise in the image. In addition, it often produces double-pixel-wide edges and cannot provide edge direction information. For the above reasons, the Laplacian operator is mainly used to determine that the edge pixel is on the dark or bright side of the edge in the image after the edge pixel is known, but it can also help determine the position of the edge according to the nature of detecting the zero-crossing point.

FIGURE 2.2   The masks of the Laplacian operator.

2.2.1.3 Marr Operator

The method of calculating the derivative is susceptible to the influence of noise in the image, especially if the second-order derivative is used. In order to reduce or eliminate the influence of noise, the image can be convolved with the Laplacian of the following 2-D Gaussian function:

$$h(x, y) = \exp\left(-\frac{x^2 + y^2}{2\sigma^2}\right) \qquad (2.5)$$

where σ is the mean square variance of the Gaussian distribution. If we let $r^2 = x^2 + y^2$ and calculate the Laplacian value by taking the second-order derivative of r, we get:

$$\nabla^2 h = \left(\frac{r^2 - \sigma^2}{\sigma^4}\right)\exp\left(-\frac{r^2}{2\sigma^2}\right) \qquad (2.6)$$

This is an axisymmetric function, and its profile is shown in Figure 2.3. It can be seen from the figure that this function has a zero-crossing point at $r = \pm\sigma$, which is positive when $|r < \sigma|$ and negative when $|r > \sigma|$.

The above function is also called *Marr operator*. It can be proved that the average value of this operator is also zero. If it is convolved with the image, it will not change the overall grayscale range of the image. On the other hand, since it is quite smooth, it will blur the image if it is convolved with the image, and the blur degree is proportional to σ. Because the smooth nature of $\nabla^2 h$ can reduce the influence of noise, when the edge is blurred or the noise is large, the use of $\nabla^2 h$ in detecting the zero-crossing point can provide a more reliable edge position. Of course, the computational complexity of this method is relatively large.

2.2.1.4 Boundary Closing

When there is noise, the edge pixels obtained by various operators are often isolated or only continuous in small segments. In order to form a closed boundary of a region to separate different regions, it is necessary to connect edge pixels. The aforementioned various edge detection operators all work in parallel. If the boundary is closed in parallel

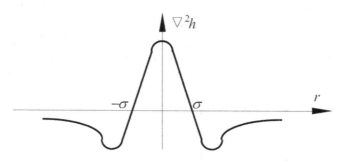

FIGURE 2.3   Profile of $\nabla^2 h$.

on this basis, the segmentation can basically be implemented in parallel. The following introduces a method for boundary closing by using the magnitude and direction of the pixel gradient.

The basis of edge pixel connection is a certain similarity between them. Therefore, if the pixel (s, t) is in the neighborhood of the pixel (x, y) and their gradient amplitude and gradient direction meet the following two conditions (where T is the amplitude threshold and A is the angle threshold):

$$|\nabla f(x, y) - \nabla f(s, t)| \leqslant T \tag{2.7}$$

$$|\varphi(x, y) - \varphi(s, t)| \leqslant A \tag{2.8}$$

Then the pixel located at (s, t) can be connected with the pixel located at (x, y). If all edge pixels are judged and connected in this way, it is hoped that a closed boundary can be obtained.

2.2.2 Sequential Boundary Class Algorithms

The sequential boundary class algorithms use a sequential mode to detect the edge of the object. Specifically, the edge detection is performed serially. In other words, detecting edge points and connecting them are performed at the same time. Typical methods include graph search, dynamic programming, etc. (Zhang 2017). The methods using the active contour model and graph cutting are commonly used sequential boundary class algorithms.

2.2.2.1 Active Contour Model

The *active contour model* approximates the contour of the object in the image by gradually changing the shape of the closed curve. In this process, the various parts of the object contour are often represented by straight-line segments. The active contour model is also called the *snake model*, because in the process of approximating the object contour, the closed curve continuously changes its shape like a snake crawling. In practice, the active contour model is often used to detect the actual contour when an approximate initial contour of the object contour in the image is given.

Referring to Figure 2.4, the sequence of points $\{v_i\}$ represents the initial points on the **active contour**, and the final segmentation result can be obtained by adjusting them one by one to the actual contour.

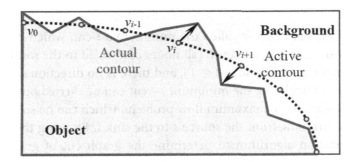

FIGURE 2.4   The movement of a point on the active contour to the actual contour.

The energy that helps the initial contour to continuously change its shape to approximate the actual contour includes *internal energy* that depends on the shape of the contour itself and *external energy* that depends on the nature of the image. The internal energy is used to promote the change of the active contour shape and keep the distance between the points on the contour not too far or too close. Commonly used internal energy includes the continuous energy used to push the shape of the active contour to change and the expansion force energy used to expand or contract the active contour in the radial direction. The external energy is used to attract the deformed mask to the features of interest (such as the edge of the object in the image). Commonly used external energy includes image grayscale energy with high or low gray levels in the corresponding region and image gradient energy proportional to the pixel gradient amplitude.

2.2.2.2 Graph Cut

Graph cut is a special segmentation method that combines the overall information and local information of the image, and uses the graph structure.

The main steps of image segmentation with the graph cut method are:

1. Mapping the image I to be segmented into arc-weighted directed graph G, which corresponds to I in both size and dimension. Among them, each pixel in the image I is regarded as a node in the graph G, that is, the node set N is composed of all pixels; and the adjacent relationship between the pixels is represented by the arc in the graph G, that is, the node pair set A represents the (weighted) connection between pixels.

2. Determining the respective seeds of the object and the background, and constructing two special graph nodes for them, namely the source node s and the sink node t. Both the object seed and the background seed are assigned corresponding object or background labels, and all seeds are connected to the source node or the sink node according to their labels. In this way, an arc-weighted graph $G_{st} = [N \cup \{s, t\}, A]$ is obtained, where the node set N corresponds to the pixel in the image I, and s and t are two special terminal nodes.

3. Calculate the arc cost function, and assign a certain arc cost to each arc in the graph G. A cut in G_{st} divides the nodes in the graph into two groups, and its cost is the sum of the costs of the arcs (the arcs that the cut traverses/crosses) corresponding to this cut.

4. The cut with the least cost is called the minimum s-t cut, which divides the nodes into two non-overlapping subsets S (all nodes connected to the source, $s \in S$) and T (all nodes connected to the sink, $t \in T$), and there is no directional path from s to t. The problem of calculating the minimum s-t cut can be carried out with the help of its dual – calculating the maximum flow problem, which can be solved by searching for the maximum flow from the source s to the sink t. By using the maximum flow graph optimization algorithm to determine the graph cut of graph G, the nodes corresponding to the object and background pixels can be distinguished.

(a)   (b)   (c)   (d)

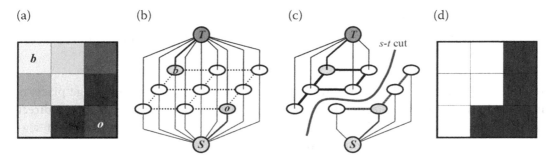

FIGURE 2.5   Schematic diagram of each step of graph cut.

The above steps can be illustrated with the help of Figure 2.5. Figure 2.5(a) shows the image I to be segmented, and the object seed o and background seed b, $o \subset N$, $b \subset N$, $o \cap b = \varnothing$ have been determined. Figure 2.5(b) is the constructed graph G_{st} (where the arc connecting adjacent pixels is represented by a dashed line, and the arc connecting the pixel and the terminal node is represented by different solid lines). Figure 2.5(c) shows the s-t cut (cutting the corresponding arc) in the picture G_{st}, in which all object pixels are connected to the object seed node and all background pixels are connected to the background seed node. Figure 2.5(d) shows the segmentation result obtained by mapping the nodes back to the image according to the s-t cut.

2.2.3 Parallel Region Class Algorithms

The parallel region class algorithms use a parallel mode to directly detect the object region, which can determine the attribution of each object pixel at the same time. *Thresholding* is the most widely used parallel segmentation method for direct detection of regions. The key step is to determine the segmentation threshold. The determination of the threshold can use different information in the image, and its general form can be written as:

$$T = T[x, y, f(x, y), q(x, y)] \tag{2.9}$$

In the formula, $f(x, y)$ is the gray value at the pixel point (x, y); $q(x, y)$ is a certain local property of the neighborhood of the pixel point. In other words, T can be a function of pixel position (x, y), pixel gray value $f(x, y)$, and pixel neighborhood local property value $q(x, y)$ in general cases. With the help of the above formula, the thresholds used in common thresholding segmentation methods can be divided into the following three categories:

1. *Global threshold*: it is selected only according to $f(x, y)$, the obtained threshold is only related to the nature of each image pixel, but the determined threshold at this time takes the pixels of the whole image into consideration;

2. *Local threshold*: it is selected according to $f(x, y)$ and $q(x, y)$. The determination of this threshold is related to the properties of the (local) region, but the obtained threshold can be used for the segmentation of whole image;

3. *Dynamic threshold*: it is selected, in addition to $f(x, y)$ and $q(x, y)$, also according to the coordinates (that is, related to x and y), that is, the threshold is different everywhere in the whole image.

It should be noted that the information about the spatial distribution of image pixels is not used in the threshold selection (only the pixel grayscale information is used). A direct result is that if there are multiple disconnected objects in the image, the result of segmentation will be multiple disconnected regions. In other words, the segmentation result with thresholding does not necessarily guarantee that the object is a connected region.

2.2.3.1 Global Threshold Selection

Assuming that the image is composed of an object and a background with a unimodal grayscale distribution, the gray values between adjacent pixels within the object or background are highly correlated, but the gray values of pixels on both sides of the boundary between the object and the background have large difference. If an image satisfies these conditions, its grayscale histogram can basically be regarded as a mixture of two unimodal histograms corresponding to the object and background, respectively. At this time, if the two distributions are close in size (number) and the means are far enough apart, and the mean square error is small enough, the histogram should be bimodal. For this type of image, the (global) thresholding can often be used to better segment the image.

In the actual image, the gray values of the object pixels and the background pixels are often partially interlaced, and even if the valley of the histogram is selected, these pixels cannot be completely separated. At this time, it is often hoped that the probability of mis-segmentation can be minimized, and selecting the optimal threshold is a common method. Assuming that an image contains only two main types of gray value regions (object and background), its histogram can be seen as an approximation of the gray value probability density function $p(z)$. This density function is actually the sum of two unimodal density functions representing the object and background. If the form of the density function is known, then it is possible to select an optimal threshold to divide the image into two types of regions to minimize the mis-segmentation error.

Given such an image mixed with additive Gaussian noise, its mixed probability density is

$$p(z) = P_1 p_1(z) + P_2 p_2(z) = \frac{P_1}{\sqrt{2\pi}\,\sigma_1} \exp\left[-\frac{(z - \mu_1)^2}{2\sigma_1^2}\right] + \frac{P_2}{\sqrt{2\pi}\,\sigma_2} \exp\left[-\frac{(z - \mu_2)^2}{2\sigma_2^2}\right]$$

(2.10)

In the formula, P_1 and P_2 are the *a prior* probability of the gray values of the background and object regions, respectively; μ_1 and μ_2 are the average gray values of the background and object regions, respectively; σ_1 and σ_2 are the mean square variance of the mean value, respectively. According to the definition of probability, $P_1 + P_2 = 1$, so there are five unknown parameters in the mixed probability density. If these parameters can be obtained, the mixture probability density can be determined.

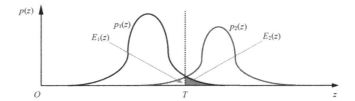

FIGURE 2.6 Optimal threshold selection schematic.

Now look at Figure 2.6. Assuming that $\mu_1 < \mu_2$, a threshold T needs to be defined so that pixels with a gray value less than T are segmented as the background, and pixels with a gray value greater than T are segmented as the object. At this time, the probability of erroneously classifying an object pixel as a background pixel and the probability of erroneously classifying a background pixel as an object pixel are, respectively:

$$E_1(T) = \int_{-\infty}^{T} p_2(z)\,dz \text{ and } E_2(T) = \int_{T}^{\infty} p_1(z)\,dz \tag{2.11}$$

The total error probability is

$$E(T) = P_2 \times E_1(T) + P_1 \times E_2(T) \tag{2.12}$$

In order to find the threshold value that minimizes the error, we can take the derivative of $E(T)$ with respect to T and make the derivative equal zero, so that

$$P_1 \times p_1(T) = P_2 \times p_2(T) \tag{2.13}$$

Applying this result to the Gaussian density (substituting Equation (2.10)), the quadratic equation can be obtained:

$$\begin{cases} A = \sigma_1^2 - \sigma_2^2 \\ B = 2(\mu_1\sigma_2^2 - \mu_2\sigma_1^2) \\ C = \sigma_1^2\mu_2^2 - \sigma_2^2\mu_1^2 + 2\sigma_1^2\sigma_2^2 \ln(\sigma_2 P_1/\sigma_1 P_2) \end{cases} \tag{2.14}$$

This quadratic equation has two solutions in general. If the variances of the two regions are equal, there is only one optimal threshold:

$$T = \frac{\mu_1 + \mu_2}{2} + \frac{\sigma^2}{\mu_1 - \mu_2} \ln\left(\frac{P_2}{P_1}\right) \tag{2.15}$$

Furthermore, if the *a prior* probabilities of the two gray values are equal (or the variance is zero), then the optimal threshold is the median of the average gray values in the two regions. The optimal threshold obtained above is also called the *maximum likelihood threshold*.

2.2.3.2 Local Threshold Selection

The actual image is often affected by noise, etc. At this time, the valleys that originally separated the peaks will be filled. According to the image model introduced above, if the peaks corresponding to the object and the background on the histogram are very close or have a large difference in size, it is very difficult to detect the valley between them. Because at this time the histogram is basically single-peak, although one side of the peak may have a gentle slope, or one side of the peak may not be steep on the other side. In order to solve this kind of problem, in addition to using the properties of the pixels themselves, the local properties of some pixels in neighborhoods can also be used.

A common local property is the gradient of pixels. In other words, the pixel grayscale and pixel gradient information can be combined to construct a 2-D histogram (called *grayscale-gradient scatter map*), where one axis is the gray value axis and the other is the gradient value axis, and its statistical value is the number of pixels with a certain gray value and gradient value at the same time. As shown in Figure 2.7(a), there are generally two large clusters that are close to the gray value axis (low gradient value) but are separated from each other along the gray value axis in the scatter map. They correspond to the interior pixels of the object and the background, respectively. The shape of these two clusters is related to the degree of correlation between these pixels. If the correlation is strong or the gradient operator is not very sensitive to noise, these clusters will be very concentrated and very close to the gray value axis. Conversely, if the correlation is weak or the gradient operator is sensitive to noise, these clusters will be far away from the gray value axis. There will also be fewer points corresponding to pixels on the boundary of the object and background in the scatter map. The positions of these points are in the middle of the first two clusters along the gray value axis, but there is a certain distance from the gray value axis along the gradient value axis due to their larger gradient value. It can be seen that according to the distribution of pixels in different regions in the scatter map, gray threshold and gradient threshold can be used to separate them.

The schematic diagram of Figure 2.7(a) is actually an abstraction of the real world. The grayscale-gradient scatter map of the grayscale image of Figure 2.7(b) is shown in Figure 2.7(c). It can be seen that in Figure 2.7(c), several of the features discussed for Figure 2.7(a) are all present.

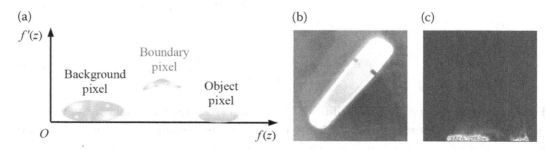

FIGURE 2.7 Schematic diagram of grayscale-gradient scatter map.

2.2.3.3 Dynamic Threshold Selection

When there are different light and dark changes in the image (for example, due to the influence of illumination) or the contrasts are different everywhere, if only a fixed global threshold is used to segment the entire image, the segmentation results will be affected because the situation in various images cannot be all taken into account. One solution is to use a set of thresholds related to coordinates to segment the image. This coordinate-related threshold is also called dynamic threshold. Its basic idea is to first decompose the image into a series of sub-images. These sub-images can overlap each other or just be adjacent to each other. If the sub-images are relatively small, the problems caused by the spatial changes in shadow or contrast will be relatively small, and a threshold can be calculated for each sub-image. At this time, the threshold for each sub-image can be selected by any fixed threshold method. By interpolating all the thresholds obtained from these sub-images, the threshold required for segmenting the pixels at each position in the image can be obtained. Here the threshold corresponding to each pixel constitutes a curved surface on the image (amplitude axis), which can also be called a threshold surface.

The following basic steps can be adopted for image segmentation using dynamic thresholding:

1. Divide the whole image into a series of sub-images with 50% overlap between each other;

2. Count the histogram of each sub-image;

3. Detect whether the histogram of each sub-image is double-peaked, if yes, use the optimal threshold method (other methods can also be used) to determine a threshold, otherwise it will not be processed;

4. According to the threshold values obtained for the sub-images whose histograms are bimodal, the threshold values of all the sub-images are obtained by interpolation;

5. According to the threshold value of each sub-image, the threshold values for all pixels are obtained through interpolation, and then the image is segmented.

Figure 2.8 shows an example of image segmentation using the dynamic thresholding (with coordinate-dependent threshold selection). Figure 2.8(a) is an image with grayscale

(a)   (b)   (c)   (d)   (e)

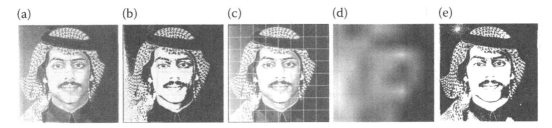

FIGURE 2.8   Dynamic thresholding example.

shading due to side illumination, and Figure 2.8(b) is the segmentation result with global thresholding. Due to uneven illumination, it is impossible to use single threshold to segment the whole image. As shown in Figure 2.8(b), the scarf and the background in the lower-left corner cannot be separated. This problem can be solved by thresholding each part of the whole image separately. Figure 2.8(c) is the partition grid (for sub-image) used, and Figure 2.8(d) is the threshold surface obtained after interpolating the thresholds of each partition. Use this threshold surface to segment Figure 2.8(a), providing the result shown in Figure 2.8(e); the problem in Figure 2.8(b) is overcome.

2.2.4 Sequential Region Class Algorithms

The sequential region class algorithm uses a sequential mode to directly detect the object region.

2.2.4.1 Region Growing

Region growing is a basic method in the sequential region class.

The basic idea of *region growing* is to combine pixels with similar properties to form regions. Specifically, a seed pixel for each region first needs to be found, which is used as the starting point for growth. Then, the pixels in the neighborhood around the seed pixel that have the same or similar properties as the seed pixel (determined according to a certain predetermined growth or similarity criterion) are selected and included into the region where the seed pixel is located. Use these new pixels as new seed pixels to continue the above process until no more pixels that meet the conditions can be included. Such a region is thus produced. Figure 2.9 shows an example. Figure 2.9(a) is an image to be segmented. The values of each pixel are shown by the values in each unit. Assume that the seed points of the two regions are known to be two shaded pixels in the figure. Take them as the center for region growing. The result after one step is shown in Figure 2.9(b), the result after two steps is shown in Figure 2.9(c), and the result after three steps is shown in Figure 2.9(d). At this time, all pixels have belonged to two regions, and the growth is over. Figure 2.9(d) is the final segmentation result.

It needs to be pointed out here that the growth criterion has a great influence on the segmentation result. The previous growth criterion is: if the absolute value of the difference between the gray value of the pixel under consideration and the seed pixel is less

(a)

1	0	4	7	5
1	0	4	7	7
0	1	5	5	5
2	0	5	6	5
2	2	5	6	4

(b)

1	0	4	7	5
1	1	4	5	7
1	1	5	5	5
2	1	5	5	5
2	2	5	6	4

(c)

1	1	4	7	5
1	1	5	7	7
1	1	5	5	5
2	1	5	5	5
2	2	5	5	4

(d)

1	1	5	7	5
1	1	5	7	7
1	1	5	5	5
1	1	5	5	5
1	1	5	5	5

FIGURE 2.9 Example of region growing process (with known seed points).

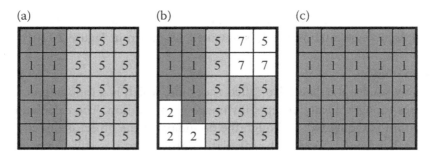

FIGURE 2.10 The results of region growing when the thresholds are selected differently.

than a certain threshold T, then the pixel is included in the region where the seed pixel is located. In Figure 2.9, the threshold is set to $T = 3$, and the whole image is better divided into two regions, as shown in Figure 2.10(a). Figure 2.10(b) shows the region growing result with $T = 2$, and some pixels cannot be determined; Figure 2.10(c) shows the region growing result with $T = 7$, and the entire image is grouped into one region. This example shows that the choice of threshold is very important.

2.2.4.2 Split and Merge
Split and merge can be considered as an improved region growing techniques.

Split and merge starts from the entire image and obtain each sub-region through continuous splitting. In practice, the image is often divided into regions of any size and non-overlapping according to a certain data structure (such as quadtree expression or pyramid structure), and then these regions are merged or split to meet the segmentation requirements. If only splitting is allowed, it is possible that two adjacent regions have the same properties but are not integrated. To solve this problem, after each split, subsequent splits or mergers are allowed. The merge here only merges those regions that are adjacent and the new region formed after the merge meets the requirements

Figure 2.11 gives a simple example. Figure 2.11(a) is an image to be segmented, and the value of each pixel is shown by the value in each unit. Assuming that the first level of quadtree expression is used to split the image into four blocks, the upper-left block and the lower-right block do not need to continue to split, while the upper-right block and the lower-left block need to continue to split, as shown in Figure 2.11(b). After the second-level split of the image quadtree, the attributes of each pixel can be determined, as shown in

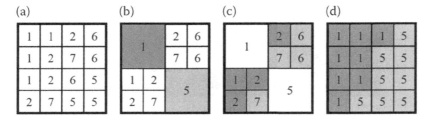

FIGURE 2.11 Example of split and merge process.

Figure 2.11(c). Combine the results of the first two levels of quadtree splits according to the attributes, and the segmentation result is obtained, as shown in Figure 2.11(d).

2.2.4.3 Watershed

The commonly used watershed (also called waterline, which is a topographical concept) algorithm uses topographical concepts for image segmentation. The calculation process of this algorithm is sequential. Although the boundary of the object is directly obtained, the regional consistency is used in the calculation process, so it is still a sequential region class algorithm. One example can be found in Dai (2003).

Think of the image as a representation of the 3-D terrain, that is, the 2-D foundation (corresponding to the image space) plus the height of the third dimension (corresponding to the image grayscale). In this way, high-brightness regions in the image correspond to mountain peaks, and low-brightness regions correspond to valleys. Suppose there is water gushing from the bottom hole of each valley and the water level gradually increases. If the level of the water gushing from two adjacent valley bottoms is higher than the mountain peak in between, these waters will converge. To prevent these waters from converging, a dam must be built on the mountain, and the height of the dam must increase as the water level rises. This process ended when all the peaks were submerged in water. The various dams built in this process divide the entire land into many regions, and these dams constitute the *watershed* of this land. Figure 2.12 gives a schematic diagram (it can be seen as a cross-section of a grayscale image), here for simplicity, only the 1-D cross-section of each object is drawn.

It can be seen from the above that if the location of the watershed can be determined, the image can be segmented into different regions with a set of closed curves. The watershed image segmentation algorithm performs image segmentation by determining the location of the watershed. Generally, considering that the gray levels of pixels in each region are relatively close, and the gray level difference between pixels in adjacent areas is relatively large, the gradient map of an image can be calculated first, and then the watershed of the gradient map can be found. In the gradient map, pixels with small gradient values correspond to the interior of the region, and pixels with large gradient values correspond to the boundary of the region. The watershed algorithm finds the position of the pixel with the large gradient value, that is, the position of the segmentation boundary.

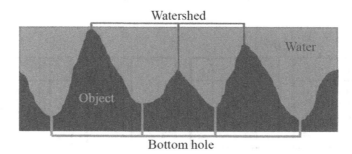

FIGURE 2.12   Schematic diagram of the principle of the watershed method.

The above discussion actually pointed out the idea of the watershed calculation; that is, gradually increase a grayscale threshold. Whenever it is greater than a local maximum, the binary image at that time (only distinguishes land and water, that is, the region with pixel values greater than the grayscale threshold and the region with pixel values smaller than the grayscale threshold) and the binary image at the previous moment (that is, the time when the grayscale threshold taking the previous value) are subjected to a logical exclusive OR (XOR) operation to determine the location of the local maximum value of the grayscale. The watershed can be determined according to the location set of all local maxima of grayscale.

2.3 COLOR IMAGE SEGMENTATION

Compared with gray-scale images, color images provide richer information and also make image segmentation more diverse and complex. With the increasing use of color images in recent years, color image segmentation has also attracted more and more attention. For example, many new technologies and methods have been introduced, such as genetic algorithm, ant colony fuzzy clustering algorithm, particle swarm optimization algorithm, pulse coupled neural network, and so on.

2.3.1 Overview of Color Image Segmentation Methods

Color images have extended attributes in comparing with gray-scale images. The attributes are no longer scalars, but vectors with three components. A 2-D color image needs to be represented as a vector image $f(x, y)$. In many practical applications, the various components of the color image can be appropriately combined to transform into a grayscale image, and then the grayscale image segmentation algorithm can be used for segmentation. Only methods dedicated to *color image segmentation* are considered here.

2.3.1.1 Color Segmentation Category

Image segmentation needs to extract the region of interest. In color images, regions can be defined in many ways (Koschan 2009).

1. Edge-based definition
   Think of a region as a collection of pixels surrounded by edge pixels that make up a color outline. These edge pixels can be determined using an extended edge detection operator. What is emphasized here is the inconsistency between the regions and the boundaries between regions.

2. Region-based definition
   Think of a region as a collection of (maximized) connected pixels on the image plane. This set satisfies the uniformity condition. Note that the combination of color signals is performed on the image plane instead of in the color space. For example, a uniform region can be obtained by splitting a large, non-uniform region, or by merging other pixels (or pixel blocks) in the neighborhood of a starting pixel. The emphasis here is on the consistency within the region.

3. Pixel-based definition

   The region is regarded as a connected component composed of a set of pixels, which is specified by a set of membership functions defined in the color space. Note that the combination of colors here is performed in color space (so the connection of pixels on the image plane is not considered). For example, a condition of the combination may be that the colors of the pixels are all on a plane or in a polyhedron in the color space.

4. The definition based on physics

   Here, the region is also regarded as the connected component of the pixel set, but the combination of this pixel set comes from the physical modeling of the color signal in the color space. The purpose of segmentation is to extract regions from the color image corresponding to the surface of the scene, and each region contains a substance. Occlusion, shadows, and highlights should not affect this image segmentation, although the color values in the image can vary.

This type of region definition can be seen as a special case of the previous type of region. However, the purpose of image segmentation and the assumption of the physical properties of the scene are different from the other three cases. For example, in this definition, the same region can contain both light red and dark red, because it is assumed that the difference in brightness is caused by occlusion and shading, and the pixels correspond to the color vector representing the same surface region. The segmentation technology using this region definition belongs to a new set of image segmentation technology categories, and is generally regarded as a *physics-based vision technology*. All segmentation techniques that use the fourth type of region definition are not extensions of the original gray-scale method, and are completely used for color images.

The segmentation technology processes corresponding to the above four types of region definitions are separately introduced below.

2.3.1.2 Edge-Based Segmentation

Edge-based segmentation techniques use non-uniformity measures or discontinuities of image functions to divide the image into regions. In principle, local or global technologies with their own characteristics can be used. Local technology only uses pixel neighborhood information to detect edge pixels, and can often be done in parallel. Global technology achieves a certain global optimization for the entire image, often requiring a large-scale serial search and multiple optimizations. There are a lof of literature about edge detection, such as Zhang (2001, 2006).

Local techniques can sometimes be based on a single color. For example, the edges can be detected independently in each component image of the color image (this is equivalent to edge detection in the grayscale image), and then the edge pixels detected in the three component images can be combined. If the union of edge pixels is used to combine edge pixels, it may be easier to obtain a closed contour using color images than using grayscale images.

2.3.1.3 Region-Based Segmentation

Many *region-based segmentation* techniques can be extended from grayscale images to color images. The extension of the thresholding technique in Sub-section 2.2.3 to color image segmentation will be discussed in the next sub-section. Here we first consider extending the watershed technique in Sub-section 2.2.4 to color image segmentation.

A three-channel color image can be expressed as $C(x, y) = [R(x, y), G(x, y), B(x, y)]$ in the RGB color space. If the waterline transformation is used in the three components of the color signal vector, then three results with different regions and waterlines will be obtained. Their information can be combined to give the segmentation result of the color image.

In practice, the original color image is regarded as a vector, and each channel is regarded as a component. A gradient image is calculated for each component, and three gradient images G_R, G_G, and G_B corresponding to the red, green, and blue channels are obtained. From the three gradient images G_R, G_G, G_B, a combined gradient image G_C can be determined. Then, the region and waterline can be calculated for the combined gradient image G_C.

2.3.1.4 Pixel-Based Segmentation

The pixel-based segmentation often using histogram that is the statistics of the gray levels of pixels in the image, and the segmentation method using histogram for thresholding can be extended to color images. In the simplest case, the RGB component values can be combined into a 1-D function (such as taking the average or weighted average of the three components), and then its histogram for thresholding can be calculated.

There is another method, two orthogonal color features obtained by linear transformation of the three components of R, G, and B:

$$F_1 = (R + G + B)/3 \qquad (2.16)$$

$$F_2 = (R - B)/2 \quad \text{或} \quad F_2 = (B - R)/2 \qquad (2.17)$$

The segmentation in this 2-D space has obtained better results for most natural images. This method can also be seen as an extension (adding an F_2 feature) to the previous method using an average (equivalent to using only one F_1 feature).

Better results can be obtained if the 1-D, 2-D, and 3-D histograms of the components are calculated in sequence. When using a 1-D histogram, one needs to calculate the histogram for each color channel separately, and determine the maximum and minimum values for each histogram. A priority list can be obtained from the maximum value obtained. This can be arranged according to frequency, or specific weighting of different components can be considered (for example, hue is often more important than brightness). The segmentation threshold is sequentially determined based on the priority list. Recent techniques determine the maximum and minimum values in a 2-D histogram (such as the chromaticity plane of a color space) or a 3-D histogram.

Cluster analysis technology can also be extended to color images that include vector values. Suppose the cluster centers of a given set of vector values in the color space are J_1, ... , J_n, where n is the number of clusters. For each pixel q_i in the color image C, an n-D probability vector $(p_{i1}, ... , p_{in})$ can be determined, where p_{ik} represents the probability that the pixel q_i belongs to the category J_k, $k = 1, ... , n$. Considering the distance between a pixel and the cluster center of its category, p_{ik} can be defined as:

$$p_{ik} = \frac{\|C(q_i) - J_k\|^{-1}}{\sum_{l=1}^{m} \|C(q_i) - J_l\|^{-1}} \tag{2.18}$$

2.3.1.5 Physics-Based Segmentation

In physics-based segmentation, physical models are often used. These models are used to divide an image into regions corresponding to the surfaces and/or objects in the scene (Koschan 2009). The purpose of these techniques is to segment the color image at the object boundary, not at the shadows, occlusions, or highlights. *Physics-based segmentation* has so far been limited to determining changes in the reflection of substances whose reflection properties are known and can be effectively modeled.

A *dual-color reflection model* (DRM) is a commonly used model. It generally refers to a mixed reflection model that does not specifically model the high light reflection component on the non-uniform opaque material in optics. The surface of these substances consists of an interface and an optically neutral medium containing color pigments. The interface separates the surface from the surrounding medium (usually air). Part of the radiation that hits the surface does not penetrate into the substance, but is reflected on the interface, which is called *interface reflection*. The light that is not reflected from the interface will penetrate into the substance. There it is scattered on the colored particles, part of it is absorbed, part of it passes through, and finally a part of the transmitted light enters the surrounding medium through the reflection of the interface. This last process is called *body reflection*. When the distribution of color pigments is uniform and the pigments show the same optical behavior, it can be assumed that the light penetrating into the substance does not have any special direction when it comes out of the surface of the substance.

The light energy, L, shining on the sensor depends on the wavelength, λ; the surface normal vector, n; the light direction, s; and the observation direction, v. L is the sum of interface reflection, L_s, and body reflection, L_b. The interface reflection describes the specular reflection component, and the volume reflection describes the scattered reflection component. The dual-color model can be written as a mathematical formula:

$$L(\lambda, n, s, v) = L_s(\lambda, n, s, v) + L_b(\lambda, n, s, v) = m_s(n, s, v)c_s(\lambda) + m_b(n, s, v)c_b(\lambda) \tag{2.19}$$

In the dual-color reflection model, it is assumed that the geometric components, m_s and m_b, can be separated from the specular components, c_s and c_b. Here, c_s represents the interface reflection color, and c_b represents the volume reflection color. Because m_s and m_b can be any scalar, the vectors c_s and c_b constitute a plane in the RGB color space, which is called a *dual-color plane*, also called a *color-signal plane*. It is possible to separate the reflection components by analyzing the clusters, so that color image segmentation can be realized.

Now consider how to distinguish between material changes in the scene and high-lights, shadows, occlusion, or mutual reflections. One method (Bajcsy 1990a, b) is to assume that the image is composed of a collection of patches on the object surface, and each patch has uniform color (not brightness) characteristics. In this way, the image can be divided into regions with uniform hue and saturation regardless of the surface structure. Using the dual-color reflection model in the HSI color space, it is assumed that the highlight is composed of the same spectrum of light. For lighting, first use a reflection map with a known reflection factor for white balance. By analyzing the structure of color clusters in the HSI color space such as shadows, occlusions, highlights, and mutual re-flections, the following observations can be obtained:

1. Shadows, highlights, occlusions, and mutual reflections all change brightness.

2. Shadows and occlusions neither change the hue nor the color saturation.

3. Highlights will reduce the saturation value.

4. Mutual reflection generally causes changes in hue and saturation.

Based on these observations, operations on the hue component and saturation compo-nent can distinguish other factors, and can realize the segmentation of the color image according to the object composition of the original material.

2.3.2 Sequence Segmentation of Color Images

The color image has three color components. If the 3-D histogram is projected onto the 1-D plane by projection, the histogram obtained will be a 3-D array, in which to de-termine the threshold would be more difficult than to determine the threshold in the corresponding 1-D arrays of grayscale image histograms.

If *hue, saturation,* and *intensity* (HSI) color space (or HSV color space or HSB color space) is used for color image segmentation, it is possible to decompose the high-dimensional calculation problem in this 3-D space into a lower-dimensional calculation problem, since the three components of H, S, and I are independent of each other.

The following introduces a method for sequence segmentation of different color component images. The idea comes from the language/method of people describing or distinguishing different colors. Under normal circumstances, when people describe a color object, people will use different methods according to the colorful of the object (corresponding to saturation). If the it is colorful (high saturation), the hue (such as red, green, blue, etc.) is used to describe; and if it is not so colorful (low saturation), the hue and brightness are both used (such as dark brown, light yellow, etc.). In other words,

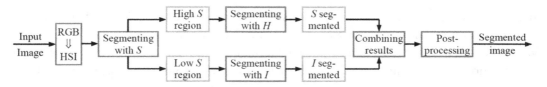

FIGURE 2.13 The algorithm flow chart for sequence segmentation of different components of color images.

people do not judge the hue, saturation, and brightness at the same time, but first use the saturation, and then use the hue or brightness to make further judgments based on the result of the saturation judgment. With reference to such an idea or strategy, the color image segmentation algorithm flow as shown in Figure 2.13 can be designed.

It can be seen from Figure 2.13 that the original RGB color image is first converted to the HSI color space. Next, a 1-D thresholding segmentation on the saturation component map is performed, and the image is divided into a high saturation part and a low saturation part. Then the obtained high-saturation part is used as a mask, and the corresponding part in the hue component map is selected for segmentation. Since the saturation value is relatively large in the high-saturation part, the quantization of the hue value is relatively fine, and the threshold value of the hue H can be selected to segment this part of the image to obtain the object. In the low-saturation part, the saturation value is small, and the quantization of the hue value is relatively coarse and cannot be directly used for segmentation. However, since the low-saturation part is closer to the grayscale image, the low-saturation part that can be obtained is used as a mask, and the corresponding part in the brightness component map is selected for segmentation, that is, the threshold value of the brightness I is used to segment this part of the image to distinguish the object with background. After respectively obtaining the segmentation results of the high-saturation part and the segmentation result of the low-saturation part, because they are complementary in the image space, the results need to be combined. The final segmentation result can be obtained by performing certain post-processing on the combined result.

Figure 2.14(a) shows a color image (here printed in black and white). The three component images of H, S and I are shown in Figure 2.14(b), Figure 2.14(c), and Figure 2.14(d), respectively.

Figure 2.15 shows images of some stages in the segmentation of the color image in the above-mentioned manner. First, segment the saturation component image to get Figure 2.15(a),

(a)　　　　　(b)　　　　　(c)　　　　　(d)

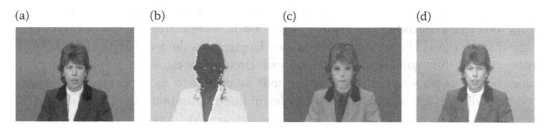

FIGURE 2.14 A color image (here printed in black and white) and its three components (H, S, I).

(a) (b) (c) (d)

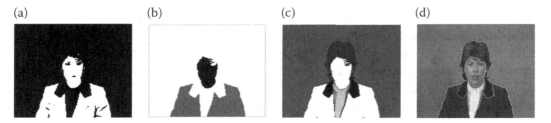

FIGURE 2.15 Example of sequence segmentation results of color image.

where the white region is the high saturation region, and the black region is the low saturation region. Threshold segmentation of the high-saturation region according to the H value is shown in Figure 2.15(b), where the white region corresponds to the low-saturation region that is not involved in the segmentation, and other regions with different gray levels represent the different hue regions obtained after segmentation by the H value. Threshold segmentation of the low-saturation region according to the I value is shown in Figure 2.15(c), where the white region corresponds to the high-saturation region that is not involved in the segmentation, and other regions with different gray levels represent the different brightness regions obtained after segmentation according to the I value. Combine the results of Figure 2.15(b) and Figure 2.15(c) and superimpose the boundaries of every segmented region on Figure 2.14(a) to obtain Figure 2.15(d).

It can be seen from the above that the strategy of this method is to transform a segmentation problem in a 3-D space into a segmentation problem in three 1-D spaces, into two steps. The physical meaning is clearer and the computational complexity is also reduced.

2.4 MEDICAL IMAGE SEGMENTATION

Medical image segmentation is the basis of various medical image applications. The purpose of medical image segmentation mainly includes: (i) recognizing objects of interest; (ii) studying the anatomical structure of organs; (iii) measuring various parameters of tissues. There are many ways or modalities of medical imaging, such as transmission computed tomography (TCT, CT for short); emission computed tomography (ECT), including positron emission tomography (PET) and single photon emission CT (SPECT); electrical impedance tomography (EIT); magnetic resonance imaging (MRI); ultrasound (US) imaging, etc. It is difficult to segment medical images. In addition to the different shapes of medical objects, complex structures, and many uncertainties, there are also many interference effects in imaging. For example, the artifacts in CT imaging include motion artifacts, bar artifacts, ring artifacts, and metal artifacts, etc.; and MRI imaging also includes Gibbs artifacts, folding artifacts, gradient artifacts, and magnetic sensitivity artifacts, etc.

2.4.1 Overview of Medical Image Segmentation Algorithms

Due to the particularity of medical images, there are special researches on its segmentation. In the segmentation of medical images, in addition to the common region-based methods that use the homogeneity of pixels within the region and the boundary-based methods that use the pixel differences between regions, the method of modeling the characteristics of the segmentation object is often considered. In addition, new mathematical models and tools are continuously introduced, and new methods are continuously proposed for segmentation.

The segmentation of medical images will encounter three problems (Withey 2007). The first is the influence of noise. Noise will change the pixel value, leading to uncertainty in pixel segmentation. Secondly, the non-uniformity of pixel values in the image makes the pixel values of each part of the same object gradually change. Finally, the image has a limited pixel size, which makes it possible for a single pixel to contain information about different objects. The value of the mixed pixel is the average of multiple object values, and may be different from the value of any type of object. It is called the partial volume average effect.

There are three stages in the development of medical image segmentation, and each stage represents a new level of algorithm design. The corresponding segmentation algorithms for the three stages can be regarded as three generations. The earliest first-generation algorithms used the lowest level of image processing methods; the second-generation algorithms used image models, optimization methods, and uncertainty models; the third-generation algorithms are characterized by a combination of knowledge.

2.4.1.1 First-Generation Algorithms

In the first-generation algorithms, the low-level technology was mainly used, and almost no *a prior* knowledge was used. The three problems encountered in the segmentation mentioned above have an impact on the algorithms at this stage. Typical methods include edge detection and tracking methods, thresholding methods, region growing methods, clustering methods, etc. (Zhang 2001).

Among these algorithms, the methods based on thresholding are relatively simple. The basic principle is that the gray value of different tissues or organs of the human body will be different when the original image data is obtained by medical imaging technology, and the appropriate threshold is selected for segmentation. Generally, the gray value of each part in the CT image is relatively uniform, and the thresholding method can often achieve better results. However, the resolution of the magnetic resonance image is relatively high, the change of the gray value will be more complicated, the unevenness of the gray level will be large, and the thresholding method cannot guarantee a better result.

Clustering-based methods are also commonly used. The underlying tissues or organs that need to be segmented are regarded as different pattern classes, and the object segmentation results are obtained by dividing and extracting the pattern classes. Segmentation algorithms based on unsupervised clustering include iterative self-organizing data analysis, unsupervised artificial neural networks, etc. The effect is more dependent on the initial value and parameter settings. Segmentation algorithms based on supervised clustering include Gaussian mixture models, supervised artificial neural networks, etc., which require a suitable training sample set.

2.4.1.2 Second-Generation Algorithms

In the second-generation algorithm, uncertainty models and optimization techniques are introduced, and intuitive heuristic methods are generally avoided, but the segmentation results depend on the data. There are several types of typical methods, as follows.

1. Statistical pattern recognition algorithm

   A hybrid model is used in which each pixel in the image is modeled as belonging to a certain known category (region). Commonly used supervised methods include Bayesian classifier, discriminant analysis, etc. K-nearest neighbor classification is also a typical representative. The algorithm using expectation maximization (EM) is a distinctive representative of unsupervised statistical clustering. They use Markov Random Field (MRF), Hidden Markov Random Field (HMRF), etc. to contain contextual information to reduce the misclassification rate.

2. Neural network

   Many neural networks need to be trained with appropriate image data before they can be used to segment other images. Neural network models are often equivalent to corresponding statistical pattern recognition methods or certain types of biological models. In addition, the fuzzy nervous system, that is, the combination of neural network and fuzzy system, has also been used for image segmentation. A related review can be found in (Boskovitz 2002).

3. Kalman filter

   The *Kalman filter* is used to automatically track the object. The Kalman filter can make full use of the dynamic information of the object to remove the noise that affects the measured value of the object position, velocity, and acceleration, and get a better estimate of the object position.

4. Deformation model

   Design contours that can expand or contract over time according to specific image characteristics. Active contour or snake model is a typical representative, and the forward propagation (it is reachable to the local optimal) model based on level set is also commonly used. The graph cut method is closely related to the active contour and level set methods. Watershed algorithm is a commonly used image search algorithm in medical image segmentation.

5. Minimum path method

   Edge tracking is performed by calculating the geodesic contour, which is similar to the deformation model based on the level set method. Algorithms using graph search, dynamic programming, graph cut, etc. also basically belong to this category. Essentially, the object image is regarded as an undirected weighted graph, the node set contains pixels and the edge set represents the connection between pixels. Generally, the computational complexity is relatively large.

6. Multi-resolution method

   The method of using scale reduction to collect pixels into groups is also called multi-scale or pyramid method. By iteratively blurring the original image and then down-sampling to reduce the scale, a set of overlapping images can be obtained. During segmentation, the pixels in one layer and the pixels in the next layer are connected according to similar attributes, and the boundary is also refined by using a multi-scale method.

7. *K*-means clustering

   It uses a set of descriptive features to group pixels together. It is generally assumed that the number of clusters is known, and the value of each feature is often normalized to between 0 and 1. In medical image segmentation, fuzzy *K*-means clustering (FCM) is used more.

2.4.1.3 Third-Generation Algorithms

Only using the uncertainty model and optimization method introduced in the second-generation algorithm is not generally enough to obtain accurate and automatic segmentation results. Combining high-level knowledge, such as *a prior* information, rules formulated by experts, and (shape) models of desired objects, constitute the third-generation algorithm.

1. Shape model

   The *Active Shape Model* (ASM) is based on the deformation model, and it also adds constraints on the deformation of the model. First, the object contour is represented by a series of landmark points, and its changes are analyzed with the help of training images. The trained active shape model can be used to detect similar objects in other images. The occurrence of deformation is similar to that in the deformation model, the difference is that it is limited to the scope of the statistical model. Some other shape-based representation methods have also been applied.

2. Appearance model

   Active Appearance Model (AAM) is a generalization of the active shape model. It not only considers the shape information of the object, but also includes the intensity information of the object, and combines them into a statistical model. A related review can be found in Beichel (2005).

3. Segmentation based on atlas

   The atlas is a combined image composed of images that are segmented and co-ordinated by multiple people. A 3-D mapping (registration) is established between the atlas and the unknown segmented image. The atlas provides the *a prior* probability of statistical pattern recognition, so that the segmentation can make better use of the *a prior* information. In many cases, it is necessary to separate the segmentation step and registration step to use the atlas method, but there are also methods for joint segmentation and registration. When the manually determined mark points limit the deformation, a semi-automatic method can also be considered.

4. Rule-based segmentation

With the aid of the first-generation algorithm and the second-generation algorithm, image primitives are obtained, and then structural information and image knowledge are used as rules to interpret these primitives. Typical examples include using probabilistic clustering and fuzzy logic, combined with expert knowledge to describe objects and features, while deforming a set of meshed surfaces, and constructing a set of rules using the shape and texture information of medical objects of interest to guide segmentation.

5. Coupling surface method

The segmentation based on the deformation model and graph cut method is improved to meet the requirements of multiple surfaces and maintaining known spatial connections at the same time. In this way, the advantages of different algorithms can be combined to improve the segmentation results.

2.4.2 Interactive Level Set Image Segmentation of Thoracic Aorta

The original image of the thoracic aorta to be segmented is obtained by magnetic resonance imaging and can be represented as a 4-D image of $128 \times 128 \times 20 \times 24$. Among them, 128×128 is the size of each layer of image. There are 20 layers in total. Such 3-D images are collected 24 times (24 time phases) in each cardiac cycle. The grayscale of the image is represented by 16 bits. In order to accurately segment the thoracic aorta, the blood flow velocity amplitude image was further collected. Figure 2.16 shows twenty 3-D images in one phase, where the faster the blood flow, the greater the gray value (the brighter the image).

It can be seen from Figure 2.16 that the thoracic aortic vessels have large deformations between the images of each layer, and are often accompanied by changes in the topological structure. On the other hand, the amount of data in 4-D images is relatively large, and the computational complexity of the segmentation method cannot be too high. To this end, an interactive level set algorithm based on a deformable model is used to directly segment the 3-D images in each phase. The algorithm flow is shown in Figure 2.17. First, the seed points belonging to the blood vessel are determined by interaction in the input image, and then the initial blood vessel region (the center of which is the polyline connecting various sub-points) is obtained by the region growing algorithm and used as the initial value of the high-dimensional scalar function (the level set method regards the change of the parameter equation of the surface with time as a high-dimensional scalar function that depends on the evolution of time) of the level set algorithm. Next, set the expansion energy constraint term, continuous energy constraint term, and external energy constraint term (including grayscale energy and gradient energy), so that the evolution equation of the function approximates to the surface of the blood vessel wall. Finally, the finite difference method is used to iterate until convergence to obtain the segmentation result of the blood vessel (Liu 2013).

Sometimes, several unnecessary protrusions or depressions appear in the segmentation results based on interactive level sets. For this reason, the interactive level set segmentation

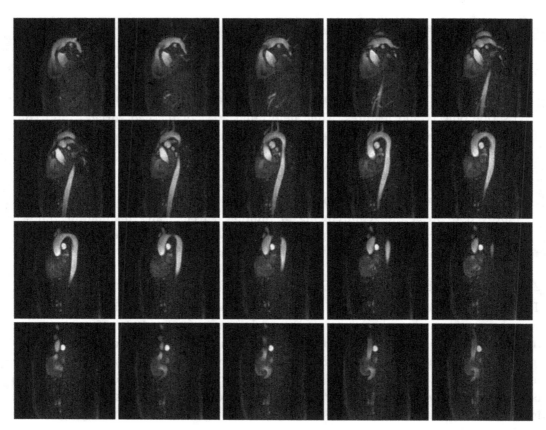

FIGURE 2.16   Twenty-layer 128 × 128 thoracic aortic blood flow velocity amplitude image in one phase.

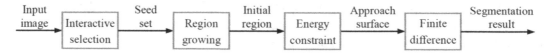

FIGURE 2.17   Flowchart of interactive level set segmentation algorithm based on deformable model.

algorithm can be improved by adding the constraints of blood vessel shape information. The shape information can be provided by means of the centerline of the blood vessel, and the calculation of the centerline of the blood vessel can be achieved by constructing an internal Voronoï diagram.

Figure 2.18 shows the images of some steps in the segmentation of the thoracic aorta image with the improved interactive level set of shape information constraints. Among them, Figure 2.18(a) is an interactive initialization step. After selecting several seed points, a polyline connecting various sub-points is obtained. By using the region growing algorithm, the initial surface can be obtained from the connection of these seed points, as shown in Figure 2.18(b), which also shows the centerline of the blood vessel. Further use of level set segmentation to obtain the segmentation result is shown in Figure 2.18(c), in which there is an obvious depression in the top vessel. Figure 2.18(d) shows the Voronoï

(a)   (b)   (c)   (d)   (e)   (f)

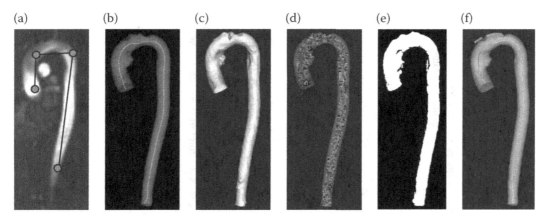

FIGURE 2.18   Some examples of image segmentation of thoracic aorta with improved interactive level set based on shape information constraints.

diagram inside the blood vessel. The segmentation result obtained after introducing the shape information of the blood vessel is shown in Figure 2.18(e), and the original top depression in Figure 2.18(c) is eliminated. Finally, Figure 2.18(f) also shows the vascular radius around the centerline of the thoracic aorta after segmentation.

2.5 SOME RECENT DEVELOPMENTS AND FURTHER RESEARCH

In the following sections, some technical developments and promising research directions in the last few years are briefly overviewed.

2.5.1 A Classification of Deep Learning-Based Segmentation Methods

Deep learning has been proved to be very effective for image segmentation. A lot of deep learning–based methods have been proposed and applied in various domains. In a recent survey for deep learning–based segmentation methods (Lateef and Ruichek 2019), the network models/methods studied have been classified into ten categories, as shown in Table 2.2.

2.5.2 U-Net Network for Medical Image Segmentation

As indicated in Section 2.4, medical image segmentation is the basis of various medical image applications. Many types of medical images are popularly used, such as transmission computed tomography (TCT, CT for short); emission computed tomography (ECT), including positron emission tomography (PET) and single photon emission CT (SPECT); electrical impedance tomography (EIT); magnetic resonance imaging (MRI); ultrasound (US) imaging, etc.

Medical imaging literature has witnessed great progress in the designs and performance of deep convolutional models for medical image segmentation (Tajbakhsh et al. 2020).

U-Net network is a network proposed initially for medical image segmentation (Ronneberger et al. 2015). Compared with other existing segmentation models, the U-Net network is a small model with fewer training parameters, mainly for the case of a small

TABLE 2.2 Deep learning–based segmentation methods

Sl. No.	Class	Brief Description
1	Feature encoder based methods	The feature maps are extracted on the basis of stacked convolution layers, ReLU layers and pooling layers. VGGNet (Visual Geometry Group Network) and ResNet (Residual Network) are mostly used.
2	Regional proposal based methods	The core idea is to detect the regions according to the variety of color spaces and similarity metrics, and then perform the classification (region proposals that might contain object). Regional Convolutional Neural Network (R-CNN) is used for Region-wise prediction.
3	RNN-based methods	Recurrent neural network capability to learn long term dependencies from sequential data and ability to keep memory along the sequence makes it applicable in semantic segmentation, scene segmentation and labeling.
4	Up-sampling/ Deconvolution based methods	The spatial information lost during down-sampling operation can be regained by up-sampling and deconvolution. The reconstruction technique for increasing spatial accuracy and refinement technique can be developed by fusing the features of a low and high level.
5	Increase resolution of feature based methods	The spatial resolution can be recovered by using atrous convolution and dilated convolution which can generate high-resolution feature maps for dense prediction. The dilated convolution has the ability to expand the receptive field without losing resolution.
6	Enhancement of features based methods	Enhancement of feature based methods include extraction of feature at multi-scale or from a sequence of nested regions. In deep networks for semantic segmentation, CNNs are applied to image square patches, often called kernel of fixed size centered at each pixel, labeling each pixel by observing small region around it.
7	Semi and weakly supervised concept	Deep CNN requires large-scale data set and massive computing power for training. Collecting labeled data set manually is time consuming and requires enormous human efforts. To comfort these efforts, semi or weakly supervised methods are applied using deep learning techniques.
8	Spatial-temporal based methods	Both spatial information along with temporal information are used for semantic segmentation. Spatial-temporal structured prediction can prove useful in both supervised and semi-supervised manner.
9	Methods using CRF/ MRF	Markov random field (MRF) and its variant Conditional Random Fields are used to smooth and refine the pixel prediction in pixel classification. CNNs can thus be trained to model unary and pairwise potentials in order to capture contextual information.
10	Alternative to CRF	The majority of CRFs uses hand constructed color-based affinities that may lead to spatial false predictions. So alternate methods have been proposed to overcome these issues.

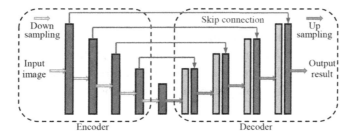

FIGURE 2.19   U-Net network structure.

number of training samples. These features make U-Net a popular model for solving various medical segmentation tasks.

2.5.2.1 U-Net Network Structure

The *U-Net network* structure consists of an encoder for acquiring class information and a decoder with a symmetrical structure of the encoder, which respectively implement the down-sampling and up-sampling process of the image. The network structure is shown in Figure 2.19. The encoder uses the typical structure of convolutional networks, alternately using multiple layers of convolution and pooling operations, gradually reducing the resolution of feature maps, and at the same time doubling the number of channels in each layer of feature maps, so as to obtain the global information of the image. Each step in the decoder corresponds to the encoder and consists of up-sampling the feature map followed by multiple convolutions. The decoder gradually increases the resolution of the output feature map while halving the number of channels of the feature map. To localize the up-sampled features, the decoder concatenates them with the same-resolution feature maps from the encoder via skip connections. The model does not have fully connected layers, and the final layer maps the number of channels to the desired categories. The network finally outputs a pixel-by-pixel label map of the same size as the input image, and the value of each pixel shows the category to which the pixel belongs.

The improvements have been proposed from different aspects, such as considering the models of network, considering the structures of network, and considering the mechanisms of network. Some typical improvements are briefly listed below. These improvements can also be combined, so in the area of medical image segmentation using U-Net, many advancements have been achieved in recent years. However, one note here is that all these improvements are taken into account the specific properties of underlying medical images, so their generalities are still pending for verification.

2.5.2.2 U-Net Network Model Improvements

The original U-Net network adopts a symmetric encoder-decoder structure, and some improvements use various numbers of encoder. Few examples are as follows.

One of them is the Y-Net network (Lan et al. 2020). The network model structure is "Y"-shaped, which consists of two encoders and one decoder. The two encoder structures can obtain more information of the original signal and beamforming image. The original signal is input to the encoder I, and then the original signal is processed by delay-and-sum (DAS) to generate a beamforming image and input to the encoder II. Encoder I and encoder II encode physical features and texture features respectively, and finally the decoder connects the features output by the two encoders to generate the final segmentation result.

Ψ-Net network is another improved network (Kuang et al. 2020). The network is in the shape of the Greek letter "Ψ", and its network has three batch encoding layers and one decoder. The encoder processes the slice to be segmented and its two adjacent slices respectively, and the self-attention block is applied in the encoding layer, the contextual attention block is applied in the decoding layer. This design not only helps to extract global feature capabilities, suppresses irrelevant information, and improves the recovery of local details through the contextual attention block.

The multi-path dense U-Net is another improved network (Dolz et al. 2019), which is suitable for extracting different brain imaging features. The network introduces ultra-dense ideas in the encoding part, and the input of the encoding path includes diffusion-weighted imaging (DWI), cerebral blood volume (CBV), CT perfusion imaging (CTP), and mean transit time (MTT). This makes full use of the lesion characteristics of each modality and alleviates the problem of vanishing gradient. In addition, all inputs are connected to each other, which can be trained with a small number training samples. It can effectively reduce the overfitting problem.

2.5.2.3 U-Net Network Structure Improvements

The improvement of U-Net structure includes data enhancement, convolution operation, down-sampling operation, up-sampling operation, model optimization strategy, and jump connection. There are many different methods for each aspect, which are summarized in Table 2.3 (Zhou et al. 2021).

2.5.2.4 U-Net Network Mechanism Improvements

Different mechanisms have been adopted for improving the performance of the U-Net network.

1. Improvements based on residual network:

In a residual network, the identity shortcut connection is introduced to solve the degradation and vanishing gradient problems of multilayer neural networks. The schematic diagram of a *residual network* is shown in Figure 2.20 (He et al. 2016).

The residual network is introduced into the U-Net network to deepen the network depth to improve the network training effect, and batch normalization is introduced to improve the segmentation speed (Tong et al. 2018).

The residual U-Net is proposed for lung CT image segmentation, integrating residual blocks into the contraction path of U-Net network, so as to reduce the computational burden (Khanna et al. 2020).

TABLE 2.3 U-Net network structure improvements

Improvement Aspects	Improvement Methods
Data augmentation	Elastic transform, geometric transformations, generative adversarial network (GAN), Wasserstein GAN (WGAN), and live enhancer, etc.
Convolution operation	Convolution block improvements: asymmetric convolution, dilated convolution, and the addition of the inception module.
	Improved convolution padding: zero padding, mirror padding, constant padding, and repeat padding.
Down-sampling operation	Max pooling, average pooling, random pooling, span convolution (the stride is greater than or equal to 2 during convolution), dilated convolution, spatial pyramid pooling, and inception module, etc.
Up-sampling operation	Nearest neighbor interpolation, bilinear interpolation, trilinear interpolation, sub-pixel convolution, and transpose convolution.
Model optimization	Activation function: rectified linear unit (ReLU), random ReLU (RReLU), parametric ReLU (PRe-LU), leaky ReLU (LReLU), hard exponential linear sigmoid squashing (HardELiSH), and exponential linear sigmoid squashing (ELiSH).
	Normalization: batch normalization (BN), group normalization (GN), instance normalization (IN), and layer normalization (LN).
Skip connection	Attention mechanism, feature reuse and attention mechanism (FRAM), deconvolution and activation function, annotation information from Siamese network, and new skip connection mode.

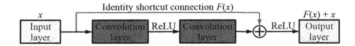

FIGURE 2.20   Residual network diagram.

The residual module is also used to replace the convolution module of U-Net, which increases the reusability of features and reduces the difficulty of model optimization (Yu et al. 2020).

In MultiResUNet network, the multi-resolution blocks are used to replace the convolution operation of contraction path and expansion path to avoid network degradation (Ibtehaz and Rahman 2020).

2. Improvements based on dense mode:

Based on ResNet, the dense convolutional network (DenseNet) is proposed (Huang et al. 2017). This network connects the output and input in parallel, which cannot only effectively alleviate the problem of vanishing gradient, but also increase the reusability of features and reduce the parameters of network calculation.

In a Dense Connected U-Net (DC U-Net) network, the dense connection blocks are applied to the encoder path, and are also used between adjacent pooling layers of the network to replace convolution operation, so as to improve the ability of the network to learn features such as position and edge (Wang et al. 2019).

In a Deep Pooling Fully Progressive Network (DPFCN), the dense mechanism to the pooling layer to avoid the computational redundancy of adjacent windows in the sliding window of pooling operation (Nasr-esfahani et al. 2019).

In a Dense-Inception U-Net network (Zhang et al. 2020), the Dense-Inception block is used in the fourth and fifth layers of the contraction path to replace the conventional convolution block, which can deepen the width and depth of the network and avoid vanishing gradient and redundant calculation.

3. Improvements based on attention mechanism:

In the Residual Attention-aware U-Net (RA-UNet), the attention mechanism is introduced into the U-Net network for CT image segmentation of liver tumors (Jin et al. 2020). The mechanism combines low-level and high-level feature maps to extract contextual information.

The dual attention CapNet (DA-CapNet) combines the squeeze and excitation (SE) module and the convolutional block attention module (CBAM). The CBAM is integrated into the decoder part of U-Net, which enables the network to focus on important locations and better capture contextual information (Hariyani et al. 2020).

In Category Attention Boosting U-Net (CAB U-Net), the CAB module combines the deep network computational graph with the gradient boosting method, pays different attention to the feature maps of different categories, and uses these features to enhance segmentation in the probability space, and finally achieves the aggregation of global location information and local texture information (Ding et al. 2020).

In the Attention-based Nested segmentation network (ANU-Net), in order to make the network focus on the object organ locations, an attention mechanism is introduced between the nested convolution blocks, making the features extracted from different layers of the encoder can be combined with the feature selection of the decoder layer (Li et al. 2020).

2.5.3 Solutions for Large Labeled Data Sets

Since the introduction of U-Net, neural architectures for medical image segmentation have transformed markedly (Tajbakhsh et al. 2020). However, to train the image segmentation model, large and high-quality annotated data sets are required, while perfectly sized and carefully labeled data sets could rarely be found, particularly for medical imaging applications, where both data and annotations are expensive to acquire.

The common limitations of medical image segmentation data sets include scarce annotations where only limited annotated data is available for training, and weak annotations where the training data has only sparse annotations, noisy annotations, or image-level annotations. The up-to-date techniques for generalizing the data sets in overcoming the above two limitations have been surveyed, and will be introduced in the following two sub-sub-sections, respectively.

2.5.3.1 Solutions for Scarce Annotations

The methodologies for solving scarce annotations try to handle data sets where only a small fraction of images are densely annotated. Currently, six categories of solutions for scarce annotation can be distinguished, as listed in Table 2.4.

Among these categories, the first four share the same philosophy to enlarge the training set but they differ in the required data resources and whether or not they require the expert in the loop. In the fifth category, the regularization can be applied to the input space by changing the image representation, to the output space by constraining the segmentation results with shape priors, or directly to the gradients by leveraging additional supervision signals through multi-task learning. In the sixth category, most methods adopt different variants of conditional random fields (CRFs), either as a post-processing or during model training, to refine segmentation masks. Here, a CRF models pixel-wise labels collectively as a random field that is conditioned upon image/volume intensities. The local CRF optimizes Gibbs energy over local patches weighing in pairwise pixel dependency. The fully connected CRF (FC-CRF) extends the local scope of the CRF to the whole image in an efficient manner. The CRF as recurrent neural networks (RNN-CRF) makes FC-CRF end-to-end trainable by replacing the iterative calculations with an RNN.

2.5.3.2 Solutions for Weak Annotations

The methodologies for solving weak annotations try to handle data sets with sparse, noisy (also inaccuracy of the object boundary), or only image-level annotations. Currently, three categories of solutions for weak annotation can be distinguished, as listed in Table 2.5.

In the category of image-level annotations, different variants of class activation maps are used to leverage weak image-level labels for image segmentation. In the category of sparse annotations, methods based on some variants of selective loss (only for labeled pixels) are used, where only sparsely labeled pixels contribute to the segmentation loss. In the category of model-generated annotations or noisy annotations, noise-resilient loss functions are used to learn from noisy annotations.

2.5.4 Panoptic Segmentation

Panoptic segmentation (PS) is a recently proposed concept (Kirillov et al. 2019). PS unifies the typically distinct tasks of semantic segmentation (assign a class label to each pixel) and instance segmentation (detect and segment each object instance). The task format for panoptic segmentation is: each pixel of an image must be assigned a semantic label and an instance ID. Pixels with the same label and ID belong to the same object; for stuff labels the instance id is ignored.

The proposed PS is based on the separation of studying "stuff" (that is, amorphous regions of similar texture or material) and "things" (that is, countable objects). Studying stuff is most commonly formulated as a task known as semantic segmentation (to classify each pixel according to the properties for belonging to different semantic objects) while studying things is typically formulated as the task of object detection or instance segmentation (to extract the specific objects directly from image).

TABLE 2.4   Solutions for scarce annotations

Category	Main Sub-categories and Their Concise Descriptions
Data augmentation	Traditional augmentation: Using spatial and intensity transforms to manipulate image properties by image appearance, or by image layout. Mixing augmentation: New training images and the corresponding labels are generated through a convex combination of pairs of training images and their labels. Synthetic augmentation: Image synthesis based on adversarial networks (such as GAN).
Leveraging external labeled data sets	Transfer learning: A large external labeled data set is used to train an initial model, which can then be fine-tuned using the target data set. Domain adaptation: To bridge the distribution gap between the different data sets by either learning a common latent representation or by learning to translate images from one domain to the other. Data set fusion: Utilizes data from one or multiple external data sets to train a general segmentation model having superior performance to those trained on each individual data set.
Cost effective annotation	Active learning: To determine the next batch of samples from unlabeled images for expert annotation so as to maximize model's performance. Interactive segmentation: To accelerate the annotation process by allowing the expert annotators to interactively correct an initial segmentation mask generated by a model.
Leveraging unlabeled data	Self-supervised pre-training: The unlabeled images are used to pre-train a segmentation network. Semi-supervised learning with pseudo labels: The unlabeled images are labeled by a segmentation model and then used as new examples during training. Semi-supervised learning without pseudo labels: Both labeled and unlabeled images are used jointly to train a segmentation model.
Regularized training	Altered image representation: projecting or trans-forming the images into a more informative or compact representation, which present deep models with an easier problem to solve, thereby reducing the need for large training sets. Multi-task learning: Under the framework of U-Net, encoder is served as feature extractor to learn a latent representation that generalizes across the required tasks, with each task serving as a regularizer for the others. The up-sampling branch produce the segmentation results. Shape regularization: Shape defines a region of interest (ROI) in segmentation problems under certain constraints Such constraints can be effectively encoded as regularization towards more realistic appearance of the segmentation output, especially when well-annotated data is scarce.
Post segmentation refinement	Locally connected CRF: The CRF is designed to induce local smoothness by restricting the pairwise potentials to neighboring pixels, or optimizes Gibbs energy over local patches. Fully connected CRF (FC-CRF): It considers all pixel pairs with an iterative mean field approximation, so to extend the local scope of the CRF to the whole image in an efficient manner. RNN-CRF: It takes a similar approach to FC-CRF, but it is now end-to-end trainable by replacing the iterative calculations with an recurrent neural networks (RNNs).

TABLE 2.5   Solutions for weak annotations

Category	Main Sub-categories and Their Concise Descriptions
Learning with image level labels	Class activation maps (CAMs): The idea is to combine the feature maps to generate class-specific saliency maps. It can be used in conjunction with image-level annotations, Multiple Instance Learning (MIL): The labels are provided for each bag of instances rather than each individual instance. Here, each image can be considered as a bag of instances where each instance can be a pixel or a patch in the image.
Learning with sparse labels	Selective loss with mask completion: The idea is to artificially reconstruct the incomplete regions of the ground truth masks and use the completed masks for training. Selective loss without mask completion: The objective function is modified to circumvent ground truth when the reconstruction of the complete segmentation mask is not required.
Learning with noisy labels	Robust loss without mask refinement: It consists of a weighted cross entropy loss function where the contribution of each pixel to the total loss is controlled by model's perception of the annotation quality for the pixels. Robust loss with iterative mask refinement: It is to identify samples, in semi-supervised learning, with noisy labels during training and then lower their impact on parameter updates by downplaying their gradients.

Compared the original definition of image segmentation (as stated in the beginning of this chapter) that indicates two aspects/stages: classify image pixels into regions, extract the required regions. It seems the panoptic segmentation divide the overall segmentation into two stages: a semantic segmentation stage for classifying image pixels, and an instance segmentation stage for detecting objects based on semantic segmentation.

2.5.4.1 Panoptic Segmentation Process

The flowchart of panoptic segmentation process is shown in Figure 2.21, which is mainly divided into four modules: feature extraction, semantic segmentation, instance segmentation, and task fusion. For an input image, first extract features. Then, the extracted features are input into semantic segmentation and instance segmentation branches to produce semantic segmentation and instance segmentation output. Finally, the task fusion is performed to fuse the results generated by the semantic and instance branch through appropriate strategies to generate the ultimate output result.

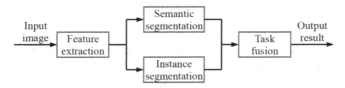

FIGURE 2.21   Flowchart of panoptic segmentation process.

Below, some brief discussions for feature extraction and task fusion are provided. Some typical techniques for semantic segmentation and instance segmentation are given in the following sub-sub-sections.

1. Feature extraction

   The main task of feature extraction is to obtain the features of the input image and provide necessary information for the subsequent semantic segmentation and instance segmentation. The commonly used backbone network includes visual geometry group network (VGGNet), residual network (ResNet), as well as DenseNet, MobileNet, etc.

2. Task fusion

   The task fusion step is to combine the output results of the semantic segmentation and instance segmentation branches to produce the final panoptic segmentation result. The main method groups are: the heuristic method (in proposed relative to the optimization method) that tries to find a solution to a problem in a short time based on limited information; and the panoptic head method in which the logical output of semantic segmentation is divided into two categories: Things and Stuff, and a new instance segmentation mask is formed by bilinear interpolation and zero-filling of the semantic segmentation mask outside the border, then the current mask is represented by the sum of the Stuff class mask and the instance mask, and the instance class is predicted by Softmax.

2.5.4.2 Semantic Segmentation

Early developed segmentation techniques are more sematic segmentation orientated. Most traditional semantic segmentation methods are based on model-driven methods, and model-driven methods can be divided into generative and discriminative methods. The generative model first learns the features and label probability of the image, and then calculates the posterior probability of each label when the features of the input image come, and labels the image according to this probability. Markov random field (MRF) is a typical generative model. The discriminative model assumes that there is a certain mapping relationship between image features and labels, and then learns the relevant parameters of the mapping relationship from historical data. Typical discriminative models include support vector machine (SVM), conditional random field (CRF), etc.

With the rapid development of deep learning technology, significant breakthroughs have been made in the research of semantic segmentation, and many convolutional neural network models for semantic segmentation have emerged:

1. Fully convolutional network (FCN)

   Unlike traditional CNN, which uses full connection layer and Softmax to classify and assign labels after convolution layer, FCN replaces the full connection layer in the network with convolution layer, and samples the output of the last convolution layer, so as to obtain the dense prediction of pixel semantic categories (Shelhamer et al. 2017).

2. U-Net

U-Net is a U-shaped semantic segmentation network and a variant of FCN (Ronneberger et al. 2015). It adopts an encoder-decoder structure, which is simple and efficient. The encoder part extracts the features of the input image, which is composed of convolution and down sampling operations. The decoder part restores the feature size to the original image size, which is mainly composed of up sampling and jump connection. Up sampling increases the feature dimension, while the expansion fuses feature with spatial information to produce accurate segmentation.

3. DeepLab

This net is based on VGG-16, the fully connected layer of VGG-16 is converted into a convolutional layer. DeepLab V2 is based on ResNet and VGG-16, and uses ASPP (Atrous spatial pooling pyramid) revise the network (Chen et al. 2018).

4. PSPNet

In this pyramid scene parsing network, after the Res-Net backbone network extracts features to form feature maps, the pyramid pooling module pools the feature maps at different scales (Zhao et al. 2017). Finally, PSPNet up-samples the pooled results, and combines them with the features of another branch map, and the segmentation result is output through the convolutional layer.

2.5.4.3 Instance Segmentation

Instance segmentation is essentially a combination of object detection and semantic segmentation. The purpose is to detect the object in the input image and assign a class label to each pixel of the object. The development of instance segmentation is relatively late, so the instance segmentation model is mainly based on deep learning technology. Some typical instance segmentation networks are:

1. DeepMask

The DeepMask (Pinheiro et al. 2015) network uses VGGNet to extract features from the input image and generate segmentation proposals. The extracted features are used by two branches. The first branch predicts the segmentation patches for the selected object, and the second branch predicts an object score for the input patch.

2. Mask R-CNN

Mask R-CNN is an instance segmentation model (He et al. 2017) extended on the basis of Faster RCNN. It first uses RPN (region proposal network) to generate ROI (region of interest) candidate regions, and then predicts the class, bounding box offset and binarization mask for each ROI.

3. PANet

PANet uses low-level accurate localization information to boost the feature pyramid, creating bottom-up path augmentation (Liu et al. 2018). It uses adaptive feature pooling to pool features from all feature layers for each candidate region, and uses fully connected layers to enhance mask predictions.

4. Mask SSD

Based on the single-stage detector SSD, Mask SSD adds an instance segmentation module, including multiple convolutional layers and a de-convolutional layer, to predict the foreground mask for each detected object (Zhang et al. 2019). The network is also optimized for feature representation and object prediction.

REFERENCES

Bajcsy, R., S.W. Lee, and A. Leonadis. 1990a. Color image segmentation with detection of highlights and local illumination induced by inter-reflections. *Proceedings of the ICPR*, 785–790.

Bajcsy, R., S.W. Lee, and A. Leonadis. 1990b. Color image segmentation and color constancy. *Proceedings of the SPIE 1250, Perceiving, Measuring and Using Color*, 245–255.

Beichel, R., H. Bischof, and F. Leberl, et al. 2005. Robust active appearance models and their application to medical image analysis. *IEEE Transactions on Medical Imaging*, 24(9): 1151–1169.

Boskovitz, V., and H. Guterman. 2002. An adaptive neuro-fuzzy system for automatic image segmentation and edge detection. *IEEE Transactions on Fuzzy Systems*, 10(2): 247–262.

Chen, L.C., G. Papandreou, I. Kokkinos, et al. 2018. DeepLab: Semantic image segmentation with deep convolutional nets, atrous convolution, and fully connected CRFs. *IEEE Transactions on Pattern Analysis and Machine Intelligence*, 40(4): 834–848.

Dai, S.Y., and Y.-J. Zhang. 2003. Color image segmentation with watershed on color histogram and Markov random fields. *Proceedings of the 4th IEEE Pacific Rim Conference on Multimedia*, 1: 527–531.

Ding, X.F., Y.X. Peng, C.M. Shen, et al. 2020. CAB U-Net: An end-to-end category attention boosting algorithm for segmentation. *Computerized Medical Imaging and Graphics*, 84: #101764.

Dolz, J., A.I. Ben, and C. Desrosiers. 2019. Dense multi-path U-Net for ischemic stroke lesion segmentation in multiple image modalities. *Proceedings of the 4th International Workshop on Brain-lesion: Glioma, Multiple Sclerosis, Stroke and Traumatic Brain Injuries*. Springer (pp. 271–282).

Hariyani, Y.S., H. Eom, and C. Park. 2020. DA-Capnet: Dual attention deep learning based on U-Net for nailfold capillary segmentation. *IEEE Access*, 8: 10543–10553.

He, K.M., G. Gkioxari, P. Dollar, et al. 2017. Mask R-CNN. *Proceedings of the 2017 ICCV*, 2980–2988.

He, K.M., X.Y. Zhang, S.Q. Ren, et al. 2016. Deep residual learning for image recognition. *Proceedings of the 2016 CVPR*, 770–778.

Huang, G., Z. Liu, L. Van Der Maaten, et al. 2017. Densely connected convolutional networks. *Proceedings of the 2017 CVPR*, 2261–2269.

Ibtehaz, N., and M.S. Rahman. 2020. MultiResUNet: Rethinking the U-Net architecture for multimodal biomedical image segmentation. *Neural Networks*, 121: 74–87.

Jin, Q., Z. Meng, C. Sun, et al. 2020. RA-UNet: A hybrid deep attention-aware network to extract liver and tumor in CT scans. *Frontiers in Bioengineering and Biotechnology*, 8: #605132.

Khanna, A., N.D. Londhe, S. Gupta, et al. 2020. A deep Residual U-Net convolutional neural network for automated lung segmentation in computed tomography images. *Biocybernetics and Biomedical Engineering*, 40(3): 1314–1327.

Kirillov, A., K.M. He, R. Girshick, et al., and P. Dollar. 2019. Panoptic segmentation. *Proceedings of the 2019 CVPR*, 9396–9405.

Koschan, A. 2009. *Digital Color Image Processing*. USA Hoboken: Wiley Publishing.

Kuang, Z., X.B. Deng, L. Yu, et al. 2020. Ψ-Net: Focusing on the border areas of intracerebral hemorrhage on CT images. *Computer Methods and Programs in Biomedicine*, 194: #105546.

Lan, H.R., D.H. Jiang, C.C. Yang, et al. 2020. Y-Net: Hybrid deep learning image reconstruction for photoacoustic tomography in vivo. *Photoacoustics*, 20: #100197.

Lateef, F., and Y. Ruichek. 2019. Survey on semantic segmentation using deep learning techniques. *Neurocomputing*, 338: 321–348.

Li, C., Y.S. Tan, W. Chen, et al. 2020. ANU-Net: Attention-based nested U-Net to exploit full resolution features for medical image segmentation. *Computers and Graphics*, 90: 11–20.

Liu, K., Y.-J. Zhang, and R. Li. 2013. A method to calculate the wall shear stress of aortas based on image segmentation with magnetic resonance imaging. *Science Technology and Engineering*, 13(25): 7395–7400.

Liu, S., L. Qi, H.F. Qin, et al. 2018. Path aggregation network for instance segmentation. *Proceedings of the 2018 CVPR*, 8759–8768.

Nasr-Esfahani, E., S. Rafiei, M.H. Jafari, et al. 2019. Dense pooling layers in fully convolutional network for skin lesion segmentation. *Computerized Medical Imaging and Graphics*, 78: #101658.

Pinheiro, P.O., R. Collobert, and P. Dollar. 2015. Learning to segment object candidates. *Proceedings of the NIPS*, 1990–1998.

Ronneberger, O., P. Fischer, and T. Brox. 2015. U-Net: Convolutional networks for biomedical image segmentation. *Proceedings of the 18th International Conference on Medical Image Computing and Computer-Assisted Intervention*, Springer (pp. 234–241).

Shelhamer, E., J. Long, and T. Darrell. 2017. Fully convolutional networks for semantic segmentation. *IEEE Transactions on Pattern Analysis and Machine Intelligence*, 39(4): 640–651.

Tajbakhsh, N., L. Jeyaseelan, Q. Li, et al. 2020. Embracing imperfect data sets: A review of deep learning solutions for medical image segmentation. *Medical Image Analysis*, 63: #101693.

Tong, G.F., Y. Li, H.R. Chen, et al. 2018. Improved U-NET network for pulmonary nodules segmentation. *Optik*, 174: 460–469.

Wang, Z.H., Z. Liu, Y.Q. Song, et al. 2019. Densely connected deep U-Net for abdominal multi-organ segmentation. *Proceedings of the 2019 ICIP*, 1415–1419.

Withey, D.J., and Z.J. Koles. 2007. Medical image segmentation: Methods and software. *Proceedings of the NFSI & ICFBI*, 140–143.

Yu, N.B., J.N. Liu, L. Gao, et al. 2020. Auto-segmentation method based on deep learning for the knee joint in MR images. *Chinese Journal of Scientific Instrument*, 41(6): 140–149.

Zhang, H., Y.L. Tian, K.F. Wang, et al. 2019. Mask SSD: An effective single-stage approach to object instance segmentation. *IEEE Transactions on Image Processing*, 29: 2078–2093.

Zhang, Y.-J. 2001. *Image Segmentation*. Beijing: Science Publisher.

Zhang, Y.-J. (ed.). 2006. *Advances in Image and Video Segmentation*. USA: IRM Press.

Zhang, Y.-J. 2014. A 50 years' review for image segmentation. *Machine Vision*, (6): 12–20.

Zhang, Y.-J. 2015. Half Century for image segmentation. In Khosrow-Pour, M. (ed.), *Encyclopedia of Information Science and Technology*, 3rd Ed., Hershey PA, USA: Information Science Reference, Chapter 584 (pp. 5906–5915).

Zhang, Y.-J. 2017. *Image Engineering. Image Analysis, Vol. 2*. Germany: De Gruyter.

Zhang, Y.-J. 2018. A critical overview of image segmentation techniques based on transition region. *Encyclopedia of Information Science and Technology*, 4th Ed., Chapter 112 (pp. 1308–1318).

Zhang, Z., C.D. Wu, S. Coleman, et al. 2020. DENSE-Inception U-net for medical image segmentation. *Computer Methods and Programs in Biomedicine*, 192: #105395.

Zhao, H.S., J.P. Shi, X.J. Qi, et al. 2017. Pyramid scene parsing network. *Proceedings of the 2017 CVPR*, 6230–6239.

Zhou, T., Y.L. Dong, B.Q. Huo, et al. 2021. U-Net and its applications in medical image segmentation: A review. *Journal of Image and Graphics*, 26(09): 2058–2077.

CHAPTER 3

Segmentation Evaluation and Comparison

A lthough people have made a lot of research on image segmentation, and have already proposed thousands of various algorithms (Zhang and Gerbrands 1994), there is no universal segmentation algorithm suitable for all images. Most algorithms are proposed for specific problems. An important reason here is that there is no general segmentation theory, yet. On the other hand, choosing a suitable segmentation algorithm for a given practical application is still a very troublesome problem, and there is no standard method or procedure. Due to the lack of general theoretical guidance, image segmentation often requires repeated trials. The existence of these problems has prompted people to carry out a lot of research works on image segmentation for a long time (Zhang 2014, 2015).

To overcome the above-mentioned problems and difficulties in image segmentation, it is necessary to conduct research on how to evaluate image segmentation technology and its performance. In fact, the performance evaluation and comparison of segmentation algorithms (Zhang 1996) has received extensive attention for a long time. *Segmentation evaluation and comparison* through the study of the performance of the segmentation algorithm to achieve the purpose of improving and enhancing the performance of the existing algorithm, optimizing the segmentation process, refining the quality of the segmentation and guiding the research on new algorithms.

The research on image segmentation can be divided into three levels. If the image segmentation is at the first level of research, then the evaluation of image segmentation constitutes the second level of research (it helps to grasp the performance of different segmentation algorithms), and a systematic comparison and characterization of evaluation methods and evaluation criteria constitutes the third level of research (it helps to grasp the performance of different evaluation methods). In other words, segmentation evaluation is to study segmentation technology, and the comparison

DOI: 10.1201/b23131-3

and characterization of segmentation evaluation methods is to study evaluation methods to better evaluate segmentation technology. In a sense, the comparison and characterization of segmentation evaluation is the evaluation of segmentation evaluation.

Generally speaking, there are many domains worthy of further study in the three levels of segmentation research. The research on the theory and accuracy of the image segmentation technology itself still needs to be improved, the evaluation research on the segmentation technology is still lacking, and the systematic research on the evaluation method is almost zero. It is worth pointing out that the study of image segmentation evaluation is to better study the image segmentation itself, and the comparison and characterization of evaluation methods is to better study the segmentation evaluation, so as to play a guiding role in the segmentation research itself. In view of the importance of this work, this chapter will summarize and discuss the existing research results of image segmentation evaluation to promote in-depth research in this domain and promote the progress of image segmentation technology from "top" to "down".

The contents of each section of this chapter are arranged as follows.

Section 3.1 first classifies the existing segmentation evaluation research tasks, including segmentation levels (divided into three layers), evaluation works (divided into two types), and evaluation methods (divided into three groups) to lay the foundation for further discussion.

Section 3.2 combines an overall framework of evaluation to introduce the mechanism of evaluation based on experiments, and discusses the various working modules of the framework, which is one of the key points of evaluation research.

Section 3.3 introduces and analyzes the various evaluation criteria used in the three groups of evaluation methods in detail, and discusses their respective characteristics, which is another focus of the evaluation research. In addition, an example of evaluating various segmentation algorithms is also given.

Section 3.4 uses the overall evaluation framework introduced in Section 3.2 to test and evaluate a typical algorithm in each of the four classes of segmentation algorithms, and conduct a specific analysis of the evaluation results to reflect the information revealed by the evaluation.

Section 3.5 raises the study of image segmentation from evaluation to comparison and characterization of evaluation. Through the characteristic analysis of evaluation methods and the experimental comparison of quantitative criteria, the order of the evaluation methods in terms of evaluation ability is provided.

Section 3.6 introduces an evaluation-based segmentation algorithm optimization system, which shows that the results of segmentation evaluation can be used to guide segmentation. It mainly introduces the idea and strategy of algorithm optimization and the realization and effect of the optimization system.

Section 3.7 provides a brief introduction to some technique developments and promising research directions in the last year.

3.1 CLASSIFICATION OF SEGMENTATION EVALUATION RESEARCH TASKS

Image segmentation evaluation work can be divided into two situations:

1. *Performance characterization:* It masters the performance of a certain algorithm in different segmentation situations, and selects algorithm parameters to adapt to the needs of segmenting images with different contents and segmenting images collected under different conditions.

2. *Performance comparison:* It compares the performance of different algorithms in segmenting some given images to help select appropriate algorithms or improve existing algorithms in specific segmentation applications.

The above two aspects are related to each other. The performance characterization can make the performance of the algorithm more comprehensive, and the performance comparison can make the performance characterization of the algorithm more purposeful.

In order to achieve the purpose of segmented evaluation, the basic requirements for evaluation methods are mainly (Zhang and Gerbrands 1994):

1. It should have a wide range of versatility, that is, the evaluation method should be suitable for evaluating different types of segmentation algorithms and suitable for various application fields.

2. Quantitative and objective performance evaluation criteria should be used. Quantitative here means that the performance of the algorithm can be accurately described, and objective means that the evaluation is free of human factors.

3. Common images should be selected for testing to make the evaluation results comparable and portable. At the same time, these images should reflect the real situation of the objective world and the common characteristics of the actual application field as much as possible.

At present, most of the methods that people have put forward in evaluating segmentation techniques and algorithms can be summarized into two categories. One type is a direct method, which directly studies the principle characteristics of the segmentation algorithm itself, and obtains the performance of the segmentation algorithm through analysis and reasoning, so it can also be called an *analytical method*; the other type is an indirect method, which indirectly judging the performance of the segmentation algorithm via the quality of the segmented image. It can also be called a test method or empirical method or *experimental method*. Specifically, it is to use the algorithm to be evaluated to segment the image, and then use a certain quality measure to determine the pros and cons of the segmentation result, and then obtain the performance of the segmentation algorithm used.

The experimental methods can be further divided into two groups: one group uses some goodness parameters (often established according to human intuition) to describe the characteristics of the segmented image, and then judges the performance of the segmentation algorithm according to the goodness value; the other group determines first the ideal or expected segmentation result (reference image), and then experimentally compare the discrepancy between the segmented image and the reference image to determine the performance of the segmentation algorithm. The former group of methods can be called **goodness experimental methods**, and the latter group of methods can be called **discrepancy experimental methods**. Based on the above discussion, the segmentation evaluation methods can be divided into three groups: analytical methods, goodness experimental methods and discrepancy experimental methods. Their respective characteristics and interrelationships can be illustrated with the help of Figure 3.1 (Zhang 1996).

The basic flowchart of image segmentation in a narrow sense is given in the dotted line box in Figure 3.1. Here, image segmentation is regarded as the process of segmenting the image to be segmented by the segmentation algorithm to obtain the segmented image. A generalized basic flowchart of image segmentation is given in the dashed box in Figure 3.1. Here, image segmentation is regarded as a series of three steps: (i) pre-processing; (ii) image segmentation in a narrow sense; (iii) post-processing. In the generalized segmentation flowchart, the image to be segmented is obtained by performing certain pre-processing on the general input image, and the segmented image also has to undergo certain post-processing to become the final output image.

From Figure 3.1, we can see the different points of action and working methods for the above three groups of evaluation methods. The analytical method only acts on the segmentation algorithm itself, and does not involve segmentation of the image and the segmentation process. The goodness experimental method is to detect the quality of the

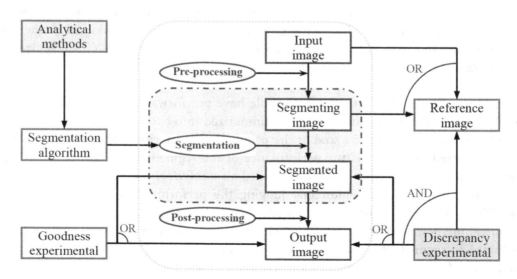

FIGURE 3.1   General scheme for segmentation and its evaluation.

segmented image or the output image to evaluate the segmentation algorithm, without considering the input of the segmentation process; while the discrepancy experimental method is to compare the quality of reference image obtained through the input image or the image to be segmented with the quality of segmented image or output image in order to evaluate the segmentation algorithm, so it is necessary to consider both the input of the segmentation process and the output of the segmentation process.

Regardless of the analytical methods or the experimental methods (including direct methods and indirect methods), they basically have two key steps or operation modules. One is the framework or mechanism as well as the approach or scheme (that is, mechanism and procedure) for analyzing or testing segmentation algorithms; the other is the *evaluation criteria* (also often called measures or indicators) used to judge the characteristics of the algorithm. The former has similarities to the same group of evaluation methods (because the main consideration is the mechanism when grouping here), while the latter has its own characteristics for each specific approach in the same group of methods. Evaluation criteria are both important for analytical methods or experimental methods. For analytical methods, to analyze certain characteristics of algorithms, it is necessary to have a measure for this characteristic, and the characteristics of the algorithm can only be distinguished and compared based on this measure. For experimental methods, because they rely on the results of image segmentation to determine the performance of the segmentation algorithm used, they are quantitative (computable and comparable) and objective (not different due to the subjective consciousness of the appraiser). The index is very important, and the pros and cons of the algorithm are determined by the index value. It can be seen that appropriate and effective performance evaluation criteria must be adopted to evaluate image segmentation. In addition, evaluation criteria also have a limiting effect on evaluation programs under certain circumstances, and certain evaluation criteria can only be used in certain evaluation programs.

3.2 SEGMENTATION ALGORITHM EVALUATION FRAMEWORK

The evaluation mechanism is mainly embodied in the evaluation framework, in which the discrepancy experimental method has to consider both the segmentation algorithm itself and the segmentation process. In the segmentation process, input and output need to be considered at the same time, which makes this group of methods relatively more complicated.

3.2.1 Evaluation Framework

Figure 3.2 shows a schematic diagram of the *evaluation framework* for the segmentation algorithm by using the discrepancy experimental methods. It mainly includes three modules: performance assessment, image generation, and test procedure (for algorithm testing) (Zhang and Gerbrands 1992a).

The evaluation framework shown in Figure 3.2 is general. On the one hand, conditions and factors related to analysis purposes, evaluation requirements, image acquisition, and processing can be selectively integrated into this framework, so it can be applied to

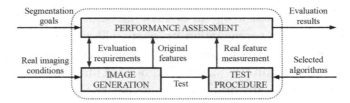

FIGURE 3.2 A general framework for segmentation evaluation.

various application fields. On the other hand, because it only needs to use the results of image segmentation when studying the segmentation algorithm and does not need to understand the internal structural characteristics of the algorithm being studied, it can be applied to all segmentation algorithms. A brief introduction to these three modules is given below.

3.2.2 Performance Assessment

Performance assessment includes three related parts (see Figure 3.3):

1. ***Feature selection:*** According to the purpose of segmentation, the corresponding object features are selected for evaluation, and the corresponding synthetic test images should be generated accordingly;

2. ***Discrepancy computation:*** Using the original and measured feature values obtained from the original image and the segmentation image to calculate;

3. ***Performance description:*** Combine the discrepancy computation result with the image synthesis conditions to give the evaluation result.

3.2.3 Image Generation

Image generation refers to the process of image synthesis process. In order to judge the segmentation algorithm based on the results of test segmentation, it is necessary to adopt some suitable segmentation test images. To ensure the objectivity and versatility of the evaluation process, synthetic images can be used to test the segmentation algorithm and serve as a reference image. This not only has good objectivity, but also has strong repeatability and stable results. If the real image was used, the test results are often limited to specific applications, and subjective bias will be introduced in the evaluation due to the need for manual segmentation to obtain the reference image. The important point in

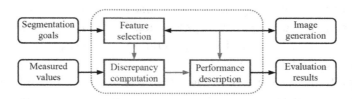

FIGURE 3.3 Schematic diagram of performance assessment module.

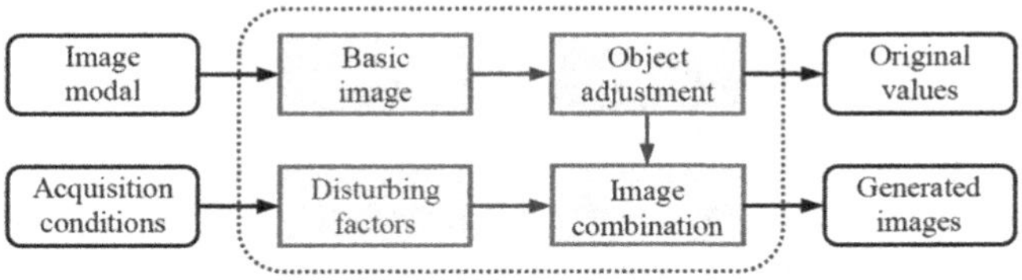

FIGURE 3.4 Schematic diagram of image synthesis module.

using synthetic images is that the generated images should reflect the objective world, which requires the integration of knowledge in the application domain. The image synthesis process should be adjustable to adapt to actual conditions such as changes in image content and various conditions for acquiring images. The image synthesis system introduced below can meet the above requirements, and it includes four related parts (see Figure 3.4):

1. ***Building the basic image:*** The basic image reflects the basic content and structure, and can be established according to the model of the actual application field. It will be the basis and starting point for generating a series of composite images.

2. ***Object adjustment:*** To simulate the actual image, the object in the basic image should be modified to generate objects of different gray scales, sizes, shapes, numbers, positions, etc.; the original data of the object can be output to the performance assessment module.

3. ***Disturbing factors:*** Various influence factors can be simulated. Noise is generated by simulating the acquisition conditions (or actual acquisition), and the simulated processing conditions (such as smoothing) to make an image blurred, and they are superimposed on images with different objects to approximate the real world.

4. ***Image combination:*** Combine various image objects and interference factors in a certain order to finally obtain a test image that is as close to the actual situation as possible.

Figure 3.5 shows a set of segmentation evaluation test images synthesized according to the process of Figure 3.4. These images are all 256 × 256 pixels, 256-level grayscale images. The basic image is composed of a bright circular object placed in the middle of a dark background. In the figure, the grayscale contrast between the object and the background is 32, and the superimposed noises are all zero-mean Gaussian random noises. This group of images can be called "size group". The object area in the eight columns from left to right is 20%, 15%, 10%, 5%, 3%, 2%, 1%, 0.5% of the whole image. The signal-to-noise ratios of the four rows images from top to bottom are 1, 4, 16, and 64, respectively.

3.2.4 Test Procedure

The flowchart of the test procedure for image segmentation algorithms is shown in Figure 3.6.

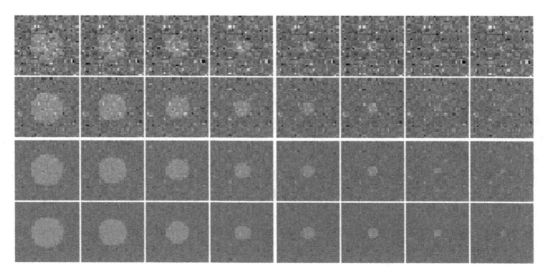

FIGURE 3.5   Examples of segmentation evaluation test images.

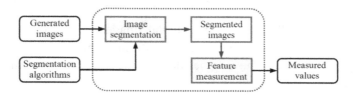

FIGURE 3.6   Test procedure flow diagram.

The flow diagram of test procedure for algorithms in Figure 3.6 is a typical image analysis module, which includes two connected steps: image segmentation and feature measurement. In the segmentation stage, the algorithm under test is regarded as a "black box", the input to it is the test image, and the output produced is the segmented image. In the measurement stage, the actual object feature values are obtained by measuring the predetermined features according to the segmented objects, and then these feature values are input into the "performance assessment" module for discrepancy calculation.

3.3 CRITERIA FOR SEGMENTATION EVALUATION

In Section 3.1, the segmentation evaluation methods are divided into three groups: analytical methods, goodness experimental methods, and discrepancy experimental methods. The evaluation criteria used by different methods to judge the characteristics of the algorithm also have their own characteristics. The following introduces some basic and typical evaluation criteria for each group.

3.3.1 Criteria for Analytical Methods

The ***analytical method criterion*** refers to the evaluation criterion suitable for analyzing the segmentation algorithm itself, which can be qualitative or quantitative.

3.3.1.1 A-1: The Combined a priori Information

Image segmentation belongs to the middle-level image analysis of image engineering. It has a certain degree of abstraction, and the guiding role of high-level knowledge is also important. When designing the segmentation algorithm, some characteristic information about the image to be segmented can be combined and used to improve the stability, reliability and efficiency of segmentation. For some algorithms, it is possible to obtain better segmentation results by combining *a priori information* or *a priori knowledge* in practical applications. Since the application of *a priori* information has a greater impact on the performance of the segmentation algorithm, it is possible to compare the advantages and disadvantages of the algorithms to a certain extent according to the types and amounts of the *a priori* information combined by different algorithms.

It should be noted that not all algorithms can effectively use this criterion to judge and compare. On the one hand, this is because there is no method that can quantitatively describe the *a priori* information, so it is difficult to compare. On the other hand, not only the type and amount of *a priori* information, but also how to use this information in the segmentation algorithm will have a great impact on the performance of the algorithm (Zhang and Gerbrands 1991). Since the use of *a priori* information is difficult to quantitatively describe, this criterion is mainly used for qualitative analysis of algorithm performance.

3.3.1.2 A-2: Processing Strategy

Image segmentation, like many image analysis techniques, can be implemented sequentially, in parallel, mixed, or iteratively. The performance of image segmentation algorithms is often closely related to these *processing strategies*, so the characteristics of the algorithm can be grasped to a certain extent according to the processing strategy of the algorithm (Zhang 1993a). For example, algorithms that work in parallel have high processing speeds, and are especially suitable for rapid implementation by computers with parallel processing capabilities. However, because all pixels are processed at the same time in parallel processing, the intermediate results in sequential and iterative algorithms cannot be used to adjust the algorithm, so it is not flexible enough, and the influence of noise and interference will be greater. On the contrary, although the algorithm of sequential working is more complicated and slow, because it makes more use of the information obtained gradually in the early stage, it can better deal with difficult situations, and the anti-noise ability is often stronger.

3.3.1.3 A-3: Computational Cost

Each segmentation algorithm is realized by a series of computational operations. The *computational cost* required to complete these operations is related to the complexity of the segmentation process, the efficiency of the algorithm (and the calculation speed), and it is also an indicator of the performance of the algorithm. In practice, the calculation cost for completing various operations is also related to many factors, such as computer hardware, image content, and so on. In order to eliminate the influence of computer hardware, the calculation cost can also be calculated according to the type and quantity of different operations (Zhang 1993a). In this case, the computational cost of certain algorithms can be quantified by analyzing the algorithms. The calculation amount of some segmentation algorithms is related to the content of the image or the region to be segmented, or the complexity of the image itself. At this time, it is necessary to use the criteria calculated according to each specific segmentation task (that is, by measuring the specific time required for the image segmentation) to determine the computational cost of the algorithm, but this is generally only applicable to certain algorithms.

3.3.1.4 A-4: Detection Probability Ratio

The **detection probability ratio** is defined as the ratio of the probability of correct detection to the probability of false detection. This criterion was originally used to compare and study various edge detection operators. Given an edge pattern, the correct detection probability P_c and false detection probability P_f of an operator when detecting such edges can be calculated by the following two Equations (3.1 and 3.2) (T is a given threshold):

$$P_c = \int_T^\infty P(t|\text{edge})\, dt \tag{3.1}$$

$$P_f = \int_T^\infty P(t|\text{no} - \text{edge})\, dt \tag{3.2}$$

Generally, the ratio of P_c and P_f for simple edge detection operators can be obtained through analysis. The larger the value, the higher the reliability of the operator in detecting the corresponding edge. Since many segmentation techniques use edge detection operators to help segment images, this criterion can be used to evaluate the performance of these algorithms.

In practice, the ratio of P_c and P_f is often expressed as a detection and false alarm curve to evaluate segmentation performance. By the way, this method can also be based on other metrics for images, objects, or algorithms.

3.3.1.5 A-5: Resolution

The **resolution** of the segmented image obtained by using different segmentation algorithms can have a variety of levels, for example, it can be a pixel, a number of pixels, or a fraction of a pixel (sub-pixel). In practice, the resolution of most algorithms is in pixels (texture image segmentation is often based on a collection of multiple pixels), but the resolution of **sub-pixels** has attracted attention in many applications, so the resolution is also an effective indicator for measuring the performance of the algorithm.

Generally speaking, for a given segmentation algorithm, its resolution can be obtained by analyzing its principles and processing steps.

3.3.2 Criteria for Goodness Experimental Methods

The **goodness experimental method** should use some **goodness criteria** when evaluating the effect of image segmentation. These criteria often represent some properties that are subjectively expected for the ideal segmentation result, and they are generally quantitative.

3.3.2.1 G-1: Inter-Region Contrast

Image segmentation needs to divide an original image into several regions. Intuitively, there should be a relatively large gap or obvious contrast between the characteristics of these regions. The quality of the segmented image can be judged according to the ***inter-region contrast*** for the given characteristics, and the pros and cons of the segmentation algorithm used can also be derived from contrast. For two adjacent regions in the image, if their respective average gray levels are f_1 and f_2, the ***gray-level contrast (GC)*** between them can be calculated as follows (Levine and Nazif 1985):

$$GC = \frac{|f_1 - f_2|}{f_1 + f_2} \tag{3.3}$$

In fact, f in Equation (3.3) can also represent other feature quantities except grayscale. In this way, the inter-region contrast of other features is obtained. When there are multiple regions in an image, Equation (3.3) can be used to calculate the contrast between two adjacent regions and then sum them up.

An indicator closely related to the inter-region contrast is called correlation (Brink 1989). Although it directly measures the correlation coefficient between the original image and the binary image obtained after thresholding, however, it has been proved that the square of the correlation coefficient here is also the class separation entropy in an entropy segmentation algorithm (Otsu 1979), so the meaning of this index is similar to the inter-region contrast (Zhang 1996).

3.3.2.2 G-2: Intra-Region Uniformity

Segmentation is often defined as decomposing an original image $f(x, y)$ into several regions with similar internal characteristics. Therefore, the uniformity of the internal characteristics of each region in the segmented image can be used to describe the quality of the segmented image. The criterion can be called ***intra-region uniformity***. If R_i is used to represent the i-th region in the segmented image and A_i represents its area, the ***uniformity measure (UM)*** within each region in the segmented image can be expressed as (Sahoo et al. 1988):

$$UM = 1 - \frac{1}{C}\sum_i \left\{ \sum_{(x,y)\in R_i} \left[f(x, y) - \frac{1}{A_i}\sum_{(x,y)\in R_i} f(x, y) \right]^2 \right\} \tag{3.4}$$

where C is the normalization coefficient. Similar to this, there are ***measures of busyness*** (Weszka and Rosenfeld 1978) and ***higher-order local entropy*** (Pal and Bhandari 1993) based on the same idea.

3.3.2.3 G-3: Shape Measure

Intuitively speaking, a good segmentation result should meet certain subjective conditions or visual requirements. Generally, it is hoped that the contour line of the object is relatively smooth, and the **shape measure (SM)** is proposed to measure the smoothness of the outer contour of the object, so it can also be called the contour index. If $f_N(x, y)$ represents the average gray level in the neighborhood $N(x, y)$ of the pixel (x, y), $g(x, y)$ represents the gradient at the pixel (x, y), and T is the threshold value used for thresholding, then the shape measure SM obtained by segmentation can be calculated with the following formula (Sahoo et al. 1988):

$$\text{SM} = \frac{1}{C}\left\{\sum_{x,y} \text{Sgn}[f(x, y) - f_{N(x,y)}]g(x, y)\text{Sgn}[f(x, y) - T]\right\} \tag{3.5}$$

where C is a normalization coefficient. $\text{Sgn}(\cdot)$ represents the unit step function, and T is a predetermined threshold.

3.3.3 Criteria for Discrepancy Experimental Methods

The evaluation criterion used in the discrepancy experimental methods is used to compare the difference between the segmented image and the reference image, so it is called the **discrepancy criterion**. Using the discrepancy criterion should be able to quantitatively measure the segmentation results, and this measurement is objective.

3.3.3.1 D-1: Pixel Distance Error

The actual segmentation results are often not perfect. In this case, there must be some pixels erroneously segmented into regions that they should not belong to. The distance between these misclassified pixels and the correct regions they should belong to (with certain spatial information) reflects the quality of the segmentation. Several measures based on the **pixel distance error** have been proposed to evaluate the segmentation results. A commonly used measure is the **figure of merit (FOM)** or **factor of merit (FOM)**:

$$\text{FOM} = \frac{1}{N}\sum_{i=1}^{N}\frac{1}{1 + p \times d^2(i)} \tag{3.6}$$

where N is the number of misclassified pixels, p is a scale factor, and $d^2(i)$ represents the distance between the i-th misclassified pixel and its correct position. A measure associated with this is the **mean absolute value of the deviation (MAVD)**:

$$\text{MAVD} = \frac{1}{N}\sum_{i=1}^{N}|d(i)| \tag{3.7}$$

There is another measure called the **normalized distance measure (NDM)**:

$$\text{NDM} = \frac{\sqrt{\sum_{i=1}^{N} d^2(i)}}{A} \times 100\% \tag{3.8}$$

where N and $d^2(i)$ are the same as above and A is the area of the image. Other similar measures include pixel spatial distribution, modified figure of merit (MFOM), probability-weighted figure of merit (PWFOM), and so on.

3.3.3.2 D-2: Pixel Number Error

For image segmentation results, the number of misclassified pixels due to segmentation errors is an important image quality indicator. In this regard, many different weighting methods have been proposed to judge the quality of the segmented image by means of the **pixel number error**. For example, there is a kind of **error probability (PE)**. When the image is composed of two parts, the object and the background, the PE can be calculated by the following formula:

$$PE = P(o) \times P(b|o) + P(b) \times P(o|b) \tag{3.9}$$

where $P(b|o)$ is the probability of mistakenly segmenting the object into the background, $P(o|b)$ is the probability of mistaken segmenting the background into the object, and $P(o)$ and $P(b)$ are the *a priori* probability of the percentages of object and background in image, respectively. When the image contains multiple objects, a more general definition of PE can be found in Lim and Lee (1990). There is also a variant of error probability called the error rate (Luo and Zhang 1997).

For some specific segmentation algorithms, the parameters obtained and used by the segmentation algorithm have a certain correspondence with the number of pixels after segmentation. In this case, the pixel number error can also be calculated with the help of parameter errors. For example, for a global thresholding algorithm, when the threshold is given, the pixel number error is also determined, so the difference between the threshold actually obtained by a certain algorithm and the ideal threshold can also be used to measure the pros and cons of this algorithm.

3.3.3.3 D-3: Object Count Consistency

Suppose S_n is the number of objects obtained by segmenting an image and T_n is the number of objects actually existing in the image. Due to the imperfection of the segmentation result, S_n and T_n may be different. The difference between them reflects an aspect of the performance of the segmentation algorithm to a certain extent. By using probability, this difference can be taken to define a measure called the **object count consistency** to evaluate the segmentation algorithm. There is also an index that uses this measure to describe the performance of the algorithm called the **number of image blocks**, denoted by F, which is defined as

$$F = \frac{1}{1 + p\,|T_n - S_n|^q} \tag{3.10}$$

where p and q are both scale parameters.

3.3.3.4 D-4: Ultimate Measurement Accuracy

A basic problem in image analysis is to obtain an accurate measurement of the characteristic value of each object in the image (Young 1993), which is the ultimate goal of segmentation and other subsequent operations in image analysis. Because the feature measurement is based on the segmentation result, its accuracy directly depends on the segmentation result and the performance of the segmentation algorithm. In addition, this accuracy that can be called the **ultimate measurement accuracy (UMA)** also reflects the quality of the segmented image and can be used to judge the performance of the algorithm (Zhang and Gerbrands 1994). From the perspective of high-level image understanding, the quality of a segmented image depends on the difference between the decision made based on it and the decision made based on the original image. This is also the original intention of the ultimate measurement accuracy.

In practice, different object characteristics can be used to describe different properties of the object, so UMA can be written as UMA_f. This gives a series of evaluation criteria with object characteristics as parameters. If R_f represents the original feature value obtained from the reference image, and S_f represents the actual feature value obtained from the segmented image, their absolute difference and relative difference can be calculated by the following two formulas:

$$AUMA_f = |R_f - S_f| \tag{3.11}$$

$$RUMA_f = \frac{|R_f - S_f|}{R_f} \times 100\% \tag{3.12}$$

From the above, the **absolute ultimate measurement accuracy** and the **relative ultimate measurement accuracy** are obtained, respectively. Note that the values of $AUMA_f$ and $RUMA_f$ are inversely proportional to the segmentation quality: the smaller their value, the better the segmentation effect, and the better the performance of the algorithm used (Zhang 1997a).

The ultimate measurement accuracy criterion can meet the three requirements for evaluation described in Section 3.1. First of all, they are oriented towards analytical purposes, and thus directly reflect people's needs for the quality measurement of analytical work. In addition, because this is the commonality of different types of segmentation algorithms and does not depend on any particular algorithm and segmentation application field, the criterion has a wide range of versatility. Secondly, they are objective, because they reflect the characteristics of the object itself rather than subjectively defined visual quality; and they are quantitative, because their values can be accurately calculated according to Equations (3.11) and (3.12). Finally, a good evaluation method should select a common image for testing to make the evaluation results comparable and portable. The ultimate measurement accuracy criterion is simple to calculate and easy to be obtained from the common image.

Various features not only have different ability to describe the object, but also have different performance in segmentation evaluation when used in UMA. Figure 3.7 shows some results obtained by using five common object features (Zhang 2017), namely the

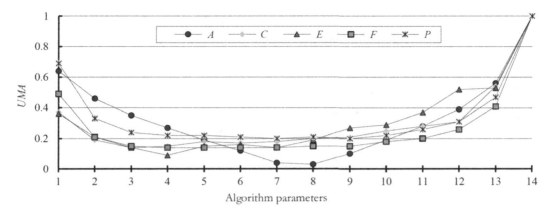

FIGURE 3.7 Feature performance study results.

object area (A), circularity (C), eccentricity (E), form factor (F), and perimeter (P). The performance of the image segmentation algorithm can be controlled by the parameters of the algorithm, so a series of actual segmentation images with different effects can be obtained by changing the algorithm parameters (a related study can see (Zhang 1995)). The horizontal axis in Figure 3.7 corresponds to the change of algorithm parameters. They correspond to the change of the segmentation effect from poor to good and from good to poor. The vertical axis corresponds to the UMA values normalized to [0, 1]. A large value indicates the poor segmentation effect, while a small value indicates a good segmentation effect.

It can be seen from Figure 3.7 that the UMA value of each feature changes from large to small and from small to large with the change of the algorithm parameters, which shows that these features can be used in UMA to indicate different segmentation quality and to judge the performance of the segmentation algorithm. However, these UMA curves are also different, which reflects the different ability of each corresponding feature to judge segmentation. Specifically, it can be analyzed from two aspects. On the one hand, look at the shape of the curve, especially the depth of the valley. Because the feature values here have been normalized to the same range, the depth of the valley reflects the dynamic range of each feature UMA value. The greater the depth of the valley, the stronger the ability to distinguish different segmentation results. Another aspect is the smoothness of the curve. It reflects the situation that the characteristic UMA value stably tracks the small change of the segmentation result. Generally speaking, the smoothness of the curve indicates that the features reflect the similar segmentation results more consistent and stable. Looking at Figure 3.7 based on the above two criteria, we can find the different characteristics of each curve. Among them, the circularity and eccentricity curves are not smooth enough, and the form factor and perimeter curves are almost horizontal in certain ranges. In contrast, the area curve has more obvious valleys and smoother rising and falling sections, which shows that in the evaluation with UMA, the area feature can often judge the segmentation result and quality better than the other features.

3.4 AN EXAMPLE EVALUATION OF SEGMENTATION ALGORITHMS

An actual evaluation experiment with the help of the previously introduced segmentation algorithm evaluation framework and its results are as follows (Zhang 1997b).

3.4.1 Algorithms and Images

First, give the evaluated algorithms. According to the classification of segmentation algorithms in Section 2.1, in order to make the evaluation more versatile and representative, one typical algorithm is selected from each type of algorithm (Zhang 2017):

1. Algorithm A (Category PB): Canny operator edge detection and boundary closing method;

2. Algorithm B (Category SB): Dynamic programming contour search method;

3. Algorithm C (Category PR): Improved histogram concavity surface analysis method;

4. Algorithm D (Category SR): Split, merge, and grouping methods.

Two sets of experimental images were used in the study: one set of experimental images is the "size group" in Figure 3.5; the other set of experimental images is called the "shape group". The two sets of images are combined as shown in Figure 3.8, where the left eight columns belong to the "size group" (numbered from left to right as circular objects No. 1–No. 8), and the right four columns belong to the "shape group". There is one column of images in these two groups that are the same, that is, the eighth column from the left.

The images of the "shape group" can be used to study the relationship between the segmentation effect with the object shape and the image signal-to-noise ratio. In the images of "shape group" in Figure 3.8, the objet shape is changed along the horizontal direction, and the image signal-to-noise ratio is changed along the vertical direction. The change of the object shape is achieved by changing the circular object in the basic image to different ellipses. The ratios of the long axis and short axis of the object in the four

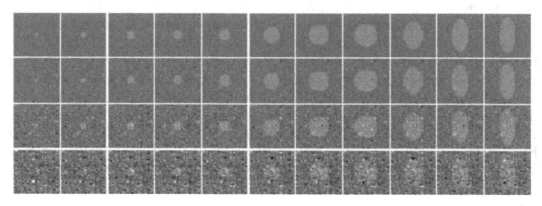

FIGURE 3.8 Experimental images for "size group" and "shape group".

columns from left to right are 1 : 1, 1.5 : 1, 2 : 1, and 2.5 : 1. They are numbered as elliptical objects No. 1–No. 4. In order to eliminate the influence of object size on segmentation, it is necessary to keep the object size as consistent as possible with the object in the basic image when changing the object shape (Zhang 1998a).

According to the results of the evaluation experiments, a lot of information about the performance of these algorithms can be obtained. The following only gives some results and analysis related to Algorithm B and Algorithm D as examples.

3.4.2 Evaluation of Algorithm B

Using Algorithm B to segment the image of the "shape group", some of the results obtained are shown in Figure 3.9. The upper and lower rows of images in Figure 3.9 correspond to various situations containing elliptical object No. 1 and elliptical object No. 4, respectively. The six columns of images from left to right are the original object (synthetic object), the segmentation results of the noise-free images, and the segmentation results of the noisy images with signal-to-noise ratios of 64, 16, 4, and 1, respectively.

The curve of the relative ultimate measurement accuracy RUMA, taking the object shape as a parameter, as a function of the signal-to-noise ratio is shown in Figure 3.10(a). Except for the curve corresponding to the image with the elliptical object No. 4, the other curves in Figure 3.10(a) are relatively similar. Note that although the shape of each object is different here, all the regions of interesting (ROI, the ring containing the elliptical outline) used in each experiment are the same, so the similarity of these curves shows that the relative shape relationship between the segmentation result and the ROI or the object is basically irrelevant. In other words, for Algorithm B, determining ROI here is not an important factor affecting segmentation. The influence of signal-to-noise ratio on segmentation is much more obvious, as shown by the curve decrease rapidly with the signal-to-noise ratio in Figure 3.10(a).

Go back and discuss the curve corresponding to the image with the elliptical object No. 4. At this time, it is clearer to use the image after the polar coordinate transformation. Figure 3.10(b) shows the result obtained by using the gradient operator and after performing the polar coordinate transformation, where the vertical axis corresponds to the polar angle and the horizontal axis corresponds to the vector radius (from the center

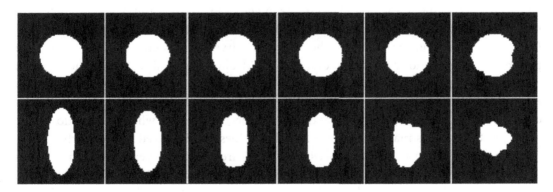

FIGURE 3.9 The segmentation result obtained by Algorithm B.

(a)　　　　　　　　　　　　　　　　　(b)

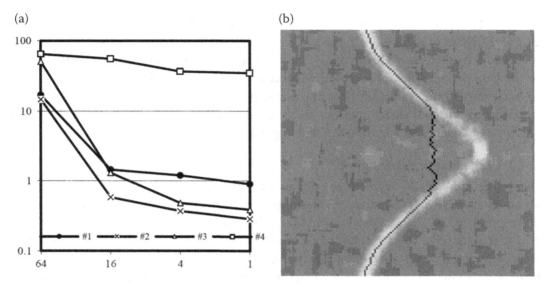

FIGURE 3.10　Algorithm B is affected by the shape of the object.

of the ROI to the object boundary). The light strips in the figure basically correspond to the boundary of the object, but the boundary line obtained from the top-down search using the dynamic programming search technology is shown as the black line in the figure, and a considerable part of it is out of the expected range. After further analysis of this problem, it is found that it is mainly caused by the insufficient sampling density during the polar coordinate transformation. For slender or irregular objects, the sampling rate needs to be appropriately increased to avoid this problem (Zhang 1993b).

3.4.3　Evaluation of Algorithm D

The following discusses the situation with the Algorithm D experiment. Here, the experimental images of the "size group" are used. In the split and merge algorithm, the consistency criteria used to determine whether to split or merge is very important. A commonly used criterion is based on the variance of the region. Since the variance of the region changes with noise, the criterion parameter V (vertical axis) of Algorithm D should be selected according to the noise level in the image. If the noise is unknown, it will lead to inaccurate selection of criterion parameters. What impact will this have on segmentation? For this reason, consider making the function curve (with signal-to-noise ratio as a parameter) of the ratio of the actual obtained RUMA and the ideal RUMA as the criterion parameter V with respect to the **standard deviation noise (SDN)**, as horizontal axis for Algorithm D, which is shown in Figure 3.11, where Figure (a) and Figure (b) are the results obtained with circular objects No. 8 and No. 5, respectively. Here, when the function value is greater than 6, it is marked as 6 so that other values are displayed more clearly.

Since the signal-to-noise ratio (SNR) and SDN are related, for each SDN, five values of V are selected so that the ratio of V to SDN is 0.5, 0.75, 1, 1.25, and 1.5, respectively. The actual RUMA is measured at different ratios of V to SDN, while the ideal RUMA is

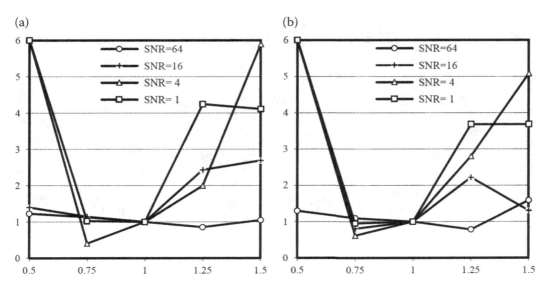

FIGURE 3.11   Evaluation results of Algorithm D.

measured when the ratio of V to SDN is 1 (that is, when the V parameter is accurately set). The larger the ratio of the actual RUMA to the ideal RUMA, the worse the segmentation result.

Figure 3.11(a) and Figure 3.11(b) have many similarities. When the ratio of V to SDN is not 1, the ratio of most actual RUMA to ideal RUMA is greater than 1. When the ratio of V to SDN is greater than 1, the segmentation algorithm tends to under-segment the image, and when the ratio of V to SDN is less than 1, the segmentation algorithm tends to over-segment the image. The valley in the middle of the two graphs indicates that setting V larger than SDN or setting V smaller than SDN will both affect the performance of the segmentation algorithm. In addition, it should be pointed out that the amount of calculation required for over-segmented images is much more than that required for under-segmented images (Zhang 1997b).

Figure 3.11(a) and Figure 3.11(b) have also some differences. The most obvious is that in Figure 3.11(a) there are only two conditions of SNR = 4 and SNR = 1, in which the ratio of actual RUMA to ideal RUMA reaches the maximum value of 6, when the ratio of V and SDN is 0.5; while in Figure 3.11(b), when the ratio of V to SDN is 0.5 under the condition of SNR = 16, it also reaches the maximum value of 6. This difference indicates that the incorrect setting of V has a greater impact when the size of object in image is small, that is, the setting of V is more critical when segmenting small objects.

Figure 3.12 shows the result of segmenting the same image when using different ratios of V to SDN. The upper and lower rows both use the circular object No. 8, but the image signal-to-noise ratios are SNR = 16 and SNR = 1, respectively. From left to right, the ratio of V to SDN is 0.5, 0.75, 1, 1.25, and 1.5, respectively. It can be seen from the figure that when the ratio of V to SDN is small (i.e., when it is over-segmentation), the segmentation result has more details, and when the ratio of V to SDN is large (i.e., when it is under-segmentation), the contour of the segmentation result is more regular.

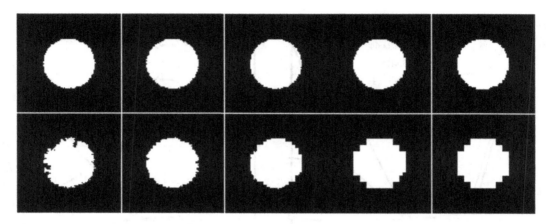

FIGURE 3.12 Segmentation results obtained by Algorithm D.

The above experimental results and discussions can provide a basis for the effective selection and use of suitable segmentation algorithms in practical applications.

3.5 COMPARISON OF EVALUATION METHODS AND CRITERIA

The previous sections have introduced various segmentation evaluation methods and evaluation criteria that have been proposed. The principles and mechanisms adopted by these methods and criteria have their own characteristics, so the evaluation performance will be different. This section discusses the performance comparison study of segmentation evaluation methods and evaluation criteria. In fact, the systematic comparison and characterization of segmentation evaluation methods is crucial for selecting effective evaluation methods, and further it is also critical for evaluating segmentation algorithms to improve segmentation quality.

As mentioned at the beginning of this chapter, if the study of image segmentation technology is regarded as the first level of content in image segmentation research, then the study of image segmentation evaluation technology can be regarded as the second level of content in image segmentation research. So how to evaluate this second level of image segmentation evaluation technology requires a third level of research, that is, to systematically characterize and compare the performance of the image segmentation evaluation technology.

Some concepts and ideas in the second level of research can also be used in the third level of image segmentation research. For example, the comparison of evaluation methods and criteria can also be carried out by means of analysis or experiment. The analytical method directly studies the evaluation methods or criteria themselves, discussing their principles, requirements, applicability, costs, etc.; while the experimental methods apply evaluation methods or criteria to the evaluation work and algorithms, to determine their pros and cons according to their performance in the evaluation process.

The following first discusses and compares the evaluation methods, then analyzes and compares various evaluation criteria, and finally compares several typical quantitative experimental criteria (including goodness experimental and discrepancy experimental criteria).

3.5.1 Discussion and Comparison of Methods

The three groups of evaluation methods in Section 3.1 can be discussed and compared from four aspects.

1. Generality

There are many types of segmentation algorithms that have been proposed, so the methods and criteria used to evaluate them should have generality, that is, they should be applicable to the study of different types of segmentation algorithms. Some methods and criteria are only suitable for studying certain segmentation algorithms due to their own restrictions, which will limit the evaluation work. For example, the calculation of the shape measure in Sub-section 3.3.2 needs to use the threshold in the thresholding algorithm, so it can only be used to study the thresholding algorithm. Another example, it is difficult to obtain analytical expressions for complex operators by only using the detection probability ratio in Sub-section 3.3.1, which also limits its application.

2. Complexity

Whether an evaluation method is practical or not has a lot to do with the complexity of its implementation, or with the operating means and workload required for evaluation, which is also very important for whether the evaluation method can be applied online. Some evaluation criteria require a series of calculations for each pixel (such as the calculation of the uniformity measurement of the region in Sub-section 3.3.2). The number of pixels in an image is usually quite large, so the amount of calculation required for evaluation will be very big. There are also some experimental indicators. In order to calculate their values, in addition to segmenting the image, additional processing and auxiliary operations are required (such as the pixel distance error introduced in Sub-section 3.3.3), so the evaluation work will become quite complicated or a lot of calculations are required.

3. Subjectivity and objectivity

For each evaluation method, there are often some subjective or objective considerations behind it, or the evaluation criteria used are determined based on specific subjective or objective factors. The criteria based on subjective factors may be consistent with human intuition, but they do not necessarily reflect actual application requirements (Zhang and Gerbrands 1994). On the other hand, the criteria based on objective factors can often provide consistent and unbiased research results (Young 1993). Image segmentation is the first step in image analysis, and objective results are more important.

4. Demand for reference images

For some evaluation methods, the evaluation conclusion depends on the comparison between the segmentation result and the reference image (truth value), and the acquisition of the reference image brings some specific problems to the applicability of the evaluation method. For actual images, accurate segmentation results are often not automatically obtainable, and manual segmentation is also difficult to ensure the consistency of evaluation. It can be seen from Figure 3.1 that neither the analytical methods nor the goodness experimental methods require a reference image, while the discrepancy experimental methods requires the use of a reference image.

In addition to the above four aspects, there are other situations worth discussing. As can be seen from the different action points and action modes of the above three groups of evaluation methods: the *analytical methods* for evaluating algorithm can only analyze the principles of the algorithm, and does not need to implement the algorithm itself (so that the evaluation will not be affected by the error or approximation produced by the implementation of the algorithm; while using the experimental methods, the algorithm needs to be implemented and the input image needs to be actually segmented to obtain the output segmented image (for the discrepancy experimental method, a reference image is also required). Another example is that the analytical methods do not consider the application environment of the algorithm at all, and the evaluation result is only related to the algorithm itself. The *goodness experimental methods* actually combine some of the expected properties of the segmented image into the goodness parameters, thus establishing a connection with the actual applications. The *discrepancy experimental methods* use the reference image obtained from the input image or the image to be segmented as the segmentation standard, and has fully considered the specific applications. In terms of combination with applications, the differences in the three groups of evaluation methods also have a great impact on their performance.

3.5.2 Analytical Comparison of Criteria

The above discussion is basically based on each group of methods, while some characteristics are specific to each group of criteria. The requirements for the reference images can be determined according to the group to which the criteria belong, and the other three aspects need to be discussed separately. Analyzing the various basic evaluation criteria introduced in Section 3.3 can be synthesized into Table 3.1 (Zhang 1993a), which also supplements some evaluation criteria (D5–D8) recently catching attention (Zhang 2015). From the table, we can see some of the main advantages and disadvantages of each group of criteria.

In the 21st century, image segmentation evaluation has made further progress (Zhang 2001, 2006, 2009, 2015). Table 3.2 shows the analysis and comparison of some segmentation evaluation methods in recent years. For each method, the main evaluation criteria used are listed (the criteria used in some methods have improved the original criteria, but they are basically the same kind). Some methods use more than one criterion in combination. All criteria are *goodness criteria* or *discrepancy criteria*. The former is mainly based on subjective factors and the latter is mainly based on objective factors. The latter also requires the use of reference images.

TABLE 3.1 Comparison of basic segmentation evaluation criteria

Lable	Criteria	Generality	Com-plexity	Subjectivity/Objectivity	Notes
A-1	*a priori* information	Some algorithms	Low	Subjectivity	Different types of knowledge are difficult to compare
A-2	Processing strategy	All algorithms	Low	Objectivity	Indicating parameters of algorithm efficiency or complexity
A-3	Computational cost	Some simple algorithms	Low	Objectivity	Relative measurement, without considering hardware and software implementation
A-4	Detection probability ratio	Some simple algorithms	Moderate	Objectivity	Difficult to analyze complex algorithms
A-5	Resolution	All algorithms	Low	Objectivity	Indicating parameters of algorithm capability
G-1	Inter-region contrast	All algorithms	Moderate	Subjectivity	Dynamic online measurement that simulates human evaluation ability
G-2	Intra-region uniformity	All algorithms	High	Subjectivity	Dynamic online measurement
G-3	Shape measure	Thresholding algorithms	High	Subjectivity	Only related to the roughness of the object boundary
D-1	Pixel distance error	All algorithms	High	Objectivity	Need to be used in conjunction with other criteria
D-2	Pixel number error	All algorithms	Moderate	Objectivity	No use of spatial information
D-3	Object count consistency	All algorithms	Low	Objectivity	Simple but rough, not very accurate when the number of objects in the image is small
D-4	Ultimate measurement accuracy	All algorithms	Moderate	Objectivity	A group of measures directly related to the purpose of segmentation
D-5	Miscellaneous object quantities	All algorithms	Moderate	Objectivity	A group of measures representing the characteristics of the segmented object
D-6	Region consistency	Some algorithms	High	Objectivity	Related to similarities between regions
D-7	Grey level difference	All algorithms	Moderate	Objectivity	Change of average gray level before and after segmentation
D-8	Symmetric divergence (cross-entropy)	All algorithms	High	Objectivity	Reflect the information connection between images

TABLE 3.2 Analysis and comparison of some new evaluation methods and criteria in the 21st century

Sl. No.	Reference	Main Criteria	Generality	Complexity
1	(Oberti et al. 2001)	D-1	All algorithms	Moderate
2	(Cavallaro et al. 2002)	D-1, D-2	Video[1]	Moderate/High
3	(Udupa et al. 2002)	D-1	All algorithms	Moderate
4	(Li et al. 2003)	D-1, D-2	All algorithms	High[2]
5	(Prati et al. 2003)	D-1	All algorithms	High
6	(Rosin and Ioannidis 2003)	D-1	Video[1]	Moderate
7	(Carleer et al. 2004)	D-1, D-3	Multi-objects[3]	Low/Moderate
8	(Erdem et al. 2004)	G-1, G-2	Video[1]	High
9	(Kim et al. 2004)	D-1	Video[1]	Moderate
10	(Ladak et al. 2004)	D-1	All algorithms	High[3]
11	(Lievers and Pilkey 2004)	G-1	Thresholding algorithm	Moderate
12	(Niemeijer et al. 2004)	D-1	All algorithms	Moderate
13	(Renno et al. 2004)	D-1, D-4	All algorithms	Moderate/High
14	(Udupa and Zhuge 2004)	D-1	All algorithms	Moderate
15	(Cardoso and Corte-Real 2005)	D-2	All algorithms	Moderate
16	(Chabrier et al. 2006)	G-1, G-2, D-1	All algorithms	Moderate
17	(Jiang et al. 2006)	D-2	All algorithms	Moderate
18	(Ortiz and Oliver 2006)	D-1	All algorithms	High
19	(Udupa et al. 2006)	D-2	All algorithms	Moderate
20	(Ge et al. 2007)	D-3	All algorithms	Low
21	(Unnikrishnan et al. 2007)	D-2	All algorithms	Moderate
22	(Philipp-Foliguet and Guigues 2008)	G-1, G-3	All algorithms	Moderate/High
23	(Xu and Gondra 2008)	D-5, D-6	All algorithms	Moderate/High
24	(Zhang et al. 2008)	G-1, G-2	All algorithms	High
25	(Cárdenes et al. 2009)	D-2, D-7	All algorithms	Moderate
26	(Hao et al. 2009)	G-1	All algorithms	Moderate
27	(Marçal and Rodrigues 2009)	D-2	All algorithms	Moderate
28	(Polak et al. 2009)	D-1, D-2, D-5	All algorithms	High
29	(Qu and Ma 2010)	D-5	All algorithms	Moderate
30	(Casciaro et al. 2012)	D-1	All algorithms	High
31	(Khan and Bhuiyan 2013)	D-8	All algorithms	High
32	(Peng and Li 2013)	D-5	All algorithms	Moderate
33	(Pont-Tuset and Marques 2013)	D-1	All algorithms	High

[1] Video means that it can only be used for video segmentation algorithms, because time information is used.
[2] The evaluation needs to be combined with the user's observation results to make judgments.
[3] More suitable for evaluating segmentation results with many objects in the image.

3.5.3 Experimental Comparison of Criteria

This section introduces the experimental comparison of some evaluation criteria. There are the following considerations when selecting criteria for comparison. First of all, the models used by various direct analysis methods are not the same and are not comparable, so only the experimental evaluation criteria are considered. Among the seven types of experimental evaluation criteria in Section 3.3, the criterion based on shape measure is only suitable for the study of thresholding algorithms, not for other types of algorithms. Moreover, it cannot actually describe the shape of the object (Zhang and Gerbrands 1992a), but only describes the smoothness of the object boundary. On the other hand, although the criterion of object count consistency can be applied to various algorithms, it is not always suitable for various practical situations. It is because when the segmentation result is relatively close to the optimal result (this is also the case in general), the number of objects obtained by the actual segmentation is often consistent with the original number of objects in the image, and the remaining problem is only that each object has not been completely segmented correctly. In this case, the object count consistency can no longer be used to identify the pros and cons of segmentation. Taking into account the above factors, the following is a comparative study with one of the other five types of criteria as a representative.

1. Criterion A: *Inter-region contrast*. It can be calculated according to Equation (3.3).

2. Criterion B: *Intra-region uniformity*. It can be calculated using Equation (3.4). But in order to compare with other criteria, only the summation part in Equation (3.4) is calculated. In this way, all index values are smaller when the segmentation result is better, and vice versa.

3. Criterion C: *Pixel distance error*. It can be calculated according to Equation (3.8). Compared with Equation (3.6), its advantage is to avoid the uncertainty caused by subjective selection of the coefficient p in Equation (3.6).

4. Criterion D: *Pixel number error*. It can be calculated according to Equation (3.10).

5. Criterion E: *Ultimate measurement accuracy*. It can be calculated according to Equation (3.12), where the object area is selected as the feature.

The comparison of different criteria can be done by evaluating a series of segmented image. Specifically, the above criteria are used to judge a series of the same segmented images, and a series of values for each criterion are calculated. From the changes of these values, different characteristics of each criterion can be obtained, and then the pros and cons of the criteria can be obtained by comparing the characteristic values. The entire experimental arrangement is somewhat similar to the feature performance study (see Figure 3.7), except that the same object feature is used here and five evaluation criteria are compared.

Figure 3.13 shows the segmented images obtained from several experiments. The image marked A is the original image (with circular object No. 8), and the images marked B–F are the results of segmentation using thresholds 112, 122, 124, 126, and 136, respectively. It can be seen from Figure 3.13 that the segmentation results change from poor to good and from good to poor with the change of thresholds, and good evaluation criteria should also have a corresponding trend with the change of threshold parameters.

Table 3.3 gives a set of experimental results for comparing the above five evaluation criteria. The label of each column corresponds to the threshold values used when

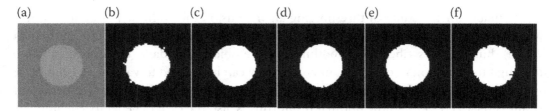

FIGURE 3.13 Experimental results obtained by segmentation with different thresholds.

TABLE 3.3 Evaluation criteria comparison data

Criteria	112	114	116	118	120	122	124	126	128	130	132	134	136	138
A	0.989	0.994	0.997	0.997	0.998	0.999	0.999	0.999	0.999	1.000	0.999	0.998	0.997	0.995
B	1.000	0.897	0.858	0.846	0.821	0.808	0.804	0.800	0.800	0.800	0.808	0.825	0.854	0.906
C	0.705	0.538	0.454	0.415	0.362	0.292	0.260	0.238	0.290	0.382	0.466	0.583	0.719	1.000
D	0.578	0.340	0.242	0.202	0.154	0.100	0.079	0.066	0.099	0.170	0.254	0.395	0.573	1.000
E	0.526	0.340	0.241	0.203	0.149	0.092	0.042	0.017	0.077	0.161	0.252	0.395	0.573	1.000

segmenting the image, and the criterion values obtained from the experiments are arranged in five rows. The values in the table have been normalized to the interval [0, 1] to facilitate the comparison of their relative sizes.

Figure 3.14 gives the values in Table 3.3 in the form of curves, so that their changing trends and characteristics can be found and studied more intuitively.

Now let's analyze the data in Table 3.3 and the curves in Figure 3.14. The analysis of Figure 3.14 can be considered from two aspects:

1. The depth of the valley of each curve

Because the maximum peak value has been normalized to 1, the dynamic range of the curve is determined by the depth value of the valley. If the valley is deeper, the dynamic range is larger, and the larger the dynamic range is, the different segmentation results that

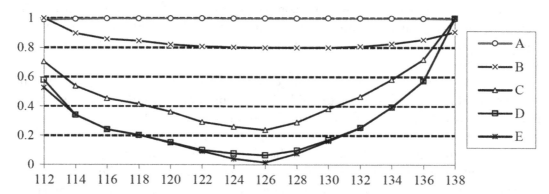

FIGURE 3.14 Evaluation criteria comparison curves.

can be represented are more and finer, or the description of the segmentation result changes is more sensitive. These five criteria are ranked E, D, C, B, A in descending order of dynamic range. The ultimate measurement accuracy is the best, and the worst is the contrast between regions. The valley and peak values on the Curve A are almost the same, so it is difficult to distinguish different segmentation results based on this criterion.

2. The shape of each curve

The shape of the curve reflects the trend of the curve. From this point of view, most of the curves are similar, they are first monotonously decreasing and then monotonously increasing, which is consistent with the arrangement of the segmented images. Note that Curve E and Curve D overlap in many places, but when it is close to the bottom (that is, when it corresponds to the optimal segmentation effect), Curve E drops more and faster than Curve D (this can also be seen in Table 3.3). This shows that the ultimate measurement accuracy can better judge the segmentation results close to the optimal, which is very meaningful in practice.

In summary, the performances of these criteria are very different. The ultimate measurement accuracy is the best, followed by the pixel number error, and the pixel distance error is behind, and finally are the intra-region uniformity and inter-region contrast. Although intra-region uniformity and inter-region contrast do not need to use reference images in practical utilization, their evaluation ability is poor. In fact, their evaluation for segmentation is mainly subjective and qualitative, and some other experimental results also support the above conclusions (Luo and Zhang 1997; Xue et al. 1998). For example, Figure 3.15 shows such an example with a set of images (Xue et al. 1998), Figure (a) is an original image to be segmented, and Figure (b) shows the result of segmentation using the threshold value selected according to the best uniformity in the region, The best uniformity in the visible region does not represent a good segmentation result. Figure (c) shows the result of segmentation using a threshold value selected according to the optimal shape measure. Similarly, the segmentation effect is not ideal. It can be seen that the value of the shape measure does not accurately reflect the actual segmentation quality.

(a)　　　　　　　　　　(b)　　　　　　　　　　(c)

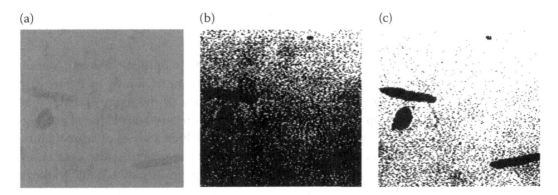

FIGURE 3.15　Examples of the evaluation ability of intra-region uniformity and shape measure.

Finally, to summarize, from the above experimental results and discussions, the discrepancy-based criteria are better than the goodness-based criteria in terms of accuracy and dynamic range. Among them, the ultimate measurement accuracy criterion can provide the largest dynamic range and describe the performance of the segmentation algorithm when it is close to the optimal segmentation in most accuracy.

3.6 ALGORITHM OPTIMAL SELECTION SYSTEM BASED ON EVALUATION

The purpose of segmentation evaluation is to guide the design and selection of segmentation algorithms, and improve the performance of segmentation algorithms. One way to connect evaluation and segmentation application is to establish a **segmentation expert system** combined with artificial intelligence technology to effectively use the evaluation results for inductive reasoning, so as to raise the image segmentation work from the current blind experimental improvement level to the systematic selection and implementation level.

3.6.1 Algorithm Optimal Selection Ideas and Strategies

At the beginning of this chapter, it was pointed out that although there are thousands of image segmentation algorithms proposed, there is no universal segmentation algorithm suitable for all images. The discussion on the evaluation of image segmentation in the previous sections further shows that even if the images belong to or conform to the same model, when the size and shape of the object change and various interference factors change, different requirements will be put on the segmentation algorithm. How can we dynamically adapt to these changes and systematically choose the appropriate algorithm to segment the underlying images?

The evaluation methods and criteria for judging the performance of the segmentation algorithm based on the accuracy of the object feature measurement in the segmented image have been introduced previously. Through this evaluation, some knowledge about the correlation between the characteristic parameters of the image to be segmented and the performance of the segmentation algorithm used can be obtained. With the further guidance of this kind of knowledge, and based on the analysis and estimation of the characteristics of the image to be segmented, the segmentation effect of different algorithms can be predicted, and the work of selecting the optimal algorithm can be carried out. This is a basic idea of optimizing the selection of algorithms based on segmentation evaluation (Zhang 1998b).

The block diagram of the image segmentation algorithm optimal selection system designed to achieve the above algorithm optimization scheme is shown in Figure 3.16 (Zhang 1998b). The input of the system (in the dashed box in the figure) includes the image to be segmented (from the image database) and various knowledge about segmentation (from the knowledge database), and can also include a series of segmentation algorithms (from the algorithm database). The output of the system is the optimal algorithm selected by the system and the resulting output image. The dotted line frame in the figure is basically a segmentation evaluation system. By segmenting the input image and judging the segmentation result, the relationship between the image characteristics

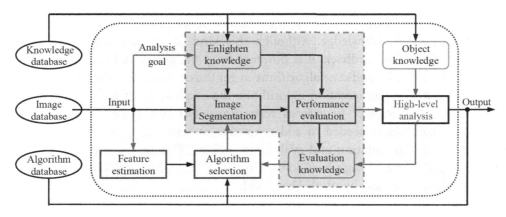

FIGURE 3.16   The block diagram of optimal selection system for image segmentation algorithms.

and the algorithm can be established. In practice, image characteristics are mainly determined by the signal-to-noise ratio and blurriness of images, the contrast between objects and background, the object area, shape and contour roughness, etc. (Zhang and Gerbrands 1992b). Some of these characteristics can be estimated from the original image. For example, the estimation of noise can be found in the literature (Olsen 1993), and the estimation of the edge parameters in the blurred image can be found in the literature (Kayargadde and Martens 1994). It should be noted that each image to be segmented in the same specific application field is inherently related, and the characteristics of many images and objects can often be roughly described with the help of some kind of image model. Accordingly, the image can be segmented along with the model structure to obtain the corresponding *a priori* evaluation knowledge through evaluation.

For a given input image, once sufficient evaluation knowledge has been obtained, algorithm optimization can be performed with the help of the corresponding relationship between image features (through feature estimation) and algorithm performance (Luo and Zhang 1998). This optimization process is a knowledge-driven "hypothesis-testing" feedback process. First, make assumptions that the *a priori* optimal algorithm based on the *a priori* image feature estimation or measurement can be produced; then, with the segmentation results obtained by using the selected algorithm for segmentation, the posterior image feature estimation can be calculated and the corresponding posterior best algorithm estimation can be obtained. If the *a priori* hypothesis is correct, then the posterior estimation should be consistent with the *a priori* hypothesis. Otherwise, the *a priori* estimation can be updated with the posterior estimation to stimulate a new round of "hypothesis-testing" process until the two meet certain consistency conditions. It can be seen that this feedback process is a process of gradual extraction and approximation of information. Algorithm selection is gradually optimized in this process, and finally tends to the best, and the best algorithm is selected. Since this feedback method is mainly driven by data to adjust the segmentation itself, it is a bottom-up processing procedure, so it is relatively quick and convenient.

In this "hypothesis-testing" approach, the choice of segmentation algorithm is mainly guided by evaluation knowledge. Although this kind of guiding ability and function needs to be adjusted in feedback, it is different from the pure "trial-feedback" model, it does not need to try all candidate algorithms to get the optimal solution. Here, due to the complexity of image segmentation algorithms, the acquisition of algorithm evaluation knowledge is often subject to various restrictions. For this reason, certain heuristic knowledge is sometimes needed to add subjective understanding of segmentation performance to the segmentation and evaluation process. Finally, from the perspective of strengthening the role of high-level knowledge in guiding the segmentation, high-level analysis methods can also be used. Here, with the help of the knowledge of the object after segmentation, through the analysis of the characteristics related to the attributes of the object region (see Figure 3.13), the optimization of the algorithm is further ensured from top to bottom.

3.6.2 The Realization and Effect of the Optimal Selection System

The segmentation algorithm optimal selection system is a knowledge-driven system. In order to improve the performance of the system and the efficiency of the system, heuristic knowledge and feedback knowledge based on high-level object analysis are also introduced in the design as a supplement to the evaluation knowledge, so a variety of knowledge sources are included in the system. The above-mentioned preferred system can also be regarded as a control system, which contains multiple control and feedback mechanisms to manage multiple knowledge sources. Based on this consideration, the control system structure based on the public data blackboard is used, and the control knowledge is divided into the form of knowledge sources, and these knowledge sources exchange information and coordinated operations through the public data blackboard. All the knowledge here can be summarized into two categories: (i) Static knowledge: including the algorithm processing method and the combination relationship between the operators, expressed by the "frame" structure; (ii) Dynamic knowledge: refers to the control knowledge related to the dynamic system states in the system, which are represented by using production rules and corresponding additional processes (Luo and Zhang 1999).

In this system, the public data blackboard is divided into four regions (Luo and Zhang 1998): image data region (place the 2-D image data processed by the segmentation algorithm), image feature region (place the parameters obtained from the estimation of the characteristics), control data region (place the historical data of the optimized operation of the recording system), and segmentation object region (record the characteristics of the segmentation region specified by the user).

There are two basic edge detection-based segmentation algorithms (they can be used to segment images with large gray gradients) and six typical thresholding algorithms in the algorithm database of the system. These six algorithms are: (i) improved histogram method, (ii) two-dimensional maximum entropy method, (iii) histogram analysis method, (iv) minimum error method, (v) moment preserving method, and (vi) simple statistical method (see the literature (Luo and Zhang 1997) for details).

With the help of the evaluation framework in Figure 3.2, the above algorithms can be tested and evaluated, and then the obtained evaluation knowledge can be incorporated into the algorithm optimal selection system (Zhang 2000).

Using this system, algorithm optimal selection experiments have been carried out on dozens of different types of images. In the experiment, for the convenience of comparison, each algorithm did not use pre-processing methods before the thresholding, and the post-processing method after segmentation (using morphological opening and closing) was the same for all algorithms. One of the typical experiments (Luo and Zhang 1999) used a slice of cancer cells within the image of a size of 256 × 256 and a grayscale of 256 (see Figure 3.17(a), Figure 3.17(b) is the grayscale histogram of Figure 3.17(a)).

Figure 3.18(a)–Figure 3.18(f) are the results obtained by segmenting Figure 3.17(a) with the above six thresholding algorithms (in the sequence described above) in order to verify the optimal effect of the system. Comparing the images in Figure 3.18, we can see that the histogram analysis method corresponding to Figure 3.18(c) gives the best segmentation results, followed by the segmentation results of the moment preservation method corresponding to Figure 3.18(e). In the experiment, the system selected histogram analysis method as the output algorithm after two attempts. That, the system correctly selected the best algorithm is this case, and only used two rounds (in contrast to six experiments for exhaustive search).

Finally, it is pointed out that in experiments with other images, the system can automatically select the optimal segmentation algorithm suitable for a given image or the sub-optimal algorithm with the closest effect to the optimal algorithm after two to three attempts. This shows that the system can achieve a relatively satisfactory optimization effect within the scope of the design expectations, the efficiency is greatly improved compared with the exhaustive method, and it can be completed automatically. In addition, the test results show that all six algorithms have been selected as the optimal algorithm, which also verifies the necessity of the optimal selection. Other types of algorithms can also be integrated into the system.

(a)   (b)

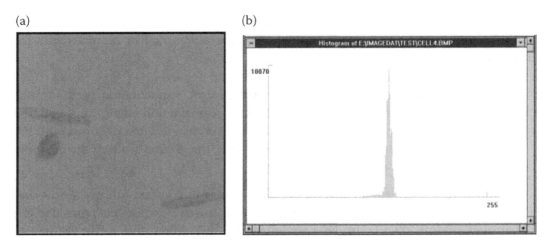

FIGURE 3.17   Cancer cell slice test image and its histogram.

(a)　　　　　　　　　　　(b)　　　　　　　　　　　(c)

(d)　　　　　　　　　　　(e)　　　　　　　　　　　(f)

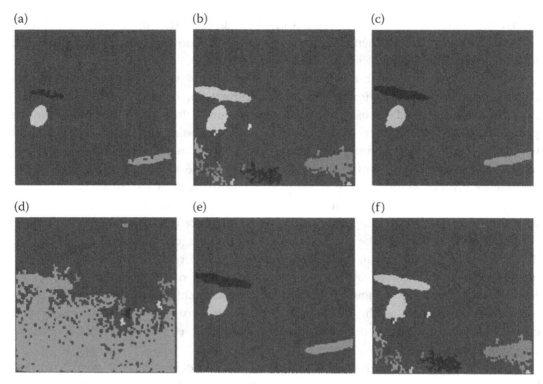

FIGURE 3.18   Results of using six thresholding algorithms to segment the image of Figure 3.17(a).

3.7 SOME RECENT DEVELOPMENTS AND FURTHER RESEARCH

In the following sections, some technical developments and promising research directions in the last few years are briefly overviewed.

3.7.1 Segmentation Evaluation Procedure

An evaluation of six semi-automatic (cranio-maxillofacial surgery) image segmentation algorithms (with open-source codes) on three platforms has been reported (Wallner et al. 2019). The study and procedure have or share some representative characteristics for current image segmentation evaluation:

1. *Supervised evaluation*: The quality and accuracy of segmentation methods was assessed by comparisons made between the segmentation algorithms and the ground truth segmentations. The ground truth results are often obtained with the help of human experts. For example, in this task, the ground truth of the anatomy structure is performed by clinical experts.

2. Limited to a specified application domain: This is in contrast to early works that only consider the segmentation algorithms themselves while not consider the images and/or objects to be segmented. In this work, the medical (cranio-maxillofacial surgery) images are considered and the lower jaw (mandible) is chosen

as the object (anatomical structure). More example can be found, for instance, specified to blood vessel (Moccia et al. 2018), high spatial resolution remote sensing image (Chen et al. 2018), or the histologic structures in the kidney cortex images (Jayapandian et al. 2021).

The reasons for this restriction could be multiple:

1. As no general segmentation theory exist, the evaluation of segmentation methods/ algorithms should consider many factors, including the application domain.

2. It seems that so many segmentation methods/algorithms with various principles have been proposed, any evaluation study could not cover all aspects of these methods/algorithms.

3. It is frequently that the segmentation methods/algorithms often take certain advantage of some *a priori* knowledge in the application domain to improve the performance of segmentation, so limiting to the specified application domain will make the evaluated methods/algorithms more comparable.

3.7.1.1 Segmentation Procedure Overview

In this study, a CT-based 3-D model of the skull is used and a schematic complete mandibular bone without teeth are taken, due to their clinical relevance in trauma and reconstructive surgery the mandible (lower jaw), as the anatomical structure.

In this study, some open-source segmentation algorithms are selected in considering the easy availability, license-free, and reproducibility of the experiments for users. More considerations are that they functionally stable and compatible with many software platforms.

In this study, some platforms are selected in considering that are easy to download, install, and use for everybody. More considerations are that they are widely used in medical imaging as well as they are very extensive and offer good documentation and user support.

Based on the above considerations, three platforms and six segmentation algorithms are selected, as shown in Table 3.4.

3.7.1.2 Evaluation Criteria and Process

The evaluation criteria used are the ***dice score coefficient (DSC)*** and the ***Hausdorff distance (HD)***.

TABLE 3.4   Multi-platforms and multi-segmentation methods

Platform	Segmentation Method
3D Slicer	GrowCut, Robust Statistics Segmenter (RSS)
MITK	3D Region Growing, Otsu & Picking
MeVisLab	Canny Segmentation, Geodesic Segmenter

The DSC is the agreement between two segmented (volumetric) objects, O_1 and O_2 (Sampat et al. 2006). It measures the relative volume overlap between O_1 and O_2. Defining $V(\cdot)$ as the volume of voxels inside an object is obtained by counting the number of voxels, and then multiplying that value by the voxel size. So,

$$\text{DSC} = \frac{2 \cdot V(O_1 \cap O_2)}{V(O_1) + V(O_2)} \tag{3.13}$$

The HD between two segmented (volumetric) objects O_1 and O_2 is defined by the Euclidean distance between the boundary voxels of the objects (Huttenlocher et al. 1993). The directed HD, $h(O_1, O_2)$, is defined as the minimum Euclidean distance from any of the points in the first set O_1 to the second set O_2, and the HD between the two sets $H(O_1, O_2)$ is the maximum of these distances:

$$h(O_1, O_2) = \max_{o_1 \in O_1}[d(o_1, O_2)] = \max_{o_1 \in O_1}\left[\min_{o_2 \in O_2} \|o_1 - o_2\|\right] \tag{3.14}$$

$$H(O_1, O_2) = \max\left[h(O_1, O_2), h(O_2, O_1)\right] \tag{3.15}$$

A schematic diagram for the geometric meaning of HD can be found in Zhang (2021).

In the evaluation process, ten ground truth segmentation sets are obtained from expert A, ten ground truth segmentation sets are obtained from expert B, and ten algorithmic segmentation sets are obtained from each of the six algorithms. The 80 segmentation sets are compared in three evaluations:

1. Algorithmic segmentation vs. Ground truth segmentation A.

2. Algorithmic segmentation vs. Ground truth segmentation B.

3. Ground truth segmentation A vs. Ground truth segmentation B (this is used to avoid bias causing variations in the ground truth segmentations).

The agreement between the ground truth segmentation A and ground truth segmentation B is, in addition to DSC and HD, also determined by volume and voxel values. Descriptive statistical calculations are performed for all above three evaluation cases to summarize the measurements and assessment parameters including minimum, maximum, and mean values and standard deviations.

Additionally, analytical statistical methods were calculated to compare the ground truth segmentations (A, B) amongst each other. These analytical statistical methods consisted of calculated paired t-tests (p) and Pearson's product-moment correlation coefficients (r) (Rodgers and Nicewander 1988). Probability values were calculated between the ground truth segmentations (A, B). p-values under 0.05 ($p < 0.05$) were assumed to be significant. In this study, the experiment shows that the Pearson's product-moment correlation coefficients (r) of volume and voxel values was close to the value one ($r > 0.99$) when comparing the ground truth segmentations.

3.7.2 Evaluation Criteria for Pixel Classification

Take into account the problem of blood vessel segmentation evaluation, a survey on the methods, datasets and evaluation metrics has been made (Moccia et al. 2018), in which a number of criteria for image segmentation evaluation are discussed. Many ideas and methods can be extended to more generalized image segmentation problems. The following is focused on the part of evaluation criteria.

Image segmentation is frequently considered as a pixel classification task. In many medical image applications, the segmentation performance is commonly evaluated with respect to golden standard (GS) or ground truth (GT) that is usually based on manual segmentation performed by one domain expert or several domain experts. In the latter case, different strategies have been proposed to combine the multiple segmentations. One approach allowing for incorporating a priori information of the structure being segmented or estimating the presence of an imperfect or limited reference standard is called STAPLE, simultaneous truth and performance level estimation (Warfield et al. 2004).

From the pixel classification point of view, four segmentation results can be counted (where positive and negative refer to pixels belonging to objects and background as in accord with the GT segmentation, respectively):

1. True positive (TP): The segmented object pixel (s_o) is classified as in the GT object pixel (g_o) class.

2. True negative (NP): The segmented background pixel (s_b) is classified as in the GT background pixel (g_b) class.

3. False negative (FN): The segmented background pixel (s_b) is classified as in the GT object pixel (g_o) class.

4. False positive (FP): The segmented object pixel (s_o) is classified as in the GT background pixel (g_b) class.

Their relation can be illustrated with the help of Figure 3.19.

3.7.2.1 Basic Evaluation Criteria

Basic evaluation criteria are simply combinations of derivations of the above four metrics. The most frequently adopted evaluation criteria are accuracy (Acc), sensitivity (Se, also named recall), and specificity (Sp). In general, the higher the Se, the lower the Sp, and the higher the FP, are the better for segmentation results (Powers 2011). In addition, other evaluation criteria are also often employed. Examples include FP rate, which is equal to

	g_o	g_b
s_o	TP	FP
s_b	FN	TN

FIGURE 3.19   The relation among TP, FP, FN, TN.

TABLE 3.5 Basic evaluation criteria

Criterion	Formula	Description
Acc	(TP+TN)/n	The proportion of true results (TP and TN) among the total number of examined cases (n).
Se	TP/(TP+FN)	The proportion of positives (TP and FN) that are correctly identified.
Sp	TN/(TN+FP)	The proportion of negatives (TN and FP) that are correctly identified.
FP rate	FP/(TN+FP)	The proportion of negatives (TN and FP) that are incorrectly identified.
PPV	TP/(TP+FP)	PPV gives an estimation of how likely it is that a pixel belongs to a vessel given that the algorithm classifies it as positive.
NPV	TN/(TN+FN)	NPV corresponds to the likelihood that a pixel does not belong to a vessel, given that the algorithm classifies it as negative.

1 − Sp, positive predictive value (PPV), also named precision, which is the proportion of TP among TP + FP, and negative predictive value (NPV), which is the ratio between TN and TN + FN. These basic evaluation criteria are listed in Table 3.5.

3.7.2.2 Extended Evaluation Criteria
Extended evaluation criteria are variant combinations of derivations of the above four metrics. The most frequently adopted evaluation criteria are the area under receiver operating characteristic (ROC) curve (precision-recall curve, or PPV-Se curve), and is denoted as AUROC, Matthews' correlation coefficient (MCC), Cohen's κ coefficient (κ), dice similarity coefficient (DSC), also called F_1 score, and Hausdorff distance (HD). These extended evaluation criteria are listed in Table 3.6.

TABLE 3.6 Extension evaluation criteria

Criterion	Formula	Description
AUROC	$AUROC = \sum_{p \in [0,1]} r(p)$	Indicating the probability that a classifier will rank a randomly chosen positive instance higher than a randomly chosen negative one.
MCC	$MCC = \dfrac{(TP \cdot TN) - (FP \cdot TN)}{\sqrt{(TP+FP)(TP+FN)(TN+FP)(TN+FN)}}$	A variation of correlation coefficient.
κ	$\kappa = \dfrac{Acc - p_e}{1 - p_e}$	In which p_e is the hypothetical probability of chance agreement, equal to the probability of GS to generate positives times the probability of the segmentation algorithm to generate positives.
DSC	$DSC = \dfrac{2 card(O \cap G)}{card(O) + card(G)} = \dfrac{2TP}{FP + FN + 2TP}$	The ratio of the number of elements (card) in the intersection of two clusters O and G by the mean label image, where O is the segmented object and G is corresponding GS object, respectively.
HD	$HD = \max[\sup_{o \in O} \inf_{g \in G} d(o, g), \ \sup_{g \in G} \inf_{o \in O} d(o, g)]$	sup represents the supremum, inf the infimum, and d can be any distance metric.

The geometric mean of the two measures is a dichotomous form of the Pearson correlation coefficient (Rodgers and Nicewander 1988), the Matthews' correlation coefficient, which is appropriate unless a continuous scale is being measured dichotomously in which case a tetrachoric correlation estimate would be appropriate. The Cohen's κ coefficient is a measure of inter-rater agreement.

3.7.2.3 More Evaluation Criteria

All above criteria are based on the pixel-to-pixel comparison between the objects of segmented image (S) and the GS (G). As stated in the beginning of Chapter 2, the image segmentation is not only for the partition of image but also the extraction of the interesting connected components (objects).

On the one hand, the point-to-point correspondence between the GS object and segmented object should be counted. In the particular case of vessel segmentation, for example, the points on the centerline of vessel can be used. Three different centerline overlap measures are thus derived as the evaluation criteria. The overlap (OV) measures the ability to track the overall vessel annotated by the observers. The overlap until first error (OF) measures the minimum radius from the first point of the GS centerline to the correspondent point of segmented centerline. More specifically, the overlap with the clinically relevant part of the vessel (OT) only measures the ability to segment vessel having a diameter equal or larger than 1.5 mm. That is, the point (p_{end}) closest to the end of the reference GS with a radius larger than or equal to 0.75 mm is determined to limit the relevant part.

On the other hand, various properties of object can also be exploited (Zhang 1996), such as connectivity (C), area (A), and perimeter (P). The factor C penalizes fragmented segmentation by comparing the number of connected components in and with regard to the total number of object pixels in G (Gegúndez-Arias et al. 2012). The factor A measures the degree of overlapping between the segmented object (O) and the object in GS (G). In the calculation of A, some morphological dilation operations are performed, which makes A, compared to the DSC, less sensitive to slight differences between the segmentation and the GS. The factor P can measure the consistency between the segmented vessel length and the GS vessel length.

The above two groups of evaluation criteria are listed in Table 3.7.

3.7.3 An Evaluation Criterion for Panoptic Segmentation

As discussed in Sub-section 2.5.4, the newly proposed ***panoptic segmentation (PS)*** considers separately the segmentation for stuff and things (Kirillov et al. 2019), so a unified metric for stuff and things will encourage the study of the unified task, or in other words, evaluating the joint task involving both stuff and thing classes.

3.7.3.1 Panoptic Quality

A suitable metric (an evaluation criterion) for PS is proposed, and is called panoptic quality (PQ). Three considerations are taken into account (Kirillov et al. 2019):

TABLE 3.7   Evaluation criteria based on pixel-to-pixel comparison or point-to-point correspondence

Criterion	Formula	Description
OV	$OV = \dfrac{TPR_{ov} + TPM_{ov}}{TPR_{ov} + FN_{ov} + TPM_{ov} + FP_{ov}}$	TPR_{ov} refers to points of the GS centerline whose distance to the correspondent points on the segmented centerline is less than the local vessel radius. Points for which this distance is higher than the radius are marked as FN_{ov}. Points on the segmented centerline are marked as TPM_{ov} if there is at least one point on the GS at a distance less than the radius, otherwise they are marked as FP_{ov}.
OF	$OF = \dfrac{TPR_{of}}{NR}$	It is the ratio of the number of TPR_{ov} before the first error (TPR_{of}) and the overall number of reference points (NR).
OT	$OT = \dfrac{TPM_{ot} + TPR_{ot}}{TPM_{ot} + TPR_{ot} + FN_{ot} + FP_{ot}}$	TPM_{ot}, TPR_{ot}, FN_{ot}, FP_{ot} are computed as TPM_{ov}, TPR_{ov}, FN_{ov}, FP_{ov} but considering only points between p_{end} and the beginning of the GS centerline.
C	$C = 1 - \min\left[1, \dfrac{\lvert card\,(G) - card\,(O)\rvert}{card\,(G)}\right]$	It assesses the fragmentation degree between G and O. In case of vessel segmentation, it is expected to have only a few connected components (ideally one).
A	$A = \dfrac{card\,\{[d_A\,(O) \cap G] \cup [d_A\,(G) \cap O]\}}{card\,(O \cup G)}$	d_A is the radius of mask used for morphological dilatations in computing A.
P	$P = \dfrac{card\,\{[d_A\,(O) \cap G] \cup [d_A\,(G) \cap O]\}}{card\,(O \cup G)}$	d_P is the radius of mask used for morphological dilatations in computing P, S represents a homotopic skeletonization.

1. Completeness: It should treat stuff and thing classes in a uniform way, capturing all aspects of the joint segmentation task.

2. Interpretability: It should have identifiable meaning that facilitates communication and understanding.

3. Simplicity: It should be simple to define and implement, so can be computed fast and efficiently.

PQ is used to measure the quality of the result of panoptic segmentation relative to the ground truth. It involves two steps:

1. Matching of corresponding patches in segmented result and ground truth, where a patch is a group of pixels (in the extreme case, one pixel) of object.

2. Computation of PQ value (after the matches between patches in segmented result and ground truth are determined).

3.7.3.2 Matching

When two matching patches have intersection, they may have the possibility to be matched. In define PQ, it is required that their ***intersection over union (IoU)*** should be strictly greater than 0.5. It has been proved (Kirillov et al. 2019) that this requirement, together with the non-overlapping property of a panoptic segmentation, can guaranty the uniqueness of matching. In other words, there can be at most one segmented patch matched with each ground truth patch.

The requirement that matches must have IoU greater than 0.5 is also agree with two of above considerations. First, it is simple and efficient as the correspondences between two patches are unique and easy to obtain. Second, it is clear and interpretable. Note that due to the uniqueness property, for IoU > 0.5, any reasonable matching strategy (including greedy and optimal) will yield an identical matching. Experiments have shown that matches with IoU ≤ 0.5 are rare in practice.

3.7.3.3 Computation

Panoptic segmentation consists of the segmentation for both stuff class and things class. The metric for the evaluation of panoptic segmentation should also consider these two classes. The proposed PQ computation treat each class independently and the final result is the average over classes.

For each class, according to the above discussions on unique matching, the segmented patches and the ground truth patches will fall into three sets:

1. TP (true positive): matched pairs (segmented, ground truth) of patches.

2. FP (false positive): unmatched segmented patches.

3. FN (false negative): unmatched ground truth patches.

According to these three sets, PQ can be defined as (g is a ground truth patch, s is a segmented patch):

$$PQ = \frac{\sum_{(s,g)\in TP} IoU(s, g)}{|TP| + |FP|/2 + |FN|/2} \tag{3.16}$$

The right side can be decomposed into two factors, that is:

$$PQ = \frac{\sum_{(s,g)\in TP} IoU(s, g)}{|TP|} \times \frac{|TP|}{|TP| + |FP|/2 + |FN|/2} \tag{3.17}$$

The first term can be called the segmentation quality (SQ), while the second term can be called the **recognition quality (RQ)**. The first term is simply the average IoU of matched patches. The second term is an estimation of detection quality, that is, F_1 score.

It is noted that the decomposition of PQ = SQ × RQ provides some perception for analysis, but the two values are not independent since SQ is measured only over matched patches.

It is also noted that all patches receive equal weight regardless of their size. It seems such a criterion may be more suitable for the evaluation of segmentation of instances of similar size.

REFERENCES

Brink, A.D. 1989. Gray-level thresholding of images using a correlation criterion. *Pattern Recognition Letters*, 9: 335–341.

Cárdenes, R., R. Luis-García, and M. Bach-Cuadra. 2009. A multidimensional segmentation evaluation for medical image data. *Computer Methods and Programs in Biomedicine*, 96(2): 108–124.

Cardoso, J.S., and L. Corte-Real. 2005. Toward a generic evaluation of image segmentation. *IEEE Transactions on Image Processing*, 14(11): 1773–1782.

Carleer, A.P., O. Debeir, and E. Wolff. 2004. Comparison of very high spatial resolution satellite image segmentations. *SPIE*, 5238: 532–542.

Casciaro, S., R. Franchini, and L. Massoptier. 2012. Fully automatic segmentations of liver and hepatic tumors from 3-D computed tomography abdominal images: Comparative evaluation of two automatic methods. *IEEE Sensors Journal*, 12(3): 464–473.

Cavallaro, A., E.D. Gelasca, and T. Ebrahimi. 2002. Objective evaluation of segmentation quality using spatio-temporal context. *Proceedings of the ICIP*, 3: 301–304.

Chabrier, S., B. Emile, and C. Rosenberger, et al. 2006. Unsupervised performance evaluation of image segmentation. *EURASIP Journal on Applied Signal Processing*, 2006(1): 1–12.

Chen, Y.Y., D.P. Ming, L. Zhao, et al. 2018. Review on high spatial resolution remote sensing image segmentation evaluation. *Photogrammetric Engineering & Remote Sensing*, 84(10): 629–646.

Erdem, C.E., B. Sankur, and A.M. Tekalp. 2004. Performance measures for video object segmentation and tracking. *IEEE Transactions on Image Processing*, 13(7): 937–951.

Ge, Y., S. Wang, and T.C. Liu. 2007. New benchmark for image segmentation evaluation. *Journal of Electronic Imaging*, 16(3): #033011.

Gegúndez-Arias, M.E., A. Aquino, J.M. Bravo, et al. 2012. A function for quality evaluation of retinal vessel segmentations. *IEEE Transactions on Medical Imaging*, 31(2): 231–239.

Hao, J., Y. Shen, and H. Xu. 2009. A region entropy based objective evaluation method for image segmentation. *Proceedings of the Instrumentation and Measurement Technology*, 373–377.

Huttenlocher, D.P., G.A. Klanderman, and W.J. Rucklidge. 1993. Comparing images using the Hausdorff distance. *IEEE Transactions on Pattern Analysis and Machine Intelligence*, 15(9): 850–863.

Jayapandian, C.P., Y.J. Chen, A.R. Janowczyk, et al. 2021. Development and evaluation of deep learning–based segmentation of histologic structures in the kidney cortex with multiple histologic stains. *Kidney International*, 99: 86–101.

Jiang, X.Y., C. Marti, and C. Irniger, et al. 2006. Distance measures for image segmentation evaluation. *EURASIP Journal on Applied Signal Processing*, 2006(10): 1–10.

Kayargadde, V., and J.B. Martens. 1994. Estimation of edge parameters and image blur using polynomial transforms. *CVGIP-GMIP*, 56(6): 442–461.

Khan, J., and S.M. Bhuiyan. 2013. Weighted entropy for segmentation evaluation. *Optics & Laser Technology*, 57: 236–242.

Kim, K., T.H. Chalidabhongse, and D. Harwood, et al. 2004. Background modeling and subtraction by codebook construction. *Proceedings of the ICIP*, 5: 3061–3064.

Kirillov, A., K.M. He, R. Girshick, C. Rother, and P. Dollar. (2019). Panoptic segmentation. *Proceedings of the 2019 CVPR*: 9396–9405.

Ladak, H.M., M. Ding, and Y. Wang, et al. 2004. Evaluation of algorithms for segmentation of the prostate boundary from 3D ultrasound images. *SPIE*, 5370: 1403–1410.

Levine, M.D., and A.M. Nazif. 1985. Dynamic measurement of computer generated image segmentations. *IEEE Transactions on Pattern Analysis and Machine Intelligence*, 7: 155–164.

Li, N., S. Li, and C. Chen. 2003. Multimetric evaluation protocol for user-assisted video object extraction systems. *SPIE*, 5150: 20–28.

Lievers, W.B., and A.K. Pilkey. 2004. An evaluation of global thresholding techniques for the automatic image segmentation of automotive aluminum sheet alloys. *Materials Science and Engineering: A*. 381(1–2), 134–142.

Lim, Y.W., and S.U. Lee. 1990. On the color image segmentation algorithms based on the thresholding and fuzzy C-means techniques. *Pattern Recognition*, 23: 935–952.

Luo, H.T., and Y.-J. Zhang. 1997. An example of image segmentation evaluation and related discussion. *Journal of Data Acquisition and Processing*, 12(1): 18–22.

Luo, H.T., and Y.-J. Zhang. 1998. Evaluation-based optimization and its system realization for segmentation algorithms. *Journal of Electronic Science*, 20(5): 577–583.

Luo, H.T., and Y.-J. Zhang. 1999. Evaluation based segmentation algorithm optimization: Idea and system. *Journal of Electronics*, 16(2): 109–116.

Marçal, A.R.S., and A.S. Rodrigues. 2009. A method for multispectral image segmentation evaluation based on synthetic images. *Computers & Geosciences*, 35(8): 1574–1581.

Moccia, S., E. De Momi, S. Hadji, et al. 2018. Blood vessel segmentation algorithms—Review of methods, datasets and evaluation metrics. *Computer Methods and Programs in Biomedicine* 158: 71–91.

Niemeijer, M., J. Staal, and B. Ginneken, et al. 2004. Comparative study of retinal vessel segmentation methods on a new publicly available database. *SPIE*, 5370: 648–656.

Oberti, F., E. Stringa, and G. Vernazza. 2001. Performance evaluation criterion for characterizing video-surveillance systems. *Real-Time Imaging*, 7(5), 457–471.

Olsen, S.I. 1993. Estimation of noise in images: an evaluation. *CVGIP-GMIP*, 55(4): 319–323.

Ortiz, A., and G. Oliver. 2006. On the use of the overlapping area matrix for image segmentation evaluation: A survey and new performance measures. *Pattern Recognition Letters*, 27(16): 1916–1926.

Otsu, N. 1979. A threshold selection method from gray-level histogram. *IEEE Transactions on Systems, Man, and Cybernetics*, 9: 62–66.

Pal, N.R., and D. Bhandari. 1993. Image thresholding: Some new techniques. *Signal Processing*, 33: 139–158.

Peng, B., and T.R. Li. 2013. A probabilistic measure for quantitative evaluation of image segmentation. *IEEE Signal Processing Letters*, 20(7): 689–692.

Philipp-Foliguet, S., and L. Guigues. 2008. Multiscale criteria for the evaluation of image segmentation algorithms. *Journal of Multimedia*, 3(5): 42–56.

Polak, M., H. Zhang, and M.H. Pi. 2009. An evaluation metric for image segmentation of multiple objects. *Image and Vision Computing*, 27(8): 1223–1227.

Pont-Tuset, J., and F. Marques. 2013. Measures and meta-measures for the supervised evaluation of image segmentation. *Proceedings of the CVPR*, 2131–2138.

Powers, D.M.W. 2011. Evaluation: From precision, recall and F-measure to ROC, informedness, markedness, and correlation. *Journal of Machine Learning Technologies*, 2(1): 37–63.

Prati, A., I. Mikic, and M.M. Trivedi, et al. 2003. Detecting moving shadows: Algorithms and evaluation. *IEEE Transactions on Pattern Analysis and Machine Intelligence*, 25(7): 918–923.

Qu, Z., and Q.W. Ma. 2010. Research on evaluation of image segmentation based on measurement method of particle's parameters. *Proceedings of the IHMSC*, 2: 232–235.

Renno, J.R., J. Orwell, and G.A. Jones. 2004. Evaluation of shadow classification techniques for object detection and tracking. *Proceedings of the ICIP*, 143–146.

Rodgers, J., and W. Nicewander. 1988. Thirteen ways to look at the correlation coefficient, *American Statistician*, 42(1): 59–66.

Rosin, P.L., and E. Ioannidis. 2003. Evaluation of global image thresholding for change detection. *Pattern Recognition Letters*, 24(14): 2345–2356.

Sahoo, P.K., et al. 1988. A survey of thresholding techniques. *Computer Vision, Graphics and Image Processing*, 41: 233–260.

Sampat, M.P., Z. Wang, M.K. Markey, et al. 2006. Measuring intra- and inter-observer agreement in identifying and localizing structures in medical images. *Proceeding of the ICIP*, 1–4.

Udupa, J.K., and Y. Zhuge. 2004. Delineation operating characteristic (DOC) curve for assessing the accuracy behavior of image segmentation algorithms. *SPIE*, 5370, 640–647.

Udupa, J.K., V.R. LeBlanc, and H. Schmidt, et al. 2002. A methodology for evaluating image segmentation algorithms. *SPIE*, 4684: 266–277.

Udupa, J.K., V.R. LeBlanc, and Y. Zhuge, et al. 2006. A framework for evaluating image segmentation algorithms. *Computerized Medical Imaging and Graphics*, 30(2): 75–87.

Unnikrishnan, R., C. Pantofaru, and M. Hebert. 2007. Toward objective evaluation of image segmentation algorithms. *IEEE Transactions on Pattern Analysis and Machine Intelligence*, 29(6): 929–944.

Wallner, J., M. Schwaiger, K. Hochegger et al. 2019. A review on multiplatform evaluations of semi-automatic open-source based image segmentation for cranio-maxillofacial surgery. *Computer Methods and Programs in Biomedicine*, 182: 105102.

Warfield, S.K., K.H. Zou, and W.M. Wells. 2004. Simultaneous truth and performance level estimation (STAPLE): An algorithm for the validation of image segmentation. *IEEE Transactions on Medical Imaging*, 23(7): 903–921.

Weszka, J.S., and A. Rosenfeld. 1978. Threshold evaluation technique. *IEEE Transactions on Systems, Man, and Cybernetics*, 8: 622–629.

Xu, T., and I. Gondra. 2008. An objective evaluation of the mean shift-based image segmentation algorithm. *Proceedings of the IPCV*, 205–211.

Xue, J.H., Y.-J. Zhang, and X.G. Lin. 1998. Feature divergence based FCM clustering for image segmentation. *Pattern Recognition and Artificial Intelligence*, 11(4): 462–467.

Young, I.T. 1993. Three-dimensional image analysis. *Proceedings of the VIP'93*, 35–38.

Zhang, H., J.E. Fritts, and S.A. Goldman. 2008. Image segmentation evaluation: A survey of unsupervised methods. *Computer Vision and Image Understanding*, 110(2): 260–280.

Zhang, Y.-J. 1993a. Comparison of segmentation evaluation criteria. *Proceedings of the 2ICSP*, 870–873.

Zhang, Y.-J. 1993b. Segmentation evaluation and comparison: A study of several algorithms. *SPIE*, 2094: 801–812.

Zhang, Y.-J. 1995. Influence of segmentation over feature measurement. *Pattern Recognition Letters*, 16(2): 201–206, 1995.

Zhang, Y.-J. 1996. A survey on evaluation methods for image segmentation. *Pattern Recognition*, 29(8): 1335–1346.

Zhang, Y.-J. 1997a. Objective image quality measures and their applications in segmentation evaluation. *Journal of Electronics*, 19(1): 1–5.

Zhang, Y.-J. 1997b. Evaluation and comparison of different segmentation algorithms. *Pattern Recognition Letters*, 18(10): 963–974.

Zhang, Y.-J. 1998a. Framework and experiments for image segmentation characterization. *Chinese Journal of Electronics*, 7(4): 387–391.

Zhang, Y.-J. 1998b. Evaluation knowledge based optimal selection system for image segmentation algorithms. *High Technology Letters*, 8(4): 21–24.

Zhang, Y.-J. 2000. Optimal selection of segmentation algorithms based on performance evaluation. *Optical Engineering*, 39(6): 1450–1456.

Zhang, Y.-J. 2001. A review of recent evaluation methods for image segmentation. *Proceedings of the 6th International Symposium on Signal Processing and Its Applications*, 148–151.

Zhang, Y.-J. 2006. A summary of recent progresses for segmentation evaluation. In Zhang, Y.-J. (ed.), *Advances in Image and Video Segmentation*. Hershey PA, USA: IRM Press, Chapter 20 (423–440).

Zhang, Y.-J. 2009. Image segmentation evaluation in this century. In Khosrow-Pour, M. (ed.), *Encyclopedia of Information Science and Technology*, 2nd Ed., Hershey PA, USA, Chapter 285 (1812–1817).

Zhang, Y.-J. 2014. A 50 years' review for image segmentation. *Machine Vision*, (6): 12–20.

Zhang, Y.-J. 2015. A review of image segmentation evaluation in the 21st century. In Khosrow-Pour, M. (ed.), *Encyclopedia of Information Science and Technology*, 3rd Ed., Hershey PA, USA: Information Science Reference (an imprint of IGI Global), Chapter 579 (5857–5867).

Zhang, Y.-J. 2017. *Image Engineering, Vol. 2: Image Analysis.* Germany: De Gruyter.

Zhang, Y.-J. 2021. *Handbook of Image Engineering.* Singapore: Springer Nature.

Zhang, Y.-J., and J.J. Gerbrands. 1991. Transition region determination based thresholding. *Pattern Recognition Letters*, 12: 13–23.

Zhang, Y.-J., and J.J. Gerbrands. 1992a. Segmentation evaluation using ultimate measurement accuracy, *SPIE*, 1657: 449–460.

Zhang, Y.-J., and J.J. Gerbrands. 1992b. On the design of test images for segmentation evaluation. Signal Processing VI, *Theories and Applications*, 1: 551–554.

Zhang, Y.-J., and J.J. Gerbrands. 1994. Objective and quantitative segmentation evaluation and comparison. *Signal Processing*, 39: 43–54.

CHAPTER 4

Saliency Object Detection

*S**aliency*** is a subjective concept associated with subjective perception. There are different perceptual saliences for different human senses. The focus here is on visual saliency associated with visual organs. Visual saliency is often attributed to the comprehensive results caused by changes or contrasts in the underlying characteristics of the surface region of the scene object, such as brightness, color, and gradient.

Saliency is a concept related to a connected component that is composed of multiple pixels, which expresses the characteristics of the image at the intermediate semantic level. Reliable estimation of saliency often does not require a high-level understanding of any actual scene content, so it is still in the middle-level semantic analysis. A typical example is when a person observes the surface of an object, the edge on it is first observed, and then the part surrounded by the contour is perceived, and the object attributes such as reflection intensity, texture, or shape are analyzed.

Salient object detection is also often referred to as salient object segmentation. The former emphasizes the direct detection of saliency objects as a whole based on the grasp of their own characteristics, and is generally not limited to a single object; the latter emphasizes classifying and forming (an) object according to the pixel attributes that make up the salient object. However, at present, they are basically not distinguished in the literature, and these two concepts are often used in alternation.

The application of saliency is inspired by the research results of physiology and psychology to a certain extent, and its thinking is closely related to human cognition. The effective extraction of saliency extreme values in the image has important significance and application value for of image analysis and processing (Duncan and Sarkar 2012). In the process of modeling the visual attention mechanism, the extraction of salient extreme values in the image is usually a key step for selective attention. For example, in the process of watershed image segmentation, the construction of labeled images is usually based on the extraction of image saliency extreme values.

The contents of each section of this chapter are arranged as follows.

Section 4.1 introduces first the connotation of saliency and the characteristics of the saliency object region; it also analyzes the evaluation of saliency map quality as well as the

DOI: 10.1201/b23131-4

relationship between visual saliency with attention mechanism and pre-attention mechanism models.

Section 4.2 first looks at the saliency detection problem from different perspectives, and classifies the primitive methods; then the basic detection process is given; after that, the detection process is given by contrast-based detection and subsequent saliency region extraction.

Section 4.3 deeply analyzes some distinctive techniques for extracting saliency regions based on contrast, including specific methods based on contrast magnitude, contrast distribution, and minimum directional contrast. It also discusses the segmentation and evaluation of saliency objects.

Section 4.4 introduces the saliency detection methods based on the background priors. Here, the boundary priors and the connectivity priors are mainly considered. A method to improve efficiency by approximate calculation of the minimum fence distance and a method to obtain the result of distance transformation based on the calculation of the minimum fence distance to detect saliency are respectively introduced.

Section 4.5 presents a technique for extracting saliency objects based on the most stable region, and discusses the overall process, the calculation of the most stable region, and the subsequent saliency calculation issues.

Section 4.6 provides a brief introduction to some technique developments and promising research directions in the last year.

4.1 OVERVIEW OF SALIENCY

As pointed out earlier, because saliency can have different applications, there are sometimes certain differences in definitions, or even ambiguity. The following is a formal definition that is more suitable for a variety of applications. **Saliency** refers to the amount or property that can make a feature, image point, image region, or object more distinctive or more conspicuous with respect to its environment. This definition can cover all domains of saliency use. The key here is that this quantity or property can make something "stand out." Although in the sense of purely based on visual stimuli, any part of the image may "stand out" from its neighborhood under the condition of measuring certain image characteristics. But in a specific task, what "stands out" can only be the object of interest (and the object is a subjective concept).

First, give some discussion and explanation on the concept of saliency and its related notions.

4.1.1 The Connotation of Saliency

Saliency can be regarded as the property of marking or annotating observable objects in an image. Such marking or labeling can be done at a single object level or object category level. As a middle-level semantic clue, saliency can help fill the gap between low-level features and high-level categories. To this end, it is necessary to construct a saliency model, and use the saliency map (a map reflecting the saliency intensity of various places in the image) generated by the saliency model to detect salient objects (regions).

Saliency is related to people's attention to the world. Attention is a psychological concept, a common feature of mental process, and the content of cognitive process. Specifically, attention refers to the process of selectively concentrating visual processing resources to certain parts of the environment and ignoring the rest. People have limited ability to perceive objects in the environment at the same time. Therefore, in order to obtain a clear, profound, and complete knowledge of things, it is necessary to make mental activities selectively point to the relevant objects.

4.1.2 Characteristics of Saliency Object

The isolated brightness extreme points, edge points/corners, etc. in the image can all be regarded as salient points in the image, but here we pay more attention to discuss the salient object in the image, that is, the connected components with saliency. Generally speaking, the salient object region in the image has the following characteristics:

1. **High-level semantic features:** Objects that people often notice during observation (such as human faces, cars, etc.) often correspond to salient regions in the image, and they themselves have certain cognitive semantic meanings.

2. **Cognitive stability:** The saliency region is relatively robust to changes in scene brightness, object position, orientation, scale, and observation conditions, etc., that is, the manifestation of saliency is not only prominent but also relatively constant.

3. **Global scarcity:** From a global perspective, the frequency of saliency regions is relatively low (local, rare), and it is not easy to be composited from other regions in the image.

4. **Local discrepancy:** The saliency region always has obvious characteristics (such as brightness, color, gradient, edge, contour, orientation, texture, shape, movement, etc.) that are different from the surrounding regions.

4.1.3 Evaluation of the Quality of the Saliency Map

In the saliency region detection process, the input is an original image, and the output is a **saliency map** composed of the salient regions of the image (that is, a saliency image whose attribute value is a saliency value, so it can also be called a saliency image). The saliency map reflects the degree to which each part of the image attracts attention, and this degree is reflected in the gray value (corresponding to the salient intensity value) of each pixel in the saliency map. The quality of the saliency map is an important criterion for evaluating the quality of the saliency detection algorithm, and it is also closely related to the characteristics of the saliency region. The quality of the saliency map is generally evaluated from the following aspects:

1. Whether it can highlight the most salient objects: The saliency map should highlight the most salient object region in the field of view, and this region should be highly consistent with human visual choices.

2. Whether it can make each part of the salient object have a relatively consistent degree of prominence: In this way, the salient region can be completely extracted and locally missed detection can be avoided.

3. Whether it can give an accurate and complete boundary of the salient object: In this way, the salient region can be completely separated from the background region, and local misdetection and missed detection can be avoided.

4. Whether it can give a full-resolution detection result: If the saliency map has the same resolution as the original image, it will help to use the detection result of the saliency region in practical applications.

In order to obtain high-quality saliency maps, detection algorithms are often required to have strong anti-noise performance. If the saliency detection algorithm is relatively robust, it will be less affected by the noise, complex texture, and cluttered background in the image.

4.1.4 Visual Attention Mechanism and Model

The concept of saliency is closely related to **visual attention (VA)** in psychology. The theory of human visual attention assumes that the **human visual system (HVS)** only deals with certain parts of the details of the environment and hardly considers the rest. The visual attention mechanism enables people to quickly locate objects of interest in a complex visual environment. The visual attention mechanism has two basic characteristics: directivity and concentration. Directivity is manifested as being selective to multiple stimuli that appear in the same time period; concentration is manifested as the ability to inhibit interfering stimuli, and its range and duration depend on the characteristics of external stimuli and human subjective factors.

Visual attention mechanisms are mainly divided into two categories: bottom-up data-driven pre-attention mechanisms and top-down task-driven post-attention mechanisms. Among them, the saliency detection driven by the underlying data without the guidance of *a priori* knowledge belongs to bottom-up processing. It corresponds to the lower-level cognitive process and does not consider the impact of cognitive tasks on the extraction of saliency, so the processing speed is relatively fast. The task-driven discovery of salient objects is a top-down process. It corresponds to the higher-level cognitive process, which needs to be processed consciously according to the task and the required domain of interest must be extracted, so the processing speed is relatively slow.

The model that uses a computer to simulate the human visual attention mechanism is called a **visual attention model**. Extracting the attention-grabbing focus that the human eye can observe from an image is to determine that the image contains a special visual stimulus distribution pattern and thus has a significant region with a higher perceptual priority, compared to a computer. The bottom-up selective visual attention mechanism that human beings have only driven by external environmental visual stimuli originates from this. In fact, bottom-up image saliency detection is based on this idea.

For example, there is a typical pre-attention mechanism model based on biological models (Itti et al. 1998). The basic idea of the model is to extract color features, brightness features, and directional features (all low-level visual features) in the image through linear filtering, and form 12 color feature maps, 6 brightness feature maps, and 24 directional feature maps, through Gaussian pyramid, ***center-peripheral difference*** operator, and normalization processing. These feature maps are combined to form an attention map of color, brightness, and direction. Then, the attention maps of the three characteristics are linearly fused to generate a saliency map, and finally the saliency region is obtained through a two-layer winner-take-all (WTA) neural network.

Another visual attention model uses a ***visual attention (VA)*** map to represent the salient regions in the image (Stentiford 2003). If the pattern composed of a certain features (such as shape, color, etc.) in an image and its surrounding region appears more frequently in other regions of the same form in the image, the VA value of the pixel will be lower, otherwise the VA value will be higher. The model can distinguish the salient features and non-salient features well, but if the image pattern is not prominent enough, the effect may not be ideal.

4.2 SALIENCY DETECTION

To obtain a saliency region or a saliency map, it is necessary to perform a saliency detection judgment.

4.2.1 Classification of Saliency Detection Methods

Saliency detection can be considered from different aspects. For example, consider the definition of saliency, application field, data set used, representation scale used, descriptive features used, computing technology used, ... Therefore, from different perspectives, the detection methods of saliency can be classified differently. Here are a few typical examples.

1. According to whether the image signal is processed in the spatial domain or in the transform domain, the detection methods can be divided into the methods based on a spatial domain model and the methods based on a transform domain model.

2. From the perspective of the flow or structure of the detection algorithm, detection methods can be divided into bottom-up methods (often based on local characteristics) and top-down methods (often based on global characteristics).

3. Considering the object of calculation, the detection methods can be divided into the calculation methods based on the saliency of the fixation point and the calculation methods based on the saliency region. The former usually obtains a small amount of human eye's attention positions in the image, while the latter can be the salient regions in the highlight image, thereby greatly improving the effectiveness of salient object extraction.

4. From the perspective of the resolution of the detection result, the detection methods can be divided into the pixel-level methods (per pixel) and the region-based method (including superpixels).

5. In practical applications, some auxiliary information (such as the description text of the picture on the Internet) is often accompanied by the input image data. In this

way, the detection methods can be divided into the internal methods that only use the image's own information and the external methods that also use the "peripheral" information of the image.

6. Saliency is related to subjective perception, so the detection methods can not only rely on the calculation model, but also consider the bionics. In addition, there is also a way to combine the two. The calculation and extraction of salient features are realized through mathematical modeling by means of calculation models. The method of considering bionics makes more use of the research results of biology and physiology.

4.2.2 Basic Detection Process

A more general *saliency detection process* is shown in Figure 4.1. There are mainly five modules. Input and output can have different forms. Some commonly used methods and techniques are also listed for the other three modules.

Feature detection can be considered separately at pixel, local, and global levels. For example, brightness can be used at the pixel level, the color histogram of the pixel neighborhood can be determined at the local level, and the global distribution of colors can be determined at the global level. The most commonly used features are color, brightness, and orientation, which mimic the mammalian visual system. Other available features include edges, corners, curvature, texture, motion, compactness, isolation, symmetry, color histograms, orientation histograms, discrete cosine transform coefficients, principal components, etc. These features can be obtained with the help of Gaussian pyramids, Gaber filters, Gaussian mixture models, etc., or can be obtained with the help of feature fusion.

The saliency measurement of an image point or region is very dependent on the previously calculated features. Different features and calculation techniques can be combined here, such as mutual information, self-information, Bayesian networks, entropy, normalized correlation coefficients, neural networks, energy minimization, maximum flow, Kulback-Leebles divergence, conditional random field, etc.

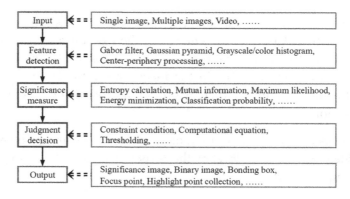

FIGURE 4.1 Saliency detection process.

Based on the data of the significance measurement, the corresponding judgment and decision can be made. The simplest method is to set a threshold to distinguish between significant regions and non-significant regions. Of course, it is also possible to obtain parameters such as the position of the salient region in the image through search and matching based on prior knowledge or limited conditions.

4.2.3 Contrast Detection

Perception research results show that: in the low-level visual saliency, **contrast** is the most important factor. Existing salient region detection algorithms mostly measure the sub-region saliency of an image by calculating the contrast between a sub-region and other surround sub-regions. According to the difference in the spatial range and scale of sub-regions used to calculate the contrast, the existing saliency region detection algorithms can be divided into two categories: algorithms based on local contrast and algorithms based on global contrast.

1. The saliency region detection algorithm based on local contrast measures the saliency of the image sub-region or pixel by calculating the contrast between each image sub-region or pixel and its surrounding sub-region or pixel in a small neighborhood.

2. The saliency region detection algorithm based on global contrast uses the entire image as the contrast region to sequentially calculate the saliency value of each image sub-region or pixel.

Contrast is at the core of many saliency calculation strategies. The current methods of calculating contrast are mainly divided into three categories:

1. Using *a priori* knowledge of local contrast

The basic idea of using local contrast is to compare each pixel or superpixel with only some pixels or superpixels in the part of the image to obtain contrast. There are mainly four common forms: (i) Comparing a pixel or superpixel with only adjacent pixels or superpixels; (ii) using a sliding window method to find the difference between the target pixel and other pixels in the window; (iii) use the multi-scale method to calculate the contrast at multiple resolutions; (iv) use the center-peripheral region relationship to calculate the contrast.

·2. Using *a priori* knowledge of global contrast

The basic idea of using global contrast is to calculate the feature difference between the object pixel or superpixel and the distribution of all other pixels or superpixels in the image, and finally add these differences as the global contrast of the target pixel or superpixel. Compared with the method based on local contrast, the method based on global contrast can produce higher saliency value at the object boundary or neighborhood when extracting large-scale objects from its surrounding environment. In addition, considering the overall situation, similar image regions can be assigned close saliency values more uniformly, so that the entire salient object can be uniformly highlighted.

3. Using various *a priori* knowledge

Some methods define the saliency of a region as the shortest weighted distance from this region to the border (frame) around the image. The **background prior** is actually used here: that is, the surroundings of the image correspond to the background. Corresponding to this, there is a **central prior** (or **foreground prior**), that is, the saliency region is often in the middle of the image and does not touch the image border. Photos taken of man-made objects generally meet this condition, that is, the object is often concentrated in the region inside the image and far away from the image border (at least not in contact with the border). The main idea of the algorithm is to first detect the background region, and then search inward to get the salient region. Or first determine the center of the image, and consider the feature that the region close to/around the center is more salient. However, these prior conditions are often not strictly met in practice.

4.2.4 Saliency Region Extraction

On the basis of calculating the saliency, the saliency region can be further extracted. Different extraction frameworks can be used here.

1. Direct segmentation with threshold

This type of method uses simple thresholding or adaptive thresholding to directly binarize the saliency map to obtain the saliency region.

2. Based on interactive image segmentation

The typical method is often based on the GrabCut algorithm. It is a popularized interactive image segmentation algorithm that can be used for salient object extraction (Rother et al. 2004). First, a fixed threshold is used to binarize the saliency map, the original image and the binarized saliency map are combined to improve the segmentation results through multiple iterations of the GrabCut algorithm, and the image is then dilated and/or eroded in the iterative process, to provides helpful assistance until the final accurate salient region is obtained.

3. Combined with rectangular window positioning

In order to avoid the influence of the saliency threshold and reduce the number of GrabCut iterations, interactive image segmentation can be combined with rectangular window positioning. For example, a rectangular window search can be performed based on the regional difference of saliency density, or a nested window search can be performed by combining saliency and edge characteristics.

The extraction of saliency regions usually includes the following steps:

1. Saliency map calculation

It is necessary to distinguish which regions are sufficiently salient and which regions are not salient enough according to the distinctive attributes of the regions.

2. Initial saliency region positioning

The most commonly used method is image binarization. The key issue is the optimization of threshold selection. In addition, the method of saliency region positioning can also be used to obtain the position of the saliency region in the image through window search.

3. Fine saliency region extraction

After locating the initial saliency region, its boundary is further refined. In specific applications, it is often necessary to use the GrabCut algorithm for multiple iterations and involve some other operations, such as dilation and erosion operations. How to reduce the number of iterations while reducing the demand for other operations and obtain better results is the key issue of this step.

4.3 EXTRACTING SALIENCY REGIONS BASED ON CONTRAST

Saliency maps have been widely used in unsupervised object segmentation. The following first introduces several specific algorithms based on contrast to calculate saliency, and then introduces the object segmentation and extraction methods based on saliency.

4.3.1 Based on Contrast Magnitude

The difference in attribute (grayscale/color) values between pixels is an important indicator to distinguish the salient pixels. The following introduces two related global saliency calculation methods using contrast magnitude.

4.3.1.1 Algorithm Based on Histogram Contrast

This algorithm uses **histogram contrast (HC)** to calculate the saliency of each pixel in the image separately. Specifically, it uses the grayscale or color difference between a pixel and all other image pixels to determine the saliency value of the pixel, which can generate a full-resolution saliency map (Cheng et al. 2015). Here, grayscale or color difference can be judged by grayscale or color histogram, and a smoothing process is used to reduce quantization artifacts at the same time.

Specifically defining the saliency of a pixel is the grayscale contrast or color contrast between the pixel and all other pixels in the image (in the following, the color contrast is considered), that is, the salient value of the pixel f_i in the image f ($i = 1, \ldots, N$, N is the number of pixels in the image) is

$$S(f_i) = \sum_{\forall f_j \in f} D_c(f_i, f_j) \tag{4.1}$$

Among them, $Dc(f_i, f_j)$ can measure the color distance between pixels f_i and f_j in the $L^*a^*b^*$ space (higher perception accuracy). Equation (4.1) is unfolded in the order of pixel label as follows:

$$S(f_i) = D_c(f_i, f_1) + D_c(f_i, f_2) + \cdots + D_c(f_i, f_N) \tag{4.2}$$

It is easy to see that pixels with the same color according to this definition will have the same saliency value (regardless of the spatial relationship between these pixels and f_i). If you rearrange the terms in Equation (4.2) and group the corresponding pixels f_i with the same color value c_i, you can get the saliency value of the pixel with this color value as

$$S(f_i) = S(c_i) = \sum_{j=1}^{C} p_i D(c_i, c_j) \tag{4.3}$$

where C corresponds to the total number of (different) colors of pixels in image f, and p_i is the probability of a pixel having color c_i.

Equation (4.3) corresponds to a histogram representation. Expressing Equation (4.1) in the form of Equation (4.3) is beneficial to increase the calculation speed in practical applications. According to Equation (4.1), the required calculation amount for the saliency value of the image is $O(N^2)$; and according to the Equation (4.3), the required calculation amount for the saliency value of the image is $O(N) + O(C^2)$. For a true color image with three channels, each channel has 256 values. If it is quantized into 12 values, a total of 1728 colors can be composed. Further considering the unevenness of color distribution in natural images, if the colors appearing in the image are arranged from most to less, generally less than 100 color values can be used to express more than 95% of the pixels in the image (the rest of the color values can be approximately quantified to less than 100 colors). In this way, using Equation (4.3) for larger-sized images can significantly increase the speed of calculating the image saliency value. For example, for an image of 100×100, the calculation amount of Equation (4.1) and Equation (4.3) are almost the same; for an image of 512×512, the calculation amount of Equation (4.3) is only 1/25 of the calculated amount of Equation (4.1).

4.3.1.2 Algorithm Based on Regional Contrast

This method improves the above-mentioned algorithm based on histogram contrast to further utilize the spatial relationship information between pixels (Cheng et al. 2015). First, the input image is preliminarily divided into multiple regions, and then the saliency value of each region is obtained by calculating the ***regional contrast (RC)***. Here, the global contrast score is used to calculate the regional saliency value, which specifically considers the contrast of the region itself and the spatial distance between it and other regions in the image (equivalent to replacing the pixels in the HC algorithm with the region as the calculation unit). This method can better combine image segmentation with saliency calculation.

First, perform a preliminary segmentation of the image, and then construct a histogram for each region. For the region R_i, measure its saliency by calculating its color contrast relative to all other regions in the image:

$$S(R_i) = \sum_{R_i \neq R_j} W(R_i) D_c(R_i, R_j) \tag{4.4}$$

Among them, take $W(R_i)$ is the number of pixels in the Region R_i, and it is used to weight the Region R_i (the weight of the larger region is greater); $D_c(R_i, R_j)$ measures the color distance in $L^*a^*b^*$ space between the Region R_i and Region R_j:

$$D_c(R_i, R_j) = \sum_{k=1}^{C_i} \sum_{l=1}^{C_j} p(c_{i,k}) p(c_{j,l}) D(c_{i,k}, c_{j,l}) \tag{4.5}$$

Among them, $p(c_{i,k})$ is the probability of the k-th color in Region R_i among all C_i colors, and $p(c_{j,l})$ is the probability of the l-th color in Region R_j among all C_j colors.

Next, the spatial information is introduced into Equation (4.4) to strengthen the weight of neighboring regions and reduce the weight of distant regions:

$$S(R_i) = W_s(R_i) \sum_{R_i \neq R_j} \exp\left[-\frac{D_s(R_i, R_j)}{\sigma_s^2}\right] W(R_i) D_r(R_i, R_j) \tag{4.6}$$

Among them, $D_s(R_i, R_j)$ is the spatial distance between the Region R_i and Region R_j; σ_s controls the strength of the spatial distance weighting (the larger the value, the greater the weighted strength of other regions far away from the region R_i); $W(R_i)$ represents the weight of the region R_i; $W_s(R_i)$ is the prior weight given to the region R_i according to how close it is to the center of the image (regions close to the center of the image have a larger weight, that is, more salient).

4.3.2 Based on Contrast Distribution

The above-mentioned algorithm based on **histogram contrast (HC)** only considers the contrast of each pixel when calculating the saliency value. The above-mentioned regional contrast (RC) algorithm also considers the distance between the pixels when calculating the saliency value, but none of the two algorithms consider the overall distribution factor of the contrast in the image. The following example illustrates the importance of this factor (Huang and Zhang 2017).

Refer to Figure 4.2, where Figure 4.2(a) is the original image. The two small boxes inside indicate two marker pixels (a foreground pixel and a background pixel). Figure 4.2(b) is the

(a)　　　　　　　(b)　　　　　　(c)　　　　　　(d)

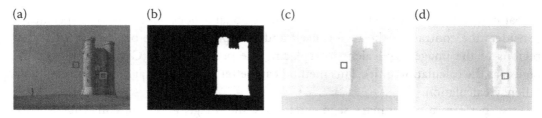

FIGURE 4.2   Influence of contrast distribution.

ideal result of foreground segmentation. The contrast maps calculated for these two pixels are shown respectively in Figure 4.2(c) and Figure 4.2(d), where the dark (green) color indicates a large contrast. It can be seen from Figure 4.2(c) and Figure 4.2(d) that although the sum of contrast can be compared, the contrast distributions in the two images are very different. With the marked pixels in Figure 4.2(c) as the center, the large saliency values are mainly distributed in the lower right. With the marked pixel in Figure 4.2(d) as the center, the large saliency values are distributed similarly around all directions. For the human visual system, the more high-contrast distribution directions (the foreground is different from the background in multiple directions), the more obvious the foreground object will appear.

An overall process flowchart taking into account the *contrast distribution* algorithm is shown in Figure 4.3. Considering that the calculation of global contrast for each pixel requires a large amount of calculation, the image is first segmented by superpixels. An example of superpixel segmentation is shown in Figure 4.4(a) and Figure 4.4(b), which are the original image and the result of super pixel segmentation, respectively. It can be seen that the superpixel segmentation results retain image structure information and image local features on a coarser scale. Then, each superpixel is taken as the unit for calculating the global contrast (that is, the color value in each superpixel is considered to be consistent). For each superpixel, calculate its maximum surround contrast (see below for details), and obtain its maximum contrast value in multiple directions. By considering the maximum contrast value in each direction, the relative contrast variance is calculated

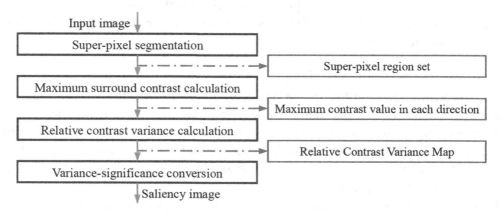

FIGURE 4.3   Flowchart of the algorithm based on the contrast distribution.

(a)   (b)

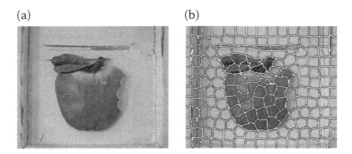

FIGURE 4.4   An image and the result of superpixel segmentation.

(see below for details). Converting the variance value into a saliency value, a saliency map corresponding to the original image is obtained.

The contrast is defined here as follows. Denote each superpixel region as R_i, $i = 1, \ldots, N$. The saliency of a superpixel region is proportional to the color contrast between this region and other regions, and also proportional to the spatial distance between this region and other regions. If a method similar to the above is adopted, the saliency between the two superpixel regions R_i and R_j can be defined as

$$S(R_i, R_j) = \exp\left[-\frac{D_s(R_i, R_j)}{\sigma_s^2} \right] D_c(R_i, R_j) \qquad (4.7)$$

Among them, $D_c(R_i, R_j)$ is the color distance between the regions R_i and R_j, $D_s(R_i, R_j)$ is the spatial distance between the regions R_i and R_j, and σ_s controls the strength of the spatial distance weighting (the larger the value, the greater the weighted strength of other regions far from the Region R_i).

Some specific steps and sample results are given below in accordance with the process in Figure 4.3. First, select two superpixel regions in the result of superpixel segmentation, one is inside the salient object, and the other is outside the salient object. They are shown in Figure 4.5(a) and Figure 4.5(c), respectively. For each superpixel region, take it as the center, calculate the contrast between it and other regions in 16 directions (interval 22.5°), and take the maximum contrast value in 16 directions (human vision often has the most maximum contrast sensitivity). By drawing these 16 values into a histogram, the standard deviation of their relative values can be calculated. The schematic diagram of calculating the superpixel region inside the salient object and the obtained relative (normalized) standard deviation histogram can be shown in Figure 4.5(a) and Figure 4.5(b), respectively. The schematic diagram of the calculation of the outer superpixel region and the obtained relative standard deviation histogram can be shown in Figure 4.5(c) and Figure 4.5(d), respectively. It can be seen from these figures that the maximum contrast values of every direction of the superpixel region belonging to the salient object are all relatively large; while for the superpixel region outside the salient object, the maximum contrast values of each direction have relatively large difference. That is, in the latter case, the maximum contrast values in some directions will be larger, while the maximum contrast values in other directions will be smaller.

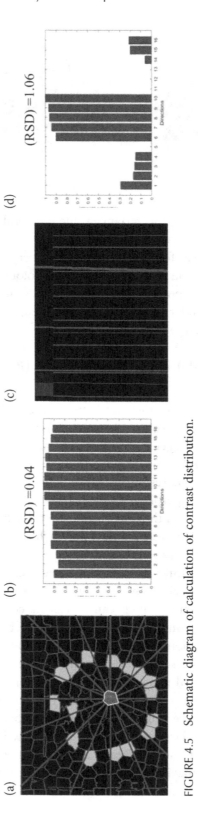

FIGURE 4.5 Schematic diagram of calculation of contrast distribution.

(a) (b) (c) (d)

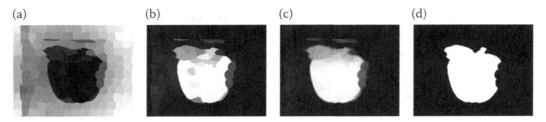

FIGURE 4.6   Salient map obtained from the contrast distribution.

(a) (b) (c) (d)

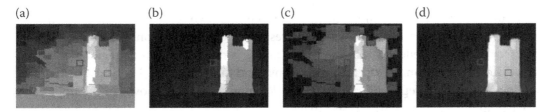

FIGURE 4.7   Comparison of two methods for detecting saliency.

From the perspective of the overall standard deviation, the relative standard deviation of the superpixel region inside the salient object will be smaller than the relative standard deviation of the superpixel region outside the salient object. The relative standard deviation obtained in this way is shown in Figure 4.6(a). The saliency of the visible region is inversely proportional to the standard deviation of the contrast. The saliency map obtained with this inverse relationship is shown in Figure 4.6(b). The result of further postprocessing the saliency map is shown in Figure 4.6(c), and Figure 4.6(d) shows the true value of the saliency map.

Figure 4.7 uses the image in Figure 4.2 to compare the methods based on contrast magnitude and the method based on contrast distribution. Figure 4.7(a) and Figure 4.7(b) are the saliency detection results obtained by the methods based on the contrast magnitude and the method based on the contrast distribution, respectively. Figure 4.7(c) and Figure 4.7(d) are the result obtained after further processing of them, respectively. It can be seen that the use of contrast distribution information has achieved better results.

4.3.3 Based on Minimum Directional Contrast

The method based on **minimum directional contrast (MDC)** is an improvement to the above method. Since the region-level method requires a large amount of calculation for image segmentation, the pixel-level method is selected to achieve fast performance.

4.3.3.1 Minimum Directional Contrast

Consider the contrast along different spatial orientations. Assuming that the object pixel i is regarded as the center of the field of view, the entire image can be divided into several regions H relative to the position of the pixel i, such as upper left (TL), upper right (TR), lower left (BL), and lower right (BR). The ***directional contrast (DC)*** from each region can be calculated as follows (H_1 = TL, H_2 = TR, H_3 = BL, H_4 = BR, i and j are the pixel indicators in the corresponding orientations):

$$DC_{i,H_l} = \sqrt{\sum_{j \in H_l} \sum_{k=1}^{K} (f_{i,k} - f_{j,k})^2} \quad l = 1, \quad 2, \quad 3, \quad 4 \tag{4.8}$$

Among them, f represents an input image with K color channels in the CIE-Lab color space. Refer to Figure 4.8, where Figure 4.8(a) is an input image, and one pixel is selected in the upper and lower images of Figure 4.8(b). One foreground pixel is selected in the upper image, which is determined by the intersection of two red lines. In the lower image, a background pixel is selected, which corresponds to the position determined by the intersection of two yellow lines. The whole image is divided into four regions by red or yellow lines, corresponding to four directions. The four-directional contrast histograms obtained by using foreground pixels and background pixels are shown in the upper and lower graphs in Figure 4.8(c), respectively.

According to the directional contrast histogram in Figure 4.8(c), it can be seen that the distributions of directional contrast between foreground pixels and background pixels are very different. Foreground pixels have quite large DC values in almost all directions, and even the smallest value is relatively large. However, the DC values of the background pixels in all directions have a large difference, especially the DC value in the lower right direction is very small. In fact, because foreground pixels are usually surrounded by background pixels, their directional contrast will have a large DC value in all directions; while background pixels usually have at least one direction connected to the image border, and a small DC value will definitely appear. This shows that the ***minimum directional contrast (MDC)***, that is, the DC value with the smallest contrast in all directions can be considered as the initial measure of saliency:

$$S_{\min}(i) = \min_{H} DC_{i,H} = \sqrt{\min_{H} \sum_{j \in H} \sum_{k=1}^{K} (f_{i,k} - f_{j,k})^2} \tag{4.9}$$

Figure 4.8(d) shows the distribution map of the MDC values obtained based on the initial saliency values of all pixels, and Figure 4.8(e) shows the true values of the saliency map. Compared with the two contrasts, the saliency detection effect obtained by the distribution of the MDC values is quite good.

4.3.3.2 Reducing Computational Complexity

In order to calculate the MDC for each pixel, it is necessary to calculate the contrast in four directions according to Equation (4.8). If calculated directly according to Equation (4.8), the computational complexity will be $O(N)$, where N is the number of pixels in the entire image. For larger-sized images, this calculation will be very large. In order to reduce the computational complexity, Equation (4.8) can be decomposed as follows:

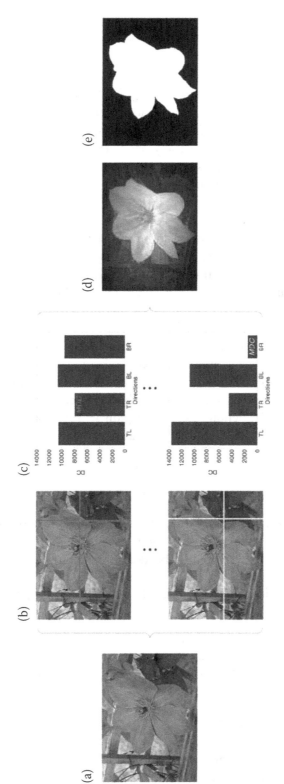

FIGURE 4.8 Saliency detection based on minimum directional contrast.

$$\sum_{j \in H_l} \sum_{k=1}^{K} (f_{i,k} - f_{j,k})^2 = \sum_{j \in H_l} \sum_{k=1}^{K} f_{i,k}^2 - 2 \sum_{k=1}^{K} \left(\sum_{j \in H_l} f_{j,k} \right) f_{i,k} + |H_l| \sum_{k=1}^{K} f_{i,k}^2 \quad l = 1, \ 2, \ 3, \ 4$$

(4.10)

where $|H|$ represents the number of pixels along the H direction. The first and second terms on the right side of the equal sign of the above equation can be calculated with the help of integral images (Viola 2001). In this way, the computational complexity for each pixel can be reduced to $O(1)$, which basically has nothing to do with the image size.

After obtaining the initial saliency, some post-processing can be performed to improve the performance of saliency detection.

4.3.3.3 Saliency Smoothing

In order to eliminate the influence of noise and improve the robustness of saliency region extraction in subsequent operations, the saliency map can be smoothed. In order to quickly achieve saliency smoothing, the prior knowledge of boundary connectivity can be used. If each color channel is quantized to L levels, the number of colors will be reduced from 256^3 to $L3$ (see Sub-section 4.3.1). Quantization of pixels with the same color can be used here.

In general, the degree of connection between the background region and the image border is much greater than the degree of connection between the foreground region and the image border. Therefore, the background can be determined with the help of **border connectivity (BC)**. This determination of the background can be calculated at the quantified color level. Let R_q denote the pixel region with the same quantized color q, then the border connectivity to R_q can be calculated as follows:

$$BC(R_q) = \frac{\sum_{j \in R_q} \delta(j)}{\sqrt{|R_q|}}$$

(4.11)

where $\delta(j)$ is 1 when the pixel j is a border pixel, otherwise it is 0; $|R_q|$ represents the number of pixels with the same quantized color q.

The average saliency of R_q weighted by border connectivity is:

$$S_{\text{average}}(R_q) = \underset{j \in R_q}{\text{average}} \{ S_{\min}(j) \bullet \exp[-W \bullet BC(R_q)] \}$$

(4.12)

Among them, $S_{\min}(j)$ is the minimum saliency (initial saliency) value in the region R_q, and W is the weight that controls the connectivity of the border. The final smoothing saliency is the combination of the average saliency and the initial saliency:

$$S_{\text{smooth}}(j) = \frac{S_{\min}(j) + S_{\text{average}}(R_q)}{2}$$

(4.13)

Figure 4.9(a) shows the result of saliency smoothing for Figure 4.8(d). It can be seen that the artifacts caused by quantization are eliminated in the saliency smoothing.

(a) (b) (c) (d)

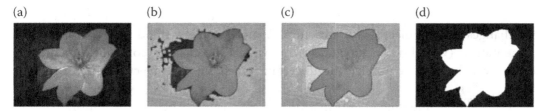

FIGURE 4.9   Saliency detection post-processing.

4.3.3.4 Saliency Enhancement

In order to further increase the contrast between the foreground and background regions, the following simple and effective watershed-based saliency enhancement method can also be used. First, the OTSU method is used to obtain the binarization threshold, T, and the smoothed saliency region, S_{smooth}, is segmented. Then, use some reliable conditions to mark some pixels as foreground (F) or background (B), and other pixels as undetermined (U):

$$M(i) = \begin{cases} F & S_{\text{smooth}}(i) > (1+p)T \\ B & S_{\text{smooth}}(i) < (1-p)T \\ U & \text{其他} \end{cases} \tag{4.14}$$

where p is the parameter that controls the initial marking region (as shown in Figure 4.9(b)). In Figure 4.9(b), the foreground pixels are marked red, the background pixels are marked green, and the undetermined pixels are without color. Next, use the marker-based watershed algorithm (Zhang 2017) to mark all pixels as foreground, background, or watershed (W). The saliency of each pixel after enhancement is

$$S_{\text{enhance}}(i) = \begin{cases} 1 - \alpha(1 - S_{\text{smooth}}(i)) & i \in F \\ \beta S_{\text{smooth}}(i) & i \in B \\ S_{\text{smooth}}(i) & i \in W \end{cases} \tag{4.15}$$

Among them, $\alpha \in [0, 1]$ and $\beta \in [0, 1]$ are used to control the degree of enhancement. Smaller values of α and β indicate that foreground pixels will be given a larger saliency value, while background pixels will be given a smaller saliency value. With the help of Equation (4.15), the saliency values of foreground pixels and background pixels are mapped to $[1-\alpha, 1]$ and $[0, \beta]$, respectively. Figure 4.9(c) is the final marked regions obtained by using the marking-based watershed algorithm. The saliency enhancement result obtained from the final marked region is shown in Figure 4.9(d).

4.3.4 Segmentation and Evaluation of Salient Objects

With the help of saliency detection, it is possible to further extract salient objects.

4.3.4.1 Object Segmentation and Extraction

The simplest method for extracting the saliency object is to perform thresholding directly on the saliency values, and extract the pixels whose saliency values are greater than a given threshold as the object pixels. This method is greatly affected by noise and changes in the object's own structure. A more stable method is to use watershed segmentation (waterline segmentation), in which the marker control segmentation method can be used to reduce the uncertain pixels on the object boundary (Zhang 2017).

A method of segmenting objects in a saliency map with the help of the improved graph cut method (Zhang 2017) has the following steps (Cheng et al. 2015):

1. Use a fixed threshold to first binarize the saliency map;

2. Regard the largest connected region with a saliency value greater than the threshold as the initial candidate region of the saliency object;

3. Mark this candidate region as unknown, and mark other regions as background;

4. Using the candidate regions marked as unknown to train the foreground color to help the algorithm determine the foreground pixels;

5. Initialize the GrabCut algorithm (an iterative method using Gaussian mixture model and graph cut) with potential foreground regions that can give high recall rate, and iteratively optimizing to improve precision;

6. Iteratively execute the GrabCut algorithm. After each iteration, the mathematical morphology dilation and erosion operations are used, and the region outside the dilated region is set as the background, and the region within the eroded region is set as undetermined.

4.3.4.2 Evaluation of the Saliency Detection Algorithms

With the aid of the extraction of the salient object, the binary mask M of the extracted object can be easily obtained. If there is a binary mask (true value) G of the original object, the effectiveness of the saliency detection can be judged and evaluated by comparing the two masks.

Commonly used evaluation indicators include precision and recall, as well as PR curves, ROC curves, F-measures, etc., obtained by combining them.

1. Precision rate: $P = |M \cap G|/|M|$;

2. Recall rate: $R = |M \cap G|/|G|$;

3. PR curve: The curve in the coordinate system that horizontal axis is the recall rate and the vertical axis is the precision rate;

4. ROC curve: The curve in the coordinate system, in which the false alarm $F_{PR} = |M \cap G^C|/|G^C|$ and the correct rate $T_{PR} = |M \cap G|/|G|$, where GC is the complement of G, are first calculated, then F_{PR} is used as the horizontal axis, T_{PR} is the vertical axis;

5. Area under the ROC curve (AUC):

$$AUC = \int_0^1 T_{PR}\, dF_{PR} \tag{4.16}$$

6. F-measure/F-score:

$$F_k = \frac{(1 + k^2) P \times R}{k^2 P + R} \tag{4.17}$$

where k is a parameter. When $k = 1$, F_1 is the harmonic mean of P and R.

4.3.4.3 Evaluation of the Minimum Directional Contrast Algorithm

The saliency calculation in the minimum directional contrast algorithm is based on the maximum contrast in each surrounding direction centered on the superpixel region. The number of surrounding directions may have a certain influence on the final result. With the help of PR curve, ROC curve and F-measure, the experiment comparison for the influence of the number of surrounding directions (the number of directions are 4, 8, 12, 16, 20 and 24, respectively) have been conducted and some results obtained are shown in Figure 4.10. Figure 4.10(a) shows the PR curve. It can be seen that when the number of surrounding directions increases from 4 to 16, the effect is improved to a certain extent. When the number of surrounding directions is more than 16, the effect does not change. Figure 4.10(b) shows the ROC curve. It can be seen that except when the number of surrounding directions is 4, the effects in other cases are basically indistinguishable. Figure 4.10(c) shows the corresponding AUC values and F-measure values, from which similar conclusions can be drawn.

4.4 EXTRACTING SALIENCY REGIONS BASED ON BACKGROUND PRIORS

The detection and extraction of saliency regions can often rely on some prior knowledge. The prior knowledge here includes prior information related to the nature of the saliency region, and prior information related to the background can also be considered. Among background-related priors, border priors and connectivity priors are commonly used. The **border priors** think that the border (contour) of the image corresponds to the background region of the image in most cases. The **connectivity priors** believe that pixels outside the saliency region are usually connected to the image border.

According to these two priors, firstly, it can be determined that the border of the image belongs to the background region, and secondly, the pixels connected to these background regions also belong to the background region, so the remaining pixels should belong to the saliency region. Based on this idea, the saliency region should be a region that is not connected to the image border, or the similarity distance between the pixels in the saliency region and the image border is large.

4.4.1 Similarity Distance

In the methods of detecting the saliency region based on the background priors, it is necessary to determine the similarity distance between each pixel in the image and the

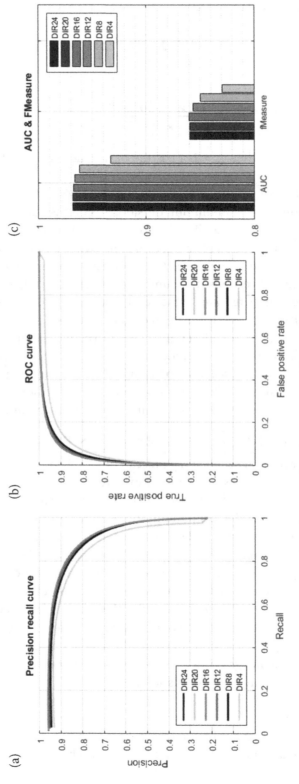

FIGURE 4.10 The influence of the number of surrounding directions on saliency detection.

image border. The commonly used distance measures here mainly include geodetic distance (Wei et al. 2012) and minimum fence distance (Strand et al. 2013).

4.4.1.1 Geodetic Distance

Geodetic distance function is a special **distance metric function**. Let A be a set of pixels, and a and b are two pixels in A. The geodesic distance $d_A(a, b)$ between pixels a and b can be represented as the infimum of all the path lengths from a to b in A. Divide the pixel set $B \subseteq A$ into K connected components B_i:

$$B = \bigcup_{i=1}^{K} B_i \tag{4.18}$$

In high dimensions, the geodesic distance is the length of the shortest path between two points along the (curved) surface. This is different from the Euclidean distance that does not consider whether the path between the start and end points is on the curved surface.

For the 2-D image $f(x, y)$, f can be regarded as the elevation corresponding to the 2-D plane XY. The geodetic distance can also be defined as follows. Consider a 4-path containing $L+1$ pixels in the image $f(x, y)$, which corresponds to a pixel sequence $G = \{g(0), g(1), \dots, g(L)\}$, where $g(i)$ and $g(i+1)$ are 4-adjacent. The geodetic distance of this path can be calculated as follows:

$$D_{GD}(G) = \sum_{i=1}^{L} |g(i) - g(i - 1)| \tag{4.19}$$

That is, the geodetic distance of a path is the sum of the absolute grayscale differences of adjacent pixels on the path. There can be N paths from a pixel p to a pixel set S, and the set of N paths can be expressed as $T = \{G_1, G_2, \dots, G_N\}$, where each G represents a pixel sequence. The geodetic distance between the pixel p and the pixel set S is the minimum of the geodetic distances of all the paths, which can be expressed as

$$D_{GD}(p, S) = \min_{G_i \in T} [D_{GD}(G_i)] \tag{4.20}$$

4.4.1.2 Minimum Fence Distance

The **minimum fence distance function** is also a special **distance metric function**. Consider a 4-path containing $L+1$ pixels in the image $f(x, y)$, which corresponds to a pixel sequence $G = \{g(0), g(1), \dots, g(L)\}$, where $g(i)$ and $g(i+1)$ are 4-adjacent. The fence distance of this path can be calculated as follows:

$$D_{BD}(G) = \max_i g(i) - \min_i g(i) \tag{4.21}$$

That is, the minimum fence distance of a path is the difference between the maximum gray level and the minimum gray level on the path (corresponding to the actual gray dynamic range). There can be N paths from a pixel p to a pixel set S, and the set of N

paths can be expressed as $T = \{G_1, G_2, \ldots, G_N\}$, where each G represents a pixel sequence. The minimum fence distance in all these paths is called the minimum fence distance between pixel p and pixel set S, which can be expressed as

$$D_{\text{MBD}}(p, S) = \min_{G_i \in T} [D_{\text{BD}}(G_i)] \qquad (4.22)$$

In the saliency detection, studies have shown that the geodetic distance is more sensitive to noise, and the minimum fence distance is more robust than the geodetic distance. In addition, the minimum fence distance is more resistant to fluctuations in pixel values in the image.

4.4.2 Approximate Calculation of Minimum Fence Distance

The minimum fence distance can be accurately calculated pixel by pixel, but this requires a large amount of calculation. According to Equation (4.22), the minimum fence distance from each pixel to the set of image border pixels should consider all paths from each pixel to the set of image border pixels, and the number of paths may be very large. In order to reduce the amount of calculation, some approximate methods can be adopted. The following first introduces the results that may be obtained by calculating the minimum fence distance, and then introduces several typical approximate calculation methods.

4.4.2.1 The Calculation Result of the Minimum Fence Distance

With the help of the calculation of the minimum fence distance, the conversion from the original image to the minimum fence distance image can be realized, that is, the minimum fence distance value of each pixel can be obtained.

Figure 4.11 shows the results obtained by calculating the minimum fence distance. Figure 4.11(a) shows an original image in which the flower is a salient object. Figure 4.11(b) shows two different (color) small blocks in the image, and their center is the example pixel (seed pixel) for calculating the minimum fence distance considered. Figure 4.11(c) shows the minimum fence distance and corresponding path calculated for these two pixels, respectively. As can be seen from the figure, the smaller the minimum fence distance, the greater the possibility that the pixel belongs to the background pixel. In addition, the path corresponding to the minimum fence distance may be a complex curve. Figure 4.11(d) is a (saliency) result obtained by transforming the distance obtained by calculating the minimum fence distance for the pixels of the whole image.

(a)   (b)   (c)   (d)

FIGURE 4.11   Calculation example of minimum fence distance.

4.4.2.2 Approximation Method Based on Raster Scanning

The method based on raster scanning (Zhang et al. 2015) is an approximate calculation method. It scans the image pixel by pixel, first forward from the upper-left corner to the lower-right corner, and then reverse from the lower-right corner to the upper-left corner. Forward scan plus reverse scan constitute a complete scan. Such scanning can be repeated. With the increase of scanning times, it can gradually approach the accurate path. Of course, multiple scans require high computational costs. In practice, three scans are generally required to achieve a good balance between operation time and calculation accuracy.

This method has a problem related to the scanning direction. Generally forward scan is carried out from the upper left corner to the lower right corner of the image. If the path corresponding to the minimum fence distance of some pixels is in the direction connecting the lower-left corner and the upper-right corner, the calculation results obtained by this method may have a relatively large error. Still considering the original image and example pixels given in Figure 4.11(a) and (b), the minimum fence distance and the corresponding path based on the raster scanning method are shown in Figure 4.12(a), while the further result obtained by distance transform is shown in Figure 4.12(b). It can be seen that the approximate path obtained is quite different from the exact path (especially for the pixel to the right), and the minimum fence distance obtained is also far from the accurate value. The distance transform result obtained under this calculation is obviously different from Figure 4.11(d).

4.4.2.3 Approximation Method Based on Minimum Spanning Tree

In this method, the image is simply represented as a ***minimum spanning tree (MST)***. The minimum spanning tree is a tree structure that can be transformed from a connected graph. Generally, an image is first represented as a 4-adjacent undirected graph (where the node corresponds to the pixel and the arc represents the grayscale difference between the pixels), and then the minimum spanning tree of the image can be obtained by eliminating the arcs with large values/weights. The minimum spanning tree of a graph with N nodes still contains the original N nodes, and retains the fewest arcs that make the graph connected, so that the path between pixels is unique (Tu et al. 2016). It is easier to search for the path with the smallest distance value in this minimum spanning tree, because the search range is much smaller. In practice, the minimum fence distance can be

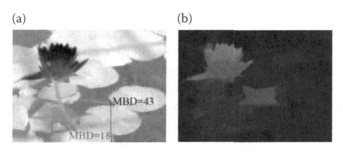

FIGURE 4.12 Approximate calculation results based on raster scanning.

(a)   (b)

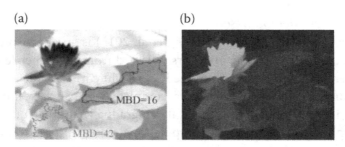

FIGURE 4.13 Approximate calculation results based on minimum spanning tree.

calculated efficiently and quickly by traversing the tree twice. First traverse once from the leaves to the root, and then traverse once from the root to the leaves.

Using the minimum spanning tree structure to represent the image simplifies the search for the path between pixels and pixel sets, but this simplification may cause some approximate paths to deviate from the exact path and cause errors. Consider again the original image and example pixels given in Figure 4.11(a) and Figure 4.11(b), the minimum fence distance and the corresponding path obtained by the minimum spanning tree method are shown in Figure 4.13(a), and the further result obtained from distance transform is shown in Figure 4.13(b). It can be seen that the approximate path obtained is quite different from the exact path (especially for the pixel to the left), and the minimum fence distance obtained is also far from the accurate value. The distance transform result obtained under this calculation is also significantly different from Figure 4.11(d).

4.4.2.4 Approximation Method Based on Water Flow Driven

In this method, the natural law of water flowing from high to low (elevation) is used (Huang and Zhang 2018). Consider the image border pixels as a pixel set S, the distance from any pixel in the image to S is measured by the minimum fence distance from that pixel to S. If S is set as the water source, and the cost of water flowing from the water source pixel to other pixels is measured by the minimum fence distance, the problem is transformed to find a path with the smallest fluctuation range (that is, the difference between the maximum value and the minimum value) of pixel gray values (for a color image, consider one of its three channels). The process of solving this problem corresponds to the process of water flowing from the water source pixel to other pixels and submerging them.

An example is shown in Figure 4.14. Figure 4.14(a) is the original image, and Figure 4.14(b) is the initialization of the image border pixels as a set of water source pixels. Figure 4.14(c) to Figure 4.14(e) are several intermediate results of water flowing to other regions in the figure according to different minimum fence distances. The red mask represents the submerged region. It can be seen that in this process, the pixels with the smallest fence distances from border of the image are submerged first. Continue the process of water flow until all regions are submerged in the end, as shown in Figure 4.14(f). The minimum fence distance of each pixel in the image is calculated in

FIGURE 4.14   Approximate calculation process based on water flow driven process.

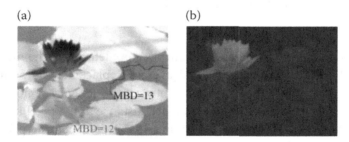

FIGURE 4.15   Approximate calculation results based on water flow driven.

this flow process, so that the original image can be converted into a minimum fence distance map, that is, the minimum fence distance value of each pixel can be obtained.

This method has a good approximation effect on the calculation of the minimum fence distance. Consider again the original image and example pixels given in Figure 4.11(a) and (b), and then use the minimum fence distance and the corresponding path based on the water flow driven method, as shown in Figure 4.15(a), and the further result obtained from the distance transform is shown in Figure 4.15(b). It can be seen that the approximate path obtained is relatively close to the exact path, and the minimum fence distance obtained is also very close to the accurate value. The distance transform result obtained under this calculation is very similar to Figure 4.11(d).

4.4.3 Saliency Region Detection by Water Flow Driven

Based on the calculation of the minimum fence distance, the minimum fence distance transform can be realized, and the result of the distance transform (that is, the salient

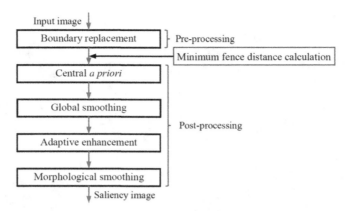

FIGURE 4.16   The overall flowchart of saliency region detection.

value of each point) can be obtained. In practice, it needs some pre-processing and post-processing steps to detect the required saliency region based on the distance transform. This sub-section introduces the related pre-processing and post-processing techniques based on the calculation method of water flow driven approximation in conjunction with the overall process. These techniques are also useful for the detection of salient regions using other approximation calculation methods.

4.4.3.1 Overall Process

See Figure 4.16 for the overall process of saliency region detection. The first step is to pre-process the input image, where a weighted average replacement is performed on the image border to adjust the salient difference between the saliency region and the image border. Then it is to calculate the minimum fence distance at the pixel level. The last is a series of post-processing operations, including the use of central priors and global smoothing, as well as morphological smoothing after adaptive enhancement to obtain the saliency region. The entire detection process can reach a speed of 180 fps when using a single thread.

An example reflecting the effects of the main steps of the above process is shown in Figure 4.17. Figure 4.17(a) is an input image and Figure 4.17(b) is the result of the minimum fence distance calculation. Furthermore, Figure 4.17(c) is the result obtained using the central priors, Figure 4.17(d) is the result obtained by performing global smoothing, Figure 4.17(e) is the result obtained with adaptive enhancement, Figure 4.17(f) is the final result obtained after morphological smoothing, and Figure 4.17(g) shows the true value of the saliency region.

The purpose and method of each step are introduced below (Huang and Zhang 2018).

4.4.3.2 Border Replacement

In the background-related priors, border priors and connectivity priors are used in the calculation based on the minimum fence distance. According to these two priors, it is determined that the pixels at the border of the image belong to the background, and the

(a)   (b)   (c)   (d)

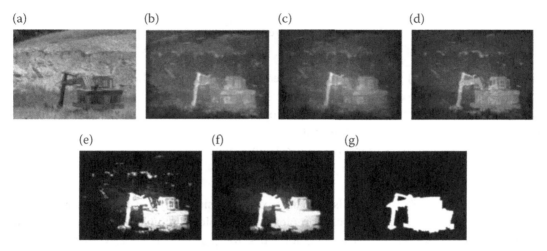

(e)   (f)   (g)

FIGURE 4.17   Examples of the results for several salient region detection steps.

pixels connected to the border also belong to the background. This judgment sometimes brings a problem, that is, the saliency value of the saliency object in contact with the image border will be quite small, and the saliency object would be misjudged as the background. To overcome this problem, the border can be replaced.

Suppose the input image is $f(x, y)$, and the average gray value of its border (which can have a width with given number of pixels) is f_b, then the border replacement can be performed as follows, that is, the new image $f_N(x, y)$ is:

$$f_N(x, y) = \begin{cases} (1 - W)f(x, y) + Wf_b & (x, y) \in \text{border} \\ f(x, y) & (x, y) \notin \text{border} \end{cases} \tag{4.23}$$

where W is a weight that controls the balance. The minimum fence distance transform map calculated from the new image is denoted as $d(x, y)$, and the saliency map $S(x, y)$ calculated from the input image is now:

$$S(x, y) = \begin{cases} |f_N(x, y) - f(x, y)| & (x, y) \in \text{border} \\ d(x, y) & (x, y) \notin \text{border} \end{cases} \tag{4.24}$$

This method of border replacement can increase the saliency values of the saliency object in contact with the image border, and reduce the possibility of misjudging the object as the background.

4.4.3.3 Central Priors

The first step of post-processing is to use the **central priors;** that is, the saliency object is more likely to be in the center of the image. To this end, the saliency value of each pixel in the image can be weighted differently according to the pixel position:

$$S_W(x, y) = S(x, y) \exp\left[-\frac{\mathrm{dis}^2(x, y)}{\sigma^2} \right] \tag{4.25}$$

Among them, dis(x, y) represents the Euclidean distance between the pixel position (x, y) and the image center coordinates (normalized by the image size), and σ^2 controls the degree of the effect of the central priors. Comparing Figure 4.17(b) and Figure 4.17(c), it is easy to see the effect of using the central priors; that is, the saliency values close to the image border region are suppressed to a certain extent.

4.4.3.4 Global Smoothing

The purpose of global smoothing is to make pixels with similar colors have closer saliency. In order to reduce the computational complexity, each color channel of the color image can be quantized into K colors, that is, all color types are quantized from 256^3 to K^3. Then, a smoothing operation is performed between pixels with the same quantized color. If $f(x, y)$ is quantized to the color $g(x, y)$, and G represents all pixels with the quantized color $g(x, y)$, then the smoothed saliency $S_S(x, y)$ of the pixel $f(x, y)$ is weighted by the average saliency $A_G(x, y)$ of the pixel set G and the saliency $S(x, y)$ of the pixel $f(x, y)$ before smoothing:

$$S_S(x, y) = \frac{1}{2}[S(x, y) + A_G(x, y)] \tag{4.26}$$

Comparing Figure 4.17(c) and Figure 4.17(d), it can be seen that after global smoothing, the saliency values of each part of the saliency region are more consistent, and the contrast between the saliency region and the background region is enhanced.

4.4.3.5 Adaptive Enhancement

The purpose of adaptive enhancement is to further increase the contrast between the saliency region and the background region. Let T be the threshold for thresholding the saliency map, then the **extended Sigmoid function** for adaptive enhancement of the saliency map is (when T is 0.5, it is the original Sigmoid function, also known as the S-shaped growth function):

$$\mathrm{Sigmoid}_E[S(x, y)] = \frac{1}{1 + \frac{1-T}{T}\exp\{-k[S(x, y) - T]\}} \tag{4.27}$$

where k is the control coefficient. After this extended Sigmoid function mapping, the saliency values of the region in the image that are greater than T will become larger; the saliency values of the region in the image that is less than T will become smaller; and the saliency value of the region equal to T will continue to remain unchanged. Comparing Figure 4.17(d) and Figure 4.17(e), it is easy to see that the contrast between the salient region and the background region has increased. More experimental statistics show that adaptive enhancement can play a great role in reducing the mean absolute deviation (MAE) between the saliency map and the true values.

4.4.3.6 Morphological Smoothing

The purpose of morphological smoothing is to remove small-sized objects or backgrounds in the image while retaining obvious edges (Zhang 2017). The smoothing operation here consists of two parts: dilation-based reconstruction and erosion-based reconstruction (Vincent 1993). Here, the mask size required for the dilation and erosion operations can be selected according to the average saliency of the image.

Comparing Figure 4.17(e) and Figure 4.17(f), after morphological smoothing, on the one hand, the small white blocks in the background region disappeared (most of them originated from the fluctuations in the background region), and on the other hand, the fluctuations in the saliency region are also reduced. Only the large part boundaries are retained.

4.4.4 Locating Object Candidate Region

Based on the detection of the saliency region, the **object candidate region** can be further located. The so-called locating object candidate region is to determine the possible object region in the image and determine its position and size.

In practice, it is generally used to scan a large number of windows with different scales and positions in the image, and quickly determine the possibility of objects in these scanning windows, which is also called **objectness**. An ideal scan window containing the object should satisfy the following two conditions:

1. The outside of the scan window is the background;

2. There are objects inside the scan window.

According to the previous discussion, the background-based border priors assume that the border of the image belong to the background region, which is consistent with the Condition (1) that the ideal scan window needs to meet. Furthermore, if each scan window is slightly enlarged, and the expanded region is regarded as the background, and the minimum fence distance from the other parts of the scan window to the background is calculated, then the saliency values of the other parts can be obtained, and the judgment about the possibility that there is an object in the scanning window can be made accordingly, so as to meet the above Condition (2).

Now use Figure 4.18 to introduce the different results obtained by calculating the saliency of different scan windows. Figure 4.18(a) is an input image that contains an object (ship). Figure 4.18(b) shows four different scanning windows. Expand these four scanning windows by one round and use them as the background, the saliency maps calculated by the minimum fence distance are shown in Figure 4.18(c)–(f), respectively. Let's analyze them separately.

1. The border of the scanning window in Figure 4.18(c) covers both the ship hull and seawater. The region obtained by expanding the scanning window by one round still covers the hull and seawater, so they will all be regarded as background. In this

(a)   (b)   (c)   (d)

(e)   (f)   (g)   (h)

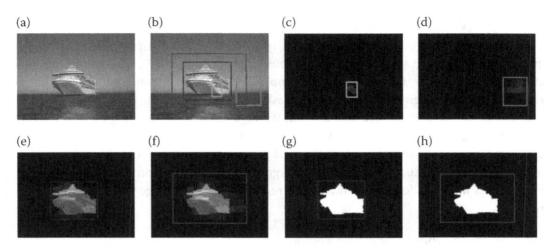

FIGURE 4.18 Saliency results in different scan windows.

way, the part in the scanning window will also be regarded as the background, resulting in a small saliency values in the scanning window.

2. The border of the scanning window in Figure 4.18(d) covers only sea water and sky, and there is only seawater and sky inside the scanning window without the hull. The region obtained by expanding the scan window by one round still contains only seawater and sky, and they are all regarded as background. In this way, the saliency values in the scan window are also very small.

3. The border of the scanning window in Figure 4.18(e) is in the sea and the sky, but there are ships in the scanning window. The region obtained by expanding the scanning window by one round still contains only seawater and sky, so the seawater and sky are regarded as the background. Since the hull is quite different in color from the sea or sky, the minimum fence distance from the hull in the scanning window to the background sea or sky will be large, so the saliency values in the scanning window will be relatively large.

4. The situation in Figure 4.18(f) is similar to Figure 4.18(e), so the saliency in the scanning window is also relatively large. Since the scanning window is larger here, the saliency values represented by the minimum fence distance (monotone increase without decrease with the path length) may also be larger. However, by thresholding Figure 4.18(e) and Figure 4.18(f), the results obtained are shown in Figure 4.18(g) and Figure 4.18(h), respectively. It can be seen that the detected salient object regions are basically the same.

To sum up, if the border of the scanning window only covers the background region and there is no object in the scanning window, or the border of the scanning window covers part of the object and part of the background at the same time, the saliency of the region in the scanning window based on the background priors will be very low. When the

FIGURE 4.19   Some results obtained in locating the object candidate region.

border of the scanning window only covers the background but there is an object inside the scanning window, it will have great saliency. The scanning window determined in this way should be the scanning window containing the object, which can distinguish the object from the background.

Figure 4.19 shows the results of locating object candidate regions for other images, where the dark (red) box indicates the true value, and the light (green) box indicates the result obtained by the above method, which is closest to the true value (Huang et al. 2018).

4.5 EXTRACTING SALIENT OBJECTS BASED ON THE MOST STABLE REGION

Calculating the saliency pixel by pixel and then grouping the pixels with large saliency to form a region based on the calculation result is a bottom-up method. When the background is more complex and the noise is relatively strong, the bottom-up approach is often not robust enough.

One way of overcoming this problem is to consider the pixels that may belong to the saliency object as a whole. In other words, when judging the saliency of a pixel, consider which object its neighborhood belongs to, and consider the saliency from the object level. Generally speaking, the interior of a pixel's neighborhood should have relatively similar properties (such as grayscale, color, etc.), but the neighborhood has significantly different properties from its exterior. Such a neighborhood is called the ***most stable region (MSR)*** below. The most stable region will be determined first and the most stable region as a whole will be used to calculate the saliency to detect and extract the saliency object (Huang et al. 2020).

4.5.1 Overall Process

The overall flowchart of extracting the saliency region based on the most stable region is shown in Figure 4.20. Firstly, the superpixel representation of the image is obtained by superpixel segmentation, and then the most stable region is calculated with the unit of superpixel, and the most stable region is calculated in the next step. The saliency map is post-processed to extract the required saliency region.

There are many algorithms for ***superpixel segmentation***. For example, the SLIC algorithm (Achanta et al. 2012) is a superpixel segmentation algorithm that can better preserve the edges in the image and has a high computational efficiency.

The other three processing modules are introduced below.

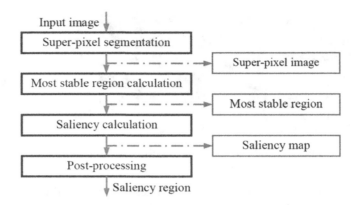

FIGURE 4.20 The flowchart of extracting the saliency region based on the most stable region.

4.5.2 Calculation of the Most Stable Region

Suppose the input image is segmented into M superpixels with the help of superpixel segmentation algorithm, denoted as P_i, $i = 1, \dots, M$. In order to calculate the most stable region, a region growing strategy is used for each superpixel P_i to find its neighborhood to indicate the object that the P_i most likely belongs to. Here, according to a pre-designed priority, let the region grow to the adjacent superpixel until it grows into the entire image. During the region growing process, a series of corresponding (that is, growing from the i-th superpixel to the j-th superpixel) regions $R_{i,j}$, $j = 1, \dots, M$ will be produced. In order to determine which of these regions can represent the object that P_i is most likely to belong to, the following three factors need to be considered:

1. Whether there is a high contrast between this region and the outer peripheral regions;

2. Whether there is good consistency within this region;

3. Whether the area of this region exceeds a certain threshold (too small may be noise).

According to the above three factors, the following evaluation function can be constructed:

$$J(R_{i,j}) = C(R_{i,j})\exp[-WH(R_{i,j})]A(R_{i,j}) \qquad (4.28)$$

Among them, $C(R_{i,j})$ represents the contrast between the region $R_{i,j}$ and its surrounding regions, $H(R_{i,j})$ represents the internal consistency of the region $R_{i,j}$, and $A(R_{i,j})$ represents the area of the region $R_{i,j}$, W is the weight parameter. The above-mentioned $C(R_{i,j})$, $H(R_{i,j})$ and $A(R_{i,j})$ correspond to the aforementioned three factors to be considered respectively, and their calculation formulas are as follows:

$$C(R_{i,j}) = \frac{1}{K} \sum_{p \in R_{i,j}} \sum_{q \notin R_{i,j}} D(p, q)\delta(q \in N_p) \qquad (4.29)$$

$$H(R_{i,j}) = \frac{1}{L} \sum_{p \in R_{i,j}} \sum_{q \in R_{i,j}} D(p, q)\delta(q \in N_p) \tag{4.30}$$

$$A(R_{i,j}) = \min\left[1, \frac{A_{i,j}}{T_A}\right] \tag{4.31}$$

Among them, K represents the number of superpixel pairs that participate in the calculation of the contrast between the regions, L represents the number of superpixel pairs that participate in the calculation of the internal consistency of the region, $D(p, q)$ represents the average distance between two superpixels p and q in the color space, $\delta(q \in N_p)$ represents the function of whether the superpixel q belongs to the neighborhood N_p of the superpixel p. If it belongs, it is taken as 1, otherwise it is taken as 0. $C(R_{i,j})$ and $H(R_{i,j})$ calculated in this way are the average contrast and average consistency, respectively. In Equation (4.31), $A_{i,j}$ is the normalized area of region $R_{i,j}$ (take the normalized total area of the image as 1), T_A is a predetermined threshold, and small regions with areas less than the threshold T_A will be suppressed.

According to the calculation of Equation (4.28), the region with the highest score (the highest evaluation function value) among a series of regions $R_{i,j}$ generated during region growing is selected, and set as $R_{i,m}$, then this region becomes the most stable region of the superpixel P_i:

$$\text{MSR}_i = R_{i,m} \quad m = \arg\max_j [J(R_{i,j})] \tag{4.32}$$

Figure 4.21 shows an example of the most stable region calculation, where Figure 4.21(a) is an input image, Figure 4.21(b) is the result of superpixel segmentation, Figure 4.21(c) shows a superpixel seed for growing (green mask), Figure 4.21(d) to Figure 4.21(h) are based on the several regions (blue mask) obtained during the growing process of this

FIGURE 4.21　The most stable region calculation example.

superpixel. From Figure 4.21(c) to Figure 4.21(h), the corresponding evaluation function values are 1.04, 4.65, 19.25, 21.94, 20.60, and 0 in order. It can be seen that the values of the evaluation function change from small to large and then from large to small. In this way, the region corresponding to the maximum value of the evaluation function can be selected as the most stable region as in Figure 4.21(f).

4.5.3 Saliency Calculation

With the help of the most stable region MSR, the regional saliency can be further calculated. Still consider the border priors and connectivity priors introduced earlier. The border connectivity can be used to measure the possibility of a region belonging to the background (Zhu et al. 2014). Here, the border connectivity B_c of a (most stable) region is defined as the ratio of the length of the overlap of the region and its border to the square root of the area of the region:

$$B_c(\text{MSR}) = \frac{\Sigma_{q \in P_b} \delta(q \in \text{MSR})}{\sqrt{\Sigma_{q \in P} \delta(q \in \text{MSR})}} \tag{4.33}$$

Among them, P represents the set of image superpixels, P_b represents the superpixels on the image border, $\delta(q \in \text{MSR})$ represents the function of whether the superpixel q belongs to the most stable region; if it belongs to it, it takes 1, otherwise, it takes 0.

Further consider the spatial distribution of the foreground and background in the image. Generally, the distribution of the foreground region will be relatively compact, so there is only a small variance in space; the color of the background region will be distributed across the entire image, so it presents a high variance in space. The spatial distribution feature (Perazzi et al. 2012) can be used to represent the possibility of the color of a certain region appearing elsewhere in the image. Therefore, for the most stable region, the following formula can be used to calculate the probability that the average color of the region appears elsewhere in the image (with the help of the weighted average variance):

$$C(\text{MSR}) = \sum_{q \in P} \|P_q - \mu(\text{MSR})\|^2 \bullet s(\text{MSR}, \ q) \tag{4.34}$$

where

$$\mu(\text{MSR}) = \sum_{q \in P} P_q \bullet s(\text{MSR}, \ q) \tag{4.35}$$

$$s(\text{MSR}, \ q) = \frac{1}{G_{\text{MSR}}} \exp\left[-\frac{D_c(\text{MSR}, \ q)}{\sigma}\right] \tag{4.36}$$

Among them, P_q represents the position of the super pixel q, $\mu(\text{MSR})$ represents the spatially weighted average position of all regions having similar MSR color; $s(\text{MSR}, q)$ represents the color similarity controlled by the parameter σ between the MSR and the superpixel q, G_{MSR} is a normalization parameter so that $\Sigma_{q \in_P} w(\text{MSR}, q) = 1$, $D_c(\text{MSR}, q)$ represents the color distance between MSR and superpixel q. The $C(\text{MSR})$ obtained in this way gives the spatially weighted average variance of all regions with similar colors to the MSR. A smaller variance indicates that the distribution is more compact and has stronger saliency; a larger variance indicates that the distribution is looser and has weaker saliency.

By comprehensively considering the border connectivity and spatial distribution, a saliency calculation formula can be obtained:

$$S(\text{MSR}) = \exp[-W_b B_c(\text{MSR})]\exp[-W_d C(\text{MSR})] \qquad (4.37)$$

Among them, W_b and W_d are the weights that control the border connectivity and spatial distribution of the border, respectively.

For a given superpixel P_i, the corresponding MSR_i can be calculated. On the one hand, a P_i may belong to multiple different MSR_i; on the other hand, in addition to P_i, a MSR_i often includes other superpixels. Therefore, take the saliency of the superpixel P_i as the average of the saliency of all MSR_i including P_i:

$$S(P_i) = \frac{\sum_{j=1}^{M} S(\text{MSR}_i)\delta(P_i \in \text{MSR}_i)}{\sum_{j=1}^{M} \delta(P_i \in \text{MSR}_i)} \qquad (4.38)$$

where $\delta(P_i \in \text{MSR}_i)$ indicates whether the superpixel P_i belongs to the function of MSR_i; if it belongs to it, then it is taken as 1, otherwise it is taken as 0.

4.5.4 Post-processing

After calculating the saliency value of each superpixel, there are two post-processing tasks: saliency smoothing and saliency enhancement.

The saliency smoothing is to make the saliency values between the regions with similar color and small distance closer. This can be achieved at the superpixel level by smoothing filter. The smoothing filtering result S_a for the superpixel p is:

$$S_a(p) = \sum_{q \in P} S(q) W_q \exp\left[-\frac{D_s(p, q)}{\sigma s^2} - \frac{D_c(p, q)}{\sigma c^2}\right] \qquad (4.39)$$

Among them, P represents the set of image superpixels; W_q represents the weight of the superpixel q belonging to P, and its value depends on the number of pixels it contains; $D_s(p, q)$ represents the average distance between two superpixels in the image space, $D_c(p, q)$ represents the average distance between two superpixels in the color space; σ_s^2 and σ_c^2 are used to control the smoothing intensity in the image space and the color space, respectively.

Saliency enhancement is to enhance the contrast between the foreground region and the background region. Here, the adaptively enhanced extended Sigmoid function of Equation (4.27) can still be used (when T is 0.5, it is the original Sigmoid function).

(a)   (b)   (c)

(d)   (e)   (f)

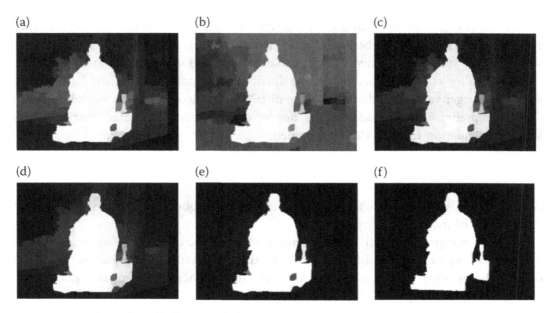

FIGURE 4.22   Examples of saliency calculation and post-processing effects.

Figure 4.22 gives examples of saliency calculations and post-processing effects. Here, after obtaining the most stable region as shown in Figure 4.21(f), the saliency calculation results obtained by using border connectivity or spatial distribution features alone are shown in Figure 4.22(a) and Figure 4.22(b), respectively. The saliency calculation result obtained by combining the features is shown in Figure 4.22(c).

Figure 4.22(d) shows the result of smooth filtering the saliency calculation result, Figure 4.22(e) shows the result of further enhancement, and finally Figure 4.22(f) shows the ideal true value.

4.6 SOME RECENT DEVELOPMENTS AND FURTHER RESEARCH

In the following sections, some technical developments and promising research directions in the last few years are briefly overviewed.

4.6.1 Saliency Detection Combining Various Characteristics

Humans consider visually distinctive saliency from a number of characteristics of image and object. Recently proposed **saliency detection processes** often combining multiple features, cues, attributes, etc. of the image and region.

4.6.1.1 A Classification of Detection Methods

A number of different **deep learning** methods for combining various **saliency properties** have been proposed. One classification of these methods can be shown in Table 4.1 (Luo et al. 2021).

Table 4.1 shows a general overview of the methods of saliency detection based on deep learning. Due to the larger granularity of processing units in sparse detection methods,

TABLE 4.1   Classification of saliency detection based on deep learning

Category	Main Sub-categories and Their Concise Descriptions
Sparse detection	With superpixels as processing units: Generating the feature sequences of units and converting them into saliency scores of superpixels; Extracting the local and global contextual information in the neighborhood centered on the superpixels for feature learning to infer each superpixel salience.
Dense detection	Based on encoding-decoding structure: The feature expression of the input image is extracted by the encoder, the image information is reconstructed by the decoder and the salency value of each pixel is obtained by using the Softmax classifier. Combing super-pixel and encoding-decoding structure: The local context cues obtained by super-pixel segmentation are used to supplement the saliency estimation with global information obtained by convolutional neural network. Based on U-Net structure: U-net structure provides a platform for generating saliency map with clear object boundary by combining the high-level semantic features of convolution layer and low-level spatial detail information.
Weakly supervised	Pseudo annotated database: Select some saliency object detection models under traditional methods to generate a corresponding series of maps for each training image, fuse them into a single sample annotation map, that is, pseudo-labels, and then compare them with the training images for network training. Weak annotated database: Use lower-cost annotations (e.g., image-level annotations, image description text) than pixel-level annotations to reduce the reliance on pixel-level annotations and avoid the limitations of traditional methods to generate pseudo-labels.

the improvement of detection accuracy is limited. In recent years, many researches have turned to dense detection methods based on deep network models. Weakly supervised models reduce the reliance on manually annotated data, but their ability to extract effective features often declines, so more current attentions have been paid to improving their detection performance relative to deeply supervised models.

4.6.1.2 An Algorithm Based on Low-Rank Background Constraints and Multi-Cue Propagation

An image saliency detection algorithm based on low-rank background constraints and multi-cue propagation is proposed (Tang et al. 2021), and the algorithm framework is shown in Figure 4.23. First, the input image is segmented into uniform superpixel blocks with the help of a *simple linear iterative clustering (SLIC)* algorithm (Achanta et al. 2012) to comprehensively capture the structural information of pixels. Second, the feature matrix of each superpixel block is extracted, and high-level background priors are used to constrain the decomposition of the feature matrix to increase the difference between the low-rank matrix and the sparse matrix, and obtain a low-rank background-constrained saliency map for the separation of foreground and background. Further, in order to explore the potential connections between superpixels, a local information graph structure that fits the human perception system is constructed. This filters out reliable label vectors with the help of low-rank background-constrained saliency maps,

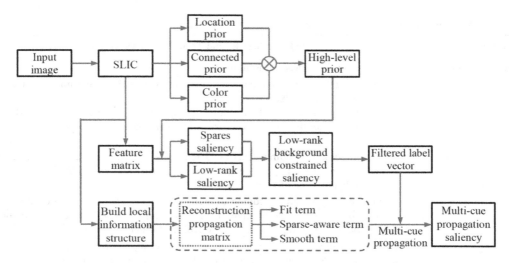

FIGURE 4.23 Framework and flowchart of the algorithm.

reconstructs the propagation matrix, and embeds sparse perception characteristics and local smoothness constraints as the regularization term. Finally, by realizing multi-cue propagation for saliency values, a fine saliency map will be obtained.

4.6.1.3 An Algorithm Fusing Boundary Connectivity and Local Contrast

A detection algorithm for **salient object detection** by fusing boundary connectivity and local contrast to overcome the problem caused by location of object region on the boundary priori or center priori is proposed (Chen et al. 2020), and the algorithm framework is shown in Figure 4.24.

The main steps of this algorithm are:

1. Constructing foreground convex hull using color-enhanced Harris corner detection.

2. The SLIC algorithm is used to suppress the background region within the convex hull to extract an accurate foreground region within the convex hull.

3. The acquired accurate foreground region is used as the absorption node of the random walk model (in model graph, the local contrast between nodes would be large), and the saliency value of the superpixel in the whole image is calculated to include all the foreground regions in the image.

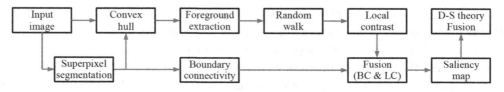

FIGURE 4.24 The diagram of algorithm flowchart.

4. Use K-means clustering algorithm to divide the whole image into multiple clusters, and optimize the saliency value of each superpixel by considering the influence of other superpixels in each cluster.

5. Use the boundary connectivity information in the image to calculate the background probability of superpixels in each region, the boundary connectivity here is defined as the ratio of the size of the region to the length of the boundary connecting the edge of the image.

6. Fusing boundary connectivity (BC) and local contrast (LC) to enhance saliency map continuity, and then suppressing the salient values of background super-pixels to produce saliency map.

7. Using weighted DS evidence theory to fuse pixel-level saliency detection algorithms to further obtain results closer to the ground truth.

4.6.2 Saliency Detection for Specific Types of Images

With the development of image acquisition technology, people have been able to obtain images of various modalities. Except the common RGB images, the depth images (Fan et al. 2021), thermal images (Jiang et al. 2021), video images (Lai et al. 2020), and depth images (Mu et al. 2020) are also widely available and (jointly) used in saliency detection.

Specific images have special properties. In saliency detection, on the one hand, specific attributes of specific images can be used to help the detection; on the other hand, special methods are also needed for treating specific images.

4.6.2.1 Saliency Detection in RGB-D Video

An RGB-D saliency detection model based on conditional random field under super-pixel is proposed, which takes the advantage of multi-modalities. Its overall framework is shown in Figure 4.25. Firstly, RGB cues, depth cues and motion cues are extracted for each frame of RGB-D video, and their corresponding saliency maps are obtained using these cues. Secondly, the **conditional random field (CRF)** model is established with the unit of super-pixels (for reducing computation and noise influence), and a global energy function is designed to combine multimodal saliency cues and consider the smoothing

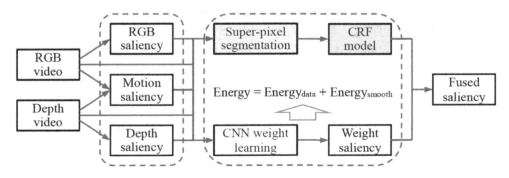

FIGURE 4.25 Overall framework of saliency detection model.

constraint of the saliency value among adjacent super-pixels. In order to make full use of the advantages of various modal saliency cues, a weight learning network based on **convolutional neural network (CNN)** is trained to learn the weight factors for each cue in the energy function. Finally, the conditional random field model and the learned weights are used to fuse the saliency maps to obtain the globally optimized saliency detection results.

From Figure 4.25, two stages can be distinguished: multimodal saliency map generation and multimodal saliency map fusion. In the first stage, the RGB saliency map is computed from RGB frame image, the depth saliency map is computed from D frame image, the motion saliency map is computed from the motion vector captured from the current and previous RGB and D frame images. For the second stage, Both RGB video and depth video, as well as the RGB, depth, and motion saliency maps are taken as input. From one side, they are used to construct the CRF model; from other side, they are used in CNN for weight learning.

In minimizing the energy function, two constraints are considered: data item energy constraint and smooth item energy constraint. Data item constraints the difference between the multi-modality saliency map and the final saliency label. Smooth item constraints the difference among nearby super-pixels.

4.6.2.2 Saliency Detection on Light Fields

Light field imaging technology can simultaneously record the position and direction information of light radiation in space (Adelson and Wang 1992) have gradually gained a lot of attention in recent years.

Traditional RGB color images cannot fully represent the human eye's perception of the world, because the general projected RGB image ignores the perception of the depth of the scene by the human binocular system. Depth information can distinguish objects located at different depth layers and reduce background interference (Wolfe and Horowitz 2004). The **RGB-D image** mentioned in the above Sub-section is the combination of RGB color image and depth image.

However, there are still two problems for using RGB-D images in saliency detection:

1. The robust of saliency detection algorithm based on RGB-D images relies heavily on the quality of the depth map. When the quality of the depth map is poor, the effective information for saliency detection are hardly provided;

2. Saliency detection algorithms based on RGB-D images often ignore the correlation between depth and appearance, when the salient objects have similar color and depth to the background, the accuracy of salient object detection will be greatly affected.

There are five types of images can be converted from light field data:

1. Micro-lens Image: It records the direction information of the light in the 4-D light field.

2. Sub-aperture image: It is an image taken of light rays passing through a sub-aperture of the main lens. The main lens can be divided into multiple sub-apertures, so the light field sensor can capture multiple sub-aperture images with different viewing angles.

3. Epipolar plane image (EPI): It is a light field image composed of straight lines projected from all points in the 3-D scene space.

4. Focus stack image: It is a series of sharply focused focal stack sequences at different depth planes obtained using the digital refocusing technique of the light field.

5. All-in-focus image: It is an image obtained by fusing all the in-focus regions in multiple focus stack images focused at different depths in which all object points are in sharp focus.

Compared with RGB images and RGB-D images, the images obtained from light field data contains more information, such as the color, intensity, position, and direction of light, so it can better reflect the geometry and reflection characteristics of natural scenes.

For the saliency detection task, compared with RGB images and RGB-D images, using light field image for saliency detection has the following advantages:

1. Both position information and angular information are included, which provides multi-view geometric information for obtaining scene depth information;

2. When using digital refocusing technology (Ng et al. 2005), a series of focal stack images focused at different depth layers can be obtained by synthesizing light field data. Individual salient object are usually located in the same depth plane. Using the focal clues of these focal stack images, it is possible to provide background cues for more complete detection of salient objects;

3. The light field data records light information in different directions, which can describe the scene from multiple angles, providing effective salient object occlusion information;

4. An all-focus image can be generated from the light field data, and each pixel in the all-focus image is clear, with clearer colors, textures, etc.

It can be seen that in saliency object detection, the light field saliency (LFS) detection algorithms based on light field image, compared with the algorithms based on RGB image or the algorithms based on RGB-D image, can provide more information for saliency detection and a way to solve the complex detection problems, such as the problem to deal with similar foreground and background, the problem of partially occluded salient objects, and the problem in clutter scenes with multiple salient objects.

In general, LFS detection can be divided into saliency detection based on human designed features and saliency detection based on learning. The former is based on the idea of contrast, which detects saliency regions by calculating the feature difference

TABLE 4.2 Classification of light field saliency detection algorithms

Category	Main Sub-categories and Their Concise Descriptions
Based on human designed features	Based on color and texture contrast: The color image is divided into superpixels, the RGB color features between the superpixels are calculated, and the directional filter is used to extract the texture features, so as to calculate the saliency of color and texture;
	Based on background probability of focus stack: A focus map was generated by detecting the focal region of each stack image using a series of band-pass filters. The background probability is calculated using a U-shaped filter on the focus map, and then the object cue is calculated using a Gaussian filter for salient object detection.
	Based on depth contrast: The center position of the object is calculated on the depth map, and then a Gaussian filter is applied in the focus stack according to the center position of the object to obtain the object-guided depth map, which is combined with the color or texture contrast information to obtain the final depth saliency map.
	Based on location priors: Implicit prior computes spatial similarity using the normalized center coordinate distance of two superpixels. Explicit prior measures the center deviation by the distance between the center coordinates of the superpixel and the image center coordinates, and uses the background prior to enhance the salient regions of the center deviation and suppress the non-salient regions.
	Based on multi-feature fusion: Various cues can be fused, such as foreground cues, color contrast cues, depth cues, focus cues, etc. Different fusion techniques have been applied, such as linear weighted fusion, least squares fusion, two-stage Bayesian fusion, random search based fusion, depth guided fusion, etc.
Based on learning	Based on sparse coding: The feature description vector of each pixel in the image is calculated, and the sparse coding framework is constructed to input the initial saliency dictionary, and the final saliency map is obtained through the optimization of dictionary.
	Based on deep convolutional networks: With the help of deep convolutional network, it is possible to learn for constructing nonlinear image representation hierarchy and extracting high-level semantic concepts. In addition, learning can be performed by combining the spatial characteristics and multi-view characteristics of light field data, or by introducing recursive attention model, or by creating memory-oriented light field, or by launching a deep light field driving method for saliency detection.

between each pixel or superpixel and other pixels or superpixels. The latter uses image feature encoding or the powerful feature learning ability of convolutional networks to obtain salient regions.

Table 4.2 provides some brief descriptions for the various classes of light field saliency detection.

Recent developments are most in the second category. One saliency detection framework (Li et al. 2015) called **weighted sparse coding (WSC)** belongs to the subcategory "Based on sparse coding" in Table 4.2. Its schematic diagram is shown in Figure 4.26. It can handle many different types of image data, such as 2-D RGB image, 3-D RGB-D image, and 4-D light field data.

In this framework, the feature description vector of each pixel in the image is firstly calculated, including the color and texture features of the RGB image, the depth value or disparity value feature of the RGB-D image, and the focus feature of the 4-D light field data. Then, according to the feature vector of the pixel, two feature matrices are

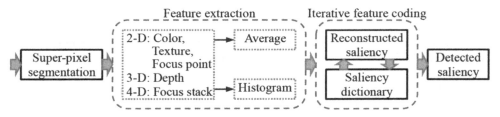

FIGURE 4.26 Schematic diagram of weighted sparse coding framework.

generated for all superpixels by calculating the vector mean (convert per-pixel feature vector to per-superpixel feature vector through averaging) and histogram over three color channels (to handle texture), and the sparse coding framework is constructed. In the following, the initial saliency dictionary is input into the sparse coding framework, and the saliency dictionary is optimized in an iterative manner. When the dictionary no longer changes, the iteration is terminated and the final saliency map is obtained.

Another saliency detection method (Zhang et al. 2020) belongs to the sub-category "Based on deep convolutional networks" in Table 4.2. This method deeply explores the positive effects of the spatial characteristics and multi-view characteristics of light field data on saliency detection, overcomes the shortcomings of light field saliency detection methods that deal with depth and color information independently, and effectively utilizes the complementarity of depth and color information.

It has been experimentally determined that the angular changes are consistent with the viewpoint variations of micro-lens images, and the effective angular changes of each pixel may increase depth selectivity and the ability for accurate saliency detection. So, a model angular changes (MAC) module is proposed in this method, trying to using convolution module to take the advantage of the relationship between viewing angle and location information through the treating of the angular information in micro-lens images. Finally, the saliency detection can be obtained by prediction. Its schematic diagram is shown in Figure 4.27.

In Figure 4.27, the MAC lock is a basic computational unit operating on a micro-lens image array input and producing an output feature map. The motivation of the MAC block is to model angular changes at one-pixel location in an explicit manner. Three different MAC block variant architectures to process light field micro-lens image arrays are used, they are MAC block-9 × 9, MAC block-3 × 3, and MAC block-star shaped (for atrous angular convolutional kernels to capture long-range angular features) with four directions (0°, 45°, 90°, 135°) to transfer the light field inputs to feature maps in different ways.

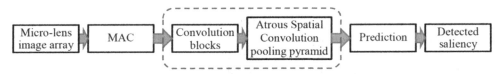

FIGURE 4.27 Schematic diagram of saliency detection method with convolution module.

REFERENCES

Achanta, R., A. Shaji, K. Smith, et al. 2012. SLIC superpixels compared to state-of-the-art superpixel methods. *IEEE Transactions on Pattern Analysis and Machine Intelligence*, 34(11): 2274–2282.

Adelson, E.H., and Wang J.Y.A. 1992. Single lens stereo with a plenoptic camera. *IEEE Transactions on Pattern Analysis and Machine Intelligence*, 14(2): 99–106.

Chen, B.C., X. Tao, H. Chen, et al. 2020. Saliency detection via fusion of boundary connectivity and local contrast. *Chinese Journal of Computers*, 43(1): 16–28.

Cheng, M.M., N.J. Mitra, and X.L. Huang, et al. 2015. Global contrast based salient region detection. *IEEE Transactions on Pattern Analysis and Machine Intelligence*, 37(3): 569–582.

Duncan, K., and S. Sarkar. 2012. Saliency in images and video: A brief survey. *IET Computer Vision*, 6(6): 514–523.

Fan, D.P., L. Zheng, Z. Zhang, et al. 2021. Rethinking RGB-D salient object detection: Models, data sets, and large-scale benchmarks. *IEEE Transactions on Neural Networks and Learning Systems*, 32(5): 2075–2089.

Huang, X.M., and Y.-J. Zhang. 2017. 300-FPS salient object detection via minimum directional contrast. *IEEE Transactions on Image Processing*, 26(9): 4243–4254.

Huang, X.M., and Y.-J. Zhang. 2018. Water flow driven salient object detection at 180 fps. *Pattern Recognition*, 76: 95–107.

Huang, X.M., Y. Zheng, and J.Z. Huang, et al. 2018. A minimum barrier distance based saliency box for object proposals generation. *IEEE Signal Processing Letters*, 25(8): 1126–1130.

Huang, X.M., Y. Zheng, and J.Z. Huang, et al. 2020. 50 FPS Object-level saliency detection via maximally stable region. *IEEE Transactions on Image Processing*, 29: 1384–1396.

Itti, L., C. Koch, and E.A. Niebur. 1998. Model of saliency based visual attention for rapid scene analysis. *IEEE Transactions on Pattern Analysis and Machine Intelligence*, 20(11): 1254–1259.

Jiang, T.T., Y. Liu, X. Ma, et al. 2021. Multi-path collaborative salient object detection based on RGB-T images. *Journal of Image and Graphics*, 26(10): 2388–2399.

Lai, Q.X., W.G. Wang, H.Q. Sun, et al. 2020. Video saliency prediction using spatiotemporal residual attentive networks. *IEEE Transactions on Image Processing*, 29: 1113–1126.

Li, N.Y., B.L. Sun, and J.Y. Yu. 2015. A weighted sparse coding framework for saliency detection. *Proceedings of the CVPR*, 5216–5223.

Luo, H.L., P. Yuan, and K. Tong. 2021. Review of the methods for salient object detection based on deep learning. *Acta Electroninc Sinica*, 49(7): 1417–1427.

Mu, H.W., M.M. Wang, J. Han, et al. 2020. Survey of depth sensitive information extraction in stereo vision perception. *Laser & Optoelectronics Progress*, 57(12): #120003.

Ng, R., M. Levoy, M. Brédif, et al. 2005. Light field photography with a hand-held plenoptic camera. *Stanford University and Duval Design*, 1–11.

Perazzi, F., P. Krahenbuhl, and Y. Pritch, et al. 2012. Saliency filters: Contrast based filtering for salient region detection. *Proceedings of the CVPR*, 733–740.

Rother, C., V. Kolmogorov, and A. Blake. 2004. "GrabCut": Interactive foreground extraction using iterated graph cuts. *ACM Transactions on Graphics*, 23(3): 309–314.

Stentiford, F.W.M. 2003. An attention based similarity measure with application to content based information retrieval. *Proceedings of the Storage and Retrieval for Media Databases*, 5021: 221–232.

Strand, R., K.C. Ciesielski, and F. Malmberg, et al. 2013. The minimum barrier distance. *Computer Vision and Image Understanding*, 117(4): 429–437.

Tang, H.M., M.Y. Bai and L.Y. Han. 2021. Image saliency detection based on background constraint of low rank and multi-cue propagation. *Journal of Electronics & Information Technology*, 43(5): 1432–1440.

Tu, W., S. He, and Q. Yang, et al. 2016. Real-time salient object detection with a minimum spanning tree. *Proceedings of the CVPR*, 2334–2342.

Vincent, L. 1993. Morphological grayscale reconstruction in image analysis: Applications and efficient algorithms, *IEEE Transactions on Image Processing*, 2(2): 176–201.

Viola, P., and M. Jones. 2001. Rapid object detection using a boosted cascade of simple features. *Proceedings of the CVPR*, 511–518.

Wei, Y., F. Wen, and W. Zhu, et al. 2012. Geodesic saliency using background priors. *Proceedings of the ECCV*, 29–42.

Wolfe, J.M., and T.S. Horowitz. 2004. What attributes guide the deployment of visual attention and how do they do it? *Nature Reviews Neuroscience*, 5(6): 495–501.

Zhang, J., Y.M. Liu, S.P. Zhang, et al. 2020. Light field saliency detection with deep convolutional networks. *IEEE Transactions on Image Processing*, 29: 4421–4434.

Zhang, J., S. Sclaroff, and Z. Lin, et al. 2015. Minimum barrier salient object detection at 80 FPS. *Proceedings of the ICCV*, 1404–1412.

Zhang, Y.-J. 2017. *Image Engineering, Vol. 2: Image Analysis*. Germany: De Gruyter.

Zhu, W., S. Liang, and Y. Wei, et al. 2014. Saliency optimization from robust background detection. *Proceedings of the CVPR*, 2814–2821.

CHAPTER 5

Motion Analysis

I n order to analyze the change information or moving objects in the image, it is ne- cessary to use an image sequence. An image sequence is composed of a series of 2-D (spatial) images that are continuous in time, or is a special type of 3-D image, which can be represented as $f(x, y, t)$. Compared with the still image $f(x, y)$, the time variable t is added here. When t takes a certain value, one frame of image in the sequence is obtained. The *video* is a sequence of images with regular changes in t (usually 20 to 30 times per second).

Unlike a single image, the continuously collected image sequence can reflect the movement of the scenery in the scene and the change of the scene. On the other hand, objective things are always in constant motion and change, motion is absolute, and stillness is relative. Therefore, an image is a special case of an image sequence. The changes of the scene and the movement of the scene are more obvious and clear appearing in the sequence images (also called dynamic images).

The analysis of the motion in the image sequence is not only based on the analysis of the objects in the still images, but also needs to be expanded in technology, changed in means, and broadened in purpose.

The contents of each section of this chapter are arranged as follows.

Section 5.1 introduces the contents of motion analysis research, including motion detection, motion object location and tracking, and motion object segmentation and analysis, as well as stereo scene reconstruction and motion/scene understanding.

Section 5.2 discusses motion detection, especially the detection of moving objects. It mainly introduces the technology and effect of background modeling and the calculation of optical flow field and its role in motion analysis; it also gives the detection status of some specific motion modes.

Section 5.3 discusses the segmentation of moving objects in sequence images. First, it analyzes the relationship between moving object segmentation and motion information extraction, and then introduces the dense optical flow algorithm based on brightness gradient as well as the ideas and methods of moving object segmentation based on parameters and models.

DOI: 10.1201/b23131-5

Section 5.4 introduces the typical techniques of motion tracking, including Kalman filter, particle filter, mean-shift and kernel tracking techniques, and tracking strategies using sub-sequence decision making.

Section 5.5 provides a brief introduction to some technique developments and promising research directions in the last year.

5.1 MOTION ANALYSIS RESEARCH CONTENTS

Compared with texture and shape, the concept of motion is more intuitive and clear, but there are more categories of motion. The research purposes and work contents of motion analysis can include the following:

1. Motion detection

Motion detection refers to detecting whether there is motion (including global and local motions) information in the scene. In this case, only a single fixed camera is generally sufficient. A typical example is security surveillance, where any factors that cause changes in the image must be taken into consideration. Of course, because the changes caused by the light are often slower and the changes caused by the movement of the object are often faster, it can be further distinguished.

2. Motion object location and tracking

The focus here is to find whether there is a motion object in the scene; if there is an object, what position and posture it is currently in (***motion object location***); it can further include determining the trajectory of the motion object, and predicting its next movement direction and trend and future motion status (***motion object tracking***), etc. In this case, it is generally possible to use only a single fixed camera (multiple cameras are often used in recent years). In practice, it can be that the camera is stationary and the object is moving or the camera is moving and the object is stationary. The most complicated thing is that both are moving. Different technologies can be used according to different study purposes. If only the location of the motion object needs to be determined, a motion-based segmentation method can be adopted, that is, a preliminary segmentation of the motion object with the help of motion information. If it is necessary to determine the movement direction and trajectory of the motion object, predict the trend of the movement, etc., then the object tracking technology will be often used to match the image data and object features, or the motion object is represented as a graph structure and the graph is matched.

The locating of motion objects is often regarded as synonymous with motion object detection, but the location focuses more on the object position rather than the characteristics of the object itself. There are often some assumptions in object location: (i) Maximum speed: if the location of the motion object in the previous frame of the video is known, the location in the current frame will be centered at the position of the previous frame and the maximum speed is the radius of the circle; (ii) small acceleration: the change of the object motion speed is limited, and there is some predictability; (iii) mutual correspondence: the rigid object maintains a stable pattern in the image sequence, and the object point in the scene corresponds to the point on the image; (iv) co-movement: if there are multiple object points, their motion modes are related (movement similarity).

3. Motion object segmentation and analysis

This is more demanding than the above requirements. It is necessary to accurately detect the movement of the objects, extract the objects, obtain their characteristics and motion parameters, analyze the motion law, determine the type of motion, and so on. In this case, it is often necessary to use a video camera to obtain sequence images to distinguish between global and local motions in the scene. It is often necessary to obtain the 3-D characteristics of the object, or to further identify the category of the motion objects.

4. 3-D scene reconstruction and movement/scene understanding

Further calculate the depth/distance of the 3-D scene through the acquired object motion information, determine the orientation of the surface and the covering/occlusion condition, etc. on the other hand. integrating motion information and information in other images can be used to determine motion causality. If further scene knowledge is available, it is possible also to explain the scene and movement. In this case, two or more stationary or moving cameras are often used. The relevant contents will be introduced in the image understanding book.

5.2 MOTION OBJECT DETECTION

The detection of motion information is the basis of the detection of motion objects. The two types of techniques introduced here are more suitable for the detection of motion objects.

5.2.1 Background Modeling

Background modeling is a general idea for motion detection, which can be achieved with the help of different technical means, so it is also regarded as a general term for a class of motion detection methods.

5.2.1.1 Basic Principles

To find the motion information in the scene, an intuitive method is to compare the current frame image that needs to be detected with the original background without motion information. The different parts represent the result of the motion. Consider a simple situation first. There is a motion object in a fixed scene (background), then in the captured video, there will be a difference in the corresponding position between the previous and next frame images due to the motion of the object. Therefore, the motion object can be detected and located by using the method of calculating the difference between the previous and current frame images.

Calculating the difference image is a simple and fast motion detection method, but the effect is not good enough in many cases. This is because when calculating the difference image, all environmental fluctuations (background clutter), lighting changes, camera shake, etc. are all detected together with the object movement (especially if the first frame is always used as the reference frame, the problem is more serious). So, only in very strictly controlled occasions (such as the environment and background are unchanged), the real object movement could be separated.

A more reasonable motion detection idea is not to regard the background as completely unchanged, but to calculate and maintain a dynamic (satisfying a certain model) background frame as a reference. This is the basic idea of **background modeling**.

A simple background modeling method mainly includes the following steps:

1. Get the previous N frames of images of the current frame, and determine their average value or median value at each pixel as the current background value;

2. Obtain the $N + 1$-th frame image, calculate the difference between the frame image and the current background at each pixel (thresholding this difference can eliminate or reduce noise);

3. Use a combination of smoothing or morphological operations to eliminate very small regions in the difference image and fill the holes in the large regions. The remaining regions represent the motion objects in the scene;

4. Update the average value or median value in combination with the $N + 1$-th frame;

5. Return to Step (2) and consider the next frame.

This method of maintaining the background based on the average value or median value of N frame periods is relatively simple and has a small amount of calculation, but the effect is not reliable when there are multiple objects in the scene at the same time or the object movement is slow.

5.2.1.2 Typical Practical Methods

Several typical practical background modeling methods are introduced below. They all divide the motion object detection procedure into two steps: model training and actual detection. Through training, a mathematical model is established for the background, and the built model is used in the detection to eliminate the background to obtain the foreground (object).

1. Methods based on a single Gaussian model

The method based on the **single Gaussian model** believes that the gray value or color value of the pixel in the video sequence obeys the Gaussian distribution. Specifically, for each fixed pixel position, calculate the mean μ and variance σ of all the pixel values at that position in the training image sequence of N frames, and thus uniquely determine a (single) Gaussian background model. In the motion detection, the background sub-traction method is used to calculate the difference between the values of the pixels in the current frame image and the background model, and then the difference is compared with the threshold T (usually three times the variance) that is, according to $|\mu_T - \mu| \le 3\sigma$ can judge the pixel as foreground or background.

This model is relatively simple, but requires stricter application conditions. For ex-ample, it is required that the light intensity does not change significantly for a long time, and the shadow of the moving foreground in the background during the detection period is small. Its disadvantage is that it is more sensitive to changes in light intensity, which will cause the model to be invalid (both the mean and variance are changed); when there is a motion object in the scene, because there is only one model, it cannot be separated from the static background, which may cause a larger false alarm rate.

2. Methods based on video initialization

In the case that the background in the training sequence is static but there is a motion object, if the background value on each pixel can be extracted first, the static background and the motion object can be separated, then the background modeling can be performed, and overcome the aforementioned problems. This process can also be seen as a *video initialization*; that is, initializing the training video before the background modeling, so as to eliminate the influence of the motion foreground on the background modeling.

Specifically, a minimum length threshold T_l can be set for N frames of training images containing moving foregrounds, and the sequence of length N at each pixel position can be intercepted to obtain several sub-sequences with relatively stable pixel values and length greater than T_l $\{L_k\}$, $k = 1, 2, \ldots$. Among them, a sequence with a longer length and a smaller variance is selected as the background sequence.

Through this initialization, the situation where the background is static but there is a moving foreground in the training sequence is transformed into a situation where the background is static and there is no moving foreground in the training sequence. After converting the background modeling problem when there is a moving foreground in a static background into a background modeling problem with no moving foreground in a static background, the aforementioned method based on the single Gaussian model can still be used for background modeling.

3. Methods based on Gaussian mixture model

When there is movement in the background in the training sequence, the method based on the single Gaussian model does not work well. At this time, a more robust and effective method is to model each pixel with a mixed Gaussian distribution, that is, to introduce a *Gaussian mixture model (GMM)* to model multiple states of the background separately. In this way, according to which state the data belongs to, the model para-meters of the state are updated accordingly to solve the background modeling problem under the motion background. According to local properties, some Gaussian distributions here represent the background and some Gaussian distributions represent the foreground. The following algorithm can distinguish them.

The basic method based on the Gaussian mixture model is to read N frames of training images in sequence, and iteratively model each pixel each time. Suppose a pixel has grayscale f (t) at time t, $t = 1, 2, \ldots, f(t)$ can be K (K is the maximum number of models allowed per pixel) Gaussian distribution $N(\mu_k, \sigma_k^2)$ to (mixed) modeling, where $k = 1, \ldots, K$. When the scene changes, the Gaussian distribution will change with time, so it is a function of time, which can be written as

$$N_k(t) = N[\mu_k(t), \sigma_k^2(t)] \quad k = 1, \ldots, K \tag{5.1}$$

The choice of K mainly considers the calculation efficiency, which is usually 3–7.

Set an initial standard deviation at the beginning of training. When a new image is read in, the pixel values of the image are used to update the original background model. Add a weight $w_k(t)$ to each Gaussian distribution (the sum of all weights is 1), so that the probability of observing $f(t)$ is

$$P[f(t)] = \sum_{k=1}^{K} w_k(t) \frac{1}{\sqrt{2\pi}} \exp \left[\frac{-[f(t) - \mu_k(t)]^2}{\sigma_k^2(t)} \right] \tag{5.2}$$

The EM algorithm can be used to update the parameters of the Gaussian distribution, but the amount of calculation is often very large. The simple method is to compare each pixel with the Gaussian function. If it falls within 2.5 times the variance of the mean, it is considered a match, that is, the pixel is considered to be suitable for the model, and its pixel value can be used to update the mean and variance of the model. If the number of current pixel models is less than K, a new model is established for this pixel. If there are multiple matches, the best one can be taken.

If a match is found, for the Gaussian distribution l, it has

$$w_k(t) = \begin{cases} (1 - a) w_k(t - 1) & k \neq l \\ w_k(t - 1) & k = l \end{cases} \tag{5.3}$$

Then renormalize w again. In the equation, a is a learning constant, and $1/a$ determines the speed of parameter change. The parameters used to match the Gaussian function can be updated as follows:

$$\mu_k(t) = (1 - b)\mu_l(t - 1) + bf(t) \tag{5.4}$$

$$\sigma_k^2(t) = (1 - b)\sigma_l^2(t - 1) + b[f(t) - \mu_k(t)]^2 \tag{5.5}$$

where

$$b = aP[f(t)|\mu_l, \sigma_l^2] \tag{5.6}$$

If no match is found, the Gaussian distribution corresponding to the lowest weight can be replaced with a new Gaussian distribution with a mean $f(t)$. Compared with other $K-1$ Gaussian distributions, this new Gaussian distribution has higher variance and lower weight, and is more likely to become part of the local background. If K models have been judged and none of them meet the conditions, the model with the smallest weight is replaced with the new model. The mean value of the new model is the value of the pixel, and then an initial standard deviation is set. Do this until all training images have been trained.

After the above steps, the Gaussian distribution that is most likely to be assigned to the pixel's current gray level can be determined, and then whether it belongs to the foreground or the background can be determined. This can be made with the help of a constant B corresponding to the entire observation process. Assume that the proportion of background pixels is greater than B in all frames. Based on this, all Gaussian distributions can be sorted by $w_k(t)/\sigma_k(t)$, and the first value of the sort indicates either a large weight, a small variance, or both. These situations correspond to situations where a given pixel is likely to belong to the background.

4. Codebook-based method

In the codebook-based method, each pixel is represented by a codebook, a codebook can contain one or more code words, and each code word represents a state (Kim et al. 2004). The **codebook** was originally generated by learning a set of training frame images. There is no restriction on the content of the training frame image, which can include a moving foreground or a moving background. Next, using a time domain filter to filter out the code words representing the moving foreground in the codebook, and retain the code words representing the background; then using a spatial filter to filter out the code words that are incorrectly filtered by the time domain filter (representing the rare background) is restored to the codebook to reduce the false alarms of sporadic foreground in the background region. Such a codebook represents a compressed form of the background model of a video sequence.

5.2.1.3 Examples of Effect
Background modeling is a training-testing process. Firstly, a background model is trained using some of the beginning frames in the image sequence, and then this model is used to test the subsequent frames, and motion is detected based on the difference between the current frame image and the background model. In the simplest case, the background in the training sequence is static and there is no moving foreground. More complicated situations include: the background in the training sequence is static, but there is a moving foreground; the background in the training sequence is not static, but there is no moving foreground. The most complicated situation is that the background in the training sequence is not static, but there is also a moving foreground. Some experimental effects of the above-mentioned background modeling methods in the first three cases are given below (Li et al. 2006).

The experimental data comes from three sequences in an open general video library (Toyama et al. 1999), with a total of 150 frames, and the resolution of each color image is 160×120. In the experiment, for each test image, the binary reference result is first given with the help of image editing software, and then the above-mentioned background modeling methods are used for object detection, and the binary detection result is obtained. For each sequence, select ten frames of images, compare the detection results with the reference results, and count the average detection rate (the ratio of the number of detected foreground pixels to the number of true foreground pixels) and the average false alarm rate (the detected foreground pixels do not belong to the foreground to the number of pixels detected as foreground).

1. The result when there is no moving foreground in the static background

Figure 5.1 shows a set of images of experimental results. In the video sequence used, there is only a ***static background*** in the initial scene, and people who enter the scene later are to be detected. Figure 5.1(a) is a scene after a person enters, Figure 5.1(b) shows the corresponding reference results, and Figure 5.1(c) shows the detection results obtained by the method based on the single Gaussian model. The detection rate of this method is only 0.473, and the false alarm rate is 0.0569. It can be seen from Figure 5.1(c) that there are many pixels in the waist and hair of the human body (all in the lower gray and relatively consistent region) that have not been detected, and there are some sporadic false detection points on the background.

2. The result when there is a moving foreground in a static background

Figure 5.2 shows a set of images of experimental results. In the video sequence used, there are people in the initial scene, and then they leave, and the people who have left the scene are to be detected. Figure 5.2(a) is a scene when a person is leaving, Figure 5.2(b) shows the corresponding reference results, Figure 5.2(c) shows the results obtained by the method based on video initialization, and Figure 5.2(d) shows the results obtained by the method based on codebook.

Comparing the two methods, the codebook-based method has a higher detection rate and a lower false alarm rate than the video initialization-based method. This is because

(a)   (b)   (c)

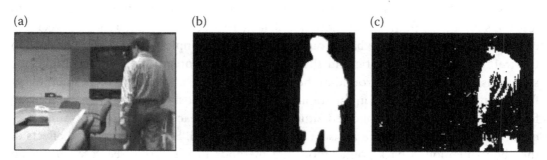

FIGURE 5.1   Result when there is no moving foreground in the static background.

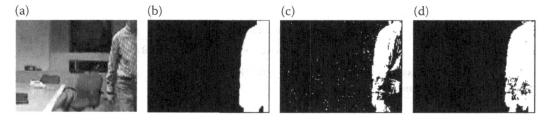

FIGURE 5.2   Result when there is moving foreground in the static background.

TABLE 5.1   Statistical results of background modeling when there is a moving foreground in a static background

Methods	Detection Rate	False Alarm Rate
Video initialization-based	0.676	0.051
Codebook-based	0.880	0.025

the codebook-based method establishes multiple code words for each pixel, thereby improving the detection rate; at the same time, the spatial filter used in the detection process reduces the false alarm rate. The specific statistics are shown in Table 5.1.

3. The result when there is no moving foreground in the moving background

Figure 5.3 shows a set of images of experimental results. In the video sequence used, the tree is shaking in the initial scene, and the person entering the scene is to be detected. Figure 5.3(a) is a scene after a person enters, Figure 5.3(b) shows the corresponding reference results, Figure 5.3(c) shows the results obtained using the method based on the Gaussian mixture model, and Figure 5.3(d) shows the result obtained using the method based on the codebook.

Comparing the two methods, the method based on the Gaussian mixture model and the method based on the codebook both have more models designed for background motion, and therefore both have higher detection rates (the detection rate of the former is slightly higher than the latter). Since the former has no processing steps corresponding to the latter's spatial filter, the false alarm rate of the former is higher than that of the latter. The specific statistics are shown in Table 5.2.

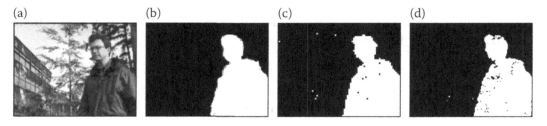

FIGURE 5.3   Result when there is no moving foreground in the moving background.

TABLE 5.2 The statistical results of background modeling when there is a moving foreground in the moving background

Methods	Detection Rate	False Alarm Rate
Gaussian mixture model	0.951	0.017
Codebook-based	0.939	0.006

Finally, it needs to be pointed out that the method based on the single Gaussian model is relatively simple, but it is less applicable, and can only be used when there is no moving foreground under a static background. Other methods try to overcome the limitations of the method based on the single Gaussian model, but their common problem is that if the background needs to be updated, the entire background model needs to be recalculated instead of a simple iterative update of parameters.

5.2.2 Optical Flow Field

The movement of the scenery in the scene will cause the scenery in the image obtained during the movement to be at different relative positions. This difference in position can be called **parallax**, which corresponds to the displacement vector (including size and direction) reflected by the scene movement on the image. If you divide the parallax by the time difference, you get the velocity vector (also called the instantaneous displacement vector). All velocity vectors (which may be different) in an image form a vector field, which can also be called an **optical flow field** in many cases.

5.2.2.1 Optical Flow Equation

Suppose a specific image point is at (x, y) at time t, and the image point moves to $(x + dx, y + dy)$ at time $t + dt$. If the time interval dt is small, it can be expected (or assumed) that the gray level of the image point remains unchanged, in other words there is

$$f(x, y, t) = f(x + dx, \ y + dy, \ t + dt) \tag{5.7}$$

Expand the right side of the above equation with Taylor series, set $dt \rightarrow 0$, take the limit and omit the higher-order terms to get:

$$-\frac{\partial f}{\partial t} = \frac{\partial f}{\partial x}\frac{dx}{dt} + \frac{\partial f}{\partial y}\frac{dy}{dt} = \frac{\partial f}{\partial x}u + \frac{\partial f}{\partial y}v = 0 \tag{5.8}$$

where u and v are the moving speed of the image point in the X and Y directions, respectively, and they form a speed vector:

$$f_x = \partial f/\partial x \quad f_y = \partial f/\partial y \quad f_t = \partial f/\partial t \tag{5.9}$$

Then, the **optical flow equation** can be obtained as

$$[f_x, \ f_y] \bullet [u, \ v]^{\mathrm{T}} = -f_t \tag{5.10}$$

The optical flow equation shows that the change rate of grayscale with time of a certain point in a moving image is the product of the change rate of spatial grayscale of that point and the spatial motion speed of that point in space.

In practice, the change rate of grayscale with time can be estimated by the first-order difference average along the time direction:

$$f_t \approx \frac{1}{4}[f(x, y, t+1) + f(x+1, y, t+1) + f(x, y+1, t+1) + f(x+1, y+1, t+1)]$$

$$- \frac{1}{4}[f(x, y, t) + f(x+1, y, t) + f(x, y+1, t) + f(x+1, y+1, t)] \qquad (5.11)$$

The change rate of spatial grayscale can be estimated by the average values of the first-order difference along the X and Y directions:

$$f_x \approx \frac{1}{4}[f(x+1, y, t) + f(x+1, y+1, t) + f(x+1, y, t+1) + f(x+1, y+1, t+1)]$$

$$- \frac{1}{4}[f(x, y, t) + f(x, y+1, t) + f(x, y, t+1) + f(x, y+1, t+1)] \qquad (5.12)$$

$$f_y \approx \frac{1}{4}[f(x, y+1, t) + f(x+1, y+1, t) + f(x, y+1, t+1) + f(x+1, y+1, t+1)]$$

$$- \frac{1}{4}[f(x, y, t) + f(x+1, y, t) + f(x, y, t+1) + f(x+1, y, t+1)] \qquad (5.13)$$

5.2.2.2 Least Square Method for Optical Flow Estimation

After substituting Equation (5.11)–Equation (5.13) into Equation (5.10), the least squares method can be used to estimate the optical flow components u and v. Take N pixels at different positions on the same object with the same u and v on two consecutive images f (x, y, t) and $f(x, y, t+1)$, let $\hat{f}_t^{(k)}, \hat{f}_x^{(k)}, \hat{f}_y^{(k)}$ represent the estimations of f_t, f_x, f_y at the k-th position ($k = 1, 2, \ldots, N$), respectively, let

$$\mathbf{f}_t = \begin{bmatrix} -\hat{f}_t^{(1)} \\ -\hat{f}_t^{(2)} \\ \vdots \\ -\hat{f}_t^{(N)} \end{bmatrix} \quad \mathbf{F}_{xy} = \begin{bmatrix} \hat{f}_x^{(1)} & \hat{f}_y^{(1)} \\ \hat{f}_x^{(2)} & \hat{f}_y^{(2)} \\ \vdots & \vdots \\ \hat{f}_x^{(N)} & \hat{f}_y^{(N)} \end{bmatrix} \qquad (5.14)$$

Then the **least squares estimations** of u and v:

$$[u \quad v]^{\mathrm{T}} = \left(\mathbf{F}_{xy}^{\mathrm{T}}\mathbf{F}_{xy}\right)^{-1}\mathbf{F}_{xy}^{\mathrm{T}}\mathbf{f}_t \qquad (5.15)$$

An example of optical flow detection is shown in Figure 5.4. Figure 5.4(a) is a side image of a sphere with a pattern, and Figure 5.4(b) is an image obtained by rotating the sphere

(a)   (b)   (c)

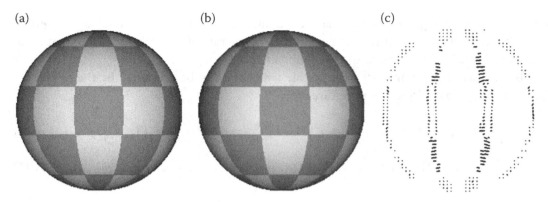

FIGURE 5.4   Optical flow detection example.

(around the vertical axis) to the right by a small angle. The movement of the sphere in the 3-D space reflected in the 2-D image is basically a translational movement, so in the optical flow detected in Figure 5.4(c), the parts with larger optical flow are distributed along the meridian, reflecting the horizontal movement result of the edge.

5.2.2.3 Optical Flow in Motion Analysis

The image difference can be used to obtain the motion trajectory, and the optical flow cannot be used to obtain the motion trajectory. However, information useful for image interpretation can be obtained via optical flow. Optical flow analysis can be used to solve a variety of motion problems, such as camera stationary object moving, camera moving object stationary, and both are moving.

The motion in the dynamic image can be regarded as a combination of the following four basic motions. The detection and recognition of them by optical flow can be carried out based on their characteristics with the help of some simple operators.

1. Translation with a constant distance from the camera (with different directions): a group of parallel motion vectors is formed, see Figure 5.5(a).

2. The translation along the line of sight in the depth direction relative to the camera (symmetric in all directions): a set of vectors with the same focus of expansion (FOE, see below) are formed, see Figure 5.5(b).

(a)   (b)   (c)   (d)

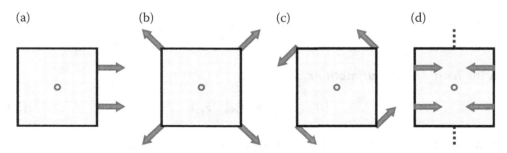

FIGURE 5.5   Recognition of motion form.

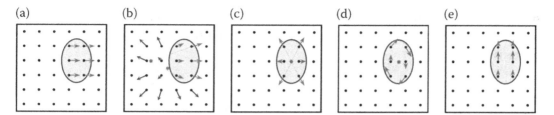

FIGURE 5.6   Interpretation of optical flow field.

3. Rotate equidistantly around the line of sight: a group of concentric motion vectors is produced, see Figure 5.5(c).

4. The rotation of the plane object orthogonal to the line of sight: one or more groups of vectors starting from the straight line are constituted, see Figure 5.5(d).

The optical flow field reflects the movement in the scene. Figure 5.6 gives some examples of optical flow fields and their explanations (the length of the arrow corresponds to the speed of movement). Only one object in Figure 5.6(a) moves to the right; Figure 5.6(b) corresponds to the camera moving forward (into the paper), at this time the fixed object in the scene seems to start outward from the *focus of expansion (FOE)* in divergent. In addition, there is a horizontal movement object that has its own focus of expansion. Figure 5.6(c) corresponds to an object moving in the direction of a fixed camera, and its focus of expansion is in its contour (if the object moves away from the camera, it appears to leave each *focus of contraction (FOC)*). Figure 5.6(d) corresponds to a situation where an object rotates around the line of sight of the camera; while Figure 5.6(e) corresponds to a situation where an object rotates around a horizontal axis orthogonal to the line of sight, the feature points on the object appear to move up and down (its contour may oscillate).

A lot of information can be obtained by analyzing motion using optical flow, such as:

1. Mutual speed

The optical flow representation can be used to determine the mutual velocity T between the camera and the object. Let the mutual velocities in the X, Y, and Z directions of the world coordinate system be $T_X = u$, $T_Y = v$, $T_Z = w$, where Z gives information about the depth ($Z > 0$ represents a point in front of the image plane). If the coordinates of an object point at $t_0 = 0$ are (X_0, Y_0, Z_0), then the coordinates of the image of that point (set the focal length of the optical system to 1 and the object moving speed is constant) at time t is

$$(x, y) = \left(\frac{X_0 + ut}{Z_0 + wt}, \frac{Y_0 + vt}{Z_0 + wt} \right)$$ (5.16)

2. Focus of expansion

Next, use the optical flow to determine the focus of expansion of the 2-D image. Assuming that the movement is towards the camera, when $t \rightarrow -\infty$, the movement starting at an infinite distance from the camera can be obtained. The movement proceeds along a straight line towards the camera, and the starting point on the image plane is

$$(x, y)_{\text{FOE}} = \left(\frac{u}{w}, \quad \frac{v}{w} \right) \tag{5.17}$$

Note that this same equation can also be used for $t \to \infty$, when the motion is in the opposite direction. Any change in the direction of motion will result in changes of the speed u, v, w, and the position of the focus of expansion on the image.

3. Collision distance

Assuming that the origin of the image coordinates moves along the direction $S = (u/w, v/w, 1)$, and the trajectory in the world coordinate system is a straight line; that is

$$(X, Y, Z) = t\,S = t \left(\frac{u}{w}, \quad \frac{v}{w}, \quad 1 \right) \tag{5.18}$$

where t represents time. Let X represent (X, Y, Z), the position of the camera closest to the world point X is

$$X_c = \frac{S(S \cdot X)}{S \cdot S} \tag{5.19}$$

When the camera is moving, the minimum distance between it and the world point X is

$$d_{\min} = \sqrt{(X \cdot X) - \frac{(S \cdot X)^2}{S \cdot S}} \tag{5.20}$$

In this way, a **collision** occurs when the distance between a point camera and a point object is less than $d_{\min}$.

5.2.3 Detection of Specific Motion Patterns

In many applications, certain specific **motion patterns** need to be determined. In this case, image-based information and motion-based information can be used in combination. Motion information can be obtained by determining the specific difference between images that are acquired sequentially. Generally, in order to improve the accuracy and use the spatial distribution information, the image is often divided into blocks, and then two moving image blocks with a time difference (one collected at time t and one collected at time $t + \delta t$) are considered. The movement direction can be calculated by using the following four kinds difference images:

$$U = |f_t - f_{t+\delta t\uparrow}|$$
$$D = |f_t - f_{t+\delta t\downarrow}|$$
$$L = |f_t - f_{t+\delta t\leftarrow}|$$ $$(5.21)$$
$$R = |f_t - f_{t+\delta t\rightarrow}|$$

where the arrow represents the direction of image movement, such as $\downarrow$ represents the image frame $I_{t+\delta t}$ moves downward relative to the previous frame I_t.

The amplitude of the motion can be obtained by summing the area of the image block, and this sum can be quickly calculated with the help of the integral image below.

Integral image (integral map) is a matrix representation method that maintains the global information of the image (Viola and Jones 2001). In the integral image, the value I (x, y) at the position (x, y) represents the sum of all the pixel values at the upper left of the positions in the original image $f(x, y)$:

$$f(x, y) = \sum_{p \leq x,\, q \leq y} f(p, q) \qquad (5.22)$$

The construction of the integral image can be carried out by scanning the image only once with the aid of a loop:

1. Let $s(x, y)$ represent the cumulative sum of a row of pixels, $s(x, -1) = 0$;

2. Let $I(x, y)$ be an integral image, $I(-1, y) = 0$;

3. Scan the entire image line by line, and calculate the cumulative sum $s(x, y)$ of the line and the integral image $I(x, y)$ for each pixel (x, y) with the help of a loop:

$$s(x, y) = s(x, y - 1) + f(x, y) \qquad (5.23)$$

$$I(x, y) = I(x - 1, y) + s(x, y) \qquad (5.24)$$

4. When the pixel in the lower-right corner is reached after a line-by-line scan of the entire image, the integral image $I(x, y)$ is constructed.

As shown in Figure 5.7, the sum of any rectangle can be calculated with the help of four reference arrays. For rectangle D, there is

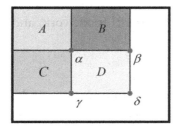

FIGURE 5.7 Schematic diagram of integral image calculation.

(a) (b) (c) (d)

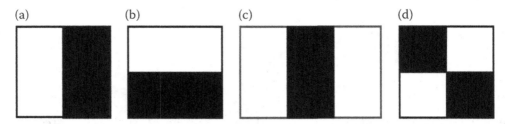

FIGURE 5.8 Haar rectangle feature in integral image calculation.

$$D_{\text{sum}} = I(\delta) + I(\alpha) - [I(\beta) + I(\gamma)] \tag{5.25}$$

where $I(\alpha)$ is the value of the integral image at point α, that is, the sum of pixel values in rectangle A; $I(\beta)$ is the sum of pixel values in rectangles A and B, and $I(\gamma)$ is the sum of pixel values in rectangles A and C. $I(\delta)$ is the sum of pixel values in rectangles A, B, C, and D. Therefore, the calculation that reflects the difference between the two rectangles requires eight reference arrays. In practice, a lookup table can be established, and calculations can be completed with the help of the lookup table.

The **Haar rectangle features** commonly used in object detection and tracking, as shown in Figure 5.8, can be quickly calculated by subtracting the shaded rectangle from the unshaded rectangle with the help of the integral image. For Figure 5.8(a) and Figure 5.8(b), we only need to look up the table six times; for Figure 5.8(c), we only need to look up the table eight times; and for Figure 5.8(d), we only need to look up the table nine times.

5.3 MOTION OBJECT SEGMENTATION

Detecting moving objects from an image sequence and segmenting them can be regarded as a space segmentation problem. For example, the segmentation of video images is mainly to detect independent moving regions (objects) in each frame. In order to solve the problem of space segmentation, you can use the time domain information in the image sequence (changes in inter-frame grayscale, etc.), or use the spatial information in the image sequence (changes in intra-frame grayscale, etc.), or use both at the same time.

5.3.1 Object Segmentation and Motion Information Extraction

The segmentation of motion objects and the extraction of regional motion information are closely related. Two strategies are commonly used: (i) Segmenting objects and then extracting motion information, and (ii) extracting motion information and then segmenting objects. There are also methods of obtaining the motion vector field and segmenting the motion region at the same time. These methods are usually related to the **Markov random field** and the **maximum posterior probability (MAP)** framework, and thus generally require a considerable amount of calculation.

5.3.1.1 Calculate Motion Information after Performing Segmentation

Performing object segmentation first and then calculating its motion information can be regarded as a direct segmentation method, which is mainly to directly use the grayscale and gradient information of the spatial-temporal image for segmentation. One method is to use the grayscale or color information (or other characteristics) of the motion region to segment the video frame image into different regions, and then use the motion vector field for each motion region to estimate the affine motion model parameters of the region. The advantage of this method is that the edges of the object region can often be better preserved. The disadvantage is that for relatively complex scenes, it often causes over-segmentation, because the same moving object may be composed of multiple different regions.

Another method is to first fit the entire change region to a parametric model according to the least mean square criterion, and then divide this region into small sub-regions for successive inspections. This hierarchical structure method includes the following steps:

1. Using the change detector to initialize the segmentation mask that can separate the changed and non-change regions.

2. Estimating a different parameter model for each spatially connected change region.

3. Using the parameters calculated in Step (2) to divide the image into a motion region and a background, the specific method is to track the pixels in the changing region in the next frame of the image (reverse the motion vector), if thus obtained pixels in the previous frame of image are also in the changing region, so the pixels in the changing region in the next frame of image can be considered as moving pixels; otherwise, it is classified as the background.

4. Verify the reliability of the model parameters corresponding to the pixels in the motion region based on the calculation of the difference between the frame images. If the corresponding parameter vector is unreliable, these regions are recorded as independent objects. Then return to Step (2), and repeat the detection until the parameter vector of each region does not change within the region.

5.3.1.2 Calculate Motion Information before Performing Segmentation

Calculating the motion information and then segmenting the object can be regarded as an indirect segmentation method. The commonly used method is to first estimate the optical flow field between two or more frames of images, and then perform segmentation based on the optical flow field. In fact, if the motion vector field of the whole image in the video frame can be calculated first, then it can be used for segmentation. According to the assumption that the entire scene is composed of a series of planes that can be represented by a 2-D or 3-D motion model, after obtaining the dense motion optical flow field, the Hough transform and split-merge process can be used to divide the motion field into different regions. In addition, the motion vector field can also be regarded as a Markov random field, and the maximum posterior probability and the simulated annealing algorithm of global optimization can be used to obtain the segmentation result. Finally, *K*-means clustering can also be used to segment the motion vector field. Segmentation on the basis of the motion vector field can ensure that the boundary of the segmented region is a position with a large difference in motion vector, which is the so-called motion boundary. For pixels of different colors or textures, as long as their motion vectors are similar, they will still be divided into the same region. This reduces the possibility of excessive segmentation, and the result is more in line with people's understanding of motion objects.

5.3.2 Dense Optical Flow Algorithm

In order to accurately calculate the local motion vector field, a ***dense optical flow algorithm based on brightness gradient*** (also called Horn-Schunck algorithm) (Ohm et al. 2000) can be used, which gradually approximates the motion vector of each pixel between adjacent frame images through an iterative method.

5.3.2.1 Solving the Optical Flow Equation

The dense optical flow algorithm is based on the optical flow equation. It can be seen from the optical flow equation; that is, in Equation (5.10) there is one equation for each pixel but two unknown quantities (u, v), so solving the optical flow equation is an ill-conditioned problem, it needs to add additional constraints to transform it into a solvable problem (Zhang 2017). Here, the optical flow equation solving problem can be transformed into an optimization problem by introducing optical flow error and velocity field gradient error. First, define the optical flow error e_{of} as the part of the motion vector field that does not conform to the optical flow equation, namely:

$$e_{of} = \frac{\partial f}{\partial x} u + \frac{\partial f}{\partial y} v + \frac{\partial f}{\partial t} \tag{5.26}$$

Obtaining the motion vector field is to minimize the sum of squares of e_{of} in the entire frame image; that is, the meaning of minimizing e_{of} is to make the calculated motion vector conform to the constraints of the optical flow equation as much as possible. In addition, define the velocity field gradient error e_s^2 as

$$e_s^2 = \left(\frac{\partial u}{\partial x}\right)^2 + \left(\frac{\partial u}{\partial y}\right)^2 + \left(\frac{\partial v}{\partial x}\right)^2 + \left(\frac{\partial v}{\partial y}\right)^2 \tag{5.27}$$

The error e_s^2 describes the smoothness of the optical flow field. The smaller the e_s^2, the closer the optical flow field is to smoothness. Therefore, the meaning of minimizing e_s^2 is to make the entire motion vector field as smooth as possible. The dense optical flow algorithm considers two constraints at the same time, hoping to find the optical flow field (u, v) that minimizes the weighted sum of the two errors in the entire frame, namely:

$$\min_{u,v(x,y)} \int_A [e_{of}^2(u, v) + \alpha^2 e_s^2(u, v)] \, dxdy \tag{5.28}$$

In the formula, A represents the image area and α is the relative weight of the optical flow error and the smoothing error, which is used to strengthen or weaken the influence of the smoothness constraint in the calculation.

5.3.2.2 Problems with the Basic Algorithm

The basic dense optical flow algorithm may encounter some problems in practical applications.

1. Aperture problem

The **aperture problem** is a common problem. Local operators can be used to calculate the grayscale changes along with space and time in the image. The scope of the local operator is equivalent to the size of its mask, but because the size of the mask is limited, an aperture problem will arise.

Figure 5.9(a) shows an example of using a circular mask to detect motion. The size of the moving object is much larger than the mask size, so within the mask, only a solid line corresponding to an edge (in the first image) can be observed moving to the dotted line (in the second image). The motion of the edge can be described by the **dispalcement vector (DV)**. In the case of Figure 5.9(a), there are different possibilities for movement, and the DV can point from a point on the solid line to any point on the dotted line. If the DV is decomposed into two directions perpendicular to the edge and parallel to the edge, only the normal component of the DV (perpendicular to the edge) can be determined, while the component parallel to the edge cannot be determined. This ambiguity problem is the aperture problem.

If the corresponding points can be determined on the images before and after the motion, then it is possible to determine the DV without ambiguity. A typical example is that a corner point of the object is in the mask range of the local operator, as shown in Figure 5.9(b). In this case, the DV at the corner point can be completely determined, and the DVs at other points can also be determined according to the parallel relationship. But this situation also shows that it is only possible to obtain motion information at some sparse point positions with the help of local operators.

The aperture problem is caused by the inability to determine the corresponding points of the front and rear edges in the sequence of images, or there is no reason to distinguish different points on the same edge. From this perspective, the aperture problem can be regarded as a more general problem, that is, a special case of the corresponding problem.

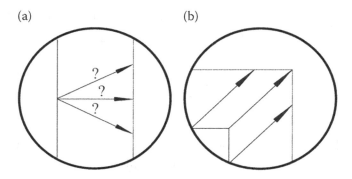

FIGURE 5.9   Aperture problem in motion analysis.

The aperture problem leads to a great increase in the amount of calculation to solve the optical flow equation. Due to the aperture problem, at strong spatial edges, the motion vector still tends to follow the normal direction of the edge, and it takes multiple iterations to propagate the motion information of the neighboring region to the local region to form a correct motion vector. Such multiple iterations make the computation loads of dense optical flow algorithm often very large. Generally, the extraction of motion information based on this algorithm can only be done off-line and non-real-time processing.

2. Approximation error problem

When the motion in the scene is violent and the motion vector has a large amplitude (the global motion vector usually has a large amplitude), the optical flow error will also be relatively large, resulting in a large error in the optimized result according to Equation (5.28).

An improvement to the dense optical flow algorithm is to replace the optical flow error term e_{of} with the displacement frame difference term $f(x + \bar{u}_n, y + \bar{v}_n, t + 1) - f(x, y, t)$, and use the average gradient term:

$$f_x = \frac{1}{2}\left[\frac{\partial f}{\partial x}(x + \bar{u}_n, y + \bar{v}_n, t + 1) + \frac{\partial f}{\partial x}(x, y, t)\right] \tag{5.29}$$

$$f_y = \frac{1}{2}\left[\frac{\partial f}{\partial y}(x + \bar{u}_n, y + \bar{v}_n, t + 1) + \frac{\partial f}{\partial y}(x, y, t)\right] \tag{5.30}$$

to replace the partial derivatives $\partial f/\partial x$ and $\partial f/\partial y$, respectively, and to better approximate larger motion vectors. In practical implementation, if the position of the pixel point does not coincide with the coordinate, the displacement frame difference value and the average gradient value need to be calculated by interpolation, such as using bilinear interpolation to interpolate from four adjacent pixels.

Using the displacement frame difference term and average gradient term obtained above, the motion vector increment in the $n + 1$-th iteration can be calculated by the following two formulas:

$$\Delta u(x, y, t)_{n+1} = -f_x \frac{[f(x + \bar{u}_n, y + \bar{v}_n, t + 1) - f(x, y, t)]}{\alpha^2 + f_x^2 + f_y^2} \tag{5.31}$$

$$\Delta v(x, y, t)_{n+1} = -f_y \frac{[f(x + \bar{u}_n, y + \bar{v}_n, t + 1) - f(x, y, t)]}{\alpha^2 + f_x^2 + f_y^2} \tag{5.32}$$

Finally, because the dense optical flow algorithm uses the global smoothness constraint, the motion vector at the boundary of the motion object will be smoothed into a gradual transition, which will blur the motion object boundary. The following first discusses how to use global motion information to perform motion compensation to obtain motion vectors caused by local objects; then it discusses how to use an algorithm based on region growing to overcome the problem of blurring of boundaries due to dense optical flow algorithms; that is, the problem of good segmentation result cannot be obtained by edge-based segmentation algorithms.

5.3.2.3 Global Motion Compensation

Based on the parameters of global motion caused by the camera motion, the global motion vector can be recovered according to the estimated motion parameters, so that the global motion vector is compensated first in the dense optical flow algorithm, and then the motion vector caused by local object can be gradually approached by iteration (Yu and Zhang 2002a).

In the actual calculation process, the **global motion vector** of each pixel is first calculated from the estimated global motion model, and then combined with the current **local motion vector** as the initial value input for the next iteration. The specific steps are as follows:

1. Set the initial local motion vector $(u_l, v_l)_0$ of all points in the image to zero;

2. Calculate the global motion vector (u_g, v_g) of each point according to the global motion model;

3. Calculate the actual motion vector of each pixel

$$(\bar{u}_n, \bar{v}_n) = (\bar{u}_g, \bar{v}_g) + (\bar{u}_l, \bar{v}_l)_n \tag{5.33}$$

   where $(\bar{u}_l, \bar{v}_l)_n$ is the average value of the local motion vector in the pixel neighborhood after the n-th iteration;

4. Calculate the correction value $(\Delta u, \Delta v)_{n+1}$ of the motion vector at this point according to Equation (5.31) and Equation (5.32);

5. If the magnitude of $(\Delta u, \Delta v)_{n+1}$ is greater than a certain threshold T, then let

$$(u_l, v_l)_{n+1} = (u_l, v_l)_n + (\Delta u, \Delta v)_{n+1} \tag{5.34}$$

and go to Step (3); otherwise, end the calculation.

Figure 5.10 shows the comparison between the calculation results of the direct block matching method (without motion compensation) and the improved dense optical flow iterative algorithm with global motion compensation. For the same original image, Figure 5.10(a) is superimposed with the motion vector field calculated by the block matching method, and Figure 5.10(b) is superimposed with the motion vector estimated by the global motion (the global smoothness constraint causes the motion boundary less obvious, and the magnitude of the motion vector is small). Figure 5.10(c) superimposes the local motion vector calculated by the dense optical flow iterative algorithm with

(a)　　　　　　　　　　(b)　　　　　　　　　　(c)

FIGURE 5.10 Comparison of the calculation results of the direct block matching method and the improved dense optical flow iterative algorithm.

global motion compensation. It can be seen from these figures that the effect of global motion in the results of the block matching method has been successfully compensated, and the erroneous motion vectors in the low-texture background region have also been eliminated, so that the motion vectors in the final result are all concentrated in the players and the ball that are moving upwards, which are more in line with the local motion contents in the scene.

5.3.3 Segmentation Based on Parameters and Models

The basic principles of the segmentation method based on parameters and models are as follows. Assuming that there are K independent motion objects in the image, each optical flow vector calculated from this corresponds to the projection of an opaque object in the 3-D space by rigid body motion. In this way, each independent motion object can be accurately described by a set of mapping parameters. On the other hand, there are K groups of parameter vectors, and each group defines an optical flow vector at each pixel. The optical flow vector defined by the mapping parameters can be called model-based or synthesized optical flow vector, so that there are K synthesized optical flow vectors at each pixel. According to this analysis, dividing the optical flow field of the image to obtain different motion regions can be regarded as assigning a composite optical flow vector label to the estimated optical flow vector at each pixel. The problem here is that the number of classes K and the mapping parameters of each group are not known in advance. If a special value is set for K, then when the estimated optical flow vectors corresponding to each category are known, the mapping parameters can be calculated in the sense of the minimum mean square error. In other words, the mapping parameters need to be known to determine the segmentation label, and the segmentation label needs to be known to determine the mapping parameter. This shows that an iterative method can be used for segmentation.

5.3.3.1 With the Help of the Hough Transform

If the optical flow is regarded as a feature of the region, the segmentation can be performed with the help of the Hough transform. The ***Hough transform*** can also be regarded as a clustering technique. Here, the most representative clusters are found by "voting" according to the selected features in the feature space. Because a plane that moves according to a rigid body generates an affine flow field under orthogonal projection, a method of directly using the Hough transform to segment the optical flow is to use a linear 6-parameter affine flow model:

$$v_1 = a_1 + a_2 x_1 + a_3 x_2$$
$$v_2 = a_4 + a_5 x_1 + a_6 x_2$$

(5.35)

where $a_1 = V_1 + z_0 R_2$; $a_2 = z_1 R_2$; $a_3 = z_2 R_2 - R_3$; $a_4 = V_2 - z_0 R_1$; $a_5 = R_3 - z_1 R_1$; $a_6 = -z_2 R_1$. Note that V_1 and V_2 are the components of the translational velocity vector; R_1, R_2, and R_3 are the components of the angular velocity vector; and z_0, z_1, and z_2 are plane coefficients. If the optical flows at three or more points are known, then the a_1, a_2, a_3, a_4, a_5, a_6 can be solved. After determining the maximum and minimum values of each parameter, the 6-D feature space can be quantified to a certain parameter state. In this way, each optical flow vector $v(x) = [v_1(x)\ v_2(x)]^T$ can be used to vote for a set of quantized parameters to minimize:

$$\eta^2(\mathbf{x}) = \eta_1^2(\mathbf{x}) + \eta_2^2(\mathbf{x})$$

(5.36)

where $\eta_1(x) = v_1(x) - a_1 - a_2 x_1 - a_3 x_2$; $\eta_2(x) = v_2(x) - a_4 - a_5 x_1 - a_6 x_2$. Obtaining a parameter set that exceeds a predetermined number of votes is likely to represent the candidate's motion, so that the number of classes K used to mark each optical flow vector and the corresponding parameter set can be determined.

The disadvantage of the above-mentioned direct method is that the amount of calculation is too large (the dimension of the parameter space is high). To solve this problem, a two-step algorithm based on *improved Hough transform* can be used. In the first step, a set of similar optical flow vectors is composed of elements consistent with a single parameter set. There are many ways to simplify the calculation, including: (i) Divide the parameter space into two non-coincident sets $\{a_1, a_2, a_3\} \times \{a_4, a_5, a_6\}$ to perform two Hough transforms; (ii) using the multi-resolution Hough transform, at each resolution level, the parameter space is quantized according to the estimation obtained in the previous stage; (iii) using multiple Hough transforms, the optical flow vector that is most consistent with the candidate parameters is first combined all togther. Then in the second step, the most consistent elements obtained in the first step are combined in the sense of least mean square to form related segments. Finally, if there are still uncombined optical flow vectors, they are attributed to adjacent segments.

To sum up, the improved Hough transform first aggregates the optical flow vectors into groups, each of which coincides with the moving small plane, and then these groups are fused into segments according to specific criteria to form the final objects.

5.3.3.2 With the Help of the Region Growing

If the optical flow is regarded as the feature of the region, the segmentation can also be carried out with the help of *region growing* (Yu and Zhang 2002b). It is assumed here that the motion objects in the scene are composed of a series of plane regions with different motion characteristics. Different regions can be represented by regional motion models with different affine parameters (Ekin et al. 2000; Ohm et al. 2000). The 6-parameter affine model of Equation (5.35) is a first-order approximate model for complex region motion. In addition to representing the translational motion of the region, it can also approximate the rotation and deformation of the region.

The two keys of the region growing algorithm are the selection of seed points and the determination of the criteria for region growing (see Sub-section 2.2.4). The difference between these two criteria can greatly affect the results of segmentation. Considering that all points in the segmented region should meet the same affine motion model as much as possible, the region growing criterion here is to judge whether the motion vector of the neighboring points to be grown can still be represented by the affine motion model of the region. In other words, whether the motion vector satisfies the affine motion model is used as the consistency criterion of the region. This judgment can be obtained by calculating the difference between the motion vector of the point and the motion vector estimated by the regional affine motion model. If the difference is greater than a certain threshold, the growing will not continue. The selection of seed points can be done according to certain sorting criteria, such as sequential selection, random selection, etc. (Yu and Zhang 2001). Since both sequential selection and random selection may select seed points where there are moving edges, if growing is performed at these seed points, a more complete consistency region cannot be obtained. For this reason, consider sorting the seed points according to the difference between the motion vectors of each current point and all points in the neighborhood. This difference $D_m(x, y)$ is defined as

$$D_m(x, y) = \sum_{(x',y')\in A} \sqrt{[u(x, y) - u(x', y')]^2 + [v(x, y) - v(x', y')]^2} \qquad (5.37)$$

where A is the neighborhood (for example, 4-neighborhood or 8-neighborhood) of the point (x, y). The smaller the value of $D_m(x, y)$, the greater the probability that the point (x, y) is located in a smooth region. Every time a seed point is selected, the point with the smallest $D_m(x, y)$ but not included in any region is selected. Such seed points are always in the middle of the smooth region, which can ensure a relatively complete growing result. In practice, in order to reduce the amount of calculation, the local motion vector can be set to 0 first; that is, the region without local motion is classified into non-motion region, so as to reduce the operation region of the segmentation algorithm.

The results obtained by the region growing algorithm are the positions of a series of motion regions and the corresponding affine motion model parameters. Figure 5.11 shows the results obtained by using the above algorithm to segment the motion vector field in Figure 5.10, except for the black regions in the figure. In the motion foreground regions, those with different colors indicate different motion model parameters.

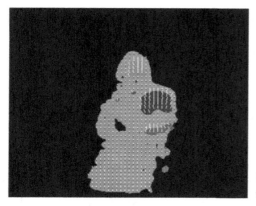

FIGURE 5.11 The segmentation result of motion vector field based on affine model.

5.4 MOTION OBJECT TRACKING

To track the motion object in the video is to detect and locate the same object in each frame of the video image. The following difficulties are often encountered in practical applications: (i) The object and the background are similar, and it is not easy to capture the difference between the two; (ii) the appearance of the object itself changes over time, on the one hand there are some non-rigid objects, and their appearances will inevitably change with time; on the other hand, changes in external conditions such as light will also cause the appearance of the object to change over time, whether the object is a rigid body or a non-rigid body; (iii) the change of the spatial position between the object and the background during the tracking process may cause the object to be tracked to be occluded and the (complete) object information cannot be obtained. In addition, tracking must take into account both the accuracy of object positioning and the real-time nature of the application.

Motion object tracking often combines the positioning and representation of the object (this is mainly a bottom-up process that needs to overcome the effects of object appearance, orientation, lighting and scale changes) with trajectory filtering and data fusion (this is a top-down process, it is necessary to consider the movement characteristics of the object, the use of various *a priori* knowledge and movement models, as well as the promotion and evaluation of the movement hypothesis).

5.4.1 Typical Technology

Moving object tracking can use many different methods, including contour-based tracking, region-based tracking, mask-based tracking, feature-based tracking, and motion information-based tracking. Tracking based on motion information is also divided into tracking using the continuity of motion information and tracking using the method of predicting the object position in the next frame to reduce the search range. Several commonly used techniques are introduced below, among which Kalman filter and particle filter are both methods to reduce the search range.

5.4.1.1 Kalman Filter

When tracking an object in the current frame, it is often desirable to be able to predict its position in the subsequent frames, so that the previous information can be utilized to the greatest extent and the least search can be performed in the subsequent frames. In addition, prediction is also helpful to solve the problems caused by short-term occlusion (Davies 2005). To this end, it is necessary to continuously update the position and speed of the tracked object points:

$$\mathbf{x}_i = \mathbf{x}_{i-1} + \mathbf{v}_{i-1} \tag{5.38}$$

$$\mathbf{v}_i = \mathbf{x}_i - \mathbf{x}_{i-1} \tag{5.39}$$

Here you need to obtain three quantities: the original position, the optimal estimated value of the corresponding variable (model parameter) before the observation (plus the mark −), and the optimal estimated value of the corresponding variable after the observation (plus the mark +). In addition, noise needs to be considered. If m represents the noise of position measurement and n represents the noise of velocity estimation, the above two equations become

$$\mathbf{x}_i^- = \mathbf{x}_{i-1}^+ + \mathbf{v}_{i-1} + \mathbf{m}_{i-1} \tag{5.40}$$

$$\mathbf{v}_i^- = \mathbf{v}_{i-1}^+ + \mathbf{n}_{i-1} \tag{5.41}$$

When the speed is constant and the noise is Gaussian noise, the optimal solution is

$$\mathbf{x}_i^- = \mathbf{x}_{i-1}^+ \tag{5.42}$$

$$\sigma_i^- = \sigma_{i-1}^+ \tag{5.43}$$

They are called predictive equations, and

$$\mathbf{x}_i^+ = \frac{\mathbf{x}_i/\sigma_i^2 + (\mathbf{x}_i^-)/(\sigma_i^-)^2}{1/\sigma_i^2 + 1/(\sigma_i^-)^2} \tag{5.44}$$

$$\sigma_i^+ = \left[\frac{1}{1/\sigma_i^2 + 1/(\sigma_i^-)^2} \right]^{1/2} \tag{5.45}$$

They are called correction equations, where $\sigma^\pm$ is the standard deviation obtained by estimating $\mathbf{x}^\pm$ with the corresponding model, and σ is the standard deviation of the original measurement $\mathbf{x}$. Here is a brief explanation why the variances in Equation (5.45) are not combined in the usual way of addition. If there are multiple error sources all acting on the same data, these variances need to be added up. If each error source contributes the same amount of error, the variance needs to be multiplied by the number of error sources M. In the opposite case, if there are more data and the error source does not change, the variance needs to be divided by the total number of data points N. So there is a natural ratio M/N to control the total error. A small-scale correlation variance is used here to describe the results, so the variances are combined in a special way.

It can be seen from the above equation that repeated measurements can improve the estimation of position parameters and reduce errors based on them in each iteration.

Since the noise is modeled as the position, the positions earlier than i–1 can be ignored. In fact, many position values can be averaged to improve the accuracy of the final estimate, which will be reflected in the values of x_i^-, σ_i^-, x_i^+ and σ_i^+.

The above algorithm is called a **Kalman filter**, which is the best estimate of a linear system with zero mean Gaussian noise. However, since the Kalman filter is based on averaging processing, large errors will occur if there are outliers in the data. This problem occurs in most motion applications, so each estimate needs to be tested to determine if it is too far from the actual situation. Furthermore, this result can be generalized to multivariable and changeable speed (or even variable acceleration) situations. At this time, define a state vector including position, velocity and acceleration, and use linear approximation to proceed.

5.4.1.2 Particle Filter

The Kalman filter requires the state equation to be linear and the state distribution to be Gaussian. These requirements are not always met in practice. The **particle filter** is an effective algorithm for solving nonlinear problems. The basic idea is to use random samples (these samples are called "particles") propagated in the state space to approximate the posterior **probability distribution function (PDF)** of the system state, thereby obtaining the estimated values of system state. The particle filter itself represents a sampling method, with which a specific distribution can be approximated through a time structure. Particle filter is also called **sequence importance sampling (SIS)**, sequence Monte Carlo method, guided filter, etc. In the research of image technology, it is also called **conditional density diffusion (CONDENSATION)**.

Suppose a system has a state $X_t = \{x_1, x_2, \ldots, x_t\}$, where the subscript represents time. At time t, there is a probability density function that represents the possible situation of x_t, which can be represented by a group of particles (a group of sampling states), and the appearance of particles is controlled by its probability density function. In addition, there are a series of observations $Z_t = \{z_1, z_2, \ldots, z_t\}$ related to the probability of state X_t, and a Markov hypothesis that the probability of x_t depends on the previous state x_{t-1}, which can be expressed as $P(x_t|x_{t-1})$.

Conditional density diffusion is an iterative process. At each step, a set of N samples s_i with weight w_i are maintained, namely

$$S_t = \{(\mathbf{s}_{ti}, w_{ti})\} \quad i = 1, 2, \cdots, N \quad \sum_i w_i = 1 \tag{5.46}$$

Together, these samples and weights represent the probability density function of the state X_t given the observation Z_t. Unlike the Kalman filter, the distribution does not need to meet the constraints of single-mode, Gaussian distribution, etc., and it can be multimode. Now it is necessary to derive S_t from S_{t-1}.

The specific steps of particle filtering are as follows (Sonka et al. 2008):

1. Suppose a set of weighted samples $S_{t-1} = \{s_{(t-1)i}, w_{(t-1)i}\}$ at a known time t–1. Let the cumulative probability of weight be

$$c_0 = 0$$
$$c_i = c_{i-1} + w_{(t-1)i} \quad i = 1, 2, ..., N \tag{5.47}$$

2. Randomly select a number r in the uniform distribution between [0 1], and determine $j = \arg[\min_i(c_i > r)]$ to calculate the n-th sample in S_t. Diffusing the j-th sample in S_{t-1} is called importance sampling, that is, adding the most weight to the most probable sample.

3. Use the Markov property of x_t to derive s_{tn}.

4. Using observation Z_t to obtain $w_{tn} = p(z_t|x_t{=}s_{tn})$.

5. Return to Step (2) and iterate N times.

6. Normalize $\{w_{ti}\}$ so that $\Sigma_i w_i = 1$.

7. Output the best estimate of x_t:

$$\mathbf{x}_t = \sum_{i=1}^{N} w_{ti} \mathbf{s}_{ti} \tag{5.48}$$

An example of particle filter iteration is given below. Consider the 1-D case, where x_t and s_t are only scalar real numbers. Suppose that at time t, x_t has a displacement v_t and is affected by zero-mean Gaussian noise e, that is, $x_{t+1} = x_t + v_t + e_t$, $e_t \sim N(0, \sigma_1^2)$. Further assume that z_t is a Gaussian distribution centered on x, and the variance is σ_2^2. The particle filter needs to make N "guess" on x_1, and get $S_1 = \{s_{11}, s_{12}, ... , s_{1N}\}$.

Now let's generate S_2. Choose a s_j from S_1 (without considering the value of w_{1i}), let $s_{21} = s_j + v_1 + e$, where $e \sim N(0, \sigma_1^2)$. Repeat the above process N times to generate particles at $t = 2$. At this time, $w_{2i} = \exp[(s_{2i}{-}z_2)^2/\sigma_2^2]$. Renormalize w_{2i}, and the iteration ends. The estimate of x_2 thus obtained is $\Sigma_i^N w_{2i} s_{2i}$.

A more detailed description of the particle filter is as follows. The particle filter is a recursive (iterative) Bayesian method that uses a set of samples of the posterior probability density function at each step. With a large number of samples (particles), it will be close to the optimal Bayesian estimation. Let's discuss it with the help of the schematic process in Figure 5.12.

Consider the observations z_1 to z_k of an object in consecutive frames, corresponding to the obtained object states x_1 to x_k. At each step, the most likely state of the object needs to be estimated. Bayes' rule gives the posterior probability density:

$$p(\mathbf{x}_{k+1}|\mathbf{z}_{1:k+1}) = \frac{p(\mathbf{z}_{k+1}|\mathbf{x}_{k+1})p(\mathbf{x}_{k+1}|\mathbf{z}_{1:k})}{p(\mathbf{z}_{k+1}|\mathbf{z}_{1:k})} \tag{5.49}$$

where the normalization constant is

$$p(\mathbf{z}_{k+1}|\mathbf{z}_{1:k}) = \int p(\mathbf{z}_{k+1}|\mathbf{x}_{k+1})p(\mathbf{x}_{k+1}|\mathbf{z}_{1:k})d\mathbf{x}_{k+1} \tag{5.50}$$

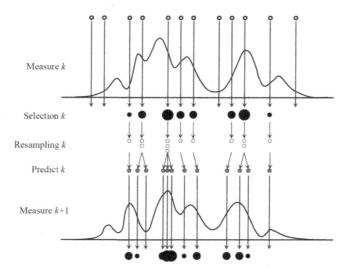

FIGURE 5.12   Schematic diagram of the whole process of particle filtering.

The prior probability density can be obtained from the last time:

$$p(\mathbf{x}_{k+1}|\mathbf{z}_{1:k}) = \int p(\mathbf{x}_{k+1}|\mathbf{x}_k)p(\mathbf{x}_k|\mathbf{z}_{1:k})d\mathbf{x}_k \tag{5.51}$$

Using the Markov hypothesis that is common in Bayesian analysis, this becomes

$$p(\mathbf{x}_{k+1}|\mathbf{x}_k, \ \mathbf{z}_{1:k}) = p(\mathbf{x}_{k+1}|\mathbf{x}_k) \tag{5.52}$$

That is, the transition probability required to update $x_k \rightarrow x_{k+1}$ depends only on $z_{1:k}$ indirectly.

There is no universal solution to the above equations, especially Equations (5.49) and (5.51), but constraint solutions are possible. For the Kalman filter, it is assumed that all posterior probability densities are Gaussian. If the Gaussian constraint does not hold, you need to use a particle filter.

To use this method, write the posterior probability density as the sum of the delta function samples:

$$p(\mathbf{x}_k|\ \mathbf{z}_{1:k}) \approx \sum_{i=1}^{N} w_k^i \delta(\mathbf{x}_k - \mathbf{x}_k^i) \tag{5.53}$$

Among them, the weight is normalized by the following formula:

$$\sum_{i=1}^{N} w_k^i = 1 \tag{5.54}$$

Substituting into Equation (5.49)–Equation (5.51), it gives

$$p\left(\mathbf{x}_{k+1}\middle|\ \mathbf{z}_{1:k+1}\right) \propto p\left(\mathbf{z}_{k+1}\middle|\ \mathbf{x}_{k+1}\right) \sum_{i=1}^{N} w_k^i p\left(\mathbf{x}_{k+1}\middle|\mathbf{x}_k^i\right) \qquad (5.55)$$

Although the above formula gives a discrete weighted approximation to the true posterior probability density, it is very difficult to directly sample from the posterior probability density. Therefore, this problem needs to use **sequence importance sampling (SIS)** to solve it with the help of a suitable "suggested" density function $q(x_{0:k}|z_{1:k})$. The importance density function is best decomposable:

$$q\left(\mathbf{x}_{0:k+1}\middle|\ \mathbf{z}_{1:k+1}\right) = q\left(\mathbf{x}_{k+1}\middle|\ \mathbf{x}_{0:k}\mathbf{z}_{1:k+1}\right) q\left(\mathbf{x}_{0:k}\middle|\ \mathbf{z}_{1:k}\right) \qquad (5.56)$$

Next, the weight update equation can be calculated:

$$w_{k+1}^i = w_k^i \frac{p\left(\mathbf{z}_{k+1}\middle|\ \mathbf{x}_{k+1}^i\right)p\left(\mathbf{x}_{k+1}^i\middle|\ \mathbf{x}_k^i\right)}{q\left(\mathbf{x}_{k+1}^i\middle|\ \mathbf{x}_{0:k}^i,\ \mathbf{z}_{1:k+1}\right)} = w_k^i \frac{p\left(\mathbf{z}_{k+1}\middle|\ \mathbf{x}_{k+1}^i\right)p\left(\mathbf{x}_{k+1}^i\middle|\ \mathbf{x}_k^i\right)}{q\left(\mathbf{x}_{k+1}^i\middle|\ \mathbf{x}_k^i,\ \mathbf{z}_{k+1}\right)} \qquad (5.57)$$

Among them, the path $xi_{0:k}$ and the observation $z_{1:k}$ are eliminated, which is necessary for the particle filter to iteratively track in a controllable manner.

Pure sequence importance sampling will make all but one particle become very small after a few iterations. A simple way to solve this problem is to resample for removing the small weights, and to replicate the doubling for enhancing the large weights. A basic algorithm for re-sampling is "systematic re-sampling", which includes the use of cumulative discrete probability distribution (CDF, in which the original delta function sampling is combined into a series of steps) and cutting between [0 1] to find the appropriate index for the new sample. As shown in Figure 5.13, this will result in the elimination of small samples and double the large samples. In the figure, regularly spaced horizontal lines are used to indicate the cuts required to find a suitable index (N) for the new sample. These cuts tend to ignore the small steps in the CDF and strengthen large samples by doubling.

The above result is called **sampling importance resampling (SIR)**, which is important for generating a stable set of samples. Using this special method, the importance density is selected as the prior probability density:

$$q\left(\mathbf{x}_{k+1}\middle|\mathbf{x}_k^i,\ \mathbf{z}_{k+1}\right) = p\left(\mathbf{x}_{k+1}\middle|\mathbf{x}_k^i\right) \qquad (5.58)$$

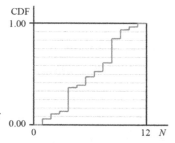

FIGURE 5.13 Use cumulative discrete probability distribution for systematic resampling.

then, substituting it back into Equation (5.57), a greatly simplified weight update equation is obtained:

$$w_{k+1}^i = w_k^i p(z_{k+1} | x_{k+1}^i) \tag{5.59}$$

Furthermore, since the index is resampled at each time, all previous weights wi_k take the value $1/N$. The above formula is simplified to

$$w_{k+1}^i \propto p(z_{k+1} | x_{k+1}^i) \tag{5.60}$$

5.4.1.3 Mean-Shift and Kernel Tracking

The mean-shift technique is a method of image segmentation through determining clusters. **Mean-shift** technology can also be used for motion object tracking. At this time, the region of interest corresponds to the tracking window, and a characteristic model of the tracked object needs to be established. The basic idea of using the mean-shift technique for object tracking is to continuously move the object model in the tracking window to search for the position with the largest correlation value. This is equivalent to moving the window to coincide (converge) with the center of gravity when determining the cluster center.

In order to track the object continuously from the previous frame to the current frame, the object model determined in the previous frame can be placed at the center position, x_c, of the local coordinate system of the tracking window, and the candidate object in the current frame is at the position y. The feature description of the candidate object can be described by the probability density function $p(y)$ estimated from the current frame data. The probability density function of the object model Q and the candidate object $P(y)$ is defined as

$$Q = \{q_v\} \quad \Sigma_{v=1}^m q_v = 1 \tag{5.61}$$

$$P(y) = \{p_v(y)\} \quad \Sigma_{v=1}^m p_v = 1 \tag{5.62}$$

where $v = 1, \ldots, m$, where m is the number of features. Let $S(y)$ be the similarity function between $P(y)$ and Q, namely

$$S(y) = S\{P(y), Q\} \tag{5.63}$$

For an object tracking task, the similarity function $S(y)$ is the likelihood that an object to be tracked in the previous frame is at the position y in the current frame. Therefore, the local extremum of $S(y)$ corresponds to the position of the object in the current frame.

To define the similarity function, an isotropic kernel can be used (Comaniciu et al. 2000), where the description of the feature space is represented by the kernel weight, then

$S(y)$ is a smooth function of y. If n is the total number of pixels in the tracking window and x_i is the position of the i-th pixel, the probability of the candidate object feature vector Q_v in the candidate window is estimated as

$$\hat{Q}_v = C_q \sum_i^n K(\mathbf{x}_i - \mathbf{x}_c)\delta[b(\mathbf{x}_i) - q_v] \tag{5.64}$$

Among them, $b(x_i)$ is the value of the feature function of the object at the pixel point x_i; the role of the δ function is to judge whether the value of x_i is the quantization result of the feature vector Q_v; $K(x)$ is a convex and monotonously decreasing kernel function; and C_q is the normalization constant

$$C_q = 1/\sum_{i=1}^n K(\mathbf{x}_i - \mathbf{x}_c) \tag{5.65}$$

Similarly, the probability of the feature model vector P_v of the candidate object $P(y)$ is estimated as

$$\hat{P}_v = C_p \sum_i^n K(\mathbf{x}_i - \mathbf{y})\delta[b(\mathbf{x}_i) - p_v] \tag{5.66}$$

where C_p is the normalization constant (which can be calculated in advance for a given kernel function), and

$$C_p = 1/\sum_{i=1}^n K(\mathbf{x}_i - \mathbf{y}) \tag{5.67}$$

The Bahattacharyya coefficient is usually used to estimate the degree of similarity between the object mask and the density of the candidate region. The more similar the distribution between the two densities, the greater the degree of similarity. The object center position is

$$\mathbf{y} = \frac{\sum_{i=1}^n \mathbf{x}_i w_i K(\mathbf{y} - \mathbf{x}_i)}{\sum_{i=1}^n w_i K(\mathbf{y} - \mathbf{x}_i)} \tag{5.68}$$

where w_i is the weighting coefficient. Note that the analytical solution of y cannot be obtained from Equation (5.68), so iterative method is needed to solve it. This iterative process corresponds to a process of finding the maximum value in the neighborhood. The characteristics of the **kernel tracking** method are: high operating efficiency, easy to modularize, especially for objects with regular movement and low speed, and new object center positions can always be obtained one by one, so as to achieve object tracking.

In the tracking of objects, in addition to tracking strategies and methods, the choice of object features is also very important (Liu and Zhang 2007). An example is given below, using the color histogram and the **edge orientation histogram (EOH)** to carry out the tracking under the frame of mean-shift, as shown in Figure 5.14. Figure 5.14(a) is a frame

(a)　　　　　　　　　(b)　　　　　　　　　(c)

(d)　　　　　　　　　(e)　　　　　　　　　(f)

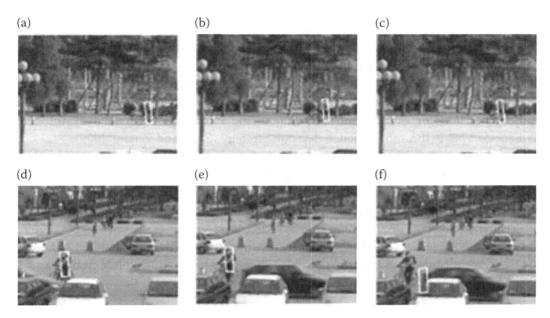

FIGURE 5.14　An example of using only one feature for tracking.

image in a video sequence, where the color of the object to be tracked is similar to the background. At this time, the color histogram does not work well (Figure 5.14(b)), but the edge orientation histogram can follow the object (Figure 5.14(c)). Figure 5.14(d) is an image in another video sequence, in which the edge orientation of the object to be tracked is not obvious. At this time, the color histogram can follow the object (Figure 5.14(e)), while the edge orientation histogram has no good effect (Figure 5.14(f)). It can be seen that the use of a feature alone will lead to the result of tracking failure under certain circumstances.

The color histogram mainly reflects the information inside the object, and the edge orientation histogram mainly reflects the information of the object contour. Combining these two features, it is possible to obtain a more general effect. Figure 5.15 gives an example of a car to be tracked. Due to changes in the size of the object, changes in the viewing angle of view, and partial occlusion of the object in the video sequence, the color or outline of the car has a certain changes over time. By combining the color histogram and the edge orientation histogram, the effect is better.

FIGURE 5.15　An example of combining two types of feature for tracking.

5.4.2 Sub-sequence Decision Strategy

The methods introduced in the previous sub-section are carried out frame by frame during object tracking. The possible problem is that there is less information to make a decision, and small errors may spread and cannot be controlled. An improved strategy is to divide the entire tracking sequence into several sub-sequences, and make a global optimal decision for each frame according to the information provided by the sub-sequences. This is the sub-sequence decision strategy (Shen and Zhang 2009).

Sub-sequence decision includes the following steps: (i) Dividing the input video into several sub-sequences; (ii) tracking in each sub-sequence; (iii) if adjacent sub-sequences overlap, then merge their results. The sub-sequence decision can also be regarded as the generation of the frame-by-frame decision. If each sub-sequence is just one frame, the sub-sequence decision becomes a frame-by-frame decision.

Let use S_i to denote the i-th subsequence, in which the j-th frame is denoted as $f_{i,j}$, and the entire S_i includes J_i frames. If the input video contains a total of N frames and is divided into M sub-sequences, then

$$S_i = \{f_{i,1}, f_{i,2}, \cdots f_{i,j}, \ldots, f_{i,J_i}\} \tag{5.69}$$

To ensure that any sub-sequence is not a subset of other sub-sequences, the following constraints are also defined:

$$\forall\, m, n \quad S_m \subseteq S_n \Leftrightarrow m = n \tag{5.70}$$

If $P_j = \{P_{j,\,k}\}$, $k = 1, 2, \ldots, K_j$ represents the K_j possible position states in the j-th frame, then the frame-by-frame decision can be expressed as

$$\forall\, P_{j,k} \in P_j \quad T(P_{j,k}) = \begin{cases} 1 & P_{j,k}\ \text{optimal} \\ -1 & \text{otherwise} \end{cases} \Rightarrow \text{output:}\ \arg_{P_{j,k}}[T(P_{j,k}) = 1] \tag{5.71}$$

while the sub-sequence decision can be expressed as

$$\forall\, P_{i,j,k} \in P_{i,1} \times P_{i,2} \times \cdots \times P_{i,j} \times \cdots \times P_{i,J_i} T_{\text{sub}}(P_{i,j,k})$$

$$= \begin{cases} 1 & P_{i,j,k}\ \text{optimal} \\ -1 & \text{otherwise} \end{cases} \Rightarrow \text{output:}\ \arg_{P_{i,j,k}}[T_{\text{sub}}(P_{i,j,k}) = 1] \tag{5.72}$$

For the subsequence S_i, it includes J_i frames in total, and there are K_j possible position states in each frame. If this optimal search problem is represented by a graph structure, it can be solved with the help of *dynamic programming* (search for an optimal path).

Figure 5.16 shows the results of three methods of tracking the object in the same video sequence (hand-held moving mouse, which moves fast and the color is similar to the background). The dark box or ellipse marks the last tracking results, light-colored boxes

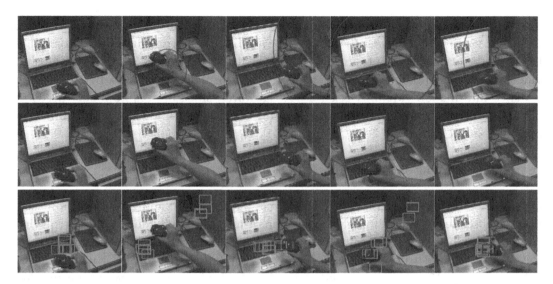

FIGURE 5.16   Results of different tracking methods and strategies.

mark candidate positions. The first line uses a method based on mean-shift technology, the second line uses a method based on particle filter technology, and the third line uses a method based on sub-sequence decision technology (only simple color histograms are used to help detect candidate positions). It can be seen from these figures that neither the method based on the mean-shift nor the method based on the particle filter can maintain continuous tracking, and only the method based on sub-sequence decision completes the entire tracking.

5.5 SOME RECENT DEVELOPMENTS AND FURTHER RESEARCH

In the following sections, some technical developments and promising research directions in the last few years are briefly overviewed.

5.5.1 Video Object Segmentation

Video object segmentation often refers to segmenting an object in subsequent video frames given the initial mask of this object in the first frame. In the semi-supervised approach, the initial mask can be obtained with some help of human-machine interaction.

5.5.1.1 Classification of Methods

A large number of methods have been developed. Different schemes for their categorization exist. One classification for these methods is divided them into three categories: online learning-based methods, offline learning-based methods, and tracking-based methods. Some examples are as follows (Li 2021):

1. Online learning-based methods

Online learning-based methods can effectively improve the discriminative ability of video object segmentation models. For example, online learning methods can be used to tune segmentation networks to distinguish objects from background and distractors. ***One-shot video object segmentation (OSVOS)*** is one such segmentation network fine-tuned on the first frame of a test video (Caelles et al. 2017). OSVOS-S (semantic one-shot video object segmentation) further enhances the performance of OSVOS by introducing instance information (Maninis et al. 2019). However, since the online model needs to update the weights of the model in the learning tasks, which leads to a large number of optimization iterations.

2. Offline learning–based methods

Offline learning–based methods use initial frame information and pass object information to subsequent frames through propagation or matching techniques without requiring computationally expensive online fine-tuning. MaskTrack stitches the predicted mask of the previous frame with the image of the current frame to provide spatial guidance (Perazzi et al. 2017). Fast end-to-end embedding learning for video object segmentation (FEELVOS) employs semantic-level semantic embedding along with global and local matching mechanisms to pass location information into subsequent frames (Voigtlaender et al. 2019). A generative appearance model for end-to-end video object segmentation (AGAMEVOS) uses a probabilistic generative model to predict the distribution of object and background features in subsequent frames (Johnander et al. 2019). Due to the low efficiency of information flow, these methods still cannot achieve high speed. Also, due to the lack of reliable object representations, they usually only achieve sub-optimal accuracy.

3. Tracking-based methods

Tracking-based methods combines the object segmentation and object tracking. Fast and accurate video object segmentation (FAVOS) adopts a part-based tracking technique to find the location regions of object objects (Cheng et al. 2018). SiamRPN (Li et al. 2018) abandons the time-consuming step of extracting multi-scale feature maps for object scale invariance, and further, SiamMask bridges the gap between tracking and segmentation by adding a mask branch on SiamRPN (Wang, Zhang et al. 2019). Since the classification branch and regression branch of the network are generated by jointly training regions, so that the running speed can meet the real-time requirements. However, SiamRPN is difficult to deal with the interference of similar-looking objects.

Another classification for these methods is divided them into four categories: unsupervised-based methods, detection-based methods, propagation-based methods, and Siamese network-based methods (Fu et al. 2021). Some typical examples for the first three categories are given below (the fourth will be discussed in the next section).

1. Unsupervision-based methods

Unsupervision-based methods often consider that both the objects and background form different clusters in feature space due to their attributes, such as color appearance or motion patterns. By first using a two-stream network to extract significant appearance features from RGB images and motion features from the optical flow, these features can then be fused to jointly predict and extract objects in a number of frames (Jain et al. 2017).

2. Detection-based methods

These methods mainly achieve video object segmentation by matching the appearance features of the given object in the first frame to the subsequent frames of video. For example, in the works proposed by (Caelles et al. 2017; Maninis et al. 2019), the VGG networor is pre-trained on the ImageNet dataset and then further trained on the DAVIS dataset as its parent network. In the detection phase, for each test video, the parent network is fine-tuned online according to its labelled first frame, and the fine-tuned network is deemed as a detector. A procedure similar to panoptic segmentation is adopted. The semantic segmentation stage is first used to annotate all objects in video frame. Then, according to the object annotated in the first frame, the same instance segmentation mask is selected from the semantic segmentation results. In addition, this selected instance mask and its corresponding semantic label are propagated to the next frame.

3. Propagation-based methods

These methods mainly provide inter-frame temporal information to the segmentation network by propagating the previous mask, that is, combining the previous mask with the current frame to form a 4-channel image, which is input into the segmentation network. In this way, it pays less attention to the useless background information and helps to separate objects from the background. For example, the first frame and its annotation can be extended to simulate the possible deformation of objects in subsequent frames and to achieve higher segmentation accuracy (Khoreva et al. 2019).

5.5.1.2 Fusion of Multi-Scale Context and Temporal Information
The continuous nature of the video sequence itself brings temporal contextual information. This information can be combined with multi-scale spatial information within deep networks for video object segmentation (Li 2021).

1. Atrous depth-wise separable convolution

The ***depth-wise convolution*** convolves the feature map for each channel separately, and then outputs and stacks the convolution result into a feature map with the same number of channels as the original feature map. The depth-wise separable convolution compresses the feature map into a single channel through the convolution operation, and then stacks the feature map to the required number of channels through the cross-channel convolution operation. Through these two steps, the parameters of the network model can be reduced, the network becomes more lightweight and the performance of the network can be maintained. Substituting the depth-wise convolution in the depth-wise separable convolution by the

atrous depth-wise convolution, and the resulting ***atrous depth-wise separable convolution*** has various receptive fields while maintaining light weight property. This provides multi-scale ability to combine temporal contextual information.

2. Multi-scale atrous spatial pyramid pooling

With the help of the atrous depth-wise separable convolution, ***multi-scale atrous spatial pyramid pooling*** modules with different atrous rates can be constructed to enable the network to capture multi-scale context. The flow chart of this module is shown in Figure 5.17. The input feature map is convolved with different receptive fields with a series of atrous rates and the feature map is adaptively pooled. Then these feature maps are stitched together, and a convolution operation with a convolution kernel of 1×1 is used to convert the channels of the transformed feature maps, so that the output feature maps have rich multi-scale context information, and so that the network has the ability to predict multi-scale objects.

3. Inter-frame mask propagation

The consistency among frames of a video sequence enables the network to efficiently transfer information from frame to frame. Furthermore, information from previous frames can pass through temporal context information and provide useful hints for subsequent predictions.

The flowchart of ***inter-frame mask propagation*** can be seen from Figure 5.18. It adds a mask propagation module to the segmentation of video objects, thereby providing localization and segmentation information to the network. The mask propagation module here consists of atrous convolution operations corresponding to different atrous rates. First, the image of the previous frame and the mask of the previous frame are stitched and input into the convolutional layer to extract the fusion features, then the fusion feature map is scaled

FIGURE 5.17 Flowchart of multi-scale atrous spatial pyramid pooling.

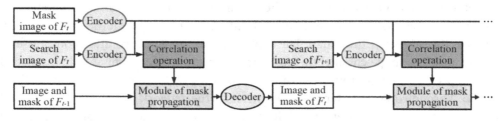

FIGURE 5.18 Flowchart of inter-frame mask propagation.

by up-sampling, and then the features manipulated by network is extracted from the current frame and correlated for inputting into the mask propagation module for fused feature extraction of the next frame. This goes on and on for the whole video.

5.5.1.3 Combining Motion-Aware ROI Prediction and Adaptive Reference Updating

To reduce the disturbance of the background to the object and to avoid excessive dependence on the appearance information of the given object in the first frame, an approach combining motion-aware ROI prediction and adaptive reference updating is proposed (Fu et al. 2021). In this approach, the directly detection instead of fine-tuning is applied to reduce the computation time.

This approach consists of three modules:

1. Motion-aware ROI prediction

In this module, see Figure 5.19, the historical motion trajectory of object region (from the image sequence) is taken as prior knowledge. Based on the motion information of the previous frame and the actual segmentation region of object, the ROI in the current frame can be dynamically predicted, with the mask propagation, ROI information can be grouped, so as to reduce the influence of the background.

2. Dynamic adaptive reference updating

In this module, see Figure 5.20, the optical flow information calculated between the previous and current frames is used to estimate the warped mask from the previous

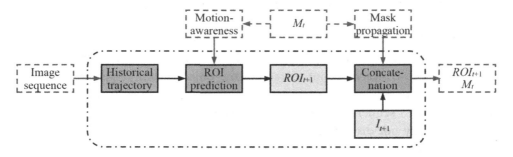

FIGURE 5.19 Motion-aware ROI prediction.

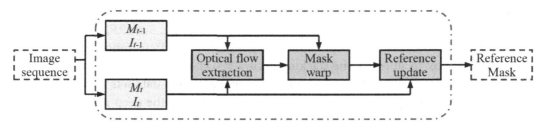

FIGURE 5.20 Dynamic adaptive reference updating.

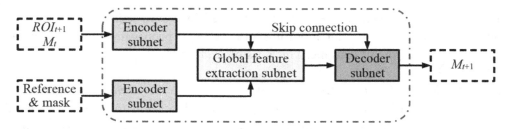

FIGURE 5.21 Siamese network.

mask, the similarity between the object mask of the current frame and the warped mask is calculated, and whether the current frame is taken as a new reference frame is determined to achieve dynamic and adaptive update of the reference frame in the process of object segmentation, so as to adapt to the appearance changes of the object in image sequence.

3. Siamese network

For this module, see Figure 5.21, the input consists of two parts. One is the object stream composed of the object ROI of the current frame and the segmentation mask of the previous frame; the other is the reference stream composed of the reference frame and its corresponding segmentation mask. A Siamese network based on the deep Xception network (Chollet, 2017) is taken as the backbone framework. This module consists of three subnets: Siamese encoder subnet (for the dimensionality reduction), global feature extraction subnet (using residual block based on the atrous convolution to extract the common global features between reference stream and object stream), and decoder subnet (for the restoration of the abstract features of the object).

5.5.2 Video Object Tracking-Based Siamese Network

Video object segmentation and video object tracking are closely related. Video object segmentation often concerns about extracting the objects from a specific frame. Video object tracking more emphasize the aspect of determining the appearance of one object in all frame of a video sequence. However, this distinction is not always strict, these two tasks are frequently not distinguished in many cases.

In the tracking of video moving objects, there have been many new advances in the method based on Siamese network in recent years. Some typical examples are ***Siamese fully convolutional (SiamFC)*** algorithm (Bertinetto et al. 2016) and a series of ***region proposal network (RPN)***–based (Ren 2015) algorithms, such as SiamRPN (Li et al. 2018), DaSiamRPN (Zhu et al. 2018), and SiamRPN++ (Li et al. 2019). SiamRPN introduces the RPN module after the correlation operation, and performs joint classification and regression on the anchor box to improve the tracking accuracy. DaSiamRPN introduces distractors with different semantics in the training, and adds some detection data sets into the training, to improve the tracking performance. SiamRPN++ introduces the deep network into the tracker, and makes predictions on multi-layer features to further improve the tracking performance. More works can also be found in (Sun et al. 2021) and (Tan, Yin, et al. 2021).

The Siamese network tracking methods express the tracking problem of video moving objects as to produce a vector obtained by cross-correlation between the object features and the search region feature to learn the similarity between the object and the search regions.

Siamese network trackers usually have two branches: classification and regression. The classification branch is responsible for outputting the similarity, which provides a rough position information of the tracked object. The regression branch is responsible for predicting the accurate state information of the object.

Most Siamese network tracking methods have similar designs for the classification branch, but there is a big difference in the sampling of training samples. SiamFC and SiamRPN only collect image pairs of the same object as input during training, due to the simple background information in the search images and non-semantic filled pixels occupy most of the area, so there are few effective negative samples, resulting in poor model discrimination ability. DaSiamRPN tries to add image pairs composed of different objects, thereby introducing different semantic distractors, which improves the discriminative ability of the model. However, it still cannot effectively discriminate distractors in the same class (with similar semantics), resulting in poor network robustness in tracking the object.

The design of the regression branch is mainly divided into two categories. SiamFC adopts a multi-scale testing method. This method sends the search image blocks after multi-scale adjustment to the tracker for detection, and selects the one with the highest classification score. The scale corresponding to the image block is used as the scale of the object. Due to the limited scales in the test, the final object scale information would be very inaccurate, while the multi-scale test will increase the computational burden and reduce the running speed of the tracker. *SiamRPN* series algorithms (SiamRPN, DaSiamRPN, SiamRPN++) could achieve quite high localization accuracy by adding a RPN after the Siamese network, which is mainly due to the fact that multiple anchor boxes can adapt to the object's shape deformation, but the setting of multiple anchor boxes increases the complexity of classification and regression tasks and further reduces the running efficiency of the tracker.

To treat these problems, various improvements for Siamese network tracking methods have been proposed. The following gives two examples.

5.5.2.1 Guided Anchoring RPN

SiamRPN combines the RPN with the Siamese network for video object tracking. In the RPN module, the candidate regions are generated by sliding windows through a large number of anchor boxes, from which the anchor region classification and bounding box regression are performed to optimize their position. This method does not consider the semantic features of the object region, resulting in inconsistency between anchor boxes and features, and generates a large number of redundant anchor boxes, resulting in a substantial increase in the amount of calculation.

In order to solve the above problems, a guided anchoring network (Wang, Chen et al. 2019) based on the Siamese RPN network to guide the generation of sparse anchor boxes

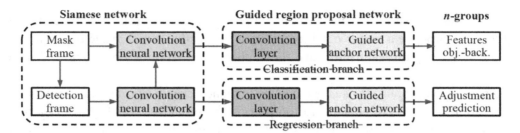

FIGURE 5.22   Siamese guided anchor RPN network.

through semantic features is proposed (Shang et al. 2021). Firstly, the semantic features extracted by CNN in the Siamese network are used to predict the position of anchor boxes as well as the length and width of anchor boxes at different positions, so as to improve the accuracy and network performance of object tracking in video.

The main modules of *Siamese guided anchor RPN network* are shown in Figure 5.22. It consists of a Siamese network for feature extraction and a guided anchor RPN network for extracting candidate regions. The upper part of the guided anchor RPN network is the classification branch, which is used to distinguish the object from the background; the lower part is the bounding box regression branch, which is used to fine-tune the candidate regions. The guided anchor module predicts the anchor box of the mask frame through the semantic features extracted by the Siamese network, and then convolves with the detection frame to obtain the response score map, which realizes end-to-end training.

In Figure 5.22, the guided anchoring network learns the shape of the anchor box according to the distribution of the object position and shape from the high-level se-mantic features extracted by the CNN in the Siamese network. The guided anchoring network includes an anchor box position prediction branch, which uses a convolution kernel to convolve the input feature map to obtain a score map about the object position information, and then obtains the probability value of each point through the Sigmoid function, and finally outputs a probability map with the same size as the input feature map. The value of each point on the probability map indicates the possibility of the detection object at that position. By setting the threshold, the possible position of the detection object can be determined. This method can filter out 90% of the regions while maintaining the recall rate, thus improving the efficiency of the network. The guided anchoring network also includes an anchor box shape prediction branch whose goal is to learn the optimal anchor box height and width given the center point of the anchor box, which is a regression problem. The shape prediction branch predicts only one anchor box whose height and width are dynamically transformed at each position through the convolutional network, which has a higher recall rate.

5.5.2.2 Anchor-Free FC Siamese Tracker

Except adding guidance to anchor, another idea is to remove anchor to simplify the complexity of classification and regression. One such a method is called, ***anchor-free fully convolutional Siamese tracker (AFST)***, which is based on the direct prediction on

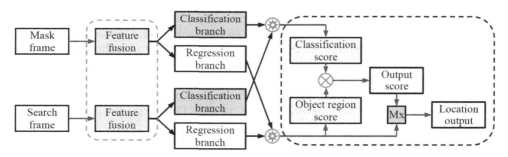

FIGURE 5.23   Framework of AFST network.

pixels (Tan, Zheng, et al. 2021). AFST network is an improvement of **SiamFC**. The framework of AFST network is drawn in Figure 5.23.

It can be seen that the AFST framework consists of a Siamese network for feature extraction and two branches for classification and regression, respectively. The classification branch is responsible for classifying the object and background, and the regression branch is responsible for predicting the state information of the object. The backbone network is ResNet50, which extracts the features of its second, third, and fourth layers that are fused as the input features of the classification branch and regression branch.

The Siamese network has two branches: the mask branch is responsible for extracting features from the input mask image, and the search branch is responsible for extracting features from the search region containing the object, and then uses the cross-correlation operation (⊛) to process the two features and output correlation vector. The correlation vector reflects how similar each region in the search image is to the mask image, so their similarity probability can be finally obtained. The classification score and the object region score are multiplied channel wise (⊗) to produce output score. The maximum (Mx) value between the object region score and the output score is used to predict the object location.

REFERENCES

Bertinetto, L., J. Valmadre, J.F. Henriques, et al. 2016. Fully-convolutional Siamese networks for object tracking. *Proceedings of the European Conference on Computer Vision*: 850–865.

Caelles, S., K.K. Maninis, J. Pont-Tuset, et al. 2017. One-shot video object segmentation. *Proceedings of the IEEE Conference on Computer Vision and Pattern Recognition*, 5320–5329.

Cheng, J.C., Y.H. Tsai, W.C. Hung et al. 2018. Fast and accurate online video object segmentation via tracking parts. *Proceedings of the IEEE Conference on Computer Vision and Pattern Recognition*, 7415–7424.

Chollet, F. 2017. Xception: Deep learning with depth-wise separable convolutions. *Proceedings of the IEEE Conference on Computer Vision and Pattern Recognition*, 1800–1807.

Comaniciu, D., V. Ramesh, and P. Meer. 2000. Real-time tracking of non-rigid objects using mean shift. *Proceedings of the CVPR*, 2: 142–149.

Davies, E.R. 2005. *Machine Vision: Theory, Algorithms, Practicalities*. 3rd Ed. Singapore: Elsevier.

Ekin, A., R. Mehrotra, and A.M. Tekalp. 2000. Parametric description of object motion using EMUs. *Proceedings of the ICIP*, 2: 570–573.

Fu, L.H., Z. Yu, X.W. Sun, et al. 2021. Video object segmentation based on motion-aware ROI prediction and adaptive reference updating. *Expert Systems with Applications*, 167: #114153.

Jain, S.D., B. Xiong, and K. Grauman. 2017. FusionSeg: Learning to combine motion and appearance for fully automatic segmentation of generic objects in videos. *Proceedings of the IEEE Conference on Computer Vision and Pattern Recognition*, 2117–2126.

Johnander, J., M. Danelljan, E. Brissman, et al. 2019. A generative appearance model for end-to-end video object segmentation. *Proceedings of the IEEE Conference on Computer Vision and Pattern Recognition*, 8945–8954.

Khoreva, A., R. Benenson, E. Ilg, et al. 2019. Lucid data dreaming for video object segmentation. *International Journal of Computer Vision*, 127(9), 1175–1197.

Kim, K., T.H. Chalidabhongse, and D. Harwood, et al. 2004. Background modeling and subtraction by codebook construction. *Proceedings of the ICIP*, 5: 3061–3064.

Li, B., W. Wu, Q. Wang, et al. 2019. Siam-RPN++: Evolution of Siamese visual tracking with very deep networks. *Proceedings of the Computer Vision and Pattern Recognition*, 4282–4291.

Li, B., J.J. Yan, W. Wu, et al. 2018. High performance visual tracking with Siamese region proposal network. *Proceedings of the Computer Vision and Pattern Recognition*, 8971–8980.

Li, H., K.H. Liu, J.J. Liu, et al. 2021. Multitask framework for video object tracking and segmentation combined with multi-scale inter-frame information. *Journal of Image and Graphics*, 26(1): 101–112.

Li, X.P., Y. Yan, and Y.-J. Zhang. 2006. Analysis and comparison of background modeling methods. *Proceedings of the NCIG'2006*, 469–473.

Liu, W.J., and Y.-J. Zhang. 2007. Real time object tracking using fused color and edge cues. *Proceedings of the9th ISSPIA*, (1–4).

Maninis, K.K., S. Caelles, Y. Chen, et al. 2019. Video object segmentation without temporal information. *IEEE Transactions on Pattern Analysis and Machine Intelligence*, 41(6): 1515–1530.

Ohm, J.R., F. Bunjamin, and W. Liebsch, et al. 2000. A set of visual feature descriptors and their combination in a low-level description scheme. *Signal Processing: Image Communication*, 16(1–2): 157–179.

Perazzi, F., A. Khoreva, R. Benenson, et al. 2017. Learning video object segmentation from static images. *Proceedings of the IEEE Conference on Computer Vision and Pattern Recognition*, 3491–3500.

Ren, S.Q., K.M. He, R. Girshick, et al. 2015. Faster R-CNN: Towards real-time object detection with region proposal networks. *Proceedings of the Advances in Neural Information Processing Systems*, 91–99.

Shang, X.R., Y.L. Wen, X.F. Xi, et al. 2021. Target tracking system based on the Siamese guided anchor region proposal network. *Journal of Image and Graphics*, 26(2): 0415–0424.

Shen, B., and Y.-J. Zhang. 2009. Subsequence-wise approach for online tracking. *Auto-Identification and Ubiquitous Computing Applications: RFID and Smart Technologies for Information Convergence. Information Science Reference*, Chapter IX (157–166).

Sonka, M., V. Hlavac, and R. Boyle. 2008. *Image Processing, Analysis, and Machine Vision*. 3rd Ed. Canada: Thomson.

Sun, R., L.F. Fang, Q.L. Liang, et al. 2021. Siamese network combined learning saliency and online leaning interference for aerial object tracking algorithm. *Journal of Electronics & Information Technology*, 43(5): 1414–1423.

Tan, J.H., W. Yin, L.M. Liu, et al. 2021. DenseNet-siamese network with global context feature module for object tracking. *Journal of Electronics & Information Technology*, 43(1): 179–186.

Tan, J.H., Y.S. Zheng, Y.N. Wang, et al. 2021. AFST: Anchor-free fully convolutional Siamese tracker with searching center point. *Acta Automatica Sinica*, 47(4): 801–812.

Toyama, K., J. Krumm, and B. Brumitt, et al. 1999. Wallflower: Principles and practice of background maintenance. *Proceedings of the ICCV*, 1: 255–261.

Viola, P., and M. Jones. 2001. Rapid object detection using a boosted cascade of simple features. *Proceedings of the CVPR*, 511–518.

Voigtlaender, P., Y.N. Chai, F. Schroff, et al. 2019. FEELVOS: fast end-to-end embedding learning for video object segmentation. *Proceedings of the IEEE Conference on Computer Vision and Pattern Recognition*, 9473–9482.

Wang, Q., L. Zhang, L. Bertinetto et al. 2019. Fast online object tracking and segmentation: a unifying approach. *Proceedings of the IEEE Conference on Computer Vision and Pattern Recognition*, 1328–1338.

Wang, J. Q., K. Chen, and S. Yang. (2019). Region proposal by guided anchoring. *Proceedings of 2019 IEEE/ CVF Conference on Computer Vision and Pattern Recognition*, 2960–2969.

Yu, T.L., and Y.-J. Zhang. 2001. Motion feature extraction for content-based video sequence retrieval. *SPIE*, 4311: 378–388.

Yu, T.L., and Y.-J. Zhang. 2002a. Summarizing motion contents of the video clip using moving edge overlaid frame (MEOF). *SPIE*, 4676: 407–417.

Yu, T.L., and Y.-J. Zhang. 2002b. A local motion information based video retrieval method. *Journal of Tsinghua University (Science and Technology)*, 42(7): 925–928.

Zhang, Y.-J. 2017. *Image Engineering, Vol. 3: Image Understanding*. Germany: De Gruyter.

Zhu, Z., Q. Wang, B. Li, et al. 2018. Distractoraware Siamese networks for visual object tracking. *Proceedings of the European Conference on Computer Vision*, 101–117.

CHAPTER 6

Mathematical Morphology Methods

M athematical morphology is a mathematical tool for analyzing images based on morphology (Serra 1982). The basic idea of mathematical morphology method is to use structure elements with a certain shape to measure and extract the corresponding shape in the image to achieve the purpose of image analysis and recognition. Using mathematical morphology techniques can simplify image data, maintain their basic shape characteristics, and remove irrelevant structures. The algorithms of mathematical morphology all have a natural parallel implementation structure.

The operating objects of mathematical morphology methods can be binary images or grayscale/color images. Although the basic principles are the same and many operations have the same names, they have different specific basic processing and application algorithms due to different objects.

The contents of each section of this chapter are arranged as follows:

Section 6.1 first reviews the mathematical foundations of mathematical morphology operations, including basic set definitions, and the sorting of grayscale images.

Section 6.2 introduces the basic operations of image mathematical morphology. The four basic operations of binary mathematical morphology and grayscale mathematical morphology, dilation, erosion, opening, and closing, are introduced in detail in combination with diagrams and examples, respectively.

Section 6.3 discusses some combined operations obtained by combining basic operations. For binary mathematical morphology, first the hit-or-miss transform is introduced, then the basic thinning and thickening, and this section also discusses the combination of basic operations, set operations, and logical operations. For grayscale mathematical morphology, it mainly discusses the operations of morphological gradient and morphological smoothing, as well as morphological filters.

Section 6.4 introduces some practical algorithms of mathematical morphology for specific image applications. For binary mathematical morphology, it includes noise filtering, corner detection, boundary extraction, region filling, and region skeleton calculation. For grayscale mathematical morphology, it includes background estimation and elimination, morphology detection of edges, fast clustering segmentation, and texture segmentation.

Section 6.5 provides a brief introduction to some technique developments and promising research directions in the last year.

6.1 MATHEMATICAL FOUNDATION

The mathematical foundation of **mathematical morphology** is **set theory**. A binary image is the spatial distribution of two sets (0 and 1), and a grayscale image is the spatial distribution of multiple sets. Any one of the three components of a color image can be regarded as a grayscale image, so the color image is still a spatial distribution of multiple sets.

6.1.1 Basic Definitions of Set

First give some definitions for the noun of set. Sets and operations are the mathematical foundation of binary mathematical morphology.

1. Set: the totality of definite, and differentiated things of a certain nature (it is also a thing in itself). Set is commonly represented by using capital letters such as A, B, ... If something does not exist, it is said that the whole of such things is an empty set. It is stipulated that any empty set is just the same set, denoted as $\varnothing$. In the following introduction, assume that A, B, ... , etc. are all sets in the Euclidean space E^N space.

2. Element: things that make up a set. Element is commonly represented by using lowercase letters such as a, b, ... , etc. Nothing is an element in $\varnothing$. If a is an element of set A, it is denoted as: $a \in A$ (pronounced a belongs to A). If a is not an element of A, it is denoted as: $a \notin A$ (pronounced a does not belong to A). Because $\in$ and $\notin$ negate each other logically, neither of the above two cases can be established at the same time, nor can they be both.

   When a set consists of only a finite number of elements, it can be written specifically, such as $A = \{a, b, c\}$. In order to indicate the characteristics of the set, the characteristics of the elements are often marked. It is generally represented by $\{x: x$ has property $P\}$ or $\{x|x$ has property $P\}$.

   If there is only one certain thing, and this thing is assumed to be recorded as a, then the whole of this kind of things is the set $\{a\}$, and a is the only element in $\{a\}$. It should be noted that a and $\{a\}$ are generally different concepts, a represents an element, and $\{a\}$ represents a set (with only one element). For another example, $\varnothing$ and $\{\varnothing\}$ are also different, $\varnothing$ refers to the empty set with no elements, and $\{\varnothing\}$ refers to the empty set with a single element $\varnothing$.

3. Subset: If and only if the elements of set A belong to set B, A is called a subset of B.

   If A is a subset of B, record it as: $A \subseteq B$ (pronounced as A is contained in B) or $B \supseteq A$ (pronounced as B contains A). A is not a subset of B, denoted as $A \nsubseteq B$

(pronounced as *A* is not included in *B*). Because ⊆ and ⊄ negate each other logically, neither of these two cases can be true, and neither of these two cases can be false.

4. **Union**: a set consisting of all elements of *A* and *B* is called the union of *A* and *B*.
   The union of *A* and *B* is marked as $A \cup B$ (i.e., $x \in A \cup B \Leftrightarrow x \in A$ or $x \in B$). Here "⇔" is read as "equivalent to".

5. **Intersection**: The set consisting of the common elements of *A* and *B* is called the intersection of *A* and *B*.
   The intersection of *A* and *B* is denoted as $A \cap B$ (that is, $x \in A \cap B \Leftrightarrow x \in A$ and $x \in B$).

6. **Complement**: the complement of *A* is denoted as A^c, and is defined as

$$A^c = \{x | x \notin A\} \tag{6.1}$$

   Figure 6.1(a) shows a diagram of set *A* and its complement A^c.

7. **Displacement**: *A* uses *x* for displacement is denoted as $(A)_x$, and is defined as

$$(A)_x = \{y | y = a + x, \ a \in A\} \tag{6.2}$$

   Figure 6.1(b) shows a diagram of the displacement set $(A)_x$ of the set *A*, where $x = (x_1, x_2)$, representing 2-D displacement.

8. **Reflection**: The reflection of *A* (also called mapping) is denoted as $\hat{A}$, and is defined as

$$\hat{A} = \{x | x = -a, \ a \in A\} \tag{6.3}$$

   Figure 6.1(c) shows the reflection (rotated by 180°) set $\hat{A}$ of set *A*. The reflection set and the original set are symmetrical, which can also be said to be transposed to each other.

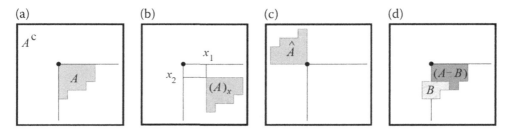

FIGURE 6.1   Some examples of basic set definitions.

9. Difference set: The difference between two sets A and B is denoted as $A - B$, and is defined as

$$A - B = \{x | x \in A, \ x \notin B\} = A \cap B^c \tag{6.4}$$

Figure 6.1(d) shows the difference set $A - B$ (not coincident with set B).

The basic operations between sets discussed above are closely related to the basic logical operations used for binary images. In fact, the concept of complement corresponds to the logical complement operation, the union operation corresponds to the logical OR operation, and the intersection operation corresponds to the logical AND operation.

6.1.2 Sorting of Grayscale Images

When discussing **mathematical morphology** for grayscale images, not only the spatial position of the pixel must be considered, but also the size (magnitude) of the pixel's grayscale. In grayscale mathematical morphology, the sorting of grayscale has a function similar to that of set operations in binary mathematical morphology. The following is an introduction to the sorting of image gray levels. For simplicity and intuition, taking 1-D signals as an example, all conclusions can be easily extended to 2-D images.

Define the **region of support** of a signal $f(x)$ as

$$D[f] = \{x : f(x) > -\infty\} \tag{6.5}$$

If there is $g(x) \leq f(x)$ for all x, then $g(x)$ is said to be below $f(x)$ and denoted as $g \perp f$. According to the convention of negative infinity, if and only if $D[g] \subset D[f]$ and x belongs to the common support region of the two signals, that is, when $x \in D[g]$, there is $g \perp f$. Figure 6.2 gives several examples, where $g \perp f$ in Figure 6.2(a); $g(x)$ is not below $f(x)$ in Figure 6.2(b), because the point x is in the region of support of $g(x)$ but $g(x) > f(x)$ at this time; in Figure 6.2(c), $g(x)$ is also not below $f(x)$, but this time because $D[g]$ is not a subset of $D[f]$.

Corresponding to the intersection and union operations in the case of binary signals, the **minimum operation** and **maximum operation** can be defined for the grayscale signal. The **minimum value** $(f \wedge g)(x)$ of the two signals $f(x)$ and $g(x)$ can be determined point by point as follows:

$$(f \wedge g)(x) = \min\{f(x), g(x)\} \tag{6.6}$$

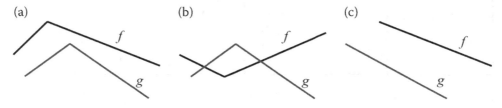

FIGURE 6.2   Sorting of 1-D signal.

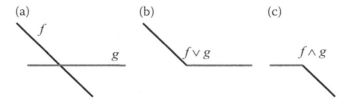

FIGURE 6.3   The maximum and minimum values of the two 1-D signals.

It should be noted here that for any value a, there is $\min\{a, -\infty\} = -\infty$. Relative to the region of support, if $x \in D[f] \cap D[g]$, then $(f \wedge g)(x)$ is the minimum of the two finite values $f(x)$ and $g(x)$; otherwise, $(f \wedge g)(x) = -\infty$.

The **maximum value** $(f \vee g)(x)$ of the two signals $f(x)$ and $g(x)$ can be determined point by point as follows:

$$(f \vee g)(x) = \max\{f(x), g(x)\} \tag{6.7}$$

Among them, for any value a, there is $\max\{a, -\infty\} = a$. If $x \in D[f] \cap D[g]$, then $(f \vee g)(x)$ is the maximum of the two finite values $f(x)$ and $g(x)$, otherwise $(f \vee g)(x) = -\infty$; if $x \in D[f] - D[g]$, then $(f \vee g)(x) = f(x)$; if $x \in D[g] - D[f]$, then $(f \vee g)(x) = g(x)$. Finally, if x is not in any region of support, that is, $x \notin D[f] \cup D[g]$, then $(f \vee g)(x) = -\infty$.

Figure 6.3 gives the examples for the minimum value and maximum value. Figure 6.3(a) shows two signals $f(x)$ and $g(x)$, Figure 6.3(b) shows $(f \vee g)(x)$, and Figure 6.3(c) shows $(f \wedge g)(x)$.

The grayscale operation corresponding to the mapping of the relative origin in the binary set on the plane is also often referred to as reflection. Consider the image $f(x, y)$; its reflection through the origin is defined as

$$\hat{f}(x, y) = f(-x, -y) \tag{6.8}$$

The above reflection can be obtained by first inverting the image with respect to the vertical axis and then with respect to the horizontal axis. It is also equivalent to turning the image 180° around the origin.

6.2 BASIC MORPHOLOGICAL OPERATIONS

The operations in mathematical morphology involve two objects. In binary mathematical morphology, these two objects are regarded as sets. Generally, A is called the input image, B is the **structure element** (it is still an image set), and the operation is recorded as to operate A with B. In grayscale mathematical morphology, these two objects are regarded as functions. Generally, $f(x, y)$ is called the input image, $b(x, y)$ is the structure element (it is also a small image), and the operation is recorded as to operate $f(x, y)$ with $b(x, y)$. By the way, each structure element has an origin, which is the reference point for the structure element to participate in morphological operations, but the origin does not necessarily belong to the structure element.

6.2.1 Basic Operations of Binary Morphology

The basic operations of binary morphology mainly include dilation, erosion, opening and closing (Russ 2016), (Zhang 2017b). In the following illustration, the shading represents the region with the value of 1, and the white represents the region with the value of 0. The calculation is performed on the region of the image with the value of 1.

6.2.1.1 Binary Dilation

The **binary dilation** operator is $\oplus$, and A uses B to dilate is written as $A \oplus B$, which is defined as

$$A \oplus B = \{x | [(\hat{B})_x \cap A] \neq \varnothing\} \tag{6.9}$$

The above formula shows that the process of dilating A with B is to map B on the origin first, and then translate its image by x, where the intersection of the image of A and B is not an empty set. In other words, the set obtained by dilating A with B is the set of the origin of B when the displacement of $\hat{B}$ intersects with at least one non-zero element in A. According to this explanation, Equation (6.9) can also be written as

$$A \oplus B = \{x | [(\hat{B})_x \cap A] \subseteq A\} \tag{6.10}$$

The above formula can help people understand the dilation operation with the help of the concept of convolution. If you regard B as a convolutional mask, the dilation is achieved by first mapping B with respect to the origin, and then moving the (mapping result) image on A continuously. An example can be seen in Figure 6.4. Among them, the shaded part in Figure 6.4(a) is set A, the shaded part in Figure 6.4(b) is structure element B (its origin is marked with "+"), and the (mapping result) image is shown in Figure 6.4(c). The two shaded parts (the darker part is the enlarged part) are combined to form the set $A \oplus B$ in Figure 6.4(d). It can be seen from the figure that the dilation expands the original region even larger.

Dilation can also be achieved by displacement operation, which can be expressed as

$$A \oplus B = \bigcup_{b \in B} (A)_b \tag{6.11}$$

(a)   (b)   (c)   (d)

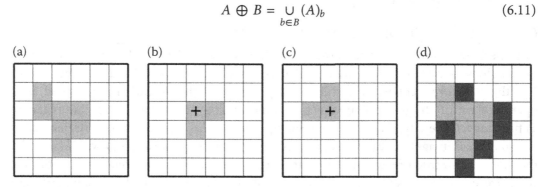

FIGURE 6.4 Example of dilation operation.

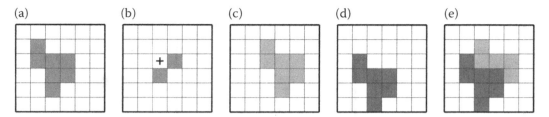

FIGURE 6.5   Example of displacement calculation for dilation.

The above formula shows that the result of $A \oplus B$ is the union obtained by shifting A by each $b \in B$. It can also be explained as: to dilate A with B is to displace A according to each b and OR the result. An example can be seen in Figure 6.5. Among them, Figure 6.5(a) is the same as Figure 6.4(a); Figure 6.5(b) is the structure element (for simplicity, here let the origin not belong to B; that is, B contains only two pixels); Figure 6.5(c) and Figure 6.5(d) show the result of shifting A with the structure element point to the right of the origin and with the structure element point below the origin, respectively. Figure 6.5(e) shows the result of the union of the results of Figure 6.5(c) and Figure 6.5(d); that is, the sum of the two shaded regions. If a coordinate system is established for the image and the origin (0, 0) is in the upper-left corner, then Figure 6.4(d) is the same as Figure 6.5(d) except for the point (1, 1). The point (1, 1) not in the dilation result is caused by the fact that B in Figure 6.5(b) does not contain the origin.

The union obtained by shifting A according to b is also equal to the union obtained by shifting B according to a, so Equation (6.11) can also be written as

$$A \oplus B = \bigcup_{a \in A} (B)_a \qquad (6.12)$$

6.2.1.2 Binary Erosion

The **binary erosion** operator is $\ominus$, and A uses B to erode is written as $A \ominus B$, which is defined as

$$A \ominus B = \{x | (B)_x \subseteq A\} \qquad (6.13)$$

The above formula shows that the result of erosion of A with B is the set of all x, where B is still in A after being translated by x. In other words, the set obtained by eroding A with B is the set of B's origin position when B is completely included in A. The above formula can also help people understand erosion operations with the help of related concepts. An example can be seen in Figure 6.6, where the set A in Figure 6.6(a) and the structure element B in Figure 6.6(b) are the same as those in Figure 6.4, and the dark-shaded part in Figure 6.6(c) gives $A \ominus B$ (light-shaded part is the part that was originally belong to A but now was eroded). It can be seen from the figure that the erosion shrinks the original region smaller.

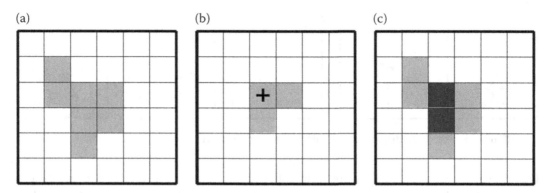

FIGURE 6.6 Example of erosion operation.

Erosion can also be realized by displacement operation, which can be expressed as

$$A \ominus B = \bigcap_{b \in B} (A)_{-b} \tag{6.14}$$

The above formula shows that the result of $A \ominus B$ is the intersection obtained by negatively shifting A for each $b \in B$. It can also be explained as: using B to erode A is to negatively shift A for each b and AND the result. An example can be seen in Figure 6.7, where Figure 6.7(a) and Figure 6.7(b) are the same as Figure 6.5. Figure 6.7(c) and Figure 6.7(d), respectively, show the result of the displacement of the structure element point at the right of the origin and the result of the opposite displacement of the structure element point at the below of the origin. The black points in Figure 6.7(e) gives the result of combining the results of Figure 6.7(c) and Figure 6.7(d), which is the same as Figure 6.6(c).

The intersection obtained by shifting A by $-b$ is also equal to the intersection obtained by shifting B by $-a$, so Equation (6.14) can also be written as

$$A \ominus B = \bigcap_{a \in A} (B)_{-a} \tag{6.15}$$

6.2.1.3 Binary Opening
If the image is eroded first and then the result is dilated (the same structure element is used here), the operation is opening.

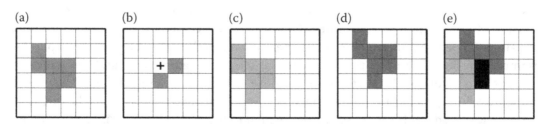

FIGURE 6.7 Example of displacement operation for erosion.

The **binary opening** operator is ○, and A uses B for opening is written as $A \circ B$, which is defined as

$$A \circ B = (A \ominus B) \oplus B \tag{6.16}$$

The opening operation can extract the shape matching its structure element from the image, thereby filtering out the thorns smaller than the structure element, cutting off the slender lap to play a separation effect. This ability can be expressed by the following opening characteristic theorem:

$$A \circ B = \{x \in A | \text{For some } t \in A \ominus B, \ x \in (B)_t \text{ and } (B)_t \subseteq A\} \tag{6.17}$$

The above formula shows that opening A with B is to select some points in A that match B. These points can be obtained by the translation of the structure element B completely contained in A.

The opening operation can be combined with the realization method of set theory to give a simple geometric explanation. Here, the structure element is regarded as a sphere (projected on a plane), and the result of opening is a set determined by the new outer edge of the structure element rolling in the opened set. According to the filling nature of the opening operation, an implementation method based on set theory can be obtained, that is, opening A with B can be obtained by translating all the results of filling B in A and then taking the union. In other words, the following filling process can be used to describe the opening:

$$A \circ B = \cup \{(B)_x | (B)_x \subset A\} \tag{6.18}$$

Figure 6.8 shows an example, where Figure 6.8(a) shows A, Figure 6.8(b) shows B, Figure 6.8(c) shows several positions of B in A, and Figure 6.8(d) shows the result obtained by opening A with B.

6.2.1.4 Binary Closing

If the image is dilated first and then the result is eroded (the same structure element is used here), the operation is closing.

The **binary closing** operator is ●, and A uses B for closing is written as $A \bullet B$, which is defined as

$$A \bullet B = (A \oplus B) \ominus B \tag{6.19}$$

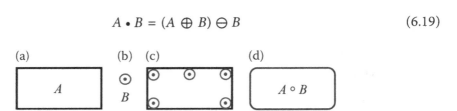

FIGURE 6.8   The geometric interpretation of opening.

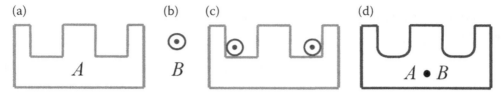

FIGURE 6.9 The geometric interpretation of closing.

The closing operation can extract shapes that match its structure elements from the image, thereby filling gaps or holes that are smaller than structure elements, and overlapping short discontinuities to play a role in connectivity. This ability can be expressed by the following closure characteristic theorem:

$$A \bullet B = \{x | x \in (\hat{B})_t \Rightarrow (\hat{B})_t \cap A \neq \varnothing\} \tag{6.20}$$

The above formula shows that the result of closing A with B includes all points that meet the following conditions, that is, when the point is covered by the mapped and displaced structure element, the intersection of A and the mapped and displaced structure element is not zero.

The closing operation can be combined with the realization of set theory to give a simple geometric explanation. Here too, the structure element is regarded as a sphere (projected on a plane), but at this time, the structure element is considered in the background. The result of closing is the set determined by the new outer edge of the structure element rolling outside the closed set.

Figure 6.9 gives an example, where Figure 6.9(a) gives A, Figure 6.9(b) gives B, Figure 6.9(c) shows several positions of B in A^c, and Figure 6.9(d) shows the result obtained by closing A with B.

6.2.2 Basic Operations of Grayscale Morphology

The basic operations of grayscale morphology mainly include dilation, erosion, opening, and closing. In a certain sense, these basic operations can be regarded as the result of the extension of the analogy method from the binary space to the grayscale space. However, unlike binary image morphology where the operation results are mainly reflected in the image plane; the grayscale morphology operation results are mainly reflected in the image amplitude axis. In other words, the operation of the input image $f(x, y)$ with the structure element $b(x, y)$ will update $f(x, y)$.

6.2.2.1 Grayscale Dilation

The **grayscale dilation** of the input image f with the structure element b is denoted as $f \oplus b$, which is defined as

$$(f \oplus b)(s, t) = \max \{f(x, y) + b(s - x, t - y) | (x, y) \in D_f \text{ and } [(s - x), (t - y)]$$

$$\in D_b\} \tag{6.21}$$

In the formula, D_f and D_b are the domains of f and b, respectively. Here, the restrictions of $(s - x)$ and $(t - y)$ within the domain of b is similar to that in the definition of binary dilation that requires two operation sets to intersect at least one (non-zero) element. Equation (6.21) is very similar to the form of 2-D convolution, the difference is that max (maximum) is used here to replace the sum (or integral) in the convolution, and the multiplication in the convolution is replaced by addition. As a result of dilating a grayscale image, regions that are brighter than the background are expanded, and regions that are darker than the background are compressed.

The following first uses 1-D function to briefly introduce the meaning and operation mechanism of Equation (6.21). When considering the 1-D function, the Equation (6.21) can be simplified as

$$(f \oplus b)(s) = \max\{f(x) + b(s - x) \mid x \in D_f \text{ and } (s - x) \in D_b\} \tag{6.22}$$

As in convolution, $b(-x)$ is the reflection of $b(x)$ corresponding to the origin of the x axis. For positive s, $b(s - x)$ moves to the right, and for negative s, $b(s - x)$ moves to the left. The requirement that x be in the domain of f and the value of $(s - x)$ in the domain of b is to make f and b coincide.

A schematic diagram of grayscale dilation is shown in Figure 6.10, where Figures 6.10(a) and Figure 6.10(b) show f and b, respectively, and Figure 6.10(c) also illustrates some positions of structure elements (after inversion) during the operation, the thick line in Figure 6.10(d) gives the final dilation result. Since the dilation is interchangeable, if f is reversed and translated, the dilation (to b) result is exactly the same.

The dilation calculation is to select the maximum value of $f + b$ in the neighborhood determined by the structure elements, so the dilation operation of the grayscale image has two types of effects:

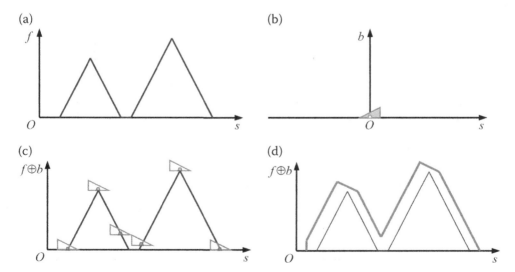

FIGURE 6.10   Grayscale dilation diagram.

1. If the values of the structure elements are all positive, the output image will be brighter than the input image;

2. If the size of the dark details in the input image is smaller than that of the structure elements, the visual effect will be weakened. The degree of weakening depends on the gray value around these dark details as well as the shape and amplitude of the structure elements.

Figure 6.11 gives a specific example of the grayscale dilation process and results. Figure 6.11 (a) is the input image f of 5×5, Figure 6.11(b) is the structure element b of 3×3, the origin is at its central element, and Figure 6.11(c) is its inversion. Since the size of b is 3×3, in order to prevent its coefficient from falling outside f during dilation, the boder pixels of f are not considered here, that is, for f of 5×5, only the center 3×3 is considered. The origin of $f(0, 0)$ is set at the upper left corner, so the coordinates of the 3 $\times$ 3 part to be considered are shown in Figure 6.11(d). If the origin of b is coincident with $f(1, 1)$, the sum of each value in b and the corresponding pixel value in f is calculated, and the result is shown in Figure 6.11(e). Take the maximum value (in bold) as the dilation result, then f is updated as shown in Figure(f) (wherein bold represents the updated value). Another example is to overlap the origin of b with $f(2, 2)$, calculate the sum of each value in b and the corresponding pixel value in f, and the result is shown in Figure 6.11(g). By taking the maximum value as the dilation result, then f is updated as shown in Figure 6.11(h). All pixels in the center 3×3 part are dilated as above, and the final result is shown in Figure 6.11(i).

Figure 6.12 gives an example of grayscale dilation. Figure 6.12(a) is the original image, and Figure 6.12(b) is the result of performing a grayscale dilation operation on Figure 6.12(a).

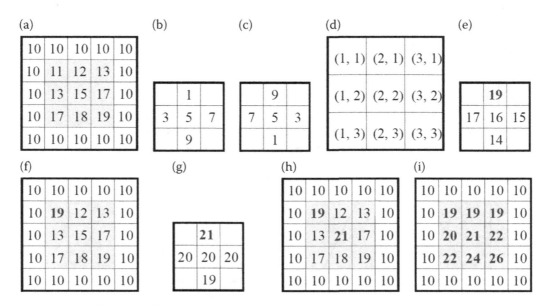

FIGURE 6.11 Grayscale dilation process and result example.

(a)   (b)

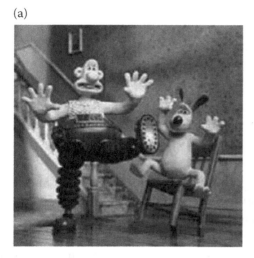 

FIGURE 6.12 Example of grayscale dilation.

The image is brighter and the dark details become smaller. The structure element used here has a center value of 2, all 4-neighbors values of 1, and all diagonal neighbors values of 0.

6.2.2.2 Grayscale Erosion

The **grayscale erosion** of the input image f with the structure element b is denoted as $f \ominus b$, which is defined as

$$(f \ominus b)\,(s,t) = \min\{f(x,y) - b(s+x, t+y) \mid (x,y) \in D_f \text{和} \,[(s+x),(t+y)] \in D_b\} \qquad (6.23)$$

In the formula, D_f and D_b are the domains of f and b, respectively. Here, the restrictions $(s - x)$ and $(t - y)$ are within the domain of b, similar to the requirement that the structure elements are completely included in the eroded set in the definition of binary erosion. Equation (6.23) is very similar to 2-D correlation. The difference is that min (minimum) is used to replace sum (or integral) in correlation, and subtraction is used to replace multiplication in correlation. Therefore, the result of the erosion of the grayscale image is that the regions darker than the background are expanded, and the regions brighter than the background are compressed.

For the sake of simplicity, as in the discussion of dilation, the following uses 1-D function to briefly introduce the meaning and operation mechanism of Equation (6.23). When using the 1-D function, the Equation (6.23) can be simplified to

$$(f \ominus b)\,(s) = \min\{f(x) - b(s+x) \mid x \in D_f \text{和} (s+x) \in D_b\} \qquad (6.24)$$

As in correlation calculations, for positive s, $f(s + x)$ is moved to the right, and for negative s, $f(s + x)$ is moved to the left. The requirement for x to be in the domain of f and the requirement for $(s + x)$ to be in the domain of b are to completely include b in the domain of f.

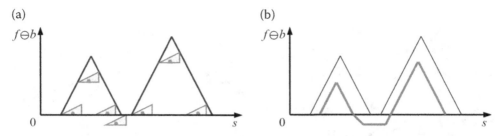

FIGURE 6.13 Grayscale erosion diagram.

A schematic diagram of grayscale erosion is shown in Figure 6.13, where f and b are the same as those in Figure 6.11; Figure 6.11(a) also illustrates some positions of structure elements in the calculation process (let b translate), and the thick line in Figure 6.11(b) gives the final erosion result.

The erosion calculation is to select the minimum value of $f - b$ in the neighborhood determined by the structure elements, so the erosion operation on the grayscale image has two types of effects:

1. If the values of the structure elements are all positive, the output image will be darker than the input image;

2. If the size of the bright details in the input image is smaller than the structure elements, the visual effect will be weakened, and the degree of weakening depends on the gray value around these bright details as well as the shape and amplitude of the structure elements.

Figure 6.14 gives a specific example of the grayscale erosion process and results. The image f and structure element b used here are still the same as in Figure 6.11. If the origin of b is coincident with $f(1, 1)$, the difference between each value in b and the corresponding pixel value in f is calculated, and the result is shown in Figure 6.14(a). Taking the minimum value as the erosion result, f is updated as shown in Figure 6.14(b). Another example is to overlap the origin of b with $f(2, 2)$, and to calculate the difference between each value in b and the corresponding pixel value in f, then the result is shown in Figure 6.14(c). By taking the minimum value as the erosion result, f is updated as shown

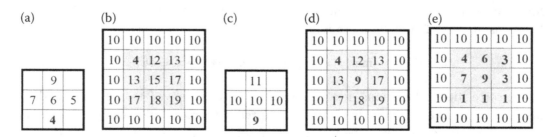

FIGURE 6.14 Grayscale erosion process and result example.

(a)

(b)

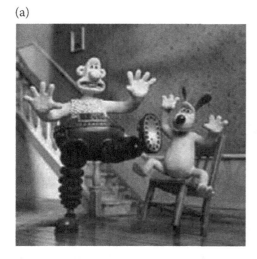 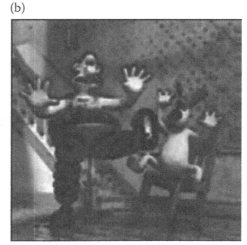

FIGURE 6.15   Example of grayscale erosion.

in Figure 6.14(d). All the pixels to be considered in f are eroded as above, and the final result is shown in Figure 6.14(e).

Figure 6.15 shows an example of grayscale erosion. Figure 6.15(a) is the original image (same as Figure 6.12(a)), and Figure 6.15(b) is the result of a grayscale erosion operation on Figure 6.15(a). The image is darker and the bright details are reduced. The structure element used here has a center value of 2, all 4-neighbors values of 1, and all diagonal neighbors values of 0.

6.2.2.3 Grayscale Opening

Both the **grayscale opening** operation and the binary opening operation are eroded first and then dilated. Opening f with b is denoted as $f \circ b$, which is defined as

$$f \circ b = (f \ominus b) \oplus b \tag{6.25}$$

There can be a simple geometric explanation for **grayscale opening**, which will be discussed below with the help of Figure 6.16. In Figure 6.16(a), a profile $f(x)$ of an image $f(x, y)$ when y is constant is given, and its shape is a series of mountain peaks and valleys. Now suppose that the structure element b is spherical and projected onto the x and $f(x)$ planes as a circle. Opening f with b, that is, $f \circ b$, which can be seen as rolling b against the bottom edge of f from one end to the other. Figure 6.16(b) shows several positions of b in the opening, and Figure 6.16(c) shows the result of the opening operation. It can be seen from Figure 6.16(c) that the height and sharpness of all peaks with a diameter smaller than b have been reduced. In other words, when b rolls against the bottom edge of f, all parts of f that are not in contact with b fall to contact b. In practice, the opening operation is often used to eliminate bright details with a smaller size compared with structure elements, while keeping the overall gray value of the image and large bright regions basically unaffected. Specifically, the erosion in the first step removes small bright

(a)

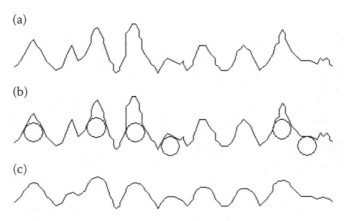

(b)

(c)

FIGURE 6.16   Grayscale opening diagram.

details and at the same time reduces the brightness of the image, and the dilation in the second step increases (basically restores) the brightness of the image but does not re-introduce the previously removed details.

The actual effect of grayscale opening can be seen in Figure 6.17, where Figure 6.17(a) is the original image and Figure 6.17(b) is the result of opening. The grayscale structure element used is the same as those in Figure 6.12 and Figure 6.15. Comparing Figure 6.17(a) with Figure 6.17(b), it is found that the handle held by the photographer has become less obvious. It can be seen that the grayscale opening eliminates some of the smaller bright details.

6.2.2.4 Grayscale Closing

Closing f with b is denoted as $f \bullet b$, which is defined as

$$f \bullet b = (f \oplus b) \ominus b \tag{6.26}$$

(a)   (b)

FIGURE 6.17   Example of grayscale opening.

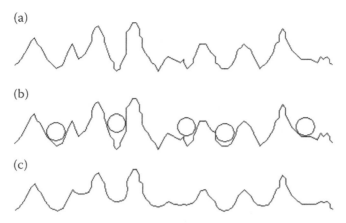

FIGURE 6.18   Grayscale closing diagram.

Grayscale closing can have a simple geometric explanation, which is discussed below with the help of Figure 6.18. Here Figure 6.18(a) is the same as Figure 6.16(a), and the structure element used is also the same. Closing f with b, that is, $f \bullet b$, which can be seen as rolling b against the upper edge of f from one end to the other. Figure 6.18(b) shows several positions of b in closing, and Figure 6.18(c) shows the result of the closing operation. It can be seen from Figure 6.18(c) that the mountain peaks are basically unchanged, and all valleys with a diameter smaller than b have been filled. In other words, when b rolls against the upper edge of f, all parts of f that are not in contact with b are filled to contact b. In practice, closing operations are often used to eliminate dark details that are smaller in size compared with structure elements, while keeping the overall gray value of the image and large dark regions basically unaffected. Specifically, the first step of dilation removes small dark details and at the same time enhances the image brightness, the second step of erosion weakens (basically restores) the image brightness but does not reintroduce the previously removed details.

The actual effect of grayscale closing can be seen in Figure 6.19, where Figure 6.19(a) is the original image and Figure 6.19(b) is the result of the closing. The grayscale structure

(a)

(b)

FIGURE 6.19   Example of grayscale opening.

element used is the same as those in Figure 6.12 and Figure 6.15. Comparing Figure 6.19(a) with Figure 6.19(b), it is found that the photographer's mouth has become a little blurred, and it can be seen that the grayscale closing eliminates some of the smaller dark details.

6.3 COMBINED MORPHOLOGICAL OPERATIONS

Combining basic operations (dilation, erosion, opening, closing) can complete some meaningful operations or realize some specific image processing functions.

The following respectively introduce some combined operation principles and methods that use binary morphology and gray morphology to complete morphological analysis.

6.3.1 Combined Binary Morphological Operations

The most basic operations in the morphological operations are dilation and erosion. In fact, both opening and closing are obtained by combining dilation and erosion, so some people regard both opening and closing as combined operations. With the help of dilation and erosion (and other operations) to carry out various combinations of different forms, many common morphological combination operations can be obtained.

6.3.1.1 Hit-or-Miss Transform

The **hit-or-miss transform** itself is a combination operation that combines dilation and erosion, and it is also the basis of many other combination operations. The hit-or-missing transform actually corresponds to two operations, so two structure elements are used. Suppose A is the original image, E and F are a pair of sets that do not coincide with each other (they define a pair of structure elements), and the hit-or-miss transform is represented by $\Uparrow$, which is defined as

$$A \Uparrow (E, F) = (A \ominus E) \cap (A^c \ominus F) = (A \ominus E) \cap (A \oplus F)^c \qquad (6.27)$$

Any pixel z in the hit-or-miss transform result satisfies: $E + z$ is a subset of A, and $F + z$ is a subset of A^c. Conversely, the pixel z that satisfies the above two items must be in the hit-or-miss transform result. In Equation (6.27), E and F are respectively called the hit structure element and the miss structure element, which are often used to limit the object to be detected in the opposite direction. It should be noted that the two structure elements must satisfy $E \cap F = \varnothing$, otherwise the hit-or-miss transform will give the result of detecting an empty set.

Figure 6.20 explains how to use the hit-or-miss transform to determine the location of a square region of a given size (Ritter and Wilson 2001). Figure 6.20(a) shows the original

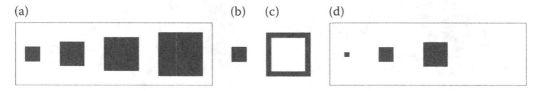

FIGURE 6.20 Use the hit-or-miss transform to detect the square regions.

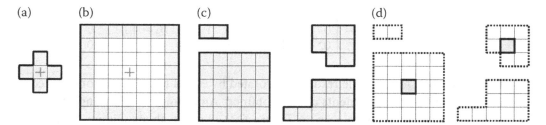

FIGURE 6.21   Use the hit-or-miss transform to detect the non-square regions.

image, including four solid squares of 3×3, 5×5, 7×7 and 9×9, respectively. The 3×3 solid square E in Figure 6.20(b) and the 9×9 box F (with a side width of 1 pixel) in Figure 6.20(c) together form the structure element $B = (E, F)$. Here, the hit-or-miss transform is designed to hit the region covering E and not hit the region covering F. The final result is shown in Figure 6.20(d), the first three squares are detected.

Not only the object size, but also the object shape will affect the detection result. Refer to Figure 6.21, where Figure 6.21(a) is the hit structure element, Figure 6.21(b) is the miss structure element, Figure 6.21(c) gives four example objects, and Figure 6.21(d) are the results of hit-or-miss transform for objects in Figure 6.21(c), respectively (two of the results are not empty sets, indicating that the hit-or-miss transform has the ability to selectively detect the shapes of the object).

6.3.1.2 Thinning

If you want to erode the object region but don't split it into multiple sub-regions, you need to use thinning. **Thinning** is used to detect pixels that are on the boundary of the object, but removing them will not split the object into disconnected sub-regions. Thinning the set A with the structure element B is denoted as $A \otimes B$, and $A \otimes B$ can be defined as follows by means of the hit-to-miss transform:

$$A \otimes B = A - (A \Uparrow B) = A \cap (A \Uparrow B)^c \tag{6.28}$$

In the above formula, the hit-to-hit transform is used to determine the pixels that should be thinned out, and then removed from the original set A. In practice, a series of structure elements $\{B\} = \{ B_1, B_2, \dots , B_n\}$ are generally defined, each of which is a small-sized mask (also called hit-or-miss mask); if B_{i+1} stands as the result of the rotating B_i, the thinning is also defined as

$$A \otimes \{B\} = A - ((\cdots ((A \otimes B_1) \otimes B_2)\cdots) \otimes B_n) \tag{6.29}$$

In other words, the thinning process is to thin the original image with B_1 first, and then thin the result with B_2, and continue until it refines with B_n. The whole process can be repeated until there is no change.

For example, the following set of four structure elements can be used for thinning ("×" indicates that its value is not important):

$$B_1 = \begin{bmatrix} 0 & 0 & 0 \\ \times & 1 & \times \\ 1 & 1 & 1 \end{bmatrix} \quad B_2 = \begin{bmatrix} 0 & \times & 1 \\ 0 & 1 & 1 \\ 0 & \times & 1 \end{bmatrix} \quad B_3 = \begin{bmatrix} 1 & 1 & 1 \\ \times & 1 & \times \\ 0 & 0 & 0 \end{bmatrix} \quad B_4 = \begin{bmatrix} 1 & \times & 0 \\ 1 & 1 & 0 \\ 1 & \times & 0 \end{bmatrix} \quad (6.30)$$

It can be seen that B_{i+1} here is the result of B_i rotated by 90°. If the mask is constructed by rotating 45°, eight structure elements can be obtained. An example of thinning using such eight structure elements can be seen in Figure 6.22. Among them, Figure 6.22(a) is a group of such eight structure elements, the origin of each element is at its center, "×" means that the value of the pixel can be any, and the white and shaded pixels take the values of 0 and 1, respectively. If the points detected by the structure element B_1 from the object is subtracted, the object will be thinned from the upper part, if the points detected by the structure element B_2 is subtracted from the object, the object will be thinned from the upper right corner, and so on. Using the above set of structure elements, symmetrical results can be obtained. Relatively speaking, the four odd-numbered structure elements have stronger thinning ability, while the even-numbered four structure elements have weaker thinning ability.

In Figure 6.22, Figure 6.22(b) shows the original object to be thinned, and its origin is set in the upper left corner. Figure 6.22(c)–Figure 6.22(k) show the results of each structure element thinned in turn (circles mark the pixels thinned in the current step).

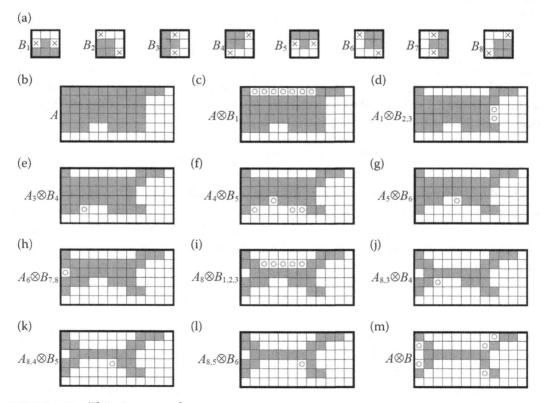

FIGURE 6.22   Thinning example.

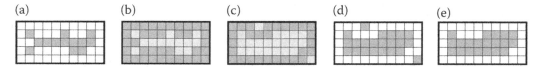

FIGURE 6.23 Use thinning to thickening.

When B_6 is used for the second refinement, the convergence result obtained is shown in Figure 6.22(l), and the refinement result is converted into mixed connectivity (Zhang 2017a) to eliminate the multi-path connectivity problem in Figure 6.22(l). The result is shown in Figure 6.22(m).

6.3.1.3 Thickening

Thickening the set A with the structure element B is denoted as $A \circledast B$. From a morphological point of view, thickening operates to thinning, and can be defined by the following formula:

$$A \circledast B = A \cup (A \Uparrow B) \tag{6.31}$$

Similar to thinning, **thickening** can also be defined by a series of operations

$$A \circledast \{B\} = ((\cdots((A \circledast B_1) \circledast B_2) \cdots) \circledast B_n) \tag{6.32}$$

The structure elements used for thickening can be similar to those for thinning, as shown in Figure 6.22(a), except that the 1 and 0 are swapped. In practice, the background can also be thinned first and then complement be made to get a thickening result. In other words, if you want to thicken the set A, you can first construct $D = A^c$, then thinning D, and finally find D^c. An example of this latter method is shown in Figure 6.23. Among them, Figure 6.23(a) is set A, Figure 6.23(b) is $D = A^c$, Figure 6.23(c) is the result of thinning D, Figure 6.23(d) is the D^c obtained by complementing the result of Figure 6.23(c), and finally after the thickening, a simple post-processing is performed to remove the discrete points and the Figure 6.23(e) is obtained.

6.3.1.4 Combination of Dilation and Erosion with Set Operations

Dilation and erosion can not only be combined with each other, but also with set operations. The combination of set operations with dilation and erosion has the following properties:

1. The order of the union operation and dilation operation for the set can be exchanged (the dilation of the union is equal to the union of the dilation):

$$B \oplus (A_1 \cup A_2) = (A_1 \cup A_2) \oplus B = (A_1 \oplus B) \cup (A_2 \oplus B) \tag{6.33}$$

2. The order of the union operation and the erosion operation for the set cannot be exchanged (the erosion of the union includes the union of the erosion):

$$(A_1 \cup A_2) \ominus B \supseteq (A_1 \ominus B) \cup (A_2 \ominus B) \quad B \ominus (A_1 \cup A_2) = (A_1 \ominus B) \cap (A_2 \ominus B)$$

$$(6.34)$$

3. The order of intersection operation and dilation operation for the set cannot be exchanged (the dilation of intersection is included in the intersection of dilation):

$$B \oplus (A_1 \cap A_2) = (A_1 \cap A_2) \oplus B \subseteq (A_1 \oplus B) \cap (A_2 \oplus B) \qquad (6.35)$$

4. The order of the intersection operation and the erosion operation for the set can be exchanged (the erosion of the intersection is equal to the intersection of the erosion):

$$(A_1 \cap A_2) \ominus B = (A_1 \ominus B) \cap (A_2 \ominus B) \qquad (6.36)$$

6.3.1.5 Combination of Dilation and Erosion with Logical Operations

Dilation and erosion can also be combined with logical operations. For example, a combination of dilation operation and logic operation can obtain a hollowed-out label, which can be used to overlay an all-black or all-white image region for labeling. The specific method is: first dilate the label text that needs to be used, and then perform a logical XOR operation between the result and the original text, so that the middle hollowed-out label can be obtained, and it can be put on the black or white region for a clear vision. Figure 6.24 shows an example (Zhang 2017b), where Figure 6.24(a) is the original text, and Figure 6.24(b) is the hollow label of the original text obtained by the above method.

6.3.2 Combined Grayscale Morphological Operations

Combining various basic grayscale morphological operations can also construct a series of combined grayscale morphological operations.

6.3.2.1 Morphological Gradient

The gradient calculation using morphology can be combined with dilation and erosion. The **morphological gradient** of an image is denoted as g:

$$g = (f \oplus b) - (f \ominus b) \qquad (6.37)$$

Morphological gradient can strengthen the sharper grayscale transition regions in the image. Different from various spatial gradient operators (for example, see Sub-section 2.2.1), the morphological gradient obtained with symmetrical structure elements is less affected by the edge direction, but generally the calculation required to calculate the

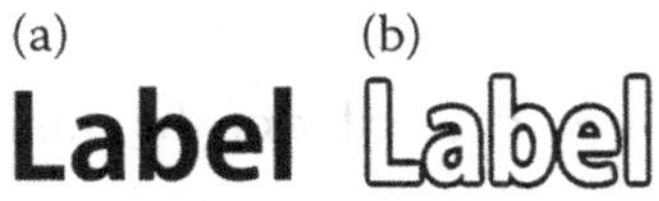

(a)　　　　(b)

FIGURE 6.24 An example of the combination of dilation and logical operations.

(a)   (b)   (c)   (d)

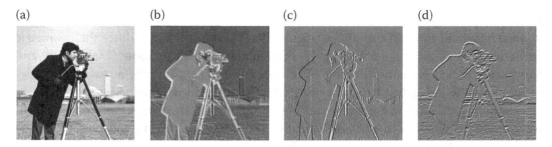

FIGURE 6.25   Morphological gradient and spatial gradient calculation results.

morphological gradient is larger. Figure 6.25 shows an example of calculation and comparison. Figure 6.25(a) is the original image, Figure 6.25(b) is the result of morphological gradient calculation, Figure 6.25(c) and Figure 6.25(d) are the results obtained by using the horizontal and vertical masks of the Sobel gradient operator, respectively.

6.3.2.2 Morphological Smoothing

Opening the image first and then closing the result is a method of smoothing the image. Let the result of **morphological smoothing** be g, and then

$$g = (f \circ b) \bullet b \tag{6.38}$$

The combined effect of the two operations in the formula is to remove or weaken all kinds of noise in the bright and dark regions, in which the opening removes or weakens the details of the bright region smaller than the structure element, and the closing removes or weakens the details of the dark region smaller than the structure element.

Figure 6.26 shows an example of morphological smoothing. Figure 6.26(a) is the original image, and Figure 6.26(b) is the result of morphological smoothing of Figure 6.26(a) with grayscale structure elements composed of 4-neighborhood. It can be seen from the picture that the ripples on the tripod are not visible after smoothing, and become smoother.

FIGURE 6.26   An example of morphological smoothing.

6.3.2.3 Morphological Filter

A *morphological filter* is a nonlinear signal filter, which locally modifies the geometric characteristics of the signal through morphological transformation (Mahdavieh and Gonzalez 1992). Given the filtering operation and filtering output, a quantitative description of the geometric structure of the input signal can be obtained.

Combining dilation and erosion can obtain opening and closing. One realization of morphological filters is to combine opening and closing. Opening and closing can be used for quantitative research on geometric features, because they have little effect on the gray levels of retained or removed features.

From the perspective of eliminating structures that are brighter than the background and smaller in size than structure elements, opening is somewhat like a nonlinear low-pass filter. However, opening is different from the frequency domain low-pass filtering that prevents various high frequencies. When large and small structures have a higher spatial frequency domain, opening only allows large structures to pass through but can remove small structures. Opening an image can eliminate excessively bright points such as islands or spikes in the image. The function of closing for darker features corresponds to the function of opening for brighter features. Closing can eliminate structures that are darker than the background and smaller in size than structure elements.

A *sieve filter* is a morphological filter that only allows structures with a size within a certain narrow range to pass through. For example, to extract bright-spot-shaped defects with a size of $n \times n$ pixels (n is an odd number), the following filter S can be used (the superscript indicates the size of the structure element):

$$S = (f \circ b^{n \times n}) - [f \circ b^{(n-2) \times (n-2)}] \tag{6.39}$$

The sieve filter is similar to the frequency domain band-pass filter. The first term in the above formula removes all bright structures with a size smaller than $n \times n$, and the second term removes all bright structures with a size smaller than $(n - 2) \times (n - 2)$. So subtracting these two items leaves those bright structures with a size between $n \times n$ and $(n - 2) \times (n - 2)$. Generally, the effect of the sieve filter is best when the size of the structure to be filtered is several pixels. In order to extract the slender object, linear (planar in 3-D) structure elements can be used for opening and closing.

6.4 PRACTICAL MORPHOLOGY ALGORITHMS

Using the various basic operations and combination operations of mathematical morphology introduced above, many practical algorithms of mathematical morphology can be constructed to solve practical image processing and analysis problems. For example, the application of detecting news headline based on morphological operation can be found in (Jiang and Zhang 2003), the application of grayscale morphological operations to distinguish the difference between various grayscale pattern regions can be used for clustering segmentation, watershed segmentation, and texture segmentation (Gonzalez and Woods 2008).

These practical algorithms can still be divided into practical binary morphology algorithms and practical grayscale morphological algorithms (Zhang 2017b), but practical grayscale morphology algorithms can also be used for binary images (think binary images as special cases of grayscale images). In many cases, grayscale images can also be converted into binary images first and then operated using practical binary morphology algorithms.

6.4.1 Practical Binary Morphology Algorithms

The object of practical binary morphology algorithm is binary image. In image analysis, it is often the result image after image segmentation.

6.4.1.1 Noise Elimination

In the binary image obtained after segmentation, there are often some small holes or islands. These small holes or islands are generally caused by system noise, pre-processing or thresholding. For example, salt and pepper noise is a typical one, causing small holes or islands in the binary image. The combination of opening and closing can form a morphological noise filter to eliminate this type of noise. For example, using a structure element consisting of a central pixel and its 4-neighborhood pixels for opening the image can eliminate pepper noise, while closing the image can eliminate salt noise (Ritter and Wilson 2001).

An example of noise elimination is shown in Figure 6.27. Among them, Figure 6.27(a) includes a rectangular object A. Due to the influence of noise, there are some noise holes inside the object and some noise blocks around the object. Now the circular structure element B shown in Figure 6.27(b) is used to eliminate noise through morphological operations. The structure element here should be larger than all the noise holes and blocks. First, B is used to erode A to get Figure 6.27(c), and then B is used to dilate the erosion result to get Figure 6.27(d). The serial combination of these two operations is the opening operation, which eliminates the noise block around the object. Now B is used to dilate Figure 6.27(d) to get Figure 6.27(e), and then B is used to erode the result of dilation to get Figure 6.27(f). The serial combination of these two operations is the closing operation, which eliminates the noise hole inside the object. The whole process is opening first and then closing, which can be written as

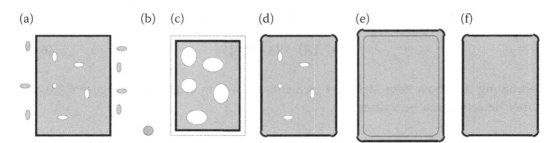

FIGURE 6.27 Example of noise elimination.

$$\{[(A \ominus B) \oplus B] \oplus B\} \ominus B = (A \circ B) \bullet B \tag{6.40}$$

Comparing Figure 6.27(a) and Figure 6.27(f), it can be seen that the noise inside and outside the object region have been eliminated, and the object itself has not changed much except that the original four right angles have become rounded corners.

6.4.1.2 Corner Detection

A **corner point** is a pixel with a sudden change in slope, that is, a position with a large absolute **curvature** value. The corner points can be extracted with the help of morphological operations. First select a round structure element of suitable size, use this structure element for opening and subtract the result from the original image. Choose two more structure elements: one is smaller than the opening region and the other is larger than the opening region. Use these two structure elements to erode the region left by the opening, and compare the two results obtained. This is equivalent to a shape band-pass filter. The size of the structure element needs to be selected according to the angle of the corner point, because the region of the opening changes with the angle of the corner point. Decrease the angle, the region left after opening increases, and the region of structure elements also increases. So first check the structure element with the largest regin, if there is no result, gradually reduce the region of the structure element until the corner point is detected, and at the same time obtain the angle information.

Corner points can also be detected by asymmetric closing (Shih 2010). Asymmetric closing involves dilating the image with one structure element and then eroding the image with another structure element. The idea is to make dilation and erosion complementary. One way is to use two structure elements, the cross "+" and the diamond "◇". The following formula represents the asymmetric closing operation on image A:

$$A_{+\diamond}^c = (A \oplus +) \ominus \diamond \tag{6.41}$$

At this time, the corner intensity is

$$C_+(A) = |A - A_{+\diamond}^c| \tag{6.42}$$

For different corners, the strength of the corners rotated by $45°$ can also be calculated (the structure elements are cross "✕" and square "□"):

$$C_\times(A) = |A - A_{\times\square}^c| \tag{6.43}$$

Combining the above four structure elements (shown in sequence in Figure 6.28), the corner detection can be written as

$$C_{+\times}(A) = |A_{+\diamond}^c - A_{\times\square}^c| \tag{6.44}$$

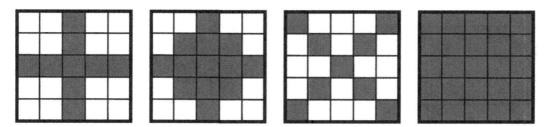

FIGURE 6.28   Four structure elements in sequence $+$, $\diamondsuit$, $\times$, $\square\,\square$.

6.4.1.3 Boundary Extraction

Suppose there is a set A, and its boundary is denoted as $\beta(A)$. By first eroding A with a structure element B, and then obtaining the difference between the erosion result and A, $\beta(A)$ can be obtained:

$$\beta(A) = A - (A \ominus B) \tag{6.45}$$

An example of boundary extraction is shown in Figure 6.29. In which, Figure 6.29(a) gives a binary object A, Figure 6.29(b) gives a structure element B, Figure 6.29(c) gives the result of eroding A with B, $A \ominus B$, and Figure 6.29(d) gives the final boundary $\beta(A)$ obtained by subtracting the Figure 6.29(a) from Figure 6.29(c). Note that when the origin of B is at the border of A, a part of B will be outside of A. In this case, it is generally set to 0 outside of A. Also note that the structure element here is 8-connected, and the resulting boundary is 4-connected.

6.4.1.4 Region Filling

Regions and their boundaries can be mutually obtained. The boundary of the known region can be obtained according to Equation (6.45), and conversely, the region can also be obtained by filling the known boundary. An example of region filling is shown in Figure 6.30. In which, Figure 6.30(a) gives a set A of regional boundary points, and its complement is shown in Figure 6.30(b). The region can be filled by dilating, complementing and intersecting it with the structure element in Figure 6.30(c). First, assign 1 to a point within the boundary (as shown by the dark dot in Figure 6.30(d)), and then fill it in according to the following iterative formula (Figures 6.30(e) and Figure 6.30(f) show the situations of two of the intermediate steps):

$$X_k = (X_{k-1} \oplus B) \cap A^c \qquad k = 1, 2, 3, \cdots \tag{6.46}$$

(a)   (b)   (c)   (d)

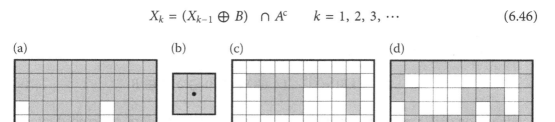

FIGURE 6.29   Example of boundary extraction.

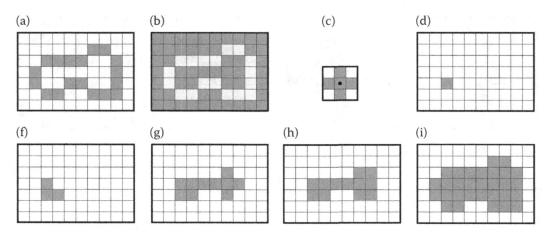

FIGURE 6.30 Example of region filling.

Stop the iteration when $X_k = X_{k-1}$ ($k = 7$ in this example, as shown in Figure 6.30(g)). At this time, the intersection of X_k and A includes the interior of the filled region and its boundary, as shown in Figure 6.30(h). The dilation process in Equation (6.46) will exceed the boundary if it is not controlled, but the intersection of each step with A^c restricts it to the region of interest. This dilation process can be called a conditional dilation process. Note that the structure element here is 4-connected, while the original filled boundary is 8-connected.

6.4.1.5 Region Skeleton Calculation

The **skeleton** is obtained by refining and simplifying a region, and has an equivalent representation to the region (the region can be reconstructed from the skeleton). Extracting the skeleton of an object is an important way to represent the shape and structure of the object, and it is often referred to as the skeletonization of the object. Mathematical morphological methods can be used to calculate the skeleton. Let $S(A)$ represent the skeleton of A, it can be represented as:

$$S(A) = \bigcup_{k=0}^{K} S_k(A) \tag{6.47}$$

$S_k(A)$ in the above formula is generally called the skeleton subset, which can be written as

$$S_k(A) = (A \ominus kB) - [(A \ominus kB) \circ B] \tag{6.48}$$

where B is a structure element; $(A \ominus kB)$ represents the erosion of A with B for k consecutive times, which can be represented by T_k, that is

$$T_k = (A \ominus kB) = ((\cdots (A \ominus B) \ominus B) \ominus \cdots) \ominus B \tag{6.49}$$

K in Equation (6.47) represents the number of the last iteration before A is eroded into an empty set, namely

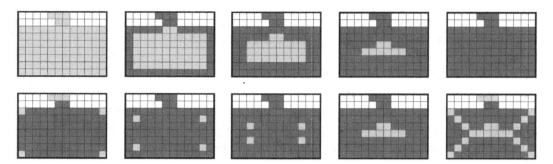

FIGURE 6.31   Example of morphological skeleton.

$$K = \max\{k \mid (A \ominus kB) \neq \varnothing\} \tag{6.50}$$

An example of a computational morphological skeleton is shown in Figure 6.31. Among them, the leftmost original image in the first row contains a rectangular object with a small add-on above it. The remaining pictures in the first row show the set T_k obtained by successive erosions, namely T_1, T_2, T_3, T_4. Because $T_4 = \varnothing$, so $K = 3$. The second line of the figure shows the skeleton set S_k obtained in sequence, namely S_0, S_1, S_2, S_3, and the final skeleton S (including two connected parts).

Equation (6.47) shows that the skeleton of A can be obtained by the union of the skeleton subset $S_k(A)$. Conversely, A can also be reconstructed with $S_k(A)$:

$$A = \bigcup_{k=0}^{K} (S_k(A) \oplus kB) \tag{6.51}$$

where B is a structure element and $(S_k(A)kB)$ represents the dilation of $S_k(A)$ with B for k consecutive times, that is

$$(S_k(A) \oplus kB) = ((\cdots (S_k(A) \oplus B) \oplus B) \oplus \cdots) \oplus B \tag{6.52}$$

An example of a computational morphological skeleton is shown in Figure 6.32. In which, Figure 6.32(a) is a binary image; Figure 6.32(b) is the skeleton obtained by using the 3 × 3 structure element in Figure 6.29; Figure 6.32(c) is the skeleton obtained by using the similar 5 × 5 structure element; Figure 6.32(d) is the skeleton obtained by using

(a)　　　　　　　(b)　　　　　　　(c)　　　　　　　(d)

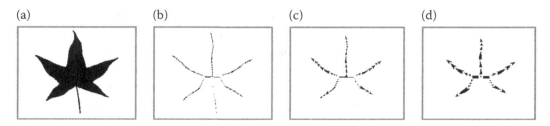

FIGURE 6.32   Example of morphological skeleton calculation.

similar 7×7 structure element. Note that the larger petiole is not retained due to using structure element masks in Figure 6.32(c) and Figure 6.32(d).

6.4.2 Practical Grayscale Morphology Algorithms

Many practical grayscale morphology algorithms can also be obtained by comprehensively using basic operations and combined operations. Here the operation object is a grayscale image, and the processing result is also a grayscale image, but for the convenience of introduction, some examples below use binary images.

6.4.2.1 Background Estimation and Elimination

The morphological filter can change the gray values of the image, but the change of the gray values depends on the geometric characteristics of the filter and can be controlled by structure elements. A typical example is **background estimation and elimination**. Morphological filtering can detect weak (less obvious) objects well, especially for images with low-contrast transition regions. The opening operation can remove regions that are brighter than the background and smaller than the size of the structure element. Therefore, by selecting appropriate structure elements for opening, only the estimation of the background is left in the image. If the estimation of the background is subtracted from the original image, the object can be extracted:

$$\text{Background estimation} = f \circ b \tag{6.53}$$

$$\text{Background elimination} = f - (f \circ b) \tag{6.54}$$

The closing operation can remove regions that are darker than the background and smaller than the size of the structure element. Therefore, by selecting the appropriate structure element for closing, only the estimation of the background can be left in the image. The object can also be extracted if the original image is subtracted from the estimation of the background:

$$\text{Background estimation} = f \bullet b \tag{6.55}$$

$$\text{Background elimination} = (f \bullet b) - f \tag{6.56}$$

It should be noted that in the estimation of the background, cylindrical structure elements are better. However, in filtering, the effect of the semi-spherical structure element is better than that of the cylindrical structure element. Because the edges are sharp, the cylinder will remove a lot of useful grayscale information, while the semi- spherical structure element rubs the surface of the original image with a gentle edge.

An example of opening the 1-D section of f using structure elements of different shapes is shown in Figure 6.33. Among them, Figures 6.33(a) and Figures 6.33(b) are schematics and results of opening with semi-spherical structure elements, and Figures 6.33(c) and Figures 6.33(d) are schematics and results of opening with cylindrical structure elements. The radii of the two structure elements are the same.

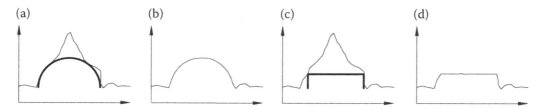

FIGURE 6.33　Comparison of opening effects with semi-spherical and cylindrical structure elements.

It can be seen from the Figure 6.33 that the result of opening with a cylinder structure elementis better, because it can minimize the residue of the structure. When opening with a semi-spherical structure element, its upper part may coincide with the structure peak part, so that the estimated background surface cannot truly reflect the gray level of the background. In this way, when the background surface is subtracted from the original gray level, the gray level near the peak of the structure will be reduced. If a cylindrical opening is used, this problem can be basically eliminated. It can also be seen from Figure 6.33 that to remove bright regions from the image, a cylinder with a diameter larger than the region must be used ftr opening the image, and to remove dark regions from the image, a cylinder with a diameter greater than the region must be used for closing the image. Of course, if a semi-spherical structure element is used with a large enough radius, a similar effect can be achieved, but the calculation time may be greatly increased.

6.4.2.2 Morphological Detection of Edges

Many commonly used edge detection operators work by calculating local differentials. Generally, this type of edge detector is more sensitive to noise and will enhance the noise. Although the ***morphological edge detector*** is also sensitive to noise, it will not enhance or amplify the noise. The concept of morphological gradient is mainly used here. The most basic morphological gradient can be defined as follows (see Equation (6.27)):

$$\mathrm{grad}_1 = (f \oplus b) - (f \ominus b) \qquad (6.57)$$

An example of applying Equation (6.57) to a binary image (using 8-neighbor structure elements) is shown in Figure 6.34. Among them, Figure 6.34(a) is the image f, Figure 6.34(b) is $f \oplus b$, Figure 6.34(c) is $f \ominus b$, and Figure 6.34(d) is grad_1. $f \oplus b$ dilates the bright region in f by one pixel width, and $f \ominus b$ shrinks the dark region in f by one pixel width, so the boundary given by grad_1 is two pixels wide.

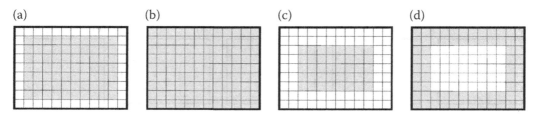

FIGURE 6.34　Example of applying morphological gradient grad_1.

The single-pixel-wide boundary can be obtained with the following two equivalent (strictly speaking, not equivalent for discrete images) morphological gradients, grad_2 and grad_3:

$$\mathrm{grad}_2 = (f \oplus b) - f \qquad (6.58)$$

$$\mathrm{grad}_3 = f - (f \ominus b) \qquad (6.59)$$

An example of applying Equation (6.58) and Equation (6.59) to a binary image (using 8-neighbor structure elements) is shown in Figure 6.35. Among them, Figure 6.35(a) is the image f, Figure 6.35(b) is $f \oplus b$, and Figure 6.35 (c) is $(f \oplus b) - f$. It can be seen that the resulting edge is one pixel wide. In addition, Figure 6.35(d) is $f \ominus b$, and Figure 6.35(e) is $f - (f \ominus b)$. It can be seen that the resulting edge is also one pixel wide.

It can be seen from Figure 6.35 that the single-pixel-wide edge obtained using Equation (6.58) is actually in the background. The single-pixel-wide edge obtained using Equation (6.59) actually belongs to the object.

It should be noted that all morphological gradients grad_1, grad_2, and grad_3 will not amplify the noise in the image, but still retain the original noise. The following gives another morphological gradient that is not sensitive to isolated noise points:

$$\mathrm{grad}_4 = \min \{ [(f \oplus b) - f], \ [f - (f \ominus b)] \} \qquad (6.60)$$

If this kind of gradient is used to detect the ideal ramp edge, a good detection effect will be achieved. Its disadvantage is that it can't (directly) detect the ideal step edge, but in this case, you can blur the image first, convert the ideal step edge into an ideal ramp edge, and then use grad_4. It should be noted here that the scope of the blurring mask should be consistent with the scope of the mask used for dilation and erosion. When the 4-neighborhood cylindrical mask is used, for a given image f, its corresponding blurred image h is

$$h(i, j) = [f(i, j) + f(i + 1, j) + f(i, j + 1) + f(i - 1, j) + f(i, j - 1)]/5 \qquad (6.61)$$

On this basis, another morphological gradient can be obtained:

$$\mathrm{grad}_5 = \min \{ [(h \oplus b) - h], \ [h - (h \ominus b)] \} \qquad (6.62)$$

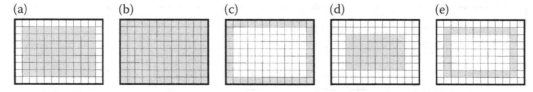

FIGURE 6.35 Example of applying two morphological gradients: grad_2 and grad_3.

Here, due to the blurring, the edge strength obtained will be weakened. Therefore, if the noise in the image is not too strong, it is best to directly use grad$_4$ without blurring the image. When choosing to use one of grad$_4$ and grad$_5$, it is necessary to take into account the requirements of both a larger signal-to-noise ratio and a sharper edge.

6.4.2.3 Clustering Fast Segmentation

The combination of conditional dilation and final erosion can realize the morphological segmentation of the image.

Conditional dilation is an extension (conditions are added) of general dilation: In the case of condition X (X can be regarded as a limited set), dilating f with b is denoted as $f \oplus b$; X, that is, conditional dilation, is defined as

$$f \oplus b; X = (f \oplus b) \cap X \tag{6.63}$$

Repeated conditional dilation (also called sequential conditional dilation) is the extension of the above-mentioned conditional dilation operation, and is denoted as $f \oplus \{b\}$; X (here $\{b\}$ represents iteratively dilate f with b until there is no more change; that is, repeat the conditional dilation):

$$f \oplus \{b\}; X = [[[(f \oplus b) \cap X] \oplus b] \cap X] \oplus b \cdots \tag{6.64}$$

Final erosion means to repeatedly erode an objet until it disappears, and retain the result of the last step before (this result is also called the seed of the object). Let $f_k = f \ominus kb$, where b is the unit circle and kb is the circle with radius k. The final erosion set g_k can be defined as the elements in f_k. If $l > k$, g_k disappears in f_l. The first step in the final erosion is repeated conditional dilation:

$$U_k = (f_{k+1} \oplus \{b\}); f_k \tag{6.65}$$

The second step in the final erosion is to subtract the above dilation result from the erosion result of f, namely

$$g_k = f_k - U_k \tag{6.66}$$

If there are multiple objects in the image, the union of their respective g_k can be obtained to provide the final eroded object set g. In other words, the final erosion image is

$$g = \underset{k=1,m}{\cup} g_k \tag{6.67}$$

where m is the total number of erosions.

Based on conditional dilation and final erosion, the **clustering fast segmentation (CFS)** of images with convex boundary objects can be realized. It is more suitable for the situation when the objects overlap and is less affected by false separation. It includes three steps: (i) Iterative erosion of f; (ii) determine the final erosion set g_k; and (iii) determine the object boundary. They are introduced separately below.

1. Using the unit circular structure element b to iteratively erode the original image f:

$$f_k = f \ominus kb \quad k = 1, \cdots, m \quad where \quad \{m: f_m \neq \varnothing\} \tag{6.68}$$

Here $f_1 = f \ominus b$, $f_2 = f \ominus 2b$, and then until $f_m = f \ominus mb$ and $f_{m+1} = \varnothing$; m is the maximum number of non-empty images.

Here is an intuitive explanation with the help of Figure 6.36. Among them, Figure 6.36(a) gives an example image. Assume that the 4-neighborhood structure element is used. The first erosion erodes the dark gray region as well as shrinks and separates the other two regions. The result is shown in Figure 6.36(b). Figure 6.36(c) shows the result of conditional dilation of Figure 6.36(b) with Figure 6.36(a) as the condition. The second erosion is carried out on Figure 6.36(b), eroding the middle gray region and shrinking the light gray region, and the result is shown in Figure 6.36(d). Figure 6.36(e) shows the result of conditional dilation of Figure 6.36(d) with Figure 6.36(b) as the condition. If the third erosion is performed, an empty set will be obtained, so no repeated conditional dilation will be performed. At this time, subtract Figure 6.36(c) from Figure 6.36(a) to get the first seed, subtract Figure 6.36(e) from Figure 6.36(b) to get the second seed, and Figure 6.36(d) to get the third seed.

2. Take the final erosion of each f_k and subtract the erosion result from f_k:

$$g_k = f_k - (f_{k+1} \oplus \{b\}; \ f_k) \tag{6.69}$$

Here, g_k is the final erosion set, or the seed of each g_k.

This step can still be explained with the help of Figure 6.36. If Figure 6.36(a) is used as condition and b is used to iteratively dilate Figure 6.36(b), then Figure 6.36(c) can be obtained. Compared with Figure 6.36(a), the only difference is the dark gray points. In order to get the dark gray points, subtract Figure 6.36(c) from Figure 6.36(a), and the result is the final erosion of Figure 6.36(a). This is the first seed. If the Figure 6.36(b) is used as condition and b is used to iteratively dilate the Figure 6.36(d), the region can be restored, and subtract the result from Figure 6.36(b) the seed of the mid-gray region can be obtained. Similarly, seeds in light gray regions can be obtained.

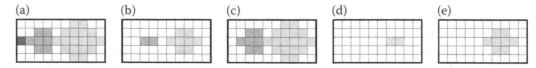

FIGURE 6.36 The steps of clustering fast segmentation.

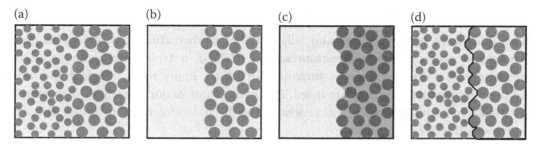

FIGURE 6.37   An example of morphological texture segmentation.

3. Finally, starting from each seed, the following formula can be used to restore the original full size of each region:

$$U = \cup g_k \oplus (k - 1)b \quad \text{for} \quad k = 1 \quad \text{to} \quad m \tag{6.70}$$

6.4.2.4 Texture Segmentation

Because grayscale closing can remove dark details in the image, grayscale opening can remove bright details in the image, so their combination can be used to segment some texture images.

Figure 6.37 provides an illustrative example of **texture segmentation**. The image given in Figure 6.37(a) includes two textured regions. The textures are formed by a combination of darker circles, but the radius of the circles in the two regions are different (representing two textures with different thicknesses). To separate these two regions, first use a series of gradually increasing circular structure elements for closing the original image in turn, until the size of the structure element is equivalent to the size of the small circles, these small circles are removed from the image during the closing process. After removing them, only the brighter background in the region remains in their original position. For the entire image, it is equivalent that only the large circle and the background of the whole image are remained as shown in Figure (b). At this time, select a structure element larger than the gap between the large circles for opening it once to remove the bright gap between the large circles and darken the entire region where the large circles are (see the result of Figure 6.37(c)). In the image obtained in this way, the region where the original small circles were located is relatively bright and the region where the large circles were located is relatively dark. The original image with two different textures are now converted into image with different brightness, and the two (texture) regions can be separated by a simple grayscale thresholding algorithm. The dividing line superimposed on the original image gives the segmented region boundary shown in Figure 6.37(d).

6.5 SOME RECENT DEVELOPMENTS AND FURTHER RESEARCH

In the following sections, some technical developments and promising research directions in the last few years are briefly overviewed.

6.5.1 Morphological Operator and Application Domain

In an illustrative review (Brunet and Sills 2017) of mathematical morphology in geosciences and *geographical information science (GISci)*, a table with some successful applications of MM operations is provided. In which, many *morphological operators* and their applications domains are listed, along with some major references. This table is up-dated here, with the recent references (omit the old references) to reflect the new progress in this area, as in Table 6.1.

6.5.2 Attribute Modification in Structure Elements

In basic operations of grayscale morphology, as in Sub-section 6.2.2, the grayscale dilation and grayscale erosion need to search the maximum value of additive sum between image and structure element and the minimum value of subtraction difference between image and structure element, respectively. For extracting the endmembers from hyperspectral images, the calculations of dilation and erosion are no longer to find the maximum and minimum

TABLE 6.1   Morphological operator and Application domain with recent major references

Morphological Operator	Application Domain	Recent Major References
Binary and grayscale morphological erosion, dilation, opening, closing, multiscale morphological operations	Petrology, GISci, geosciences, remote sensing	(Iglesias-Rey et al. 2021) (Kong et al. 2021) (Lopez-Molina et al. 2021)
Geodesic morphological operations	Remote sensing, GISci, geography, petrology	(Challa et al. 2018) (De Oliveira et al. 2019) (Sagar 2018)
Hit-or-miss transformation	Geomorphology, hydrology	(Cao and Cai 2018) (Nagajothi and Sagar 2019) (Szczepanska et al. 2020)
Morphological thinning, thickening, pruning	Hydrology, cartography	(Frejaville et al. 2018) (Macey et al. 2018) (Patricio 2020)
Morphological skeletonization	Cartography, hydrology, geomorphology	(Mihelic et al. 2021) (O'Sullivan et al. 2021) (Zhang et al 2022)
Skeletonization by zones of influence and weighted skeletonization by zones of Influence	Cartography, hydrology, geomorphology	(Nagajothi and Sagar 2019) (Sun 2020) (Torres 2019)
Granulometries and anti-granulometries	Petrology, geomorphology, hydrology	(Legentil et al. 2022) (Nagajothi and Sagar 2019) (Zhu et al. 2022)
Morphological distances, Hausdorff dilation (erosion) distances	GISci, limnology, biogeography, spatial planning	(Das et al. 2019) (Drazic 2019) (Li et al. 2021)
Morphological interpolations and extrapolations	Geophysics, atmospheric science, geology, remote sensing, cartography	(Challa et al. 2018) (De Oliveira et al. 2019) (Szczepanska et al. 2020)
Watershed transformation	Hydrology, remote sensing, mapping, borehole studies, seismic data processing	(Ghose and Mitra 2021) (Lyu et al. 2022) (Mahmoudi et al. 2020)

gray values of pixels, but to find the purest pixel and the pixel with the maximum mixing degree (the most impure pixel) in structure elements.

6.5.2.1 Pure Pixel Index

One index used to measure the purity of pixel is ***pure pixel index (PPI)***. The basic idea for computing PPI is based on convex geometry theory. According to the theory of convex geometry, the corresponding sample points of all pixels of hyperspectral image in the high-dimensional spectral feature space are distributed in a scatter diagram, all sample points are contained in a convex simplex, and those pure pixels (***endmembers***) are located at the vertex of the convex simplex.

The characteristics of convex simplex determine that the projection of sample points located at the apex of simplex on any straight line in the feature space must be the two endpoints of the projection line. Taking the 2-D space shown in Figure 6.38 as an example, the three endmembers e_1, e_2, and e_3 are located at the vertex of the triangle, and the mixed pixels are mixed by the end elements, which are all located inside the triangle. In this 2-D space, a straight line is randomly generated, and all sample points are projected on the straight line. The vertices of the triangle will be mostly projected to both ends of the line segment, and the points inside the triangle will be projected to the inside of the line segment.

Accordingly, a large number of random straight lines can be generated in the feature space for projection, and the number of times each pixel falls on the two endpoints of the line segment is counted as the PPI. The higher the PPI corresponds to a pixel, the more likely it is to be endmember. As the straight lines are generated randomly, the extracted endmembers may be different. The computation of PPI just counts hyperspectral image as a collection of disordered spectral vectors, only the spectral information of the image is used, and the spatial distribution of the objects in the image is ignored.

6.5.2.2 Morphological Eccentricity Index

Another index is the ***morphological eccentricity index (MEI)***. It is defined as the spectral angular distance between the pure pixel and the most mixed pixel.

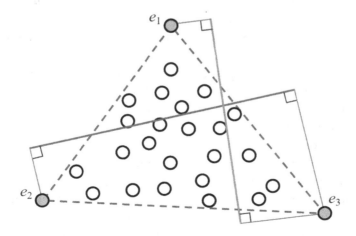

FIGURE 6.38   Using projection to computer PPI.

In practice, MEI can be obtained by calculating the distance from a pixel within a structuring element to the center of the structuring element. Assuming that the number of pixels in the structure element S is N, then the center of S can be defined as

$$C(x, y) = \frac{1}{N}\Sigma_s \Sigma_t f(s, t) \quad \forall\, (s, t) \in S \tag{6.71}$$

The distance from the pixel $f(x, y)$ in the structuring element S to the center of S can be expressed as

$$D[f(x, y), S] = dist[f(x, y), C(x, y)] \tag{6.72}$$

At this time, the dilation and erosion operations can be expanded and defined, respectively, as

$$d(x, y) = (f \oplus S)(x, y) = \arg\left\{\max_{(s,t)\in S}[D(f(x + s, y + t), S)]\right\} \tag{6.73}$$

$$e(x, y) = (f \ominus S)(x, y) = \arg\left\{\min_{(s,t)\in S}[D(f(x - s, y - t), S)]\right\} \tag{6.74}$$

where $d(x, y)$ is the pixel farthest from the center of S, that is, the relatively purest pixel; $e(x, y)$ is the pixel closest to the center of S, that is, the pixel with the largest mixing degree.

The morphological eccentricity index (MEI) can be defined by the spectral angle distance between $d(x, y)$ and $e(x, y)$:

$$\text{MEI}(p, q) = \text{dist}[d(x, y), e(x, y)] \tag{6.75}$$

6.5.2.3 Automated Morphological Endmember Extraction

Based on MEI, the **automated morphological endmember extraction (AMEE)** algorithm is proposed (Plaza 2002). AMEE algorithm uses MEI value to represent the relative purity and assigns this value to the purest pixel in structure element. This algorithm starts from the minimum structure element S_{min}, and scans the whole image. At each position, a purest pixel and a pixel with the largest mixing degree can be found, and they are used to computer MEI value that is assigned to the purest pixel. This process is repeated for the structure elements with increasing size, until the pre-defined maximum iterative number. Finally, an MEI image is obtained, and the endmember is selected according to the MEI values from high to low.

The AMEE algorithm takes the mean spectrum of all pixels in the structuring element as the spectrum of the pixel with the largest mixing degree, which is reasonable when the majority pixels are the mixed pixels in the structuring element, but when there are many pure pixels in the structuring element, the mean spectrum of all pixels will be closer to the pure pixels, and the pixels farther from the mean spectrum are the more mixed pixels, not the pure pixels (that is, the higher the MEI of the pixel, the lower the purity), so the dilation and erosion operations are not correct at this time. Besides, the AMEE algorithm defines the spectral angular distance between the purest pixel and the most mixed pixel in the structure element as MEI to represent the pixel purity, but the most mixed pixel in different structure elements may also be different, so the reference standards for calculating the MEI value are different, and the MEI value could not truly and effectively represent the purity of the pixel.

6.5.2.4 Embedding PPI into AMEE

One improved AMEE algorithm has been proposed (Xu et al. 2019). The basic idea is to embed the PPI (in replacing the MEI) into the AMEE algorithm to find the purest pixel in the structure element. Such a PPI-based morphological endmember extraction algorithm

With the introduction of PPI into AMEE, and the utilization of PPI for find the purest pixel, the purest pixel will have more possibility than other pixels to be extracted in statistics. In addition, with the increase of the number of structure elements, the PPI of real pure pixel will continuously increase, while the PPI of mixed pixel will not increase. In other words, with the increase of the number of projection lines, the possibility of extracting real endmembers will increase, while the possibility of extracting false endmembers will decrease. So the most purified pixel will certainly be found.

Based on PPI, the definitions of dilation operation and erosion operation can be redefined as:

Dilation operation: Project the pixels within the coverage of the ***structure element*** on a randomly generated line, and count the number of times each pixel falls on both ends of the line segment. The one with the highest counting number is considered to have the highest purity, and this count number is assigned to the corresponding pixel as the purity index.

Erosion operation: Count the pixels closest to the midpoint of the line segment for each projection, and record the count number, those with the most count number are considered the most mixed.

When computing the PPI in a structure element, a projection vector is first generated, the projection P_s of the pixel of the structure element on the projection vector is calculated, and the positions of the maximum and minimum values in P_s: $i_{\max} = \mathrm{argmax}(P_s)$, $i_{\min} = \mathrm{argmin}(P_s)$ are determined. The corresponding pixel purity index $P_{i_{\max}} = P_{i\max} + 1$, $P_{i\min} = P_{i\min} + 1$ are continuously updated. Here, the cumulative sum of the PPI values obtained after the projection of a certain pixel $f(x, y)$ in the structural element S is defined as:

$$P[f(x, y), S] = \sum_{(x,y)\in S} P_{i_{\max}} + P_{i_{\min}} \tag{6.76}$$

The corresponding dilation and erosion operations can be extendedly defined as:

$$D_{\mathrm{PPI}}(x, y) = (f \oplus S)(x, y) = \arg\left\{ \max_{(s,t)\in S} [P(f(x + s, y + t), S)] \right\} \tag{6.77}$$

$$e_{PPI}(x, y) = (f \ominus S)(x, y) = \arg \left\{ \min_{(s,t) \in S} [P(f(x-s, y-t), S)] \right\} \qquad (6.78)$$

In fact, the erosion operation is not needed in the improved AMEE algorithm, only dilation operation is enough for extracting the endmembers.

REFERENCES

Brunet, D., and D. Sills. 2017. A generalized distance transform: Theory and applications to weather analysis and forecasting. *IEEE Transaction on Geoscience and Remote Sensing*, 55(3): 1752–1764.

Cao, W., and Z.C. Cai. 2018. Improved multiscale roughness algorithm for lunar surface. *IEEE Journal of Selected Topics in Applied Earth Observations and Remote Sensing*, 11(7): 2336–2345.

Challa, A., S. Danda, B.S.D. Sagar, et al. 2018. Some properties of interpolations using mathematical morphology. *IEEE Transactions on Image Processing*, 27(4): 2038–2048.

Das, J.K., P.P. Choudhury, N. Chaturvedi, et al. 2019. Ranking and clustering of Drosophila olfactory receptors using mathematical morphology. *Gennomics*, 111(4): 549–559.

De Oliveira, W.A.A., D. Guliato, D.C.B. Oliveira, et al. 2019. New technique for binary morphological shape-based interpolation. *International Journal of Image and Graphics*, 19(2): #1950007.

Drazic, S. 2019. Advanced morphological distances based on dilation and erosion. *Fundmenta Informaticae*, 164(1): 17–39.

Frejaville, T., A. Vila-Cabrera, T. Curt, et al. 2018. Aridity and competition drive fire resistance trait covariation in mountain trees. *Ecosphere*, 9(12): e02493.

Ghose, P., and M. Mitra. 2021. Colon cancer detection using watershed transformation technique. *Advances in Medical Physics and Healthcare Engineering, Lecture Notes in Bioengineering* (LNBE), 221–231.

Gonzalez, R.C., and R.E. Woods. 2008. *Digital Image Processing*. 3rd Ed. New Jersey: Prentice Hall.

Iglesias-Rey, S., F. Antunes-Santos, and C. Hagemann, 2021. Unsupervised cell segmentation and labelling in neural tissue images. *Applied Sciences-Basel*, 11(9): #3733.

Jiang, F., and Y.-J. Zhang. 2003. A caption detection algorithm based on morphological operation. *Journal of Electronics & Information Technology*, 25(12): 1647–1652.

Kong, Y., X.S. Wang, Y.H. Cheng, et al. 2021. Multi-stage convolutional broad learning with block diagonal Constraint for hyperspectral image classification. *Remote Sensing*, 13(17): #3412.

Legentil, C., J. Pellerin, P. Cupillard, et al. 2022. Testing scenarios on geological models: Local interface insertion in a 2D mesh and its impact on seismic wave simulation. *Computers & Geosciences*, 159: #105013.

Li, W.X., R.G. Zhou, and H. Yu. 2021. Quantum image edge detection based on multi-directions gray-scale morphology. *International Journal of Theoretical Physics*, 60(11-12): 4162–4176.

Lopez-Molina, C., S. Iglesias-Rey, H. Bustince, et al. 2021. On the role of distance transformations in Baddeley's Delta Metric. *Information Science*, 569, 479–495.

Lyu, P.F., A. Benlarbi-Delai, Z.X. Ren, et al. 2022. Angular clustering of millimeter-wave propagation channels with watershed transformation. *IEEE Transactions on Antennas and Propagation*, 70(2): 1279–1290.

Macey, P.M., L. Kheirandish-Gozal, J.P. Prasad, et al. 2018. Altered regional brain cortical thickness in pediatric obstructive sleep apnea. *Frontiers in Neurology*, 9: #4.

Mahdavieh, Y., and R.C. Gonzalez. 1992. *Advances in Image Analysis*. Bellingham: SPIE Optical Engineering Press.

Mahmoudi, R., N. Ben Ameur, A. Ammari, et al. 2020. Left ventricular segmentation based on a parallel watershed transformation towards an accurate heart function evaluation. *IET Image Processing*, 14(3): 506–517.

Mihelic, S.A., W.A. Sikora, A.M. Hassan, et al. 2021. Segmentation-less, automated, vascular vectorization. *Plos Computational Biology*, 17(10): e1009451.

Nagajothi, K., and B.S.D. Sagar. 2019. Classification of geophysical basins derived from SRTM and Cartosat DEMs via directional granulometries. *IEEE Journal of Selected Topics in Applied Earth Obeservation and Remote Sensing*, 12(12): 5259–5267.

O'Sullivan, J.D.B., S.M. Cruickshank, P.J. Withers, et al. 2021. Morphological variability in the mucosal attachment site of Trichuris muris revealed by X-ray microcomputed tomography. *International Journal for Parasitology*, 51(10): 797–807.

Patricio, C.V. 2020. Silvicultural considerations for the production of poles in Pinus radiata D. Don plantations in Chile. *Revista Cubana de Ciencias Forestales*, 8(2): 375–391.

Plaza, A., P. Martínze, P. Pérez, et al. 2002. Spetial/spectral endmember extraction by multi-dimensional morphological operations. *IEEE Transactions on Geoscience and Remote Sensing*, 40(9): 2025–2041.

Ritter, G.X., and J.N. Wilson. 2001. *Handbook of Computer Vision Algorithms in Image Algebra*. UK: CRC Press.

Russ, J.C. 2016. *The Image Processing Handbook*. 7th Ed. Boca Raton: CRC Press.

Sagar, B.S.D. 2018. Mathematical morphology in geosciences and GISci: An illustrative review. *Handbook of Mathematical Geosciences: Fifty Years of IAMG*, 703–740.

Serra, J. 1982. *Image Analysis and Mathematical Morphology*. USA: Academic Press.

Shih, F.Y. 2010. *Image Processing and Pattern Recognition – Fundamentals and Techniques*. USA: IEEE Press.

Sun, S.P. 2020. Applying forces to generate cartograms: A fast and flexible transformation framework. *Cartography and Geographic Information Science*, 47(5): 381–399.

Szczepanska, A., D. Gosciewski, and M. Gerus-Gosciewska. 2020. A GRID-based spatial interpolation method as a tool supporting real estate market analyses. *ISPRS International Journal of Geo-Information*, 9(1): #39.

Torres, M., D.A. Pelta, and J.L. Verdegay. 2019. Towards adaptive maps. *International Journal of Intelligent Systems*, 34(3): 400–414.

Xu, J., C.L. Wang, and L. Wang. 2019. An improved endmember extraction method of mathematical morphology based on PPI algorithm. *Acta Geodaetica et Cartographica Sinica*, 48(8): 996–1003.

Zhang, K.Z., S.L. Wang, L. Wang, et al. 2022. 3D visualization of tectonic coal microstructure and quantitative characterization on topological connectivity of pore-fracture networks by Micro-CT. *Journal of Petroleum Science and Engineering*, 208: #109675.

Zhang, Y.-J. 2017a. *Image Engineering, Vol.1: Image Processing*. Germany: De Gruyter. 2017.

Zhang, Y.-J. 2017b. *Image Engineering, Vol.2: Image Analysis*. Germany: De Gruyter. 2017.

Zhu, N.N., S.Y. Xu, C.D. Li, et al. 2022. An improved phase-derived range method based on high-order multi-frame track-before-detect for warhead detection. *Remote Sensing*, 14(1): #29.

CHAPTER 7

Face Recognition

F ace recognition (FR), also known as *automatic face recognition (AFR)*, is a typical biometric recognition. To use biological characteristics to identify or confirm a person's identity, biological characteristics should mainly satisfy universality (everyone owns), uniqueness (different from person to person), and stability (not affected by changes in time, age, or environment) and convenience of collection (easy collection, simple equipment, little impact on people), etc. Human faces are owned by everyone and are universal; and different people have different faces, which are unique. Face recognition can be performed passively, without the cooperation of objects (such as proximity or contact sensors), so it is more friendly to people and has a relatively small impact on people. However, the face model will change with speech, posture, age, makeup, fat and thin, etc., and the stability is not high, so the requirements for technology are relatively high.

Face recognition has a wide range of applications, such as Olympic security checks, bank monitoring, ATMs, border inspections, ID cards, bank security, suspect photo comparison, face identification, eyewitness memories, storage and retrieval of suspect photos, human-computer interaction system, smart house (identifying and tracking people in the conference room), access control system, security and surveillance, e-commerce, entertainment, photo and video program labeling, designing professional identification systems, witnesses to reconstruct the face, electronic suspicion people comparison, and so on.

The contents of each section of this chapter are arranged as follows:

Section 7.1 gives an introduction of face recognition, including related research and application domains, the basic process of face recognition and the composition and characteristics of main modules, and some main factors that affect the effect of face recognition.

Section 7.2 introduces the principles of the widely used subspace technology in face recognition, reviews the categories and characteristics of the methods that have been proposed and applied over the years, and gives some results of their comparisons.

Section 7.3 discusses a face localization method based on Hausdorff distance and symmetry measure. The definition of Hausdorff distance and its typical improvements, as well as the principle and realization of symmetry measure are respectively described in detail.

Section 7.4 introduces the principles and methods of dimensionality reduction of face features, including supervised linear dimensionality reduction based on discriminant projection embedding and nonlinear dimensionality reduction based on non-negative matrix factorization and non-negative matrix set factorization.

Section 7.5 discusses a subspace method of face recognition based on class-dependent feature analysis; in addition to introducing the basic framework and commonly used correlation filters, it also specifically analyzes the process of correlation filter training.

Section 7.6 introduces a face recognition method based on the weighting of edge eigenvectors, analyzes and compares the Hausdorff distance weighted by edge eigenvectors, and the frequency weighted Hausdorff distance used in face localization.

Section 7.7 provides a brief introduction to some technique developments and promising research directions in the last year.

7.1 INTRODUCTION TO FACE RECOGNITION

In face recognition, face generally refers to the surface part of human head other than hair. The information obtained from this part contains extremely rich meanings, such as people's gender, age, health status, even occupation, emotion, psychological state, temper, and the names of acquaintances. Existing physiological studies have shown that the perception of the face can not only distinguish it from other people or objects, but also activate the identity information about the person stored in the long-term memory of the human brain, such as occupation, age, hobbies, name, and so on. Because of this, face perception computing represented by face recognition has become one of the hot research topics in many disciplines.

7.1.1 Research and Application Overview

Face recognition involves many research contents, including computer technology, image technology, recognition technology, database technology, physiology, psychology, legal ethics, optics, neuroscience, psychophysics, and so on. In recent years, the research includes not only the research of sample collection, but also the research of information processing technology, as well as the research combined with specific applications. With the deepening of research, not only a large number of documents have been published, but also some special books, such as the books (Zhang et al. 2009; Zhang 2011).

Because face recognition is an important means of identity recognition, it has been first applied in business and law, including static matching of photos under controlled conditions (such as passport, credit card and driver's license) to real-time matching of surveillance video. In recent years, its application field is still expanding.

The difficulties encountered in automatic face recognition include inconsistent lighting conditions, noise in the image, changes in facial expressions, occlusion of glasses and masks, etc., and the influence of head posture (pitch, rotation, etc.). In addition, the face mode changes with speech, pose, age, makeup, fatness and thinness, etc., so the stability is low. In addition, there are problems caused by race, skin color, etc. To solve these problems, one way of thinking is to obtain more information from the scene, such as collecting 3-D images (including video images and 3-D spatial images) (Yan and Zhang 2009; Zhang 2009).

With the advent of high-performance computers and the improvement of image acquisition and processing capabilities in the 1990s, face recognition methods have made major breakthroughs and have gradually entered the stage of real automatic machine recognition. Not only can it automatically recognize frontal, well-lit, and unobstructed faces, but also through the development of face recognition based on multiple gestures/expressions, face recognition based on dynamic tracking, face recognition based on 3-D models, etc., the recognition performance of faces with different posture changes, different lighting conditions, different ages, and different expressions has been greatly improved. Entering the 21st century, especially in recent years, the accumulation of research results, the improvement of technology and the further requirements for safety have led to increasing attention and rapid development in the field of face recognition, and face recognition has been widely used in many fields.

As in many biometric measurement systems, the purpose of automatic face recognition is to achieve a high level of performance when matching a given face image with a face database image. The performance of an automatic face recognition system can be comprehensively evaluated by matching accuracy (low false alarms, low underreporting), robustness (for some unfavorable factors), fast speed, and low cost.

7.1.2 Face Recognition Process

To complete the work of face recognition requires a series of steps, which are combined to form a complete process. Because researchers come from different disciplines, have different backgrounds, and different face recognition applications have different recognition goals and requirements, the process of face recognition is not completely unified. A more general face recognition process is shown in Figure 7.1. Its main steps include: *face detection* or *face tracking, face feature extraction, face feature dimensionality reduction*, and *face matching recognition*. The relationship between them is basically serial. In practice, there are also processes that combine different steps or add feedback.

Some general introductions are given below for each step.

7.1.2.1 Face Detection/Tracking

Face detection/tracking is the first step to complete the face recognition work. The purpose of this step is to accurately, efficiently and reliably determine the face and give its position in the input image. Face detection/tracking is also called face positioning, but the narrower sense of face positioning often refers to a specific situation of a single face. It assumes that there is only one face in the image, but the background is often more complicated, which is often encountered in human-computer interaction, etc. Some people also define face detection as, given an image, the goal of face detection is to

FIGURE 7.1   The process of face recognition.

determine all image regions that contain faces, regardless of the person's position, orientation, and imaging lighting conditions in 3-D space (Yang et al. 2002).

The face detection/tracking step uses information shared by face images. If the input is a still image, each image is generally tested. If the input is a video, it is needed to get the face part in every frame in the entire sequence. Except that each frame can be detected as a still image, the common strategy is to detect only the first frame of the sequence and track the subsequent frames with the detection results of the previous frame. Although it is easier for humans to recognize faces in chaotic scenes, it is still very challenging to use machines to automatically complete the corresponding work. The following factors are closely related to face detection:

1. Imaging conditions: Illumination (light source distribution and intensity) and camera parameters (sensor response, lens) will affect the appearance of a person.

2. Pose: Due to the different poses of the face image relative to the camera (such as front, 45°, side, upside down, etc.), certain facial features will be deformed, resulting in changes in the appearance of the person, and face detection becomes difficult.

3. Facial expressions: Facial expressions directly affect the appearance of the human face, thereby changing the recognition result.

4. Occlusion: The face may be partially occluded by other objects. If there are multiple people in the image, some faces may partially block other faces. The occlusion of the lost information will affect the judgment of the face.

5. Facial features: The presence or absence of beard and glasses, will cause changes in the color, shape, and size of the face.

In practical applications, the collection or acquisition of face images is often carried out under uncontrolled conditions, so that the face in the obtained image has many differences in size, orientation, brightness, occlusion, resolution, etc., making the same person with various deformations of the face, which may lead to various misunderstandings, missed recognition and other failures. In order to correct the changes of the face in terms of scale, illumination, and rotation, it is often necessary to use some methods including **geometric normalization** (spatial scale normalization) and **illumination normalization** (grayscale amplitude normalization) to adjust the difference of face images in order to facilitate the use of a unified algorithm for recognition.

7.1.2.2 Face Feature Extraction

In order to distinguish different faces, the unique properties of each face need to be extracted. That is to extract a set of numerical representation samples that reflect the features of the face from the face image. Here, it is first needed to adopt a certain representation method to represent the detected face and the known face in the database. Common representations include geometric features (such as Euclidean distance, curvature, angle), algebraic features (such as matrix or eigenvector), fixed feature masks, eigenfaces, etc.

At present, face recognition often uses parts of the face that are not easily changed, such as the contour of the eye socket and the contour of the chin. In face recognition, some people associate facial features with facial organs (such as eyes, nose, mouth, etc.). Among these features, some features (such as hairline, eyes, mouth) play a greater role in recognition than others (such as nose). However, this conclusion is mainly true for frontal face images. If you consider a side face image, the nose is also very important.

In order to improve the face recognition ratio, similar to many recognition tasks, both the global and local features of the representation and recognition of the face should be considered. Also note that although the selection of features is related to human anatomy and physiology, it does not require an explicit physiological explanation for the extracted features (Wayman 2002). There is a certain regularity in the number and distribution of face organs, and building a face model is a commonly used method. However, although model-based methods can compensate for changes between faces, they are not necessarily universal.

7.1.2.3 Face Feature Dimensionality Reduction

The human face is a non-rigid natural object (flexible body). Many different features can be extracted from the face image. Therefore, the original features representing the human face correspond to the data in the high-dimensional space (for an image of $M \times N$, the spatial dimensions can reach $M \times N$). In addition to the need for a lot of matching calculations to directly use such high-dimensional data for recognition, it is difficult to make effective judgments on the descriptive ability of each high-dimensional data, so the accuracy of the recognition results based on so many data cannot be guaranteed. In addition, from a psychological point of view, high-dimensional image data can be projected into a low-dimensional subspace, and the information in this subspace is sufficient for the computer to complete the identification and classification of facial features. Therefore, after feature extraction, a compact face representation method needs to be selected, the original features are filtered and combined, the information is concentrated, and the dimensionality is reduced, so that the effectiveness of these low-dimensional spatial features is improved to facilitate the subsequent matching and classification.

It should be pointed out that feature extraction and feature dimensionality reduction are closely related. In many face recognition methods, especially face recognition based on subspace, these two tasks are closely combined.

7.1.2.4 Face Matching and Recognition

On the basis of feature extraction and dimensionality reduction, an appropriate matching strategy can be selected to compare the face to be recognized with the known face in the database, to establish the correlation between them, and to output the judgment decision made (recognition result). Unlike face detection, the information used here is mainly the difference between individual faces. There are two recognition purposes and situations that need to be distinguished: one is to verify the face image, that is, to confirm whether the person in the input face image has an image in the database, which belongs to supervised recognition; the other is to recognize the person from the face image, that is, to confirm the identity of the person in the input face image, this belongs to unsupervised recognition.

With the establishment of large-capacity databases, the speed and efficiency of matching and searching methods cannot be ignored. In addition to finding a solution on the matching algorithm itself, it is also to consider using information about a person's race, gender, etc. to narrow the search scope. In addition, some recognition only needs to obtain relatively qualitative results or coarser quantitative results, such as the recognition of human gender, the recognition of age groups, and so on. Corresponding simplified methods can also be used at this time.

7.1.3 Factors Affecting Face Recognition

The recognition of human faces will be affected by many factors. For example, changes in the lighting environment will change the brightness of different parts of the face image, different expressions will change the appearance of the face in the image, and the posture of the face during imaging may also produce a certain amount of occlusion. The same recognition method has different recognition effects for people of different ages and genders, or as the person's age changes, the recognition success rate will also change. The research on face recognition also requires objective evaluation of the recognition effect and fair comparison of different methods. Among them, the use of a unified database can facilitate the comparison work.

The influencing factors on face recognition can be divided into two categories: expression, gender, makeup, glasses, race, facial hair, weight change, age change, etc. are all *internal factors* (intrinsic factors) that lead to changes in the appearance of the face; while lighting (light source intensity, direction, color), camera viewpoint, camera radiation response, etc. are *external factors* that cause changes in the appearance of a human face. These factors ultimately lead to obvious image changes.

The external factors that affect face recognition mainly come from the environment. Environmental conditions can be divided into two types: *controllable environment* and *uncontrollable environment*. In an uncontrollable environment, the collected face images may have changes in illumination, changes in facial posture, and changes in facial expressions.

A preliminary discussion of several influencing factors is as follows.

7.1.3.1 Illumination Changing

In face recognition, changes in lighting conditions often cause obvious changes in the appearance of the face. Shadows, occlusions, bright and dark regions, dark lights, and highlights caused by changes in lighting will greatly reduce the recognition rate. The change in illumination can come from the difference in light direction or energy distribution, and it can also be affected by the 3-D structure of the human face. The changes in the appearance of the face caused by these factors may be more obvious than the changes in the appearance of the face due to different identities.

Existing methods for solving illumination changes can be divided into two categories: one can be called a *passive method*, which tries to reduce the impact of illumination changes by learning the changes in the visible spectrum image caused by the illumination changes; the other class can be called *active method*, which uses active imaging technology to make the acquired image have the characteristics of the image acquired under fixed lighting conditions, or the image acquired by the acquisition method that is not affected by lighting changes.

At present, the existing passive methods can be divided into four types: methods for modeling changes in illumination, methods for extracting invariant features of illumination, methods for normalizing luminosity, and methods for 3-D deformation models.

In the active method, some additional devices or additional equipment (such as optical filters, active light sources or special sensors, etc.) are often used. In many cases, different imaging methods can be used to acquire face images to obtain images that are not sensitive to changes in illumination or are independent of illumination. In this regard, 3-D face information (such as (Bowyer et al. 2004)), non-visible spectrum (such as thermal infrared image (Kong et al. 2005), and near-infrared hyperspectral image (Pan et al. 2003)) are commonly used.

7.1.3.2 Posture Changing

When collecting face images, if people's posture changes, the resulting projection deformation will cause the lifting, compression and occlusion of different parts of the face, which will greatly change the image. There are six degrees of freedom in the *posture changing* in 3-D space: translation along the X, Y, and Z axes and rotation around the X, Y, and Z axes. Among them, the translation along the X and Y axes is represented as the change of face position in the image, and its correction can be realized by using appropriate detection methods to obtain the change, and then by coordinate transformation; The change along the Z-axis is represented as the change of scale in the image, and its correction can be realized by scaling the 2-D image or 3-D face. The variation around the axis can be divided into plane rotation, vertical depth rotation and lateral depth rotation. The plane rotation is the rotation around the Z axis; the vertical depth rotation, also known as up-down rotation or pitch deflection, is a rotation around the X-axis; the lateral depth rotation is sometimes called left-right rotation or horizontal deflection, is rotation around the Y axis. Among the changes of the above six degrees of freedom, the rotations around the X and Y axes are difficult to be determined directly from the image.

One way to overcome the problem caused by pose change is to estimate the different pose of the face from the image, and try to transform it back to the standard pose of the face, then use the standard face recognition method for recognition. Another method is to learn and memorize the features under multiple postures, which is equivalent to establishing multiple standard postures, and the workload will be larger. Finally, the 3-D geometric model of the head can also be constructed to extract pose independent features to recognize the face.

Unrestricted illumination and pose changes can lead to significant changes in face images and hinder the wide use of face recognition systems. It is challenging to obtain a wide range of conditions from a limited number of images of a person. In recent years, significant progress has been made in the modeling of illumination and pose changes with the help of 3-D shape information and reflection model, including the non-existence of illumination changes, the characterization of object images with a given pose but different illumination, and the introduction of spherical harmonic function and low dimensional linear space. In order to generalize to the new conditions, it is necessary to use multiple images, or only one image but with prior knowledge of 3-D shape and appearance. As a general model, 3-D deformable model can be used to predict human appearance, and its parameters can be estimated from a single image. Due to these advances, the common changes of illumination and pose have also been studied (Romdhani et al. 2006).

7.1.3.3 Expression Changing

Expression changing can have a great impact on the appearance of human face, but the classification of expression is also a difficult work (see Chapter 8). On the one hand, there is no clear formal definition of facial expression, and people often use different languages to explain it. On the other hand, the psychological research on facial expression is not perfect. The requirements for automatic facial expression classification system include: the system should be able to process all facial images, regardless of gender, age, and race; the classification result of the system should be independent of the pose of the face; the system should be able to classify facial expressions in real time.

There are common points and similarities between the classification of facial expressions and the recognition of face. For example, facial expression classification and face recognition are consistent in face detection/tracking and positioning, and image normalization. Some technologies for facial expression classification can easily be extended to face recognition, and vice versa. Furthermore, removing the impact of facial expression differences from facial features and removing the impact of individual differences from facial expression features is also a dual problem. For example, in the framework of high-order singular value decomposition, facial features weighted by facial expression similarity can be used to reduce the impact of facial expression differences in facial features, which can effectively improve the robustness of facial features on facial expression differences (Tan et al. 2010). However, in terms of feature extraction, face recognition needs to extract individual characteristics of a person from a face image to distinguish different people, while facial expression classification needs to extract common features of expressions from a face image to summarize the specialty of each expression.

Expression classification is closely related to expression synthesis. The international standard MPEG-4 extends the **facial action coding system (FACS)** and provides two parameter systems: **facial definition parameters (FDP)** system and **facial animation parameters (FAP)** system. Among them, FAP system has good parameterization characteristics and compressibility, and is widely used in the research of face animation.

In facial expression classification, the movements of the eyebrows, eyelids, and cheeks play an important role, and the movements of the mouth (especially the movements of the lips and chin) sometimes reflect a certain expression (such as opening the mouth when surprised, and upturning the corners of the mouth when happy, etc.), but sometimes these only indicate that they are speaking, not necessarily related to facial expressions. One of the solutions is to divide the movement features of the face into two categories: visual speech features and expression features. The FAP reflecting the movement of the mouth is used as the visual speech feature vector, while the FAP representing the movement of other parts of the face is classified as the expression feature vector.

7.1.3.4 Age Influence

The shape and texture of the face will change with age, which will also lead to a decline in the recognition rate in face recognition. Data shows (Phillips et al. 2003) that the recognition rate will decrease significantly as the age difference between the image to be recognized and the database image increases. Generally, if the age difference reaches three years, the recognition rate will drop by about 20% on average.

The idea of solving the *age influence* is somewhat similar to the first idea of solving the influence of posture, that is, to estimate the age of the face from the image, and then try to transform it back to the age of the face originally used to train the recognition algorithm. Age-related facial features include both shape and texture features. The shape feature can be obtained from the contour of the human face and the texture feature can be obtained from the surface of the human face. In training, the correspondence between facial features and age can be established first; that is, the age function is established. Using the age function combined with the classification of the way the face grows old, the age of the face in the image can be automatically estimated.

Recently, people have discovered that according to the temporal characteristics of age changes, face images will show a sequential pattern of low-dimensional distribution. This pattern can be effectively extracted with the help of a learning algorithm for discriminating subspaces and can be regarded as a manifold structure. Using the manifold analysis of the face image, the dimensional redundancy of the original image space can be greatly reduced. After dimensionality reduction, the linear regression method can be used to effectively express the manifold space with discriminative characteristics (Fu and Huang 2008).

7.2 SUBSPACE METHODS

Face recognition methods can be divided into subspace method (Zhang et al. 2009) and non-subspace method. The basic idea of the *subspace* method is to compress the high-dimensional face image features into a low-dimensional subspace for recognition through spatial transformation (linear or non-linear). In the subspace method, the most significant features in each category must be individually extracted to form a feature set corresponding to the category. In decision-making, the distance between the feature vector of the pattern to be classified and the subspace corresponding to each category is used as the discriminant function of the classification.

7.2.1 Classification of Subspace Methods

Many subspace face recognition methods have been proposed. These methods can be divided into linear subspace methods and non-linear subspace methods. Among them, *linear subspace* methods can be divided into *unsupervised linear subspace* methods (from which expressive features are obtained) and *supervised linear subspace* methods (from which discriminative features are obtained). Typical unsupervised linear subspace methods include principal component analysis and independent component analysis. Typical supervised linear subspace methods include linear discriminant analysis, class dependency analysis, etc. (Some researchers combine different supervised linear subspace

TABLE 7.1 Classification of subspace methods

Linear subspace method	Unsupervised linear subspace method	Principal component analysis
		Independent component analysis
	Supervised linear subspace method	Linear discriminant analysis
		Class dependency analysis
Non-linear subspace method	Kernel method	Kernel principal component analysis
		Kernel linear discriminant analysis
		Kernel manifold analysis
	Non-negative matrix factorization method	See Section 7.4
	Non-negative matrix set decomposition method	See Section 7.4

methods to form the so-called hybrid supervised linear subspace methods). On the other side, *non-linear subspace* methods include *kernel* methods, *non-negative matrix factorization (NMF)* , and *non-negative matrix set factorization* methods. Typical kernel methods include kernel principal component analysis, kernel linear decision analysis, and kernel manifold analysis. There are many methods for non-negative matrix factorization and non-negative matrix set factorization, some of which will be introduced in Section 7.4. A classification table for subspace methods can be found in Table 7.1.

In addition, there are many non-subspace methods, such as neural network-based methods, elastic matching methods, deformation model methods, and hidden Markov model methods.

The following mainly discusses some situations and characteristics of the subspace method.

The initial subspace is regarded as a set of orthogonal normalized basic vectors, so the method of statistical orthogonal expansion (the expansion of a vector to a set of orthogonal normalized non-random vectors) has been applied earlier. In the late 1980s, researchers introduced the idea of KL transformation into the field of image representation, and developed an optimal technology for describing face images in the sense of minimum mean square error. Inspired by this, the researchers used the reconstruction weight vector as the feature for recognition, and proposed the *"eigenface"* (the name comes from that image form of each eigenvector extracted is similar to a human face) recognition technology (Sirovich and Kirby 1987), promoted the development of characterization-based subspace analysis methods, and gradually extended to *eigen-analysis*. In eigen-analysis, the overall features and local features are unified into various eigen-features (such as eigen-eyes, eigen-mouths, etc.).

7.2.2 List of Subspace Methods

After years of efforts by researchers, subspace analysis methods have made comprehensive development. Some typical methods for face recognition and related research are listed in Table 7.2 (Zhang 2015).

TABLE 7.2 List of typical subspace analysis methods

Abb.	Full Name	Abb.	Full Name
1D-CFA	1D Class-dependence Feature Analysis	LDE	Local Discriminant Embedding
2D-CFA	2D Class-dependence Feature Analysis	LF	Laplacian Face
2D-KDA	2D Kernel Discriminant Analysis	LFA	Local Feature Analysis
2D-LDA	2D Linear Discriminant Analysis	LLE	Locally Linear Embedding
2D-PCA	2D Principal Component Analysis	LPP	Locality Preserving Projection
APCA	Adaptive PCA	MFA	Marginal Fisher Analysis
B2D-PCA	Bidirectional 2D-PCA	NDA	Nonparametric Discriminant Analysis
Bayesian	Bayesian	NLDA	New LDA
CFA	Class-dependence Feature Analysis	NLPCA	Non-Linear PCA
DLDA	Direct LDA	NMF	Non-negative Matrix Factorization
DPE	Discriminant Projection Embedding	NMSF	Non-negative Matrix Set Factorization
DSDA	Dual Space Discriminant Analysis	NN	Neural Networks
EFM	Enhance Fisher Linear Discriminant Model	NPE	Neighborhood Preserving Embedding
EPCA	Empirical PCA	NSC	Non-negative Sparse Coding
F2D-KDA	Frame 2D-KDA	NSLDA	Null Space LDA
FDA	Fisher Discriminant Analysis	OFLD	Optimal LDA
FF	Fisher Faces	PCA	Principal Component Analysis
FNMF	Fast Non-Negative Matrix Factorization	PM	Principal Manifold
GLDA	Generalized LDA	PSA	Probabilistic Subspace Analysis
GSVD	Generalized Singular Value Decomposition	SLDR	Supervised Linear Dimensionality Reduction
ICA	Independent Component Analysis	SR2D-KDA	Sampling and Regrouping 2D-KDA
K2D-PCA	Kernel 2D-PCA	SR2D-LDA	Sampling and Regrouping 2D-LDA
KFDA	Kernel Fisher Discriminant Analysis	SVD	Singular Value Decomposition
KLDA	Kernel LDA	TCF-CFA	Tensor Correlation Filter Based CFA
KPCA	Kernel-based PCA	TPCA	Topological PCA
KTS	Kernel Tensor-subspace	UPCA	Unified PCA
LDA	Linear Discriminant Analysis		

7.2.3 Characteristics of Subspace Method

The subspace method has some unique points, and its effectiveness in face recognition has certain guarantees. Previous research work has shown that changes in face images obtained under different lighting conditions, even with multiple light sources and multiple shadows, can be effectively modeled using low-dimensional linear space (Lee et al. 2005).

The subspace method can represent high-dimensional pattern vectors compactly. In other words, the dimension of the subspace is often much less than that of the pattern space. Therefore, the calculation amount of the vector inner product is reduced, which can speed up the classification. For example, in face recognition, separate eigen subspaces can be established for facial organs, such as eyes, nose, and mouth, to effectively represent the characteristics of these organs. For another example, the changes of a face image under different lighting conditions, including multiple light sources and shadows, can be modeled by a low-dimensional linear subspace. The base image in this space can be obtained in three ways:

1. Making use of a large number of images with objects under different lighting conditions, the method of principal component analysis can be used to estimate a subspace;

2. According to the 3-D model illuminated by the point source (which can be constructed from the image) to synthesize the image, and then use the principal component analysis method to estimate a subspace;

3. Using the 3-D model obtained based on the spherical harmonic function under diffused light directly as the base image.

The subspace method is based on the linear orthogonal expansion, so the linear subspace methods, such as statistical subspace, eigenspace, discriminant subspace, independent component subspace, etc., are first applied. With the help of local feature analysis method, factor analysis method, etc., hybrid linear subspace and non-linear subspace methods have also been developed. These many subspaces and methods can also be combined. For example, some face recognition methods perform discriminant analysis in the principal component subspace and the null space at the same time, and merge the discriminative features of these two subspaces in the feature layer. By extracting the most discriminative features in each subspace, and using their complementary characteristics to achieve the purpose of using as much discriminative information as possible.

7.3 FACE LOCALIZATION BASED ON HAUSDORFF DISTANCE AND SYMMETRY METRIC

In the process of face detection and localization, Hausdorff distance (HD) and symmetry metric have been widely used.

7.3.1 Hausdorff Distance

The **Hausdorff distance (HD)** is suitable for measuring the distance between two point sets. For example, in the face detection and localization method based on mask matching (Liu et al. 2008), it is necessary to perform correlation calculations between the preestablished face mask and the face region in the image. The face mask can be constructed with the help of face edge images, so that the average face mask is obtained (as shown in Figure 7.2). Afterwards, a certain coordinate transformation (translation, rotation, or scaling) of the mask is required to register the average face mask with the face region in the image. Finally, in order to measure the degree of correlation, it is necessary to calculate the (similarity) distance between the average face mask after coordinate transformation and the face region in the image. This correlation calculation can then be performed using the Hausdorff distance.

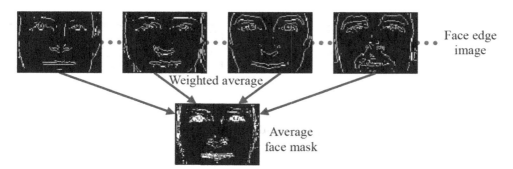

FIGURE 7.2   Using multiple face edge images to obtain an average face mask.

7.3.1.1 Basic Hausdorff Distance

The face as an object is composed of pixel points, and the correlation calculation of the two objects is a match of the two point sets in a certain sense. The method of using HD to describe the similarity of point sets and matching through feature point sets is widely used. Given two finite point sets $A = \{a_1, a_2, \ldots, a_m\}$ and $B = \{b_1, b_2, \ldots, b_n\}$, the HD between them is defined as follows:

$$H(A, B) = \max[h(A, B), h(B, A)] \tag{7.1}$$

where

$$h(A, B) = \max_{a \in A} \min_{b \in B} \|a - b\| \tag{7.2}$$

$$h(B, A) = \max_{b \in B} \min_{a \in A} \|b - a\| \tag{7.3}$$

In Equation (7.2) and Equation (7.3), the norm $\|\bullet\|$ can take different forms. The function $h(A, B)$ is called the directed HD from the set A to B, which describes the longest distance from the point $a \in A$ to any point in the point set B; similarly, the function $h(A, B)$ is called the directed HD from B to A, which describes the longest distance from point $b \in B$ to any point in the point set A. Since $h(A, B)$ and $h(B, A)$ are asymmetric, the maximum value between them is generally taken as the HD between these two point sets. The geometric meaning of HD can be explained as follows: If the HD between two point sets A and B is d, then for any point in each point set, at least one point in another point set can be found in a circle with the point as the center and d as the radius. If the HD between the two point sets is 0, it means that the two point sets are coincident. In the schematic diagram in Figure 7.3: $h(A, B) = d_{21}$, $h(B, A) = d_{22} = H(A, B)$.

The HD defined above is very sensitive to noise points or outliers of a point set. This is because the point with the most serious mismatch between the two point sets is selected as a measure of distance, so it is very sensitive to noise interference. In order to overcome this problem, the concept of statistical average can be used, the maximum value is

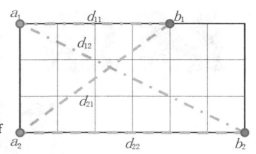

FIGURE 7.3 The geometric meaning of Hausdorff distance.

replaced with the average value to obtain the average value improved **modified Hausdorff distance (MHD)**. That is, Equation (7.2) and Equation (7.3) are modified as follows, respectively:

$$h_{\mathrm{MHD}}(A, B) = \frac{1}{N_A} \sum_{a \in A} \min_{b \in B} \|a - b\| \tag{7.4}$$

$$h_{\mathrm{MHD}}(B, A) = \frac{1}{N_B} \sum_{b \in B} \min_{a \in A} \|b - a\| \tag{7.5}$$

where N_A represents the number of points in point set A and N_B represents the number of points in point set B. Substituting them into Equation (7.1), it gives

$$H_{\mathrm{MHD}}(A, B) = \max [h_{\mathrm{MHD}}(A, B), \; h_{\mathrm{MHD}}(B, A)] \tag{7.6}$$

7.3.1.2 Hausdorff Distance Modified with Standard Deviation
The MHD introduced above has the advantage of being insensitive to noise points or outliers of a point set, but it is more sensitive to the distribution of each point in the point set. This problem can be introduced with the help of Figure 7.4, where the MHD values between the two point sets represented by the two parallel line segments in the left figure and the two intersecting line segments in the right figure are both d. However, the two images should be different from the perspective of matching. The distribution of points in the left figure should give a smaller HD than the distribution of points in the right figure to meet the perception of ordinary people (Gao and Leung 2002). This problem may cause errors in some face matching problems, because the mask and the test image

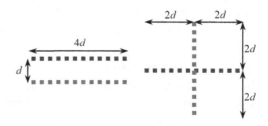

FIGURE 7.4 Problems in modified Hausdorff distance calculation.

are usually not exactly the same. Individual differences, changes in postures and re-presentations will cause a certain difference between the face in the test image and the mask. For example, when a person is surprised, he raises his eyebrows, and the position of the eyebrows is different from the standard face. These changes in position may also be caused by changes in posture. In this case where the mask is different from the test image, the mask and the image cannot be completely overlapped, so it may cause the problem that the two cases need to be distinguished, as shown in Figure 7.4.

An improvement of MHD metric is to distinguish the above two cases with the help of the standard deviation of the distance between point sets, and make the HD obtained in the right figure greater than that obtained in the left figure (Liu et al. 2008). Specifically, the **standard deviation modified Hausdorff distance (STMHD)** is defined; that is, Equation (7.2) and Equation (7.3) are modified as follows, respectively:

$$h_{\text{STMHD}}(A, B) = \frac{1}{N_A} \sum_{a \in A} \min_{b \in B} \|a - b\| + k \times S(A, B) \tag{7.7}$$

$$h_{\text{STMHD}}(B, A) = \frac{1}{N_B} \sum_{b \in B} \min_{a \in A} \|b - a\| + k \times S(B, A) \tag{7.8}$$

where parameter k is the weighting coefficient; $S(A, B)$ represents the standard deviation of the average distance from a point in point set A to each point in point set B:

$$S(A, B) = \sqrt{\sum_{a \in A} \left[\min_{b \in B} \|a - b\| - \frac{1}{N_A} \sum_{a \in A} \min_{b \in B} \|a - b\| \right]^2} \tag{7.9}$$

$S(B, A)$ represents the standard deviation of the average distance from a point in point set B to each point in point set A:

$$S(B, A) = \sqrt{\sum_{b \in B} \left[\min_{a \in A} \|b - a\| - \frac{1}{N_B} \sum_{b \in B} \min_{a \in A} \|b - a\| \right]^2} \tag{7.10}$$

For example, for Figure 7.4(a), $S(A, B) = S(B, A) = 0$, and for Figure 7.4(b), $S(A, B) = S(B, A) = d/3^{1/2}$. It seems more reasonable.

Substituting Equation (7.7) and Equation (7.8) into Equation (7.1), it gets

$$H_{\text{STMHD}}(A, B) = \max\left[h_{\text{STMHD}}(A, B), h_{\text{STMHD}}(B, A) \right] \tag{7.11}$$

The above STMHD not only considers the average distance between the two point sets, but also adds the distribution information of the points in the point set by introducing the standard deviation of the distance between the point sets (considering the consistency of the point distribution between the two point sets), so the description of the point set is more detailed (Liu et al. 2008).

7.3.1.3 Hausdorff Distance Weighted by Edge Frequency

By the way, when using HD to calculate the distance between two point sets and perform face mask matching, since different positions in the face region contribute differently to the matching, it is possible to consider weighting respectively each item in HD, namely the Equation (7.4) and Equation (7.5) can be changed to (Lin et al. 2003)

$$h_w(A, B) = \frac{1}{N_A} \sum_{a \in A} w(b) * \min_{b \in B} \|a - b\| \tag{7.12}$$

$$h_w(B, A) = \frac{1}{N_B} \sum_{b \in B} w(a) * \min_{a \in A} \|b - a\| \tag{7.13}$$

Among them, $w(a)$ and $w(b)$ are weight functions, and each point corresponds to a spatial position (x, y). The weight function can be determined by using the training set. For example, the weight function can be determined by counting the edge information in the image, so as to more directly and effectively reflect the structural information of the human face.

A specific implementation method is as follows (Tan and Zhang 2006). First, normalize the face images in the training set, including spatial scale normalization and gray scale normalization. Next, the edge detection operator is used to calculate the edge images corresponding to them, and the edge images are thresholded to obtain a binary image. Here, the threshold is selected so that the number of pixels with a value of 1 in the binary image is 20% of the entire image, so that the contribution of each binary image in the training set can be more consistent. Using the binary images obtained from the face images in the training set, the weight functions $w(a)$ and $w(b)$ can be obtained by calculating the average of their points. The weight function calculated in this way is proportional to the frequency of the edge points of each image in the training set at the corresponding position. Substituting the weight functions $w(a)$ and $w(b)$ calculated in this way into Equations (7.13) and (7.12), respectively, the **edge frequency weighted Hausdorff distance (EFWHD)** is obtained.

$$H_{EFWHD}(A, B) = \max[h_w(A, B), h_w(B, A)] \tag{7.14}$$

The weight function calculated above can be represented as a grayscale image that expresses the frequency of edge points. Binarizing this grayscale image to obtain a binary image of the face edge model. Figure 7.5(a) shows the grayscale image of the weight function (the brighter points correspond to the points with higher frequency of edge points), and Figure 7.5(b) shows the binary image of the face edge model (where the white ones are the point represents the edge point after binarization).

A comparison experiment of several face detection and localization methods using different Hausdorff distances is as follows (Tan and Zhang 2006): The comparison methods are based on the basic HD, MHD, and EFWHD; the comparison uses a total of 2007 images, including 1521 images of all 23 people in the BioID database (https://www.bioid.com/facedb/), plus 486 images with different lighting (size 640 × 490) selected from

(a) (b)

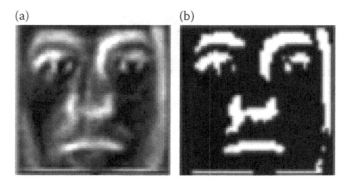

FIGURE 7.5   Images of weight function and face edge model.

about 2000 image sequences of 210 people in the Cohn-Kanade database (Kanade et al. 2000). In the training phase for the face masks, about 10% of the face images are randomly selected for training. When comparing the localization accuracy of each method, the relative error of eye detection is used (Josorsky et al. 2001). This relative error index is defined as

$$d = \frac{\max \{d_l, d_r\}}{\|C_{lt} - C_{rt}\|} \tag{7.15}$$

Among them, C_{lt} and C_{rt} are the true values of the centers of the left and right eyes, respectively; d_l and d_r are the differences between the true values and the detected values of the centers of the left and right eyes, respectively. The average results obtained from the experiments of the two databases are shown in Table 7.3. It can be seen that EFWHD has a smaller error than MHD, and MHD has a smaller error than HD.

7.3.2 Symmetry Metric

One of the key issues in face detection and localization is to find some representative features that can characterize the characteristics of the face, and to distinguish the face from other objects. Commonly used features, such as the fixed structure of the facial features, skin color, etc., while an important feature of the frontal face is a high degree of symmetry. The flow of *symmetry detection* on a human face is shown in Figure 7.6, where the symmetry metric is completed by calculating the similarity between the left half and the right half of the image. Here, the similarity between the left half of the image and the right half of the image with the Hausdorff distance is considered as the symmetry metric S of the image I. So the symmetry metric can be written as

TABLE 7.3   Comparison of the average errors of several Hausdorff distance detections

	HD	MHD	EFWHD
BioID Database	0.9788	0.4962	0.2513
Cohn-Kanade Database	0.6037	0.5157	0.1153

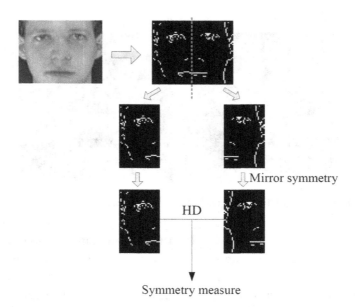

FIGURE 7.6   Schematic diagram of the detection process of face symmetry.

$$S(I) = \max[H(I_l, I_r), H(I_r^*, I_l)] \tag{7.16}$$

Among them, $H(\cdot)$ represents the Hausdorff distance, I_l and I_r represent the left half and right half of the face image, respectively, and I_r^* represents the mirror image symmetry part of I_r.

Since other objects (non-faces) in the actual scene may also have the characteristics of symmetry, the above-mentioned symmetry metric method cannot be used alone to locate human faces. However, combining the *symmetry metric* with the *similarity metric* based on mask matching, as shown in Figure 7.7, can improve the performance of face localization.

Assuming that the faces to be detected are all frontal faces and there is no rotation outside the plane, the problem of face positioning can be written as

$$D_p = \min\{H[T_p^*(I), T_p(J)] + w \bullet S[T_p^*(I)]\} \tag{7.17}$$

Among them, $H(\cdot)$ represents the Hausdorff distance, T_p represents the affine change to the face mask (such as translation, scaling and rotation), p represents the transformation

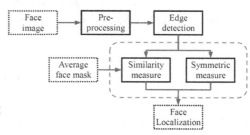

FIGURE 7.7   The face location process combining similarity metric and symmetry metric.

parameter, and $T_p{}^*(I)$ represents the transformed mask J corresponding to the part in the image I, w is a parameter representing the weight. The goal of a face localization system is to find a set of transformation parameters p, so that the final measurement result is minimized, so as to locate the face.

7.4 FACE FEATURE DIMENSIONALITY REDUCTION

Face feature dimensionality reduction is a key step in subspace face recognition, which is closely related to face feature extraction. In many face recognition methods, especially face recognition based on subspace, the two are often combined consider.

The following separately selects a linear method and a non-linear method for introducing.

7.4.1 Supervised Linear Dimensionality Reduction Based on Discriminative Projection Embedding

This **supervised linear dimensionality reduction (SLDR)** method can overcome the so-called "small sample set" (that is, the number of training samples is less than the sample dimension) problem, which is often encountered in face recognition (Yan and Zhang 2008d).

7.4.1.1 Supervised Linear Dimensionality Reduction

Now let's first analyze how the supervised linear dimensionality reduction method extracts discriminative information useful for classification. Assuming that there is a face sample x to be recognized, if the nearest neighbor classifier is used, the difference between x and each face category in the database needs to be calculated, and the face category with the smallest norm difference (*i.e.*, the smallest face distance) is counted as the result of recognition (the result of classification). There are two different types of face image differences: the intra-face difference D_W and the inter-face difference D_B. D_W is composed of transform difference component T (corresponding to face changes under different lighting, postures, and expressions) and noise component N. D_B is composed of identity difference component I (corresponding to different identity changes), transformation difference component T and noise component N. For simplicity, let $D_W = T + N$ and $D_B = I + T + N$. If the intra-class distance calculated for the face to be recognized is less than the inter-class distance, then the face will be correctly identified and classified. However, in practice, due to the influence of various factors such as noise, light, posture, expressions, etc., the distance within a class may be greater than the distance between classes, resulting in recognition errors.

It can be seen from the above that direct distance comparison is not the best method. Face recognition needs to extract identification information that characterizes different identities, and the change factors (transformation difference component T and noise component N) such as illumination, posture, and expression are all interference factors that should be removed. For this reason, the subspace that the transformation difference components and noise components in the intra-class difference and the inter-class difference can be reduced and removed, and the identity difference component of the inter-class difference can also be well preserved and enhanced should be found through the training set. This is equivalent to make a projection, the key is to determine the projection matrix. Generally, the intra-class metric matrix is mainly used to describe the transformation difference component (often also including the noise component), and the inter-class metric matrix is used to describe the identity difference component (often including a certain transformation difference component and the noise component). Therefore, most SLDR methods obtain the projection subspace by maximizing the ratio of the traces of the inter-class metric matrix and the intra-class metric matrix after projection (the identity difference component is enhanced, the transformation difference component and the noise component are reduced), that is, the following criterion function is used to find the best linear projection matrix P_{opt}:

$$P_{opt} = \arg\max_{P} \frac{\text{tr}(P^T B P)}{\text{tr}(P^T W P)} \tag{7.18}$$

Among them, B and W represent the inter-class metric matrix and the intra-class metric matrix, respectively, and tr(·) represents the trace operation. When the intra-class metric matrix W is not singular, the optimal projection matrix of SLDR is equal to the characteristic matrix of $W^{-1}B$. But in the case of "small sample set", W becomes a singular matrix. Therefore, it is not possible to directly calculate the projection matrix for SLDR.

7.4.1.2 Discriminative Projection Embedding

In order to solve the above practical problem, it is necessary to use different methods to describe the intra-class metric matrix and the inter-class metric matrix. Specifically, ***neighbor preserving embedding (NPE)*** is used to characterize intra-class changes, and the idea of ***non-parametric discrimination analysis (NDA)*** is used to extract the discriminative structure information between classes.

1. Intra-class metric matrix

There is a relatively close relationship between the data in the class. ***Local linear embedding (LLE)*** assumes that each point in the data within the class can be represented by a linear combination of surrounding K-nearest neighbors. After reducing the dimensionality in this way, the geometric positional relationship between the data can be preserved by maintaining the relationship of this linear combination. LLE should be minimized as follows:

$$\min \sum_i \| x_i - \sum_j a_{ij} x_j \|^2 \tag{7.19}$$

The constraints are that the weight $a_{ij} = 0$ between nodes of different types, and that the sum of weights between nodes of the same type $\sum_j a_{ij} = 1$.

Under the above constraints, the weight a_{ij} is invariant to translation, rotation and scale transformation. The original LLE is only defined on training data and cannot be generalized to test data. NPE is a linearized form of LLE, which can be defined on training data and test data at the same time. Assuming that P is a linear projection matrix, in order to ensure that the spatial position relationship between the original high-dimensional spaces is maintained between the projected vectors, the loss function becomes:

$$J_{\min}(P) = \min \sum_i \|y_i - \sum_j a_{ij}y_j\|^2 = \min \sum_i \|P^Tx_i - \sum_j a_{ij}P^Tx_j\|^2 = \min_p \mathrm{tr}(P^TWP)$$

(7.20)

where y is the projected data.

2. Inter-class metric matrix

Non-parametric discriminant analysis (NDA) uses a non-parametric structural form, so it can retain structural information useful for classification. The definition of the inter-class metric matrix in NDA is (n is the total number of training samples):

$$B = \frac{1}{n} \sum_{i=1}^{n} w_i D_i D_i^T = \frac{1}{n}DD$$

(7.21)

where $D = [D_1\sqrt{w_1}, D_2\sqrt{w_2}, \ldots, D_n\sqrt{w_n}]$, D_i is the difference between $x_i \in C_k$ and the mean of its K neighbors, and w_i is the weight of the i-th sample.

3. Discriminative projection embedding

By combining Equation (7.20) and Equation (7.21), Equation (7.18) can be calculated. Equation (7.20) uses the neighborhood to maintain the embedding to describe the pattern changes within the class. Equation (7.21) uses the idea of discriminant analysis, so together they form the ***discriminative projection embedding (DPE)***. DPE uses the local manifold changes within a class to effectively describe the change of the transform difference component, and uses the nearest neighbor difference between the classes to describe the change of the identity difference component. Minimizing the local manifold changes within a class can better retain the local geometric position information within the class, thereby effectively reducing the transformation difference component; while maximizing the nearest neighbor difference between the classes can pay more attention to and distinguish the face category of people who are close in distance, so it can enhance the identity difference component. Unlike linear discriminant analysis and other methods in which the number of projection vectors is less than the total number of categories, because the inter-class metric matrix is in a non-parametric form, the number of projection vectors obtained by DPE is greater than the total number of categories, so more discrimination vectors can be obtained. This method has not only achieved good results in face recognition, but also in fingerprint recognition (Yan and Zhang 2008b).

7.4.2 Nonlinear Dimensionality Reduction Based on Nonnegative Matrix Decomposition

When **nonnegative matrix factorization (NMF)** realizes the non-linear dimensionality reduction of the vector, it is also necessary to keep all the components of the decomposition to be non-negative (Lee and Seung 1999). The psychological and physiological structure of NMF is based on the perception of the whole being constituted by the perception of the parts that make up the whole (pure additive) (Palmer 1977; Biederman 1987; Wachsmuth et al. 1994; Logothetis and Sheinberg 1996; Ullman 1996). This view is also in line with the intuitive understanding: the whole is composed of parts (Lee and Seung 1999). In addition, the limitation of the non-negativity of NMF leads to a certain degree of sparseness of the corresponding description (Lee and Seung 1999), and the expression of sparseness has been proved to be a form of effective data description between the description with fully distribution and the description of a single active component (Field 1994).

7.4.2.1 Basic Concepts of NMF

Consider making N observations on an M-dimensional positive random vector v, denote these observations as $v_j, j = 1, 2, \ldots, N$, denote $V = [V_{\bullet 1}, V_{\bullet 2}, \ldots, V_{\bullet N}]$, where $V_{\bullet j} = v_j, j = 1, 2, \ldots, N$. In this way, V represents all the observation data, and the dimensionality reaches $M \times N$. Suppose that the dimension of the data after dimensionality reduction is L, and NMF is to solve

$$\min_{0 \leq W, H} f_V (W, H) \tag{7.22}$$

($f_V (W, H)$ describes the difference between V and WH) to find the non-negative $M \times L$ basis matrix W and the non-negative $L \times N$ coefficient matrix H, so that

$$V \approx WH \tag{7.23}$$

Since $L << \min(M, N)$ is usually set, that is, it is desirable to describe a large amount of data with only a few bases, it is possible to make $V \approx WH$ only when W contains the essential characteristics of random vector v (Lee and Seung 2000).

From the algebraic point of view, NMF is an inherent non-negative algebraic decomposition form or representation method for discovering data; from the point of view of dimensionality reduction, because the coefficient matrix H is not the linearity projection results of the data matrix V in the space represented by the base matrix W, so NMF realizes nonlinear dimensionality reduction; from the perspective of multivariate statistics, NMF is to reduce the high-dimensional random pattern V to low-dimensional random pattern H under non-negative constraints and keeping the information as unchanged as possible., and the basis of this simplification is to estimate the essential structure W in the data.

7.4.2.2 NMF Model

The NMF model can be classified into a **basic NMF (BNMF)** model and an **improved NMF (INMF)** model. The former only imposes non-negative restrictions on W and H, while the latter also imposes some restrictions other than non-negative restrictions on W and H according to certain needs.

In order to realize NMF, it is necessary to construct an objective function reasonably, thereby alternately optimizing W and H, so as to obtain a local optimal solution of NMF. This is the basic idea of constructing NMF algorithm at present.

According to the different types of objective functions on which the algorithm is based, BNMF algorithms can be divided into two types: algorithms based on a single objective function and algorithms based on objective function families (see also [Li and Zhang 2008]). Typical algorithms based on a single objective function include: (i) the maximum likelihood algorithm under the Poisson distribution assumption, (ii) the smallest generalized Kullback-Leibler (KL) divergence algorithm, and (iii) the least square algorithm. Typical algorithms based on objective function families include: (i) algorithms based on αdivergence (αD), (ii) algorithms based on β divergence (βD), (iii) algorithms based on Bregman divergence.

The INMF model introduces more new restrictions, so that the decomposition results can meet more expected properties (see also [Li and Zhang 2008]). INMF algorithms mainly include three categories: NMF algorithms with enhanced sparsity; weighted NMF algorithms; discriminative embedded NMF algorithms. Typical NMF algorithms with enhanced sparsity include: (i) NMF algorithms with enhanced feature sparsity, (ii) NMF algorithms with enhanced coefficient sparsity, and (iii) NMF algorithms with enhanced feature and coefficient sparsity. Typical weighted NMF algorithms include: (i) Weighted least squares algorithm and (ii) weighted least KL divergence algorithm.

The above classification is summarized in Table 7.4.

7.4.2.3 NMSF Model

NMF is suitable for processing non-negative vector sets, but the image data is matrix data. Although the matrix data can be converted into long vectors (*i.e.*, vectorization) by

TABLE 7.4 NMF model and algorithm classification table

Basic NMF	Algorithm based on a single objective function	Maximum likelihood algorithm under the assumption of Poisson distribution
		Minimal generalized KL divergence algorithm
		Least squares algorithm
	Algorithm based on objective function family	Algorithm based on α divergence
		Algorithm based on β divergence
		Algorithm based on Bregman divergence
Improved NMF	NMF algorithm with enhanced sparsity	NMF algorithm with enhanced feature sparsity
		NMF algorithm with enhanced coefficient sparsity
		NMF algorithm with enhanced feature and coefficient sparsity
	Weighted NMF algorithm	Weighted least squares algorithm
		Weighted minimum KL divergence algorithm
	Discriminative embedded NMF algorithm	

line-by-line scanning, the spatial connection information between pixels is lost in this way, and the dimensionality reduction effect is not ideal (Lee and Seung 1999).

In fact, W is the learned parameter of the NMF learning process. At this time, the process of learning W is a process of using N samples to learn $MN \times L$-dimensional parameters, which is often called typical small-sample learning. There is a huge gap between the dimensionality of the learned object and the sample size. The ratio of the two is $MN \times L/N$, and its value is often hundreds or even thousands. According to statistical learning theory, small-sample learning usually leads to insufficient accuracy and poor generalization of learning results. Therefore, when dealing with data matrix sets, NMF's ability to describe data matrix sets is often not strong, and the generalization of NMF results is often poor.

For this reason, people have extended the NMF model and realized the nonnegative matrix set factorization (NMSF) model, which can directly process the matrices in the data matrix set. With reference to NMF model research methods and application needs, and inheriting the structural characteristics of NMF, different NMSF algorithms can be constructed and designed under the framework of NMSF (Li and Zhang 2011).

Consider making N observations on a random matrix A of $M \times N$ dimensions, and record these observations as a matrix set $\{A^k, k = 1, 2, \dots, N\}$. After NMSF specifies the non-negative weight matrix set $\{W^k, k = 1, 2, \dots, N\}$, the non-negative $l_1 \times l_1$ sparseness adjustment matrix S_1 and the non-negative $l_2 \times l_2$ sparseness adjustment matrix S_2, then the difference between $W^k \otimes A^k$ and $W^k \otimes LS_1 f(A^k)S_2R$ can be described by $g_{A^k}[W^k, L, S_1, f(A^k), S_2, R]$ (in principle, g_{A^k} it can be any distance measure or divergence); that is, NMSF uses

$$\min_{0 \le L, R, f(A^k), k=1,2,\dots,N} \sum_{k=1}^{N} g_{A^k}(L, S_1, f(A^k), S_2, R) \tag{7.24}$$

to find the non-negative $M \times l_1$ characteristic matrix L, the non-negative $l_2 \times N$ characteristic matrix R and the non-negative $l_1 \times l_2$ coefficient matrix set $\{f(A^k), k = 1, 2, \dots, N\}$, such that

$$W^k \otimes A^k \approx W^k \otimes \{LS_1 f(A^k)S_2R\}, \quad k = 1, 2, \dots, N \tag{7.25}$$

Here L, R and $\{f(A^k), k = 1, 2, \dots, N\}$ can have other characteristics (such as sparsity, discriminative, etc.) as needed.

Usually $l_1, l_2 << \min(M, N)$, so only when L and R contain the essential characteristics of the random matrix A, it is then possible to make $W^k \otimes A^k \approx W^k \otimes \{LS_1 f(A^k)S_2R\}$, $k = 1, 2, \dots, N$ (that is, a small amount of data $\{f(A^k), k = 1, 2, \dots, N\}$ can describe a large amount of data $\{A^k, k = 1, 2, \dots, N\}$). In addition to being used to describe training data, L and R are used to describe non-training data. After L and R are determined, the difference measurement criterion $\{f(A^k), k = 1, 2, \dots, N\}$ between $W^k \otimes A^k$ and $W^k \otimes \{LS_1 f(A^k)S_1R\}$ is also determined, so L and R contain all the content of the NMSF learning results, they are the parameters learned in the learning process.

The process of learning parameters L and R is the process of learning $M \times l_1 + l_2 \times N$-dimensional parameters with N samples. Because l_1, $l_2 << \min(M, N)$, this is no longer a small sample learning problem. Moreover, no matter the value of N is, the ratio of the sample size to the dimension of the learned parameter must be much smaller than the ratio of the sample size to the dimension of the learned parameter in NMF. Therefore, when dealing with data matrix sets, NMSF will describe more accurately and has generality better than NMF.

In the following, some comparative experiments and analyses taking face recognition as an example to show the superiority of NMF over NMF are presented.

1. Comparison of descriptive power between NMF and NMSF

The reference index used here is the compression ratio. Assuming that the decomposed data matrix set is $\{A^k, \quad k = 1, 2, \ldots, N\}$, A^k is $M \times M$-dimensional. According to the definition of compression ratio [Zhang 2017], it is known that the compression ratio in NMSF is $mnN/[(ml_1 + nl_2) + l_1 l_2 N]$, while the compression ratio of NMF is $mnN/(mnL + LN)$. The descriptive power depends on the relative error between the original data and the processed data, which can be measured by the reconstruction effect under a given compression ratio.

The images used in the experiment come from the ORL face database having a total of 400 images. With the help of these images, the descriptive power of the dimensionality reduction effect of the two compared methods at different compression ratios (compression ratios are from first to the seventh power of 2) is calculated. Figure 7.8 shows the reconstructed images obtained by these two comparison methods. Among them, the leftmost image in the first row is the original image; the next seven images correspond to the results obtained using NMSF with compression ratios of 2, 4, 8, 16, 32, 64, and 128; the seven images in the second row correspond to the results obtained by using NMF with compression ratios of 2, 4, 8, 16, 32, 64, and 128. According to the clarity of the image, it can be seen that the ***descriptive power*** of NMSF is significantly better than that of NMF.

2. Comparison of generality of NMF and NMSF

The reference index used here is the number of description coefficients. Because under the same number of descriptive coefficients, the compression ratio of NMSF is often

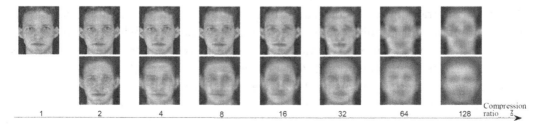

FIGURE 7.8 Comparison results of the descriptive power of the two methods.

much higher than that of NMF, that is, the descriptive power of NMSF for training data is usually worse than that of NMF. If the NMSF's descriptive power on the test data is better than the NMF at this time, then the difference between the NMSF's descriptive power on the training data and the descriptive power on the test data is less than the difference between the NMF's descriptive power on the training data and the descriptive power on the test data. That is, NMSF has higher generality than NMF.

The training data used in the experiment are 400 images from ORL face database, and the test data used in the experiment are from Yale database, PIE database and UMIST database. Table 7.5 lists some example images and the corresponding reconstruction errors. When 225 description coefficients are retained, the compression ratio of NMSF (44.3) is much higher than that of NMF (1.71), that is, the descriptive power of NMSF on training data is worse than that of NMF on training data (see the reconstruction examples under "training results" for the images and the corresponding reconstruction relative error). However, NMSF's ability to describe the images of YALE database, PIE database and UMIST database is much better than NMF's ability to describe the images of these databases (see the reconstruction examples under " generality test results" for the images and the corresponding reconstruction relative error). The conclusion is that when the training data is matrix set, the generalization of NMSF result is much better than that of NMF result.

7.5 FACE RECOGNITION BASED ON CLASS-DEPENDENCY FEATURE ANALYSIS

Typical supervised linear subspace methods include linear decision analysis, class dependency analysis and so on. The ***class-dependency feature analysis (CFA)*** method (Xie et al. 2005; Kumar et al. 2006) is different from the traditional linear subspace method. A projection axis obtained by CFA only tries to distinguish a certain category from all other remaining categories. The different projection axes distinguish different specific categories. CFA is similar to treating multi-class problems as to treating multiple two-class problems. Each projection axis is equivalent to a classifier, which only classifies a specific face category and other remaining face categories.

7.5.1 Basic Framework

The projection matrix obtained by many linear subspace methods (such as PCA, ICA, LDA, etc.) is related to the statistical characteristics of all training samples. The projection axis attempts to preserve (such as PCA and ICA) or distinguish (such as LDA) all face categories.

The CFA face recognition method uses a correlation filter technology. For each face category in the training set, a correlation filter is trained. The correlation filter has the largest output for the training samples of the current category, while suppressing the output for the training samples of other categories. Different design criteria can be used to obtain correlation filters with different properties.

The design block diagram of the 2-D correlation filter in face recognition based on class-dependent feature analysis is shown in Figure 7.9. The filter works in the frequency domain. The extraction of discriminative features with the help of filters is shown in Figure 7.9 (Xie et al. 2005; Kumar et al. 2006). The process of extracting feature vectors by

TABLE 7.5 Comparison results of generalization of the two methods

Method	Example of training results			Examples of generality test results											
	Taken from ORL database			Taken from YALE database			Taken from PIE database				Taken from UMIST database			
Ori. image															
NMSF Reconstructed															
Error	0.101	0.125	0.120	0.117	0.093	0.101	0.105	0.107	0.121		0.152	0.141	0.115	
NMF Reconstructed															
Error	0.092	0.106	0.103	0.268	0.268	0.244	0.180	0.196	0.173		0.249	0.227	0.233	

$l_1 \times l_2 = 15 \times 15$/Compression ratio = 44.3

$L = 225$/ Compression ratio = 1.71

Notes

(1) The training data is all 400 images in the ORL database; (2) the compression ratio refers to the compression ratio of the training data; (3) error refers to the relative error during reconstruction

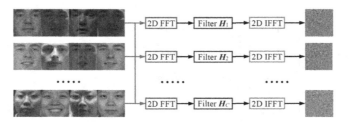

FIGURE 7.9   The design of 2-D correlation filter.

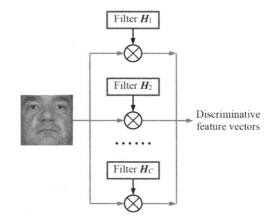

FIGURE 7.10   Discriminative feature extraction.

CFA is as follows: First, the training set is used to obtain the basis function (*i.e.*, correlation filter) of the 2D-CFA, where each category in the training set corresponds to a basis function. Each correlation filter distinguishes a certain category from other categories (Figure 7.9). Then, the relevant filters obtained from each category in the training set are formed into a filter bank and used as the basis function of 2D-CFA for feature extraction (Figure 7.10). It can be seen that the core of the recognition framework is the design of related filters.

7.5.2 Commonly Used Correlation Filters

Correlation can usually be used to characterize the similarity between two patterns. Here, the correlation filter is a filter designed in the frequency domain. The frequency domain includes frequency and phase. The phase is generally considered to contain more structural information that is conducive to perception. Generally, a certain number of training samples are used to design the correlation filter, so that the output response to the authentic training sample is the largest, and the output response to other false training samples (also known as the imposter sample) is the smallest.

The following briefly introduces several commonly used correlation filters.

7.5.2.1 Matched Filter

The simplest **correlation filter** is the matched filter (VanderLugt 1963), which is usually the conjugate transpose of the 2-D Fourier transform of the mask image. If the input test image is a mask image plus Gaussian noise, the output result of the **matched filter** is optimal. However, in the face recognition problem, due to the influence of factors such as illumination, expression, age, etc., the face image will have various changes (not a simple mask image plus Gaussian noise), so the theoretically optimal method must design a matched filter for every possible face sample, but in fact this is not feasible, so the matched filter is not suitable for the problem of face recognition.

7.5.2.2 Synthetic Discriminant Function Filter

The **synthetic discriminant function (SDF)** filter reflects the changes between the modes within the class (Hester and Casssant 1980). The filter assumes that there are a certain number of typical samples in the training set. SDF is the weighted sum of matched filters of these typical samples. It selects the weight by controlling the output value at the origin. For example, the output of the real sample at the origin is set to 1, and the output of the false sample at the origin is set to 0. The correlation filter designed in this way has an expected value of 1 for real samples at the origin, and an expected value of 0 for false samples at the origin.

It can be proved that the frequency domain representation of the filter designed by SDF is

$$H_f = X \, (X^H X)^{-1} p \tag{7.26}$$

where X is the data matrix, p is the expected peak value (vector) of each training sample, and the superscript H represents the conjugate transpose operation.

7.5.2.3 Minimum Average Correlation Energy Filter

Although SDF can generate a setting value at the origin, it cannot control the values of non-origin points. The design principle of the **minimum average correlation energy (MACE)** filter is to minimize the average output correlation energy of all training images while controlling the peak value of the output image at the origin (Mahalanobis et al. 1987). That is, the value of training samples of a specific category is 1 at the origin of the output image, and the values of training samples of other categories are 0 at the origin of the output image. The MACE filter can not only generate spikes for real samples, but also suppress output values other than the origin, so as to ensure that the location of the spikes can be easily found. As shown in Figure 7.11, spikes can be generated for real samples, while the output for false samples is random, and the output values are relatively small.

The frequency domain expression of MACE filter is

$$H_f = D^{-1} X \, (X^+ D^{-1} X)^{-1} p \tag{7.27}$$

where X is the data matrix, p is the expected peak value (vector) of each training sample, and D is the diagonal matrix (the elements on the diagonal are the average power spectrum of all training images).

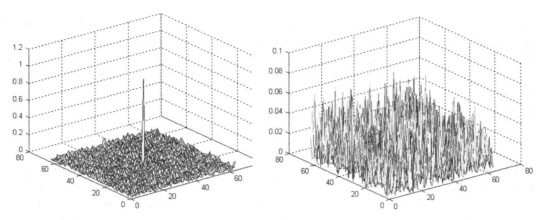

FIGURE 7.11 A typical output image of real samples (left) and a typical output image of fake samples (right).

7.5.2.4 Minimum Variance Synthetic Discriminant Function Filter

The design principle of the **minimum variance synthetic discriminant function (MVSDF)** filter is to minimize the noise variance of the average output while controlling the peak value of the output image at the origin (Kumar 1986). Unlike MACE, the MVSDF filter minimizes the output noise. When the input noise is white noise, the MVSDF filter is equivalent to a synthetic discriminant function filter.

The spatial expression of the MVSDF filter is

$$H_s = C^{-1}X\,(X^+C^{-1}X)^{-1}p \tag{7.28}$$

where C is the diagonal matrix (the elements on the diagonal are the noise power spectrum of all training images).

7.5.2.5 Optimal Trade-off Filter

Comparing the above two filters, it can be seen that in order to generate spikes, the MACE filter emphasizes high-frequency components (the time-domain correlated signal output of the spikes requires the filter to support signals in a wide frequency domain), which causes the MACE filter to be very sensitive to high-frequency noise. In order to suppress high-frequency noise, the MVSDF filter emphasizes low-frequency components, and it is not easy to obtain spikes. The optimal tradeoff filter (optimal tradeoff filter, OTF) combines the two filters, and achieves the purpose of generating spikes and suppressing noise by controlling the weights of the two filters (Refregier 1990).

The frequency domain expression of the filter designed by OTF is

$$H_f = T^{-1}X\,(X^H T^{-1}X)^{-1}p \tag{7.29}$$

where X is the data matrix, p is the expected peak value (vector) of each training sample, $T = aD + \sqrt{1 - a^2}\,C$ is the diagonal matrix, $a = 1$ corresponds to the MACE filter, and $a = 0$ corresponds to the MVSDF filter.

Using OTF, good recognition results have been achieved on the FRGC (face recognition grand challenge) 2.0 database (Xie 2005; Kumar 2006).

7.5.2.6 Optimal Extra-Class Origin Trade-off Filter

The basic idea of optimal extra-class origin trade-off filter (OEOTF) is to optimize two different objective functions at the same time (Yan and Zhang 2008a; Yan and Zhang 2008c). Both objective functions optimize the output statistics (energy and variance) of the inter-class training samples at the origin of the relevant output plane, and at the same time make the output values of the intra-class training samples at the origin of the relevant output plane meet certain constraints. Specifically, OEOTF combines the minimum average extra-class origin correlation energy (MAEOCE) filter and the minimum extra-class origin variance synthetic discrimination function (MEOVSDF) filter.

The spatial domain expression of the filter designed by OEOTF is

$$H_s = D^{-1}X^I (X^{IH}D^{-1}X^I)^{-1}u \qquad (7.30)$$

Among them, $D = aR_Y + \sqrt{1 - a^2}\,C$, $0 \le a \le 1$, where $R_Y = (\sum_{i=1}^{N-N_c} X_i^E X_i^{EH})/(N - N_c)$, X_i^E ($i = 1, 2, \ldots, N - N_c$) is the Fourier transform of the inter-class feature (E) of the face; and N_c represents the number of training samples in the class. C is a diagonal matrix, and the elements on the diagonal represent the noise power spectral density function of the characteristics between classes. $X_c^I = [X_1^I, X_2^I, \ldots, X_{Nc}^I]$, where X_i^I ($i = 1, 2, \ldots, N_c$) is the Fourier transform of the intra-class feature (I) of the c-th face. $u = [1, 1, \ldots, 1]^T$ is a vector of $N_c \times 1$.

The following qualitatively compares the difference between OTF and OEOTF.

Both OTF and OEOTF try to generate spikes and suppress noise output at the same time, but OTF and OEOTF are designed in completely different ways. OTF optimizes the trade-off between the energy and noise variance of all training samples at all points in the relevant output plane, and at the same time constrains the value of these samples at the origin of the relevant output plane (the output of the training samples in the class is 1, while the output of the training samples between the classes is 0). OEOTF minimizes the trade-off between the energy and noise variance of the inter-class training samples at the origin of the relevant output plane, and constrains the value of the training samples within the class at the origin of the relevant output plane. It can be seen that OTF optimizes and constrains all training samples in the same manner, while OEOTF optimizes and constrains training samples respectively between and within classes. OTF constrains the entire correlation output plane, while OEOTF only constrains the origin of the correlation output plane. Therefore, the constraints of OEOTF are simpler (only the training samples in the class are constrained), but OEOTF still assumes that the peak value of all training samples in the class is 1.

From the perspective of pattern recognition, OEOTF's design criteria are simpler than OTF (the value of all points on the relevant output plane is not considered), so OEOTF may be more generalizable. Moreover, the OEOTF goals for criteria designing and the extraction of the identification feature vector are more consistent, so the features extracted by OEOTF are more effective.

According to Parseval's theorem (Oppenheim and Schafer 1996), the inner product in the frequency domain is proportional to the inner product in the time domain, namely

$$\sum_{i=0}^{P-1} x(i)y^*(i) = \frac{1}{P} \sum_{j=0}^{P-1} X(j)Y^*(j) \tag{7.31}$$

Since the design of OEOTF is only for the value of the origin of the relevant output plane (the inner product of the input signal and the correlation filter), OEOTF can design the filter in the time domain. However, due to the need to optimize the energy and variance of the entire correlation output plane, OTF can only design filters in the frequency domain.

7.5.3 Correlation Filter Training

The training flow diagram of the correlation filter is shown in Figure 7.12. First, extract the original features (such as grayscale features or *Gabor wavelet features*) of the training images, and treat the extracted features as a point in the high-dimensional space after vectorization, and then use the linear dimensionality reduction method to reduce the dimensionality, and then the 1-D Fourier transform of low-dimensional features (think as 1-D signals) is used to train the correlation filter H in the dimensionality reduction space. Suppose there are L categories, so L filters need to be trained. If there are N training images, the original feature matrix can be expressed as $X = [x_1, x_2, \ldots, x_N]$, where x_i is the vectorized feature obtained by extracting the original feature from the training image. Then use the projection matrix obtained by *linear dimensionality reduction* methods (such as PCA and LDA) to reduce the dimensionality of the original feature matrix, so that the low-dimensional feature matrix obtained after linear reduction can be expressed as $Y = [y_1, y_2, \ldots, y_N]$, the feature dimension of the post-dimensionality reduction is M.

After training the correlation filter, the feature vector can be extracted, as shown in Figure 7.13. Here, the original feature extraction, vectorization and dimensionality reduction are also performed on the recognition image, and then the feature vectors are produced by inner-production of L correlation filters and the obtained low-dimensional features.

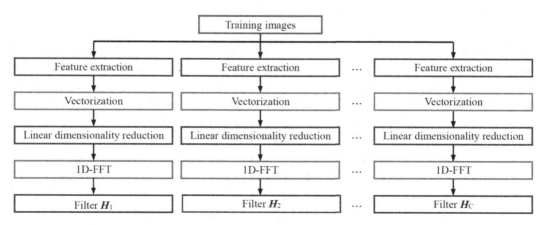

FIGURE 7.12 The training process of the correlation filter.

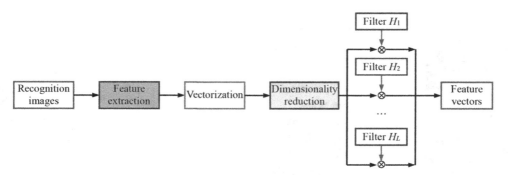

FIGURE 7.13 Feature vector extraction process.

7.6 FACE RECOGNITION BASED ON EDGE EIGENVECTOR WEIGHTING

There are many methods for face matching and recognition. Here, we only briefly introduce a method of calculating the weighted Hausdorff distance of the edge eigenface based on the eigenface of the face edge image to match the image for recognition (Tan and Zhang 2007). It considers that different face regions have different importance for face recognition and Hausdorff distance is a feature of calculating the distance between binary point sets.

The face matching recognition method uses edge masks for matching recognition. This is similar to the process of face localization based on the average face mask matching obtained from the edge image introduced in Section 7.3. It is necessary to match the tested image/candidate image region with the pre-defined face mask to measure the similarity between them. But it should be noted that their goals are different. In face localization, the goal is to search for features shared by various faces in the test image to detect the position of the face; while in face recognition, the goal is to find the unique characteristics of each person in the test image to identify the person's identity. Therefore, the two tasks have different requirements for the face masks used. In face localization, the face mask needs to reflect the commonality of all faces (so the average face mask is used). In face recognition, the face mask needs to reflect the difference between different faces.

In addition, different regions of the face have different importance in face recognition, so different face regions need to be weighted. The weight function can be established on the basis of the grayscale domain or the gradient domain. A Hausdorff distance weighted by the weight function calculated based on the first eigenface of the human face edge image can be called the ***edge eigenvector weighted Hausdorff distance (EEWHD)***. The weight function calculated in this way can be written as

$$W(x, y) = \left(\frac{255}{\max(E) - \min(E)} \right) E(x, y) \qquad (7.32)$$

Among them, $E(x, y) = |E_1(x, y)|$, $E_1(x, y)$ is the first eigenvector of the face edge image in the training set; $\max(E)$ and $\min(E)$, respectively, represent the maximum and minimum

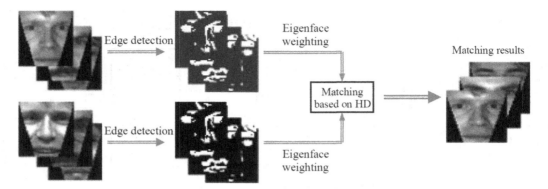

FIGURE 7.14 Schematic diagram of face recognition process based on EEWHD.

values of $E(x, y)$. Here, according to the definition of eigenface, a point with a larger amplitude in a eigenface image means that the image in the training set has a larger grayscale change at this position. Face recognition needs to find the difference between the test face and other faces. In this way, it should be appropriate to use the amplitude of the first feature face as the weight function.

The system framework diagram of applying EEWHD to face recognition is shown in Figure 7.14. After extracting all the face edge images in the training set, the first feature face in the edge domain can be calculated. Then, the required weight function is calculated according to Equation (7.32). In Figure 7.14, the weight function used by the system is also represented by a grayscale image, where white represents points with large weights.

Finally, it is pointed out that the edge eigenvector weighted Hausdorff distance (EEWHD) discussed here is different from the edge frequency weighted Hausdorff distance (EFWHD) introduced in Section 7.3. Although they are all calculated on the edge image, the Hausdorff distance weighted by the edge frequency reflects the commonality of the edge image, and the Hausdorff distance weighted by the edge eigenvector reflects the personality of the edge image, which is just suitable for face recognition in which it is necessary to fit the requirements of different characteristics between different faces.

7.7 SOME RECENT DEVELOPMENTS AND FURTHER RESEARCH

In the following sections, some technical developments and promising research directions in the last few years are briefly overviewed.

7.7.1 Face Liveness Detection

A spear makes a shield. With the wide application of face recognition, the security of face recognition technology has become increasingly prominent. One of the problems is that the impostors cheat the face recognition system by presenting the facial camouflage of legitimate users. This behavior is called *face spoofing*.

Among the face spoofing means, the most common methods are based on *prosthetic face*. That is, in order to cheat the face recognition system, low-cost and simple and feasible attacks mostly appear in the form of a fake face presented in front of the camera.

This is often called "presentation attack", which is a typical way of face spoofing. So, ensuring that the object in front of the camera is a real face is the first step for the face recognition system to make a correct judgment.

To meet this challenge, the process of **face liveness detection** (also called **face anti-spoofing**) is considered. Face liveness detection refers to the process of identifying whether the currently acquired face image is from a living face or a prosthetic face. The living face refers to a real face in living, and the prosthetic face refers to a face counterfeit posing as a real person. With the wide application of face recognition technology, face liveness detection becomes the key to ensure the security of face recognition utilization. It is often embedded into the face recognition system and placed before the face recognition module, that is, the input image needs to be verified first (determining whether a real face or a false face), then the actual face recognition starts.

7.7.1.1 Face Spoofing

Face spoofing with a prosthetic face has various fashions. The following types can be distinguished (Jiang et al. 2021):

1. Photo-like prosthetic face

Photo-like prosthetic face refers to the printed black and white or color face photo on the photo paper or ordinary printing paper.

2. Video-like prosthetic face

Video-like prosthetic face refers to pre-recorded face videos played through mobile phones, computers, or other electronic display devices.

3. Mask-like prosthetic face

Mask-like prosthetic face refers to 3-D face masks of molds of various materials that include plastic, latex, silicone, etc. It can be customized based on user-provided photos.

4. Model-like prosthetic face

The most used form is the **synthetic prosthetic face** with a 3-D face model, which refers to a 3-D face model synthesized by using legal user photos using 3-D face manipulation software. This type of face model usually uses electronic equipment as a medium, and attacks face recognition after being displayed by electronic equipment.

Another categorization considering the face spoofing modes and their providing information is shown in Table 7.6 (Xie et al. 2022).

Some other spoofing modes are also reported (Hu et al. 2021), such as occlusion (part of the real face has been covered in various degrees of transparency), using eyeglasses with adversarial noise, etc.

TABLE 7.6 Common spoofing modes and information provided

Spoofing Mode	Information Provided		
	Texture	3-D Structure	Interactive Action
Printed photo	Yes	No	No
Curved printed photo	Yes	Simple	No
Printed photos with real facial features	Yes	Simple	Open mouth, blink eye, turn head
On-screen photo	Yes	No	No
On-screen video	Yes	No	No
On-screen 3-D model	Yes	No	Yes
3-D rigid body mask	Yes	Complex	Open mouth, blink eye, turn head
3-D flexible mask	Yes	Complex	Many facial expressions

7.7.1.2 Non-Interactive Face Anti-Spoofing

Existing face liveness detection methods are dedicated to distinguishing live face images from prosthetic face images in considering various perspectives. Regarding the classification of face live detection methods, different classification schemes can be obtained according to different criteria. For example, considering the modality of input information, single-frame image-based face liveness detection, video-based face liveness detection, 3-D model-based face liveness detection, and depth coordinate points-based face liveness detection can be distinguished.

According to the application form of the current mainstream face liveness detection methods, they can be divided into two categories: interactive face liveness detection (cooperation type) and non-interactive face liveness detection (silent type).

The interactive face liveness detection takes the human into the detection loop. Since the host of a living face is a living human and humans can make actions or make sounds as required, while this could be a difficult task for a prosthetic face. Interactive face liveness detection uses action commands to interact with users, and the system determines whether the face in front of the camera is a live face or a prosthetic face by judging whether the user has accurately completed the specified required action. The performance of interactive face detection algorithms mainly depends on the recognition of action instructions and results. Through carefully designed interactive actions, the interactive face liveness detection techniques can effectively reduce the impact of prosthetic faces on the detection performance, and its recognition rate and versatility have met the needs of many practical business scenarios.

However, the interactive *face liveness detection* needs a large amount of calculation and calculation time to identify whether the user has completed the action from the multi-frame images, and it requires the user to complete multiple specified actions in the specified region, the detection process is cumbersome, and the restrictions and requirements for the user are high. So the user experience is not good, which offsets the convenience and natural advantages of face recognition technology. In addition, the requirement for the user's cooperation makes it can only be used in the scenarios where users actively cooperate, not suitable for cases in which users are in a state of natural behavior, such as face analysis in video surveillance.

Non-interactive face liveness detection can distinguish live faces and prosthetic faces without the user's active perception, and without interacting with the user. Non-interactive face liveness relies on detection and analysis of the difference between the real live face images and the prosthetic image captured by cameras to distinguish live faces and prosthetic faces. Following (Xie et al. 2022), the main existing anti-spoofing method categories, and their principles and characteristics, are summarized in Table 7.7.

7.7.1.3 Face Anti-Spoofing Technique Classification

Face anti-spoofing techniques can also be classified, according to their principles and characteristics, into seven groups (Hu et al. 2021), as shown in Table 7.8.

7.7.2 Occlusion Face Recognition

When the face is partially occluded, the performance of face recognition system may considerably be decreased. In real-world scenarios, many occlusion situations often occur. Various occlusions will lead to difficulties in face detection, decrease of positioning and detection accuracy, incomplete feature extraction, and reduction of recognition rate.

7.7.2.1 Occlusion Face Detection

In order to enhance the detection effect of occluded faces, an occluded face detection method based on convergent CNN and attention augmentation network is proposed (Xiang and Yang 2021). When detecting an occluded face, it is first necessary to determine whether the detection region is a face, which requires reference to the context information around the face, that is, to learn face features by setting the anchor frame size reasonably. However, due to the influence of occlusion, only referring to the context information around the face may still not enough, it is necessary to refer to the visible part of the face to help confirm whether the detection region is a face. The framework detection model is shown in Figure 7.15, which mainly consists of three parts: the main network, the attention enhancement network, and the additional enhancement network. Finally, the face bounding box detected in parallel (the main network and the additional enhancement network are set in parallel) is processed by fast non-maximum suppression (NMS) to output the face detection results.

The main network uses the *single shot detector (SSD)* algorithm to extract multi-scale feature maps on multiple consecutive convolutional layers, and then performs face/non-face classification and face bounding box regression on multiple feature maps, respectively. The SSD algorithm is a one-stage detection algorithm, which can directly obtain the predicted object category and candidate frame position after a single detection stage, and has the characteristics of fast detection and high precision. The core of the algorithm is to use convolution kernels on multi-scale feature maps to predict the categories and positions of a series of default detection boxes.

The attention enhancement network is formed by concatenating multiple convolution layers, and introduces hierarchical supervised learning to improve the response values and identification degree of the visible part of the face in the original feature map, so as to obtain the enhanced feature map to assist the face/non-face detection. In the training of

TABLE 7.7 Classification of non-interactive face anti-spoofing methods

Method Category	Classification Features	Anti-spoofing Principle	Facial Spoofing
Based on image texture	LBP, HOG, Gabor descriptors and their variations Feature extracted with LPQ, BSIF, DOG, GLCM, etc.	Different textures between facial spoofing and the photo paper or electronic display screen (due to print quality, display resolution, plane structure, etc.)	Photos, Videos, Masks
Based on image quality	Image quality features in terms of specular reflection, color distribution and clarity	Different materials (differences in reflection attributes) between the media properties of facial spoofing and living face	Photos, Videos
Based on life information	Information from remote optical plethysmography (rPPG) Optical flow and motion component decomposition	Different vital characteristics The object to be tested has or not heart rate The involuntary blinking of the living body and the micro movement of the face and lip	MasksPhotos
Based on other image capturing hardware	Near, short wave, thermal infrared image, multiple bands image, light field image, depth image	Different images may make large discrimination, intra class difference for materials with different reflection properties in visible light, to obtain high recognition accuracy and simultaneously combats multiple types of fraudulent attacks	Photos, Videos, Masks
Based on depth feature	Depth features from CNN, resnet-50, VGg, etc. Fusion of depth features and manual features	Deep learning method can extract high-level semantic features (manual design features are mostly shallow features), and can effectively represent the difference between living face and spoofing face	Photos, Videos, Masks
Based on combined features	Combine information from texture, motion life, face structure, image quality, background, etc., as well as other features	More information can provide more classification cues, and extend the feature dimensionality, so as to effectively distinguish living face and spoofing face	Photos, Videos, Masks

TABLE 7.8 Technique classification of anti-spoofing methods

Method Category	Principle and Description	Advantages and Disadvantages
Based on image feature	Using Chromatic Co-occurence of Local Binary Pattern (CCoLBP) feature, Central Difference Convolution (CDC) deep feature, etc., to capture the difference between a real face and a prosthetic face.	More direct and intuitive. How to ensure that the extracted features in the source domain can be adapted to new target domain.
Based on material difference between living organisms and prosthetic faces	The living face has the characteristics that the prosthetic face does not have, such as body temperature, pulse, facial movement, etc., while the prosthetic face contains the characteristics that the living face does not have, such as the reflection of materials other than skin, the distortion artifact caused by face image recapture, and the Mole pattern produced by light interference on the screen.	Simple principle and good interpretability, and has certain potential to overcome the decline of cross library performance. Additional hardware is required, so the system hardware size is relatively large and the complexity of calculation increases.
Based on auxiliary information of software manufacturing	Use local feature blocks and global depth maps to assist face images, or use the Residual Spatial Gradient Block (RSGB) to better represent spatial information, and the Spatial-Temporal Propagation Module (STPM) to better represent temporal information, to guide the detail extraction of face images and improve detection performance.	No need for hardware coordination, low cost. Auxiliary information cannot be obtained directly, so it is necessary to use face images for estimating auxiliary information before use, the performance needs to improve.
Based on multimodal information acquired by hardware	Through the combined use of face information of various modalities such as visible light images, infrared images, and depth maps, more abundant and effective classification features can be mined, thereby further improving the classification accuracy and detection performance for prosthetic face.	Relatively higher accuracy Additional hardware is required, and maybe application domain dependent.
Based on domain adjustment with semi supervised or unsupervised learning	Domain adaptation can narrow the difference between training samples and actual detection samples. Domain generalization can use multiple existing source domains to train the model and learn a generalized feature space without having to use target data.	It has certain promotion and can improve cross-domain capability. The method research is still in the heuristic exploration stage, and the basic common sense of real and prosthetic faces are used empirically to design the loss function for supervision.

(Continued)

TABLE 7.8 (*Continued*)

Method Category	Principle and Description	Advantages and Disadvantages
Based on learning of decouple/disentangle to separate prosthetic traces	Disentanglement Learning can express complex data and features, so use decoupling learning networks, such as Spoof Trace Disentanglement Network (STDN), can disentangle between prosthetic and real faces to isolate "prosthetic traces" for improving detection performance.	It can effectively distinguish the features of living and non-living faces, is conducive to the design of a general detection model. Due to the complexity of application scenarios, the diversity of prosthetic types, and the lack of ground truth, such methods currently have insufficient description of prosthetic traces, inconsistent metrics, and the extraction of prosthetic features is vulnerable to the external environment, etc.
Based on detection of signal abnormity	Take the real face as one type of signal/data, and all non-real faces as abnormal signal/data, so the detection problem is solved by the classification method.	The progress and results of deep learning in classification problems can be used. If there is no prosthetic face information at all, performance may drop significantly.

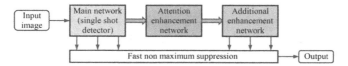

FIGURE 7.15   The framework of detection model.

network, the supervised information needs to be distributed to multiple size feature maps for supervised learning. Because the shallow feature map is suitable for detecting small-size faces, and the deep feature map is suitable for detecting large-size faces, it is necessary to add small-size face supervision information to the large-size shallow feature map, and add large-size face supervision information to the small-size deep feature map.

The detection layer of the additional enhancement network is obtained after the processing of theattention enhancement network, including multiple enhanced feature maps. These enhanced feature maps have the same size as the original feature map, but have a higher response value to the visible part of the face.

7.7.2.2 Removing Glasses for Face Recognition

Glasses is a common face occlusion object, especially for eyes. Usually glasses can be divided into three categories: full frame, half frame and frameless. In practical applications, due to the influence of occlusion by glasses, the accuracy of face recognition will drop significantly. In recent years, many different methods have been tried to remove glasses from face images. One of the methods (Mao et al. 2021) draws on the idea of mapping between low-resolution images and high-resolution images in super-resolution reconstruction (Zhang 2022), and designs a deep convolutional neural network for *removing glasses (eyeglasses removal CNN, ERCNN)* through the end-to-end learning to automatically construct the mapping relationship between the face image with glasses and the face image without glasses, finally realizing the automatic glasses removal from the face image.

The network structure is shown in Figure 7.16. First, the face image with glasses is normalized to 128 × 128 as the input image, and the 64 × 128 part of the input image that contains the complete glasses-wearing region is taken as the input of the convolution layer, theconvolution result is used for the *max feature map (MFM)* unit in the network to performs feature selection and maximum element operation for improving the model performance. After that, the deconvolution, average pooling, and element-by-element weighted summation operations are performed to reconstruct back the 64 × 128 image part. Further processing can produce the eye region after removing glasses and overlap on the original input image, and a complete face image without glasses is obtained.

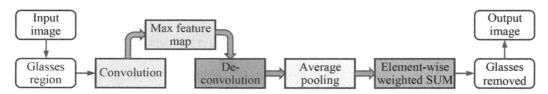

FIGURE 7.16   The structure of glasses removing network.

REFERENCES

Biederman, I. 1987. Recognition-by-components: A theory of human image understanding. *Psychological Review*, 94(2): 115–147.

Bowyer, K.W., K. Chang, and P. Flynn. 2004. A survey of approaches to three-dimensional face recognition. *Proceedings of the ICPR*, 1: 358–361.

Field, D.J. 1994. What is the goal of sensory coding? *Neural Computation*, 6(4): 559–601.

Fu, Y., and T.S. Huang. 2008. Human age estimation with regression on discriminative aging manifold. *IEEE Transactions on Multimedia*, 10(4): 578–584.

Gao, Y., and M.K.H. Leung. 2002. Line segment Hausdorff distance on face matching. *Pattern Recognition*, 35(2): 361–371.

Hester, C.F., and D. Casssant. 1980. Multivariant technique for multiclass pattern recognition. *Applied Optics*, 19(11): 1758–1761.

Hu, Y.J., Y.F. Wang, B.B. Liu, et al. 2021. A survey on the latest development and typical methods of face anti-spoofing. *Journal of Signal Processing*, 37(12): 2261–2277.

Jiang, F.L., P.C. Liu, and X.D. Zhou. 2021. A review on face anti-spoofing. *Acta Automatica Sinica*, 47(8): 1799–1821.

Josorsky, O., K.J. Kirchberg, and R.W. Frischholz. 2001. Robust face detection using the Hausdorff distance. *Proceedings of the Third International Conference on Audio- and Video-based Biometric Person Authentication*, 90–95.

Kanade, T., J.F. Cohn, and Y. Tian. 2000. Comprehensive database for facial expression analysis. *Proceedings of the Fourth International Conference of Face and Gesture Recognition*, 46–53.

Kong, S.G., J. Heo, and B. Abidi, et al. 2005. Recent advances in visual and infrared face recognition – A review. *Computer Vision and Image Understanding*, 97(1): 103–135.

Kumar, B.V.K.V. 1986. Minimum variance synthetic discriminant functions. *Journal of the Optical Society of America A*, 3: 1579–1584.

Kumar, B.V.K.V., M. Savvides, and C. Xie. 2006. Correlation pattern recognition for face recognition. *Proceedings of IEEE*, 94(11): 1963–1976.

Lee, D.D., and H.S. Seung. 1999. Learning the parts of objects by non-negative matrix factorization. *Nature*, 401(6755): 788–791.

Lee, D.D., and H.S. Seung. 2000. Algorithms for non-negative matrix factorization. *Advances in Neural Information Processing Systems*, 556–562.

Lee, K.C., J. Ho, and D.J. Kriegman. 2005. Acquiring linear subspaces for face recognition under variable lighting. *IEEE Transactions on Pattern Analysis and Machine Intelligence*, 27(5): 684–698.

Li, L., and Y.-J. Zhang. 2008. A survey on algorithms of non-negative matrix factorization. *Acta Electronica Sinica*, 36(4): 737–743.

Li, L., and Y.-J. Zhang. 2011. FastNMF: Efficient NMF algorithm for reducing feature dimension. In Zhang, Y.-J., (ed.). *Advances in Face Image Analysis: Techniques and Technologies*, Hershey PA, USA: IGI Global, Chapter 8 (137–162).

Lin, K.H., K.M. Lam, and W.C. Sui. 2003. Spatially eigen-weighted Hausdorff distances for human face recognition. *Pattern Recognition*, 36: 1827–1834.

Liu, X.M., Y.-J. Zhang, and H.C. Tan. 2008. Hausdorff distance based similarity measure and symmetry measure and their applications in face localization. *Signal Processing*. 24(1): 118–121.

Logothetis, N.K., and D.L. Sheinberg. 1996. Visual object recognition. *Annual Review of Neuroscience*, 19(1): 577–621.

Mahalanobis, A., B.V.K.V. Kumar, and D. Casasent. 1987. Minimum average correlation energy filters. *Applied Optics*, 26: 3630–3640.

Mao, L., Y.J. Xue, Y.H. Wei, et al. 2021. An eyeglasses removal method for fine-grained face recognition. *Journal of Electronics & Information Technology*, 43(5): 1448–1456.

Oppenheim, A.V., and R.W. Schafer. 1996. *Signals and Systems*. 2nd Ed. New York: Prentice Hall.

Palmer, S.E. 1977. Hierarchical structure in perceptual representation. *Cognitive Psychology*, 9(3): 441–474.

Pan, Z., G. Healey, and M. Prasad, et al. 2003. Face recognition in hyperspectral images. *IEEE Transactions on Pattern Analysis and Machine Intelligence*, 25: 1552–1560.

Phillips, P.J., P. Grother, and R.J. Micheals, et al. 2003. Face recognition vendor test 2002: Evaluation report. http://www.frvt.org/FRVT2002/documents.htm

Refregier, P. 1990. Filter design for optical pattern recognition: Multi-criteria optimization approach. *Optics Letters*, 15: 854–856.

Romdhani, S., J. Ho, and T. Vetter, et al. 2006. Face recognition using 3-D models: Pose and illumination. *Proceedings of the IEEE*, 94(11): 1977–1999.

Sirovich, L., and M. Kirby. 1987. Low-dimensional procedure for the characterization of human faces. *Journal of the Optical Society of America A*, 4(3): 519–524.

Tan, H.C., and Y.-J. Zhang. 2006. A novel weighted Hausdorff distance for face localization. *Image and Vision Computing*, 24(7): 656–662.

Tan, H.C., and Y.-J. Zhang. 2007. Computing eigenface from edge images for face recognition based on Hausdorff distance. *Proceedings of the 4th ICIG*, 639–644.

Tan, H.C., Y.-J. Zhang, H. Chao, et al. 2010. Person-independent expression recognition based on person-similarity weighted expression feature. *Journal of Systems Engineering and Electronics*. 21(1): 118–126.

Ullman, S. 1996. *High-Level Vision: Object Recognition and Visual Cognition*. Cambridge: MIT Press.

VanderLugt, A. 1963. Signal detection by complex spatial filtering. *Proceedings of the IEEE*, 51(7): 1016–1027.

Wachsmuth, E., M.W. Oram, and D.I. Perrett. 1994. Recognition of objects and their component parts: Responses of single units in the temporal cortex of the macaque. *Cerebral Cortex*, 4(5): 509–522.

Wayman, J.L. 2002. Digital signal processing in biometric identification: A review. *Proceedings of the ICIP*, 1: 37–40.

Xiang, L.P., and H.J. Yang. 2021. Occlusion face detection based on convergent CNN and attention enhancement network. *Journal of Data Acquisition and Processing*, 36(1): 95–102.

Xie, C., M. Savvides, and B.V.K.V. Kumar. 2005. Redundant class-dependence feature analysis based on correlation filters using FRGC2.0 data. *Proceedings of the CVPR*, 153–158.

Xie, X.H., J.T. Bian, and J.H. Lai. 2022. Review on face liveness detection. *Journal of Image and Graphics*, 27(1): 63–87.

Yan, Y., and Y.-J. Zhang. 2008a. A novel class-dependent feature extraction for face recognition. *Pattern Recognition Letters*, 29(14): 1907–1914.

Yan, Y., and Y.-J. Zhang. 2008b. Discriminant projection embedding for face and palmprint recognition. *Neurocomputing*, 71(16-18): 3434–3438.

Yan, Y., and Y.-J. Zhang. 2008c. 1D correlation filter based class-dependence feature analysis for face recognition. *Pattern Recognition*, 41(12): 3834–3841.

Yan, Y., and Y.-J. Zhang. 2008d. Discriminant projection embedding with its application to face recognition. *Journal of Electronics & Information Technology*, 30(12): 2902–2905.

Yan, Y., and Y.-J. Zhang. 2009. State-of-the-art on video-based face recognition. *Chinese Journal of Computers*, 32(5): 878–886.

Yang, M.H., D.J. Kriegman, and N. Ahuja. 2002. Detecting faces in images: A survey. *IEEE Transactions on Pattern Analysis and Machine Intelligence*, 24(1): 34–58.

Zhang, Y.-J., et al. 2009. *Subspace-Based Face Recognition*. Beijing: Tsinghua University Press.

Zhang, Y.-J. (ed.). 2011. *Advances in Face Image Analysis: Techniques and Technologies*. USA: Medical Information Science Reference, IGI Global.

Zhang, Y.-J. 2015. A comprehensive survey on face image analysis. In Khosrow-Pour, M., *Encyclopedia of Information Science and Technology*, 3rd Ed., Hershey PA, USA: IGI Global, Chapter 47 (491–500).

Zhang, Y.-J. 2017. *Image Engineering, Vol. 1: Image Processing*. Germany: De Gruyter.

Zhang, Y.J. 2022. *A Selection of Image Processing Techniques: From Fundamentals to Research Front*. England: CRC Press.

CHAPTER 8

Expression Classification

Facial expressions are a basic way for humans to express emotions and an effective means of nonverbal communication. On the one hand, rich expressions can show the authenticity of emotions better than language, and on the other hand, they can complement language well to convey the communicator's thoughts and feelings more completely. People can accurately and subtly express their thoughts and feelings through facial expressions, and they can also recognize the other's attitude and inner world through facial expressions. Regarding the important role of *facial expressions* in conveying information, someone once proposed a formula: emotional expression = 7% of words + 38% of voice + 55% of facial expressions (Mehrabian 1968). In text chats on the Internet, the widespread use of emoticons, even to the point where it is necessary, just shows that emoticons play an important role in conveying information in human communication. How to make better use of the information conveyed by facial expressions and propose an automatic, reliable, and efficient analysis method is the research content of facial expression recognition and classification.

Facial expression recognition and classification have broad application prospects. For example, it is conducive to the development of more efficient human-computer interaction interface, and can also be used as an auxiliary means of human behavior research. Facial expression recognition and classification is also the key technology in video face retrieval and low bandwidth face data transmission. In addition, facial expression recognition and classification are widely used in many fields, such as face image synthesis and animation, facial paralysis diagnosis, intelligent robot, intelligent monitoring, and so on. In addition, because human face is a kind of non-rigid natural object with complex detail changes, the study of facial expression will provide important enlightenment for solving other similar complex pattern recognition and classification and related problems (such as face recognition).

The contents of each section of this chapter are arranged as follows:

Section 8.1 introduces the principle of expression classification, including different expression categories and the basic process of expression classification; discusses the similarities and differences between expression feature extraction and feature extraction

DOI: 10.1201/b23131-8

in face recognition, and analyzes its unique technology; also provides an overview of expression classification methods; and, in addition, the performance of some existing facial expression classification systems on two common databases are compared.

Section 8.2 discusses the problem of facial organ detection, which is a characteristic problem in facial expression classification. Taking into account the commonly used features of facial expression classification, a detailed analysis of eye positioning and tracking, as well as a combination of lip positioning and tracking, are carried out.

Section 8.3 discusses the principles and characteristics of the application of Gabor transform in facial expression feature extraction. It introduces a feature extraction method that combines Gabor transform coefficients and hierarchical histograms. It also compares the performance of some related features in facial expression classification.

Section 8.4 introduces a vector input multi-class output expression classification method. Firstly, the principle and implementation steps of multi-class and multi-label adaptive boosting are discussed; then an adaptive boosting algorithm with vector input and multi-class output is given.

Section 8.5 provides a brief introduction to some technique developments and promising research directions in the last year.

8.1 EXPRESSION CLASSIFICATION PRINCIPLE

Since the 1990s, especially in this century, the work of facial expression recognition and classification has attracted extensive attention, and there are many research results. There are also some review articles that systematically summarize the existing technologies and methods of facial expression recognition and classification from different angles, such as (Liu et al. 2006; Yan and Zhang 2009; Ekundayo and Viriri 2021; Wei et al. 2021).

8.1.1 Expression Category

The research results of psychology and biology provide an objective basis for facial expression analysis. The ***facial action coding system (FACS)*** proposed on the basis of anatomy has greatly promoted the research of facial expressions based on vision (Ekman and Friesen 1978). Using FACS and observing the facial behavior of the video, the encoder can manually encode all possible facial displays, and with 44 basic "***action units***" (AUs), more than 7000 combinations can be obtained. Here, each basic "action unit" corresponds to a certain piece or pieces of facial muscle from an anatomical point of view. A specific combination of FACS action units can represent the expressions with specific emotions (Friesen and Ekman 1984), including six categories: happy, sad, angry (anger), disgust, fear, and surprise. A work on obtaining action units from the video can be seen in (Zhu et al. 2011). Corresponding to FACS, CMU has constructed the ***Cohn-Kanade (CK) database*** as a standard for algorithm comparison (Kanade et al. 2000). The Cohn-Kanade database is a database based on AU encoding. It contains about 2000 image sequences of 210 objects. Each person has a series of facial activities, including a single AU or a combination of AUs.

FACS is a widely accepted facial expression evaluation system, but it also has some disadvantages: Manual FACS coding is a time-consuming and laborious work. After special training, human observers can achieve the ability of coding face display, but this training takes about 100 hours. At the same time, coding based on manual is inefficient, and the coding criterion is not easy to maintain stability. In order to avoid the heavy work of human facial expression coding, psychologists and computer vision researchers use computers for automatic facial expression recognition and classification. However, there are some problems in automatic recognition and classification of these objective facial expressions by computer. For example, when using computer for automatic facial expression recognition and classification, because FACS and six basic emotion categories are descriptive, some language expressions used to describe these expressions (such as "upper eyelid tightening, lip trembling, tightening or shrinking mouth" etc.) are difficult to calculate and model. These descriptions are quite instinctive for human beings, but it is quite difficult to translate them into computer programs.

Another commonly used database in facial expression classification is the *Japanese female facial expression (JAFFE) database* (Lyons et al. 1999). The facial expression images are obtained from ten Japanese women, and the facial expression images of each person include the above six types. The database also provides a neutral expression image of each person, so some people say that the database is a database based on seven basic expressions. Figure 8.1 shows an example of the seven basic expressions of the same person. The database has a total of 213 images, and each person has an average of about three images for each expression.

In addition, psychological research shows that from a recognition perspective, certain expressions are easy to recognize and classify, while some expressions are not easy to recognize and classify. The most recognizable expressions are happiness and sad, the more difficult to recognize are fear and sorrow, and the most difficult to recognize are doubt and pity. Moreover, many expressions in real life are often mixed expressions, and

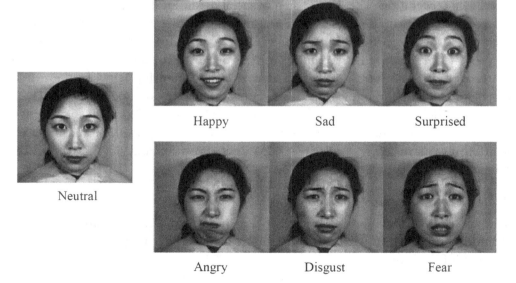

FIGURE 8.1   An example set of basic expressions in JAFFE database.

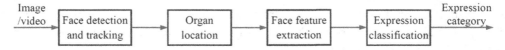

FIGURE 8.2   Block diagram of facial expression classification system.

some expressions are not necessarily exaggerated or obvious, which brings difficulties to expression recognition and classification.

Finally, by the way, sociologists also have different criteria for the classification of facial expressions. They divided expressions into 18 specific categories: laughter, smile, ridicule, disappointment, worry, worry, rage, consternation, disgust, dislike, hurried, terror, fear, doubt, anxiety, disdain, contempt, and pleading.

It can be seen from the above that the purpose of analyzing facial expression images is to classify the facial expressions appearing on the image into predetermined categories, so it is more appropriate to use facial expression classification to represent related work and technology.

8.1.2 Expression Classification Process

A process of facial expression analysis generally includes four stages: face detection, organ location, feature extraction, and expression classification. As shown in Figure 8.2, to establish a facial expression classification system, the first step is to detect (and track) the face, the second step is to determine the position of the eyes, mouth, etc. on the face, the third step is to extract from the face or the facial features that can characterize the nature of the input expression, and the fourth step is to classify the expressions according to the extracted features.

In principle, the techniques in these four steps are similar to the image techniques in many other fields. The first step is *face detection and tracking*, which is also a necessary step of face recognition. The second step of facial organ localization is often implicit in face recognition or combined with face feature extraction. *Organ localization* itself is a typical object detection work, but the object here is somehow special, which is a part of the face. The *face feature extraction* for expression in the third step is similar to that in face recognition. The fourth step is to analyze the relationship between the extracted features and classify the input facial expressions into corresponding categories (such as AU combination of six or seven basic emotion categories). From the perspective of pattern classification and classifier design, the *expression classification* and the face recognition also have many similarities. The difference is mainly in the pattern to be distinguished and its description.

8.1.3 Expression Feature Extraction

There are relatively many differences between facial expression features and face recognition features, which will be discussed more below. The main purpose of this stage is to extract information that can characterize the nature of the input expression from the face image or image sequence, and discard other useless factors that may cause interference, thereby improving the classification effect.

FIGURE 8.3   Three modules of expression feature extraction.

The **expression feature extraction** process can be further subdivided into three steps to complete, respectively using the three modules (original feature generation, expression feature dimensionality reduction, expression feature decomposition) to complete, as shown in Figure 8.3. The difference between feature extraction in facial expression classification and feature extraction in face recognition is mainly in the purpose of original feature generation and feature decomposition. First of all, it is necessary to use some form of information to represent the characteristics of expressions, such as characteristic shapes and geometric relationships, local textures, optical flow fields, and so on. Because these features generally have problems such as information redundancy, high dimensionality, insufficient discrimination, etc., these features are called original features, and the process of extracting original features is called original feature generation. In order to be able to more effectively characterize the nature of the input facial expressions, some post-processing of the original features is required. The first is to reduce the dimensionality of features to reduce the amount of data while retaining the necessary information, so that subsequent work can be carried out effectively. Finally, it is necessary to decompose the extracted features to further remove the interference of factors such as illumination and individual on the expression features, so as to obtain feature data that is more favorable for classification.

Some typical original feature generation, feature dimensionality reduction and feature decomposition methods are shown in Table 8.1 (Liu et al. 2006), and more examples can be seen in the literature related to face recognition.

The following gives a general introduction to the different methods in the three modules.

TABLE 8.1   Some typical methods in the three modules of facial expression feature extraction

Original Feature Generation	Feature Dimensionality Reduction	Feature Decomposition
Geometric feature: datum point	Principal Component Analysis (PCA)	Bilinear decomposition
Appearance features: Gabor coefficient, High-order Local Auto-Correlation (HLAC), Local Binary Pattern (LBP), Scale Invariant Feature Transform (SIFT), Speeded-Up Robust Feature (SURF)	Linear Discriminant Analysis (LDA) Independent Component Analysis (ICA)	Higher order singular value decomposition (HOSVD)
Hybrid features: Active Appearance Model (AAM)	Cluster-based Discriminant Analysis (CDA) Sequence PCA+LDA	
Sequence features: optical flow, motion unit	Mixed Probability PCA (MPPCA)	

8.1.3.1 Original Feature Generation

There are many ways to generate original features, and there are many ways to classify them, each with its own focus. For example: according to the nature of the input image, they can be divided into the methods for static images and the methods for image sequences (video); according to the range (on the image) for feature extraction, they can be divided into the overall methods and the partial methods; according to the different levels of feature abstraction, they can be divided into the model-based methods and the image-based methods; according to the different nature of the extracted features, they can be divided into the geometric feature-based methods, the appearance feature-based methods, the deformation feature-based methods and the motion feature-based methods, etc. Here is only a general introduction to the methods based on geometric features, the methods based on appearance features and their combination methods.

1. Method based on geometric features

When a specific expression occurs, the position and shape of the main organs of the human face will endure certain geometric changes under the traction of muscles. This is the most prominent feature that can express the facial expression and is the easiest to observe. Different from face recognition, for facial expression classification, the change in facial appearance is the most useful information to characterize facial expressions. At this time, a large range of inherent information of the face will become redundant and may affect the classification result. If the geometric features of the various organs and contours of the human face can be accurately extracted, it can provide a simple and effective feature representation method for expression analysis. In order to easily obtain the geometric relationship of the features, the extraction of geometric features is usually based on fiducial points. For example, the ASM model uses 152 fiducial points to represent the face (Cootes et al. 1995).

The fiducial points for facial organs and contours can be automatically extracted (Pantic and Rothkrantz 2004). First, use the morphological gradient algorithm and the labeled watershed algorithm to segment the face region; then use the multi-detector method to extract the contour of the front face, and perform spatial sampling to obtain a total of 19 feature points, and extract ten feature points from the side face at the same time, as shown in Figure 8.4.

If the input is an image sequence, these feature points need to be tracked to obtain the position or shape information of the facial features. Tracking based on feature points usually selects feature points only in regions where the gray level changes are more obvious, such as corners of the eyes, corners of the mouth, and so on. In the process of tracking feature points, two methods can be combined with **Kalman filter** and **infrared (IR)** equipment to locate the eyes to determine the predicted feature location, and then the similarity of the Gabor kernel between the two points can be matched near the predicted location, to detect the location of the feature (Zhang and Ji 2005). Due to the introduction of IR equipment, this method can also obtain robust tracking results for

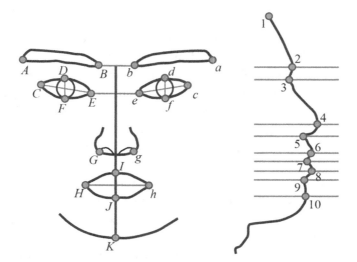

FIGURE 8.4   Face organs and contour feature points.

FIGURE 8.5   An example of tracking based on feature points.

large head movements. It is also possible to use different models for lips, eyes, eyebrows and cheeks, and use the feature point tracking method to change the contour of the model during movement to match the movement and geometric changes of the feature, as shown in Figure 8.5 (Tian et al. 2001).

Methods based on geometric features have high requirements for the accuracy of fiducial point extraction, which is often difficult to achieve when the image quality is low and the background is complex. At the same time, the extraction of geometric features ignores some useful information of other parts of the face, such as skin texture changes, etc., and the discrimination is not high enough when recognizing some subtle changes in expressions. In recent years, geometric features have been increasingly used in combination with other features.

2. Method based on appearance features

The *appearance feature* here generally refers to the features of using all face image pixels, including the grayscale feature or grayscale change feature of each point of the face, such as the most basic grayscale image and edge image. Appearance features are often obtained by filtering face images or partial images pixel by pixel, reflecting the underlying information of the face image. The extraction methods of appearance features include two types based on grayscale values and based on local features.

The gray value-based method is the simplest method of appearance feature representation. It can extract features from a full face image, or it can only extract features from the local regions such as eyes, nose, mouth and other regions. The direct use of grayscale images will have the problem of too high dimensionality, and the pixels are greatly affected by illumination and noise, so certain better preprocessing methods are required, and PCA and DCT transform methods are combined for further extraction.

The method based on local features is the main method in appearance feature extraction. Different from directly using the gray value of pixels, this type of method uses the relationship between local pixels (gradient, correlation, texture, etc.) to define features, and these features need to be calculated for each pixel. Therefore, each element in the local feature extraction result actually represents an image feature near a local point. The most typical methods include wavelet transform method, edge and high-order local auto-correlation (HLAC), local binary pattern (LBP), scale invariant feature transform (SIFT), speed-up robustness feature (SURF), non-negative matrix factorization (NMF), and local non-negative matrix factorization, etc. If the input is an image sequence, these appearance features need to be tracked. The commonly used methods are mainly based on optical flow.

3. Method based on mixed features

Geometric features and appearance features have their own advantages in representing facial expressions. Geometric features can concisely represent changes in the macroscopic structure of a human face, while appearance features can extract local subtle changes that are closely related to expressions. Therefore, geometric features can be combined with appearance features to form mixed features. For example, geometric features can be combined with the Gabor wavelet coefficients of local points or regions as expression features (Tian et al. 2001; Wen and Huang 2003); geometric features can also be fused with wrinkles and forehead region edges that are features of instantaneous changes in the face (Zhang and Ji 2005); or the geometric features (Tian et al. 2001) and the texture features composed of Gabor wavelet coefficients can be used successively (Wen and Huang 2003; Tan and Zhang 2007a).

The hybrid feature-based method often uses various models in combination, especially to describe the structure of the human face by means of a model. Typical work includes using ***active appearance model (AAM)*** to extract facial features and ***active wavelet network (AWN)*** for face alignment. Compared with the methods based on the image and the local features of the image, the model-based method can obtain more reliable facial feature parameters, but it also has the disadvantages of more complicated in calculation and difficulty in obtaining the initial point.

On the other side, due to the adaptability of 3-D model posture and illumination, the methods of using 3-D model have also been paid more and more attention. The 3-D model can be used to track the head rotation in the natural scene, and then use the 3-D deformation technique to convert the face image to a standardized posture, so that facial expression recognition is more convenient. It is also possible to use a multi-resolution 3-D deformable face model to model the face, and adopt a multi-level tracking method. This method is suitable for 3-D face depth scan data, and can extract and track subtle expression details. It should be pointed out that accurate acquisition of 3-D information is not a problem that has been successfully solved. Using professional scanning equipment such as cyberware can directly and accurately obtain the 3-D geometric information and texture information of the human head, but such equipment is expensive and inconvenient to use, and the results obtained are only suitable for specific people. The 3-D data reconstructed from image pairs or video sequences using stereovision methods have certain errors, and the robustness and anti-interference of the optimization algorithm need to be improved. There are also many problems in the automation of model generation. Model initialization and model adjustment often require a lot of manual assistance. At the same time, in the process of model tracking, there is also the disadvantage of a large amount of calculation, and it is difficult to achieve real-time requirements.

8.1.3.2 Dimensionality Reduction of Expression Features

Expression analysis relies not only on the overall analysis of the face, but also on the analysis of facial organs and their changes. In order to perform facial expression classification, many different features need to be extracted, so the original features often have a high dimensionality. In practice, it is necessary to project high-dimensional image data into a low-dimensional subspace, reduce the dimensionality and save the necessary information, so as to improve the effectiveness of the feature.

Commonly used feature dimensionality reduction and extraction methods mainly include PCA, LDA, ICA, etc. PCA considers that the changes within the class are concentrated in a subspace of the image space (the aggregation form of the class is convex), and then linear dimensionality reduction and segmentation are performed on the clusters. If the dimensionality is reduced for the class first, and then a simple classifier is used in the feature space after dimensionality reduction, it is possible to achieve better results than PCA. This is the principle of LDA. The Fisher linear discriminant function is a typical example. It selects the correlation matrix to maximize the ratio of the inter-class dispersion to the intra-class dispersion (to make the intra-class sample points more closely clustered, and the inter-class sample points dispersed further), so as to obtain the best classification result. A generalized form of Fisher's linear discriminant function can be seen in (Cheng et al. 2009a). One problem with the above method is that the correlation matrix may be singular. To solve this problem, you can first use PCA to project the training set to a relatively low-dimensional space, so that the matrix is non-singular in this space, and then use LDA to continue to reduce dimension. This way of using LDA is also called PCA+LDA. More typical subspace analysis methods can be found in (Zhang 2011).

The above-mentioned methods have their own advantages in feature dimensionality reduction and extraction. For example, PCA extracts the most representative features, which can effectively eliminate redundancy and reduce data dimensionality, but it does not consider the distinction between different types of data. However, LDA selects the appropriate projection direction by maximizing the inter-class dispersion and minimizing the intra-class dispersion of the data, focusing on finding the direction with the greatest resolution.

The PCA and other methods discussed above are mostly applied in 1-D signals, and then extended to 2-D images. For this purpose, it is necessary to convert the image line by line scan into a 1-D signal. In order to improve efficiency and effectiveness, PCA is often directly performed on 2-D images. This is generally called 2-D PCA. Whether it is better than PCA has certain criteria to be determined (Cheng et al. 2009b).

8.1.3.3 Expression Feature Decomposition

The face image contains a wealth of information, and the information used are also different for different recognition and classification tasks. Face detection looks for the common consistency of face images. Face recognition needs to use information representing individual differences in faces, while facial expression classification needs information representing differences between various expressions. When accomplishing a goal of face analysis, the information co-exist in the face image, and information that is beneficial to one recognition task will interfere with other tasks. In recent years, a new solution is to separate the different factors of the face (also called feature decomposition), such as expression factors and individual (identity) factors, so that recognition and classification can be performed in the corresponding subspace and avoid interference by other factors.

There are many types of *feature decomposition*; the commonly used ones include:

1. Using the bilinear model to decompose the appearance of the face, that is, first use AAM to obtain the parameters of the face features, and then use the asymmetric bilinear model to decompose the face feature parameters into the product of individual expression components and individual related linear mappings (Abboud and Davoine 2004);

2. Using the *high-order singular value decomposition (HOSVD)* method for the decomposition of facial expressions (Tan and Zhang 2007b). It first extracts features with AAM, and then decomposes the extracted features with HOSVD method to obtain the individual subspaces, the expression subspace and the feature subspace, as shown in Figure 8.6.

This kind of method is a multi-factor analysis method. Due to the decomposition of various factors of the face, it can not only be better applied to facial expression classification, but also can be easily synthesized for facial expressions, and even new factors can be added to meet the synthesis requirements of different lighting and different angles, in orer to solve more complex problems.

8.1.4 Expression Classification Methods

The classification of facial expressions refers to defining a set of categories, and designing a corresponding classification mechanism to recognize the expressions and classify them into

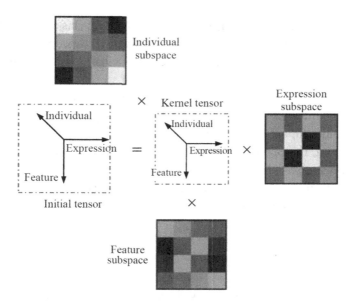

FIGURE 8.6   High-order singular value decomposition is used for facial expression decomposition.

corresponding categories. It can be divided into 44 basic action units (AUs) according to the facial action coding system (FACS); it can also be divided into six basic expressions according to the emotion classification: happy, sad, surprise, fear, anger, and disgust.

According to the technology used, facial expression classification methods are often divided into rule-based methods and statistical learning-based (machine learning-based) methods.

1. Rule-based methods

In the rule-based method, a judgment rule (or dictionary) is first established for each expression based on human prior knowledge, and then the input facial expressions are classified into corresponding categories according to this rule (Pantic and Rothkrantz 2000b). Specifically, the corresponding AU codes can be derived from the language descriptions of the six basic expressions, and compared with the AU codes of the input expressions for classification (Pantic and Rothkrantz 2000a, 2004). Compared with the method of directly categorizing expressions into six basic categories, the rule-based method can describe facial expressions more accurately, so as to better recognize mixed non-prototype expressions. At the same time, because it encodes the expressions, it also makes the synthesis of facial expressions easier.

2. Statistical learning–based methods

The method based on statistical learning is the main method used in facial expression classification. Commonly used methods include **neural network** (NN), decision tree, Bayesian classification, **support vector machine** (SVM), adaptive boosting (**Adaboost**), and hidden Markov process theory and technology. Among classifiers based on machine learning theory (including Bayesian classifiers, decision trees, support vector machines, **K-nearest neighbor** (KNN) classifiers, etc.), the KNN classifier often has the best effect, but its calculation speed is slower and it needs a lot of storage space. In the classification methods using machine learning (including support vector machines, adaptive boosting, and linear discriminant analysis), the combination of adaptive boosting based on Gabor wavelet features and support vector machines has achieved better results.

On the other hand, the presence of human facial expressions is a dynamic process, in terms of facial appearance, there are both spatial and temporal changes. Therefore, according to whether time information is used for analysis in expression classification, facial expression classification methods can also be divided into two types: methods based on spatial analysis and methods based on space-time combination.

1. Spatial analysis method

There are many categories of methods based on spatial analysis. For example, the expert rule-based method first formulates some rules from the perspective of human observation, and then uses the parameters derived from feature extraction to determine which type of rule the expression conforms to, and classifies it into the corresponding category. This type of method can accurately describe facial expressions, which is conducive to the recognition of mixed expressions. In addition, since the expressions are encoded, it is also convenient to synthesize facial expressions. Various machine learning-based methods, such as Bayesian classifiers, decision trees, K-nearest neighbor classifiers, etc., can also be used for spatial analysis.

2. Space-time analysis method

The main method commonly used is **hidden Markov model (HMM)**. Classification using the HMM method needs to determine its initial state and final state, so it is generally used for a single expression sequence or a segmented expression sequence.

8.1.5 Performance of Expression Classification Systems

Based on and combined with the various technologies introduced above, many facial expression classification systems have been constructed. Due to the using of different databases, experimental settings and classification goals, it is difficult to give a unified evaluation of all systems. Table 8.2 and Table 8.3, respectively, list the test classification results of some developed systems on the **Cohn-Kanade database** and **JAFFE database** (Liu et al. 2006), giving an overall overview of the characteristics and effects of various methods and systems.

For each system, the used feature extraction method, classification method and classification target (AU or basic expression) are listed, and the used data type (static, sequence or several frames extracted from the sequence), data volume, and the objective conditions of the experiment such as the training/test ratio are also lists. For the test

TABLE 8.2 Some facial expression classification systems and their test results on the Cohn-Kanade database

Sl. No.	Feature Extraction	Classification	Classification Task	Data Volume	Training/Test Ratio	Data Type	Test Results (/%)[a]	(/%)[b]
1	Optical flow, feature point tracking, edge detection	HMM	3 upper part AU 7 lower part AU	100–270 sequences	5: 8–4: 5	Continuous sequence Continuous sequence	85–92 81–92	— —
2	Facial organ modeling and tracking, wrinkle detection	Artificial neural networks	10 lower part AU and neutral	463 sequences	400: 63	Extract two frames per sequence: start, peak	95.6	—
3	ACM tracking, conversion to FAPs	Semi-continuous HMM	6 expressions 6 expressions + "speak"	90 persons	89: 1 repeat	Continuous sequence Segmented sequence Continuous sequence	84 81 64	— — —
4	PBVD tracks human faces and extracts motion units	Bayesian network	7 expressions	53 persons	1: 4 repeat	Static frame by frame	73.22	—
5	Infrared camera detects the iris and restores the shape parameters of the eyebrow area	SVM	5 upper part AU and neutral	25 persons	24: 1	Unknown	81.22	—
6	PBVD tracks human faces, extracts geometric features + local texture features	Gaussian mixture model (GMM)	4 expressions	47 persons, 2981 frames	i. 6: 4 ii. 1: 1	Static frame by frame	75.4	87.6
7	Boosting method locates features and extracts Gaber amplitude	SVM	7 upper part AU 7 expressions	90 persons, 625 frames	—	Extract two frames per sequence: start, peak Extract two frames per sequence: start, peak	92.9 93.3	— —
8	Representation of partial facial asymmetry-asymmetrical face	Ordered forward feature selection algorithm and LDA	3 expressions (Happy, Angry, Sad)	55 persons	6: 5 repeat	Extract 3 frames per sequence: start, middle, peak	FNR 3.6, FPR 1.8	—
9	Optical flow of image sequence	Two-step method: kNN+ HMMs	6 expressions	97 persons, 488 frames	—	Continuous sequence	90.9	—

[a] Indicates that the people in the experimental test set do not appear in the training set.
[b] Indicates that the people in the experimental test set may appear in the training set.

TABLE 8.3 Some facial expression classification systems and their test results on the JAFFE database

Sl. No.	Feature Extraction	Classification	Classification Task	Data Volume	Training/Test Ratio	Data Type	Test Results (%)[a]	(%)[b]
1	Manually annotated 34 points + 18 Gaber filters	LDA	6 expressions + neutral	9 persons, 193 frames	i. 9: 1 ii. 8: 1	Static salient expression	75	92
2	HOLA feature + Fisher weighted mapping	Fisher linear discriminant	6 expressions + neutral	9 persons	8: 1 repeat	Static salient expression	69.4	—
3	Local binary pattern (LBP)	Improved mask matching method, two-step classification	6 expressions + neutral	9 persons	8: 1 repeat	Static salient expression	77	—
4	Manually annotated 34 points + 18 Gaber filters	Feature selection linear programming	6 expressions + neutral	10 persons	9: 1 repeat	Static salient expression	—	91

[a] Indicates that the people in the experimental test set do not appear in the training set.
[b] Indicates that the people in the experimental test set may appear in the training set.

result, the recognition rates are provided, where "a" indicates that the people in the experimental test set do not appear in the training set, and "b" indicates that the people in the experimental test set may appear in the training set. They correspond to the data of the training/testing ratio.

8.2 FACIAL ORGAN DETECTION

The detection of facial organs is very important for face recognition and expression classification. For face recognition, facial organs are the main clues to distinguish different faces; while for facial expression classification, not only the identification of facial organs itself is very important, but also the changes in the characteristics of these organs provide important clues for judging facial expressions. Therefore, after determining the existence and location of the human face in the image, further detection, tracking, and description of the position, shape, and movement changes of the facial organs are required.

The eyes and mouth are the main organs that play a more important role in face recognition and expression classification, while the role of nose, ears, and eyebrows is relatively small. The following describes the typical methods of eye and mouth detection.

8.2.1 Eye Positioning

The eyes are the windows of the soul, and the condition of the eyes plays a great role in expressing feelings or emotions. To obtain the states of the eyes, the eyes must be detected first, or the position of the eyes must be determined on the face.

The detection of the eyes can be carried out with the aid of the model of the eyes. From the perspective of positioning, the eye model needs to be able to express geometric information such as the position and radius of the iris, the position of the corner of the eye, and the shape of the eye contour (upper and lower eyelids).

A typical *eye geometric model* is deformable model (Tian et al. 2000), also known as deformable mask. It uses a circle to represent the outline of the iris and two parabolas to represent the outline of the upper and lower eyelids respectively. An improved model is shown in Figure 8.7 (Tan et al. 2003). This model can be represented by a 7-tuple (O, Q, a, b, c, r, θ), where O is the geometric center of the eye (set as the coordinate origin), Q is the center of the iris circle, a and c are the height of the upper and lower parabola, respectively, b is the length of the parabola, r is the radius of the iris circle, and θ represents the angle between the connecting line of the intersection of the two parabolas

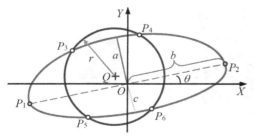

FIGURE 8.7   Eye geometric model.

and the x-axis. The intersection of two parabolas gives two corners (P_1 and P_2). In this improved model, considering that the iris circle has two intersections with the upper and lower parabola respectively, another two pairs (four) corners (P_3 and P_4, P_5, and P_6) are added. The information of P_1 and P_2 can help to adjust the overall width of the eye, and the information of P_3 to P_6 can help to determine the height of the eyelids and help to accurately and robustly calculate each eye parameter.

To detect corners, the SUSAN operator (see, for example, (Zhang 2017)) can be used. The SUSAN operator calculates the detection response value $R(x, y)$ obtained by the operator mask at the image (x, y):

$$R(x, y) = \begin{cases} G - S(x, y) & S(x, y) < G \\ 0 & \text{otherwise} \end{cases} \tag{8.1}$$

where G is a fixed geometric threshold, which can be taken as $3S_{\text{max}}/4$, and S_{max} is the maximum value that S can obtain (equal to the number of pixels contained in the detection mask minus 1). The commonly used SUSAN operator mask (plus the center) contains 37 pixels, that is, $S_{\text{max}} = 36$, so $g = 27$. For the detected corner, the obtained response value is used as the corner strength for further judgment.

Figure 8.8 shows an example of eye corner detection (Tan et al. 2007), where Figure 8.8(a) is a composite eye image, Figure 8.8(b) is the result of corner detection, and the white regions are the positions (basically distributed around the six real corner points) of high response value for corner intensity after thresholding. Figure 8.8(c) is the result of superimposing the finally detected corner points on the original image.

According to the detected corner points, the method based on **active contour model** (see, for example, (Zhang 2017)) can be used to further determine the geometric model of the eye. Here, the corresponding energy term can be defined by the detection response value calculated above as

$$E_c = 1 - \frac{1}{N} \sum_{i=1}^{N} R(x_i, y_i) \tag{8.2}$$

where N is the number of detected corners (the number of intersections between iris and eyelid is not fixed in practice and N is generally 4–6); $R(x_i, y_i)$ is the detection response value at the i-th corner.

(a)   (b)   (c)

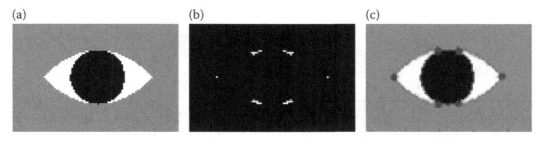

FIGURE 8.8   An example of detecting six corners of eyes.

(a) (b) (c) (d) (e)

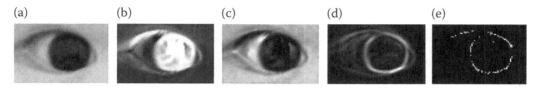

FIGURE 8.9   Various feature points detected by the same eye image.

(a) (b) (c) (d) (e)

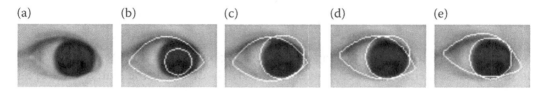

FIGURE 8.10   Eyes (including iris and eyelids) detection process and example results.

In practice, in addition to corner points, there are other points of information that can help determine energy terms and detecting eyes, such as (grayscale) valley points, peak points, and edge points. Figure 8.9 shows the valley point domain (bright region in Figure 8.9(b)), peak point domain (white region in Figure 8.9(c)), edge point domain (bright region in Figure 8.9(d)), and corner domain (white region in Figure 8.9(e)) detected for the same eye image (Figure 8.9(a)) (Tan and Zhang 2009).

Figure 8.10 shows a set of images obtained by detecting the eyes (including iris and eyelid) with the aid of the above eye model. Figure 8.10(a) is the original image, and Figure 8.10(b) is the contour determined according to the initial parameters. Figure 8.10(c), Figure 8.10(d), and Figure 8.10(e) are the results obtained by adjusting the contour of the iris, adjusting the contour of the eyelid and the final detail adjustment with the aid of the minimum energy term, respectively. It can be seen from the figure that the corner energy term plays an important role in adjusting the contour of the eyelid (Tan and Zhang 2006a).

8.2.2 Eye Tracking

In expression classification, in addition to locating the eyes, it is often necessary to track the changes of the eyes. To do this, one needs to use sequence images or video images. The degree of eye opening and closing is an important indicator reflecting the changes of the eyes. The following discussion takes the detection of the blinking process as an example, which includes two parts: the detection of the iris (including the detection of the state of the eye open and close) and the tracking of eyelid when the eye is reopened after blinking.

8.2.2.1 Iris Detection and Tracking

The detection of the iris can help determine the open and/or close states of the eye. There is a dual-state eye model based on a deformable mask that believes that the open and close states of the eye can be distinguished according to whether the iris can be detected (Tian et al. 2000). Specifically, after locating the eye mask in the first frame of image, the

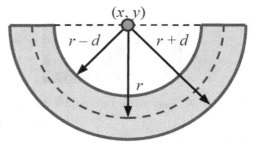

FIGURE 8.11 Schematic diagram of region mask for iris detection.

grayscale and edge information changes of the eye region are used to detect and track the iris in the subsequent frames of images. If the iris is detected, the state of the eye is considered to be open, and the midpoint of the eyelid is used to track the position of the eyelid; otherwise, the state of the eye is considered to be closed, and a straight line is used to describe the eye.

The iris is basically round, so only the lower semicircle needs to be considered in the detection of the iris. As shown in the template in Figure 8.11, if the center coordinates of the iris is (x, y) and the radius is r, the detection range (that is, the possible position of the iris contour) to be considered is the region from the semicircle with radius $r - d$ to the semicircle with radius of $r + d$, as shown in the shaded part in the figure. Here the smaller the value of d, the higher the accuracy of iris positioning, but the influence of noise and other interference will be stronger at this time. In general, d can be taken as $r/3$.

The specific **detection of iris** includes the following steps:

1. Calculating the average gray level I_0 of the region corresponding to the lower semicircle of the iris (detection region) in the first frame of image;

2. Extracting the contour of the eye region in each subsequent frame of image, and calculate the number N_0 of edge points in the iris detection region (it is considered that the iris contour has a higher gradient value);

3. In the eye region between the inner corner point and the outer corner point, searching with the semicircle mask under the iris to find the position with the largest number of edge points $N(x, y)$, it should satisfy:

$$N(x, \ y)/N_0 > T_N \tag{8.3}$$

where T_N is the threshold of the number of edge points;

4. Calculating the average mask gray level $I(x, y)$ at the mask position with the largest number of edge points, if

$$|I(x, y) - I_0| < T_I \tag{8.4}$$

then it is considered that the iris is detected, its central position is (x, i), where T_I is the grayscale difference threshold.

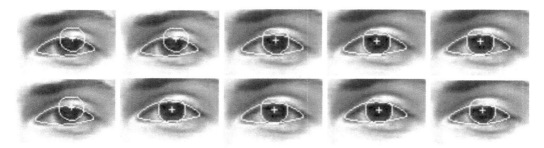

FIGURE 8.12   Example of iris tracking results.

In the previous detection process, the edge information of the iris region was used sequentially, that is, the edge point number Equation (8.3) and the grayscale information Equation (8.4). An improvement to this method is to use both types of information at the same time (Tan and Zhang 2006b). To this end, the iris detection process can be transformed into an optimization process that calculates the location of the maximum number of edge points under certain grayscale and edge constraints. Regarding Equation (8.3) and Equation (8.4) as the constraint conditions, optimization is to find the appropriate (x, y) to maximize the function $N(x, y)$. This problem can be solved with the help of Lagrange function

$$L(x, y) = N(x, y) - \alpha \left[|I(x, y) - I_0| - T_I \right] - \beta \left[N(x, y) T_N/N_0 \right] \qquad (8.5)$$

to proceed, where α and β are both coefficients greater than 0.

In some practical situations, the method of simultaneously using the grayscale and edge information of the iris region can give better results than the method of using the two types of information sequentially. Figure 8.12 shows two groups of examples of the results of eye tracking using the grayscale and edge information of the iris region at the same time. The upper and lower eyelids detected are superimposed on the original image with a parabola. The contour of the detected iris is represented by a circle and the center is represented by a cross. The two sets of images are the images of the first five frames in the tracking process. It can be seen that even if the initial position of the iris detected in the first frame of image is not very accurate, with the help of grayscale and edge information at the same time, the position of the iris is continuously adjusted in subsequent frames, and the final result is gradually tending to an accurate position.

8.2.2.2 Eyelid Tracking

Eyelid tracking can be performed on the basis of iris tracking. According to the previous geometric model of the eye, the contour of the eyelids can be represented by a parabola, so that the parameters of the parabola can be determined by detecting the position of the corner of the eye. However, when the eyes are closed during blinking, the upper and lower eyelids will overlap, and the parabola representing the contour of the eyelids will become a straight line. Then, when the eyes are reopened, due to the different movement directions of the upper and lower eyelids, it often causes problems with the tracking of the eyelids and the errors may propagate to subsequent frames of images.

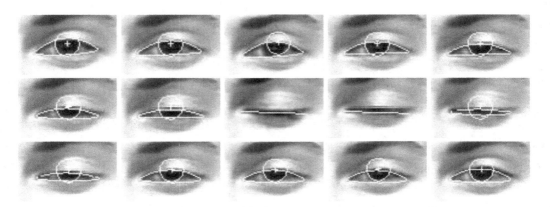

FIGURE 8.13 Example of eye tracking results during blinking.

In order to solve the above problems, the prediction mode can be considered, that is, the state mode of the eyelid before the eye is closed to predict the state of the eyelid after the eye is reopened. If k is used in an image sequence to represent the number of the first frame detecting the close of eyes, l is the number of frames with closed eyes, and p is the number of frames used for prediction ($p < k$), then the state mode M_{k+l+1} that eye is reopened is

$$M_{k+l+1} = \sum_{i=1}^{p} w_i M_{k-i} \tag{8.6}$$

where w_i is the prediction weight.

Figure 8.13 shows a set of results (a total of 15 frames) obtained by tracking the eye contour during blinking (Tan and Zhang 2006b). As can be seen from the figure, the eyes are closed in Frame 8 and reopened in Frame 10. With the help of prediction mode, the eyes have been correctly tracked immediately.

8.2.3 Lip Detection and Tracking

The changes and status of the mouth (mainly the lips) also play a great role in expressing feelings or emotions. A method for lip contour detection and tracking is introduced below (Tan et al. 2009).

8.2.3.1 Basic Lip Geometric Model

There are many methods for geometric modeling of lips. A basic model is shown in Figure 8.14 (Rabi and Si 1997), which is mainly composed of four curves from top to bottom, each of which is left and right symmetrical. The outer edge of the upper lip is represented by Z_1, which is a fourth-order curve with a height of h_1 and a half width of w_1. The inside edge of the upper lip is represented by Z_2, which is a parabola with a height of h_2 and a half width of w_2. The inside edge of the lower lip is represented by Z_3, which is also a parabola, with a height of h_3 and a half width of $w_3 = w_2$. The outer edge of the lower lip is represented by Z_4, which is also a fourth-order curve with a height of h_4 and a half width of $w_4 = w_1$.

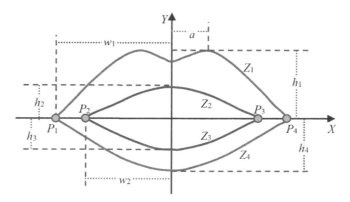

FIGURE 8.14 Lip geometry model.

8.2.3.2 Introducing Corner Information

According to the deformation mask, **lip detection** needs to be adjusted and optimized with the help of energy function. The energy function includes internal energy term and external energy term. The former is related to the geometry of the deformable masks and plays a role in maintaining the elasticity and smoothness of the lip curve; The latter is related to the characteristics of the image. Its function is to make the lip curve converge to the edge points in the image, in which the grayscale and gradient information are often used. In addition, *a priori* knowledge such as lip structure and gray level of surrounding region can also be considered. Structurally, the four corner points P_1 to P_4 on the lip contour in the figure are very helpful to determine the width of the lip, and the corresponding corner energy term can be defined:

$$E_c = \frac{1}{4} \sum_{i=1}^{4} M_i \tag{8.7}$$

where M_i represents the energy of the corresponding corner P_i. Secondly, the tooth region, R_t, surrounded by the inner contour of the upper and lower lips has rich textures, which can define the corresponding tooth region energy term:

$$E_t = 1 - \frac{1}{A_t} \sum_{t \in R_t} [kN_i^{(f)} + lN_i^{(g)} + (1 - k - l)M_i] \tag{8.8}$$

where A_t represents the area of the corresponding tooth region R_t, $N_i^{(f)}$ represents the gray value of the pixels in the region R_t, and $N_i^{(g)}$ represents the gradient value of the pixels in the region R_t.

8.2.3.3 Detection and Tracking Steps

Combining the above energy terms with the internal energy term and the external energy term determined according to the lip image, the position of the lip mask can be determined through an optimization process that minimizes the energy function. Specific optimization can be divided into three steps:

(a)   (b)   (c)   (d)

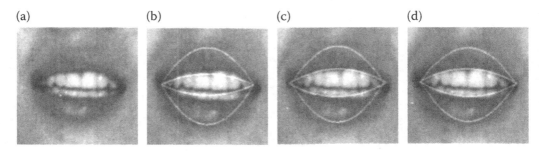

FIGURE 8.15   Examples of lip detection results.

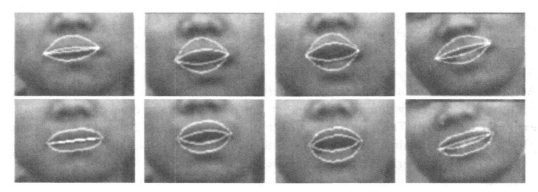

FIGURE 8.16   Example of tracking result of lip image sequence.

1. Extracting the outer contour of the lips: At this time, only the parameters related to the outer contour of the lips are adjusted while keeping other parameters unchanged;

2. Adjusting the parameters of the inner contour of the lips: At this time, only the parameters related to the inner contour are adjusted;

3. Fine-tuning the parameters of the inner and outer contours of the lips: On the basis of the above two steps, the final fine-tuning of all the parameters are performed.

A set of results obtained from each step in the above lip contour extraction process is shown in Figure 8.15, where Figure 8.15(a) is the original image, Figure 8.15(b) is the result of the outer contour adjustment, Figure 8.15(c) is the result of the inner contour adjustment, and Figure 8.15(d) is the result of fine-tuning.

Figure 8.16 shows some results obtained by tracking a sequence of lip images, where the upper row corresponds to the initial masks, and the lower row corresponds to the final result.

8.3 FACIAL EXPRESSION FEATURE EXTRACTION WITH THE HELP OF GABOR TRANSFORM

Based on the detection and tracking of facial organs, features for facial expression classification can be further extracted. Gabor transform is often used in expression feature extraction, which is a special short-time Fourier transform, and its window function is Gaussian function. When extracting features with the help of Gabor transform, a group of Gabor filters of different scales and directions are often used (a variety of sampling methods can be selected for this group of filters, and only part of the results are used to reduce the time and space demands of feature extraction and classification (Xu and Zhang 2011)). Using a set of such filters can analyze image grayscale changes in various scales and directions, and can further detect the corner points of objects and the end points of line segments.

8.3.1 Gabor Transform in Facial Expression Recognition

The **Gabor transform** has the ability to extract local subtle changes in the expression feature extraction, which is very consistent with the feature that the expression information is mainly reflected in the local region. In addition, the result of Gabor transform is not sensitive to illumination changes, and it can tolerate a certain degree of image rotation and deformation, and has good robustness.

There are many different methods for selecting the kernel function of the 2-D Gabor transform. For example, the following kernel function can be selected (Lyons et al. 1999):

$$\kappa_l(\boldsymbol{x}) = \frac{p_l^2}{\sigma^2} \exp\left(\frac{p_l^2 x^2}{2\sigma^2}\right) \left[\exp(\mathrm{j}\, \boldsymbol{p}_l \bullet \boldsymbol{x}) - \exp\left(\frac{-\sigma^2}{2}\right) \right] \tag{8.9}$$

Among them, the part outside the square brackets is a Gaussian function with a variance of σ; the first part inside the square brackets is the Gabor transform function, and after the minus sign is an additional DC term to reduce the influence of light; here σ determines the bandwidth of the transform filter and can be taken as $\sigma = 2\pi$; $\boldsymbol{p}_l$ is the wave vector (p_l is its modulus), and its different values constitute different wave functions with similar energy in the function family; $\boldsymbol{p}_l$ is defined as $\boldsymbol{p}_n \bullet [\cos\theta, \sin\theta]^{\mathrm{T}}$, where θ represents the different directions of the wave; $\boldsymbol{p}_n$ is along the X axis, and the size is $2^{-(n+2)/2}\pi$, which represents the different kernel frequencies of the wave. Since facial expressions are characterized by high frequency, a higher frequency wave function can be convolved with the expression image to extract high frequency information and shield low frequency information that has nothing to do with expression changes. If $n = 0, 1, 2, \theta = 0, \pi/6, 2\pi/6, 3\pi/6, 4\pi/6, 5\pi/6$, then 3×6 Gabor transform filter banks for Extract facial features can be obtained. In practice, in order to speed up the calculation, only some filters can be selected from them (Xu and Zhang 2011).

After defining a set of **Gabor filters**, these kernel functions can be used to convolve with the original expression image (or the organs in it):

$$G_l(\boldsymbol{x}) = \int I(\boldsymbol{x}')\kappa_l(\boldsymbol{x} - \boldsymbol{x}')\, \mathrm{d}^2\boldsymbol{x}' \tag{8.10}$$

The results obtained by each kernel function constitute a Gabor coefficient image. For example, the image of angry expression in Figure 8.1 is filtered with 18 kernel functions

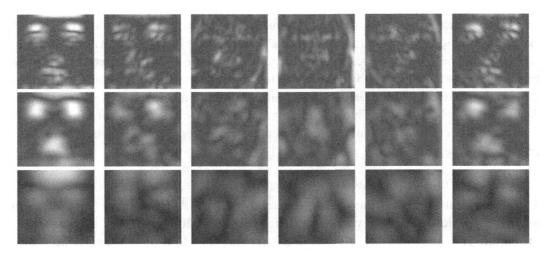

FIGURE 8.17   Examples of 18 Gaber coefficient images obtained with a set of Gabor filters.

(3 scales × 6 directions) to obtain 18 Gaber coefficient images, as shown in Figure 8.17, from which the structural information and texture information on the different scales of the human face can be observed.

8.3.2 Combination of Gabor Transform Coefficients and Hierarchical Histogram

The Gabor filter has a very strong ability to analyze local texture changes, but it lacks the ability to express global features. The histogram is a commonly used feature that represents the global characteristics of an image, but using the histogram feature directly on the full image will lose a lot of structural details. If the Gaber transform is combined with the histogram, it is possible to obtain a better overall effect. Specifically, the image can be first decomposed into blocks step by step, and then after the decomposition, the histogram distribution of the Gabor coefficients obtained in each block is calculated, so that the Gabor coefficients and histogram statistics are combined in each block, as shown in Figure 8.18 (Liu and Zhang 2007). In practice, the image is cropped and normalized first, the Gabor transform is calculated for the pre-processed image in this way, and then the hierarchical blocking is performed, and the histogram is counted separately for each block. The characteristics of the whole image are obtained by combing all the histograms of these blocks. Compared with the direct use of Gabor coefficients, this feature contains more information in the neighborhood, and the hierarchical blocking takes into account both the local subtle changes and the overall macro changes.

8.3.3 Comparison of Different Features

The above feature is to use the histogram to count the results of the Gabor transform, and obtain the histogram feature based on the Gabor transform. It is compared with other three histogram features in terms of expression classification performance: (i) Histogram feature based on *local binary pattern (LBP)*; (ii) histogram feature based on *local Gabor*

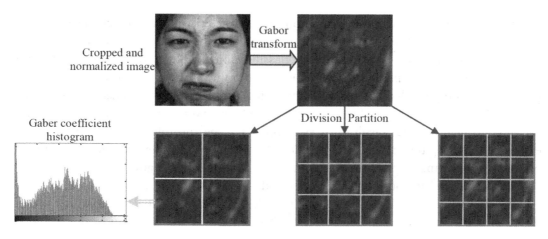

FIGURE 8.18 Hierarchical histogram representation based on Gabor features.

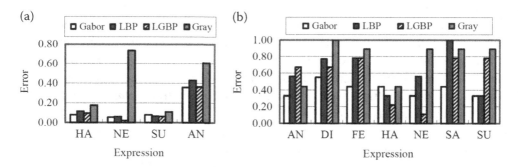

FIGURE 8.19 Comparison of four histogram features in facial expression recognition: (a) CMU database; (b) JAFFE database.

binary pattern (*LGBP*, a combination of Gabor transform + local binary pattern); and (iii) histogram feature based on gray value.

Figure 8.19(a) and Figure 8.19(b) show the results of using these four histogram features to perform expression classification on the CMU library and the JAFFE library, respectively. In Figure 8.19, HA stands for happy, SA stands for sad, AN stands for angry, DI stands for disgust, FE stands for fear, SU stands for surprise, and NE stands for neutral. It can be seen from the figures that on the CMU database, the recognition rates of the histogram feature based on Gaber transform, the histogram feature based on LBP and the histogram feature based on LGBP are similar; while on the JAFFE database, the histogram feature based on Gaber transform is obviously better than the other three histogram features for most expressions.

8.4 VECTOR INPUT MULTI-CLASS OUTPUT EXPRESSION CLASSIFICATION

Expression classification refers to defining a set of categories, and designing a corresponding classification mechanism to distinguish expressions and classify them into corresponding categories. For example, the facial expressions can be classified into six or seven basic expressions according to emotional characteristics, and the changes in facial expressions can be described by 44 action units and their combinations according to facial movements. This is a multi-class classification problem. If a general two-class adaptive boosting classifier is used, it is needed to train multiple two-class classifiers and provide the voting results. For example, for k-class problems, k binary classifiers for 1: all, or $k(k–1)/2$ binary classifiers for 1: 1 are required, and voting on the output of a single classifier to get the final result. However, there will be the following problems in the experiments: using the 1: 1 classifier will lead to too many classifiers, so the training time of adaptive boosting is much longer than the general learning algorithm, and too many classifiers will lead to too long training period; while using the 1: all classifier, the data volume of positive samples and negative samples will be very unbalanced, which makes the poor accuracy of the classifier on the test set.

8.4.1 Adaptive Boosting

Adaptive boosting, that is, Adaboost, is a commonly used and typical boosting algorithm. In practice, the classification effect of many classifiers is only slightly higher than 50% for two types of samples, which is called a ***weak classifier***. It is necessary to combine multiple such independent classifiers to achieve better results. Specifically, these classifiers are applied to different training sample subsets in turn, which is called boosting. The boost algorithm combines multiple weak classifiers into a new ***strong classifier*** that is better than each of the weak classifiers.

Suppose the pattern space is X, the training set contains m patterns x_i, and their corresponding class identifiers are c_i. In the two types of classification problems, $c_i \in \{-1, 1\}$. The main steps of the adaptive boosting algorithm are as follows:

1. Initialize K, where K is the number of weak classifiers to be used;

2. Let $k = 1$, and initialize the weight $W_1(i) = 1/m$;

3. For each k, use the training set and a set of weights $W_k(i)$ to train the weak classifier C_k, and assign a real number to each pattern x_i, namely $C_k: X \rightarrow R$;

4. Select coefficient $a_k > 0 \in R$;

5. Update the weight (where G_k is the normalized coefficient to make $\sum_{i=1}^{m} W_{k+1}(i) = 1$), where

$$W_{k+1}(i) = \frac{W_k(i) \exp\left[-a_k c_i C_k(\mathbf{x}_i)\right]}{G_k} \tag{8.11}$$

6. Set $k = k + 1$;

7. If $k \le K$, go back to Step (3);

8. The final strong classifier is

$$S(\boldsymbol{x}_i) = \text{sign}\left[\sum_{k=1}^{K} a_k C_k(\boldsymbol{x}_i)\right] \tag{8.12}$$

In the above algorithm, the weak classifier C_k is used for the training set, and the importance of correct classification of a single sample in each step is different, and each step k is determined by a set of weights $W_k(i)$, and the sum of the weights is 1. At the beginning, the weights are all equal. But in every iteration, the weight of the sample that is misclassified will relatively increase (the exp-term in Step (5) is positive for wrong classification, making $W_k(i)$ bigger weight), that is, the weak classifier C_{k+1} will pay more attention to the samples misclassified in k-th iterations.

At each step, the weak classifier C_k should be determined to adapt its performance to the weight distribution $W_k(i)$. In the case of two-class classification, the objective function to be minimized for weak classifier training is

$$e_k = \sum_{i=1}^{m} P_{i \sim W_k(i)}[C_k(\boldsymbol{x}_i) \neq c_i] \tag{8.13}$$

where $P[\cdot]$ represents the empirical probability obtained from the training sample. The error e_k depends on the weight distribution $W_k(i)$, and the weight distribution $W_k(i)$ is related to whether the classification is correct. Each classifier is trained to be better than random classification for every part of the training set.

There are different methods for determining a_k, and it is advisable for two classification problems:

$$a_k = \frac{1}{2} \ln\left(\frac{1 - e_k}{e_k}\right) \tag{8.14}$$

8.4.2 Multi-Class and Multi-Label Adaptive Boosting

In order to adapt to the multi-class problems involved in expression classification, the general two-category adaptive boosting algorithm needs to be extended to a ***multi-class multi-label*** algorithm, and the multi-class problems involved in expression classification are actually degenerated from multi-class multi-label, that is, the multi-category single-label problem, in which each sample can only belong to one category.

Given a sample space X and a label set Y, each sample x can be expressed as (x, y), where $x \in X$ and $y \in Y$, for the l-th category:

$$y[l] = \begin{cases} 1 & \text{if } l \in y \\ -1 & \text{if } l \notin y \end{cases} \tag{8.15}$$

Then the multi-class and multi-label adaptive boosting learning algorithm is:

1. Given sample set $S = \{x_1, y_1\}, \ldots, (x_m, y_m)\}$, and the number of iterations T of the final strong classifier. The probability distribution of the initial sample is $D_1(i, l) = 1/mk$, $i = 1, \ldots, m$, $l = 1, \ldots, k$, where m represents the total number of samples and k represents the number of categories.

2. The following operations are performed in the t-th iteration:

   a. Train a weak classifier with multiple outputs for each feature x_i;

   b. Under the weight distribution D_t, select an optimal classifier h_t from the weak classifiers of each feature, so that the classification error under D_t is the smallest, that is, the following formula attends the maximum value:

$$r_t = \sum_{i,l} D_t(i, l) y_i(l) h_t(x_i, l) \tag{8.16}$$

   c. Calculate the weight of the classifier according to the classification performance r_t:

$$w_t = \frac{1}{2} \ln\left(\frac{1 + r_i}{1 - r_i}\right) \tag{8.17}$$

   d. Update and normalize the distribution of samples:

$$D_{t+1}(i, l) = \frac{D_i(i, l) \exp(-w_t y_i[l] h_t(x_i, l))}{N_t} \tag{8.18}$$

where N_t is the normalization constant, so that D_{t+1} is a probability density distribution.

3. The final strong classifier is as follows:

$$H(x, l) = \text{sign}\left(\sum_{t=1}^{T} w_t h_t(x, l)\right) \tag{8.19}$$

In this result, x can belong to multiple categories at the same time; that is, multiple categories and multiple labels. Further, the definition of strong classifier is rewritten as the case of multi-class single-label:

$$H(x) = \arg\max_{l}\left(\sum_{t=1}^{T} w_t h_t(x, l)\right) \tag{8.20}$$

Expression classification can be performed with such a classifier.

8.4.3 Vector Input Multi-Class Output Adaptive Boosting Algorithm

In the face image analysis system, the input is generally a feature vector with several dimensions, which can be written as $x = [x_1, x_2, \ldots, x_n]$. For a high-dimensional input feature vector, either the entire vector x can be used as the input of the classifier, or each component x_i in the vector can be used as the input of the classifier. Take the feature based on the block histogram in the previous section as an example, each block feature is a vector, and the corresponding weak classifier is also a weak classifier for vector input; namely, $h(x, l)$. Since the vector feature contains more information than the 1-D component feature, more information is updated in each iteration, so a smaller number of iterations can converge to a lower error rate.

For the case where a single feature is a vector in the two-class adaptive boosting algorithm, a method to determine the decision surface is to determine the hyperplane between the positive sample average vector and the negative sample average vector weighted under the weight D_t (Howe 2003).

If V_P represents the weighted average vector of all positive samples, V_N represents the weighted average vector of all negative samples:

$$V_P = \sum_{i \in J^P} D(i) x_{k,i} \tag{8.21}$$

$$V_N = \sum_{i \in J^N} D(i) x_{k,i} \tag{8.22}$$

where $J^P = \{j | y_j = 1\}$ and $J^N = \{j | y_j = -1\}$ represent the positive and negative sample sets, respectively, D represents the weight distribution on the sample set in the aforementioned adaptive boosting classification process, and k represents the first k features, i represents the i-th sample. Then the decision hyperplane of the two classifications is determined by the sum vector $V_P + V_N$ of the vectors V_P and V_N. This decision face does not necessarily provide the best decision, but its performance can always meet the requirement that the correct rate of the weak classifier is greater than 50% (Howe 2003).

Find the normal vector $V_\perp$ perpendicular to the above hyperplane as follows:

$$V_\perp = V_P - \frac{V_N \bullet (V_P + V_N)}{\|V_P + V_N\|} \tag{8.23}$$

Then the output of the weak classifier can be given by the dot product value of the input feature vector x and the normal vector $V_\perp$:

$$h(x) = sign(x \bullet V_\perp - b) \tag{8.24}$$

This method can be extended to multi-class situations, that is, **vector input multi-class output adaptive boosting algorithm (MVBoost)**, so that the weak classifier can give multi-class output results in the case of vector input. Note that each input feature vector in the aforementioned algorithm represents the distribution of a histogram; that is, the vector

$$x = [x_1, x_2, \ldots, x_n] \tag{8.25}$$

and satisfies

$$\sum_i x_i = 1 \tag{8.26}$$

Then consider the vector

$$z = [\sqrt{x_1}, \sqrt{x_2}, \ldots, \sqrt{x_n}] \tag{8.27}$$

Then z is a unit vector that satisfies

$$\sqrt{\sum_i z_i^2} = 1 \tag{8.28}$$

If z is used as the feature vector, all types of feature vectors are distributed on the sphere of modulus 1 in the feature space, so the distance between two vectors can be measured by their inner angle. Calculate the weighted average vector of each class sample, take it as the weighted class center of the class. Therefore, the angle between the sample and the weighted average vector of each type of sample can be used as the criterion for judging that the sample belongs to a certain type.

Define the weighted average vector of each category as:

$$\begin{aligned}
V_1 &= \sum_{i \in J^1} D(i) z_{k,i} \\
V_2 &= \sum_{i \in J^2} D(i) z_{k,i} \\
&\vdots \\
V_L &= \sum_{i \in J^L} D(i) z_{k,i}
\end{aligned} \tag{8.29}$$

Then the intersection angle of each sample to various weighted average vectors is

$$\begin{aligned}
\cos \theta_1 &= z_{k,i} \bullet \frac{V_1}{\|V_1\|} \\
\cos \theta_2 &= z_{k,i} \bullet \frac{V_2}{\|V_2\|} \\
&\vdots \\
\cos \theta_L &= z_{k,i} \bullet \frac{V_L}{\|V_L\|}
\end{aligned} \tag{8.30}$$

Define the weak classifier as

$$h(x, l) = 2z_{k,i} \cdot \frac{V_l}{\|V_l\|} - 1 \tag{8.31}$$

Then this formula can make the output of $h(x, l)$ be between $[-1, 1]$.

Note that when the size of the block is 1×1, its histogram feature is $z \in \{[1, 0, 0, \ldots 0, 0], [0, 1, 0, \ldots 0, 0], \ldots [0, 0, 0, \ldots 0, 1]\}$, that is, the feature of the i-th dimension is 1, and the other dimensions are all zero. The weighted average vector of each histogram feature is equivalent to a statistical weighted distribution of 1×1 feature, then the output of the weak classifier is the same as Equation (8.31).

8.5 SOME RECENT DEVELOPMENTS AND FURTHER RESEARCH

In the following sections, some technical developments and promising research directions in the last few years are briefly overviewed.

8.5.1 Sparse Representation for Expression Features

There are many factors involved in expression classification and recognition, and the extracted expression features are often of high dimensionality. In response to this problem, many sparse representation methods have been proposed and used in expression classification and recognition.

8.5.1.1 Group Sparse Representation Classification

In expression classification and recognition, occlusion and the small number of expression samples will affect the effect of classification and recognition. Using **sparse representation classification (SRC)** to model occlusion expressions, it is feasible to find as few atoms as possible from an over-complete dictionary to linearly represent the object sample, so that it is robust to occlusion. The sparse representation technique can also alleviate the problem of model overfitting caused by small number of expression samples, as it is relatively less affected by the number of samples.

By extending the sparse representation to the **group sparse representation** obtained by the group dictionary, (Xie et al. 2021) proposed a **group sparse representation classification (GSRC)** method based on feature selection and dictionary optimization. In terms of feature selection, a criterion for feature selection is proposed to pre-screen various features, and to select complementary features with the same class-level sparsity pattern and different sparsity patterns within the class to build a dictionary. In terms of dictionary optimization, the **maximum scatter difference optimization learning (MSDOL)** is performed on the feature dictionary represented by group sparse, and the dictionary is optimized class-by-class under supervision to make it have undistorted reconstruction features. The maximum divergence difference criterion constraint is added to the sparse coefficient, so that the dictionaries of similar samples are closer, and the difference between the dictionaries of heterogeneous samples is greater, which improves the discriminating ability of the dictionary.

The flowchart of the GSRC method is shown in Figure 8.20. It includes the following module:

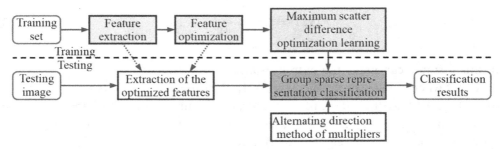

FIGURE 8.20   Flowchart of the GSRC method.

1. Feature extraction

The features to be extracted include texture features and geometric features. Based on the intensity information of image, the texture features can be extracted, which can be further classified as global texture features (based on the *gray-level co-occurrence matrix (GLCM)*) and local texture features (such as LBP and *local phase quantization (LPQ)*). The geometric features can be obtained by measuring the distance and morphing geometric forms, which can also be further classified as global geometric features (such as *active shape model (ASM)*) and local geometric features (such as *histogram of oriented gradient (HOG)*).

2. Feature selection

Directly using all the features in the feature set for classification by group sparse representation will increase the computational burden. Therefore, the extracted features can be formed into feature sets and test sample vectors. According to the criteria of having the same class-level sparsity pattern and different intra-class sparse patterns, the optimal features are selected. The most suitable feature combination that can provide complementary information is obtained.

3. Maximum scatter difference optimization learning

In order to improve the classification performance, the optimized features are further enhanced. Two considerations are to ensure that the dictionary can reconstruct features without distortion, and to make the dictionary more discriminating. Maximum scatter difference constraint is used to force the samples of homogeneous dictionaries closer and the differentiation between heterogeneous dictionaries greater.

4. Group sparse representation classification

In the testing phase, according to the optimally extracted features during training, the relevant features of the samples to be tested are extracted. Then, based on the group dictionary constructed by maximum scatter difference optimization learning, the joint coefficients can be obtained by using the ***alternating direction method of multipliers (ADMM)***. Finally, by using the minimum mean square error, the category of the sample to be tested is determined.

8.5.1.2 Sparse Subspace Transfer Learning

In practical applications, expressions used for training and testing are usually sampled from different scenes, with different resolutions, lighting, backgrounds, races, genders, etc., which will cause the source and target domain data to obey different distributions, resulting in a significant drop of recognition rate.

Many ***transfer learning*** methods have been proposed for cross-domain image classification. One method is the cross-domain facial expression recognition method based on sparse subspace transfer learning (Zhang et al. 2021). This method can be introduced with the help of Figure 8.21, in which three main modules are: Transfer feature representation, local discriminate learning, and label regression.

1. Transfer feature representation

A common subspace is learned by transferring feature representation learning while imposing sparse constraints on the reconstruction coefficient matrix. Considering the difference in the data distribution of the source domain and the target domain, the idea of subspace data reconstruction can be introduced to find an ideal projection matrix $P \in \mathbb{R}^{d \times c}$, which projects the emotional features of the source domain $X_s \in \mathbb{R}^{d \times ns}$ and the sentiment features of target domain $X_t \in \mathbb{R}^{d \times nt}$ onto a common subspace where the distributions of source data and target data are roughly the same. By learning a reconstructed coefficient matrix $Z \in \mathbb{R}^{ns \times nt}$, the data in the target domain can be linearly represented by the data in the source domain. This can be represented by

$$\min_{P,Z} \|P^{\mathrm{T}}X_t - P^{\mathrm{T}}X_s Z\|_{\mathrm{F}}^2 + k\|Z\|_{2,1} \tag{8.32}$$

where $\|\bullet\|_{\mathrm{F}}$ is F-norm, $\|\bullet\|_{2,1}$ is $L_{2,1}$ norm, k is a scale factor used to adjust the balance between the transfer feature representation and the sparse representation.

2. Local discriminate learning

A simple SVM classifier is used to obtain the initial pseudo-label Y_t for the target domain (originaly without label information), and then the pseudo-label is updated in the

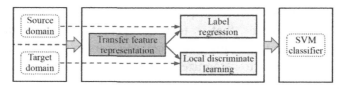

FIGURE 8.21 Schematic diagram of sparse subspace transfer learning.

iterative learning of the target subspace. The Laplacian graph regularization term is introduced to fully consider the local discriminative geometric structure of the source domain and target domain, and the source domain and target domain data are mapped with labels respectively, finally, the local discriminant learning term is expressed as the following form:

$$\min_{P} \left[\mathrm{tr}(P^{\mathrm{T}} X L X^{\mathrm{T}} P) \right] \tag{8.33}$$

where $\mathrm{tr}(\bullet)$ represents the trace of the matrix, $X = [X_s, X_t]$ and L is the Laplacian graph matrix.

3. Label regression

The label regression method is used to map the source domain samples with rich label information into a subspace guided by the source domain label information, thereby ensuring that the source domain data and target domain data have the same or similar distribution in the subspace:

$$\min_{P} \| Y_s - P^{\mathrm{T}} X_s \|_{\mathrm{F}}^2 \tag{8.34}$$

Combine the transfer feature representation term in Equation (8.32), the local discriminative learning term in Equation (8.33), and the label regression term in Equation (8.34) to get the final objective function:

$$\min_{P,Z} \| P^{\mathrm{T}} X_t - P^{\mathrm{T}} X_s Z \|_{\mathrm{F}}^2 + k \| Z \|_{2,1} + l\, \mathrm{tr}(P^{\mathrm{T}} X L X^{\mathrm{T}} P) + m \| Y_s - P^{\mathrm{T}} X_s \|_{\mathrm{F}}^2 \quad \mathrm{s.t.} \ \ P^{\mathrm{T}} P = I \tag{8.35}$$

8.5.2 Micro-Expression Recognition

Facial expressions can have various forms and be presented in many ways. Micro-expressions are subtle and unconscious facial expressions, and are often produced when people want to suppress their emotions. Micro-expressions belong to spontaneous expressions (Mostafa and Levine 2014). Micro-expressions usually occur within 1/25–1/2 s (which is different from normal facial expressions that usually last 0.5–4 s), and change uncontrollably during this period. In addition, the corresponding facial changes are limited to a few small regions on the face.

The occurrence of a person's micro-expressions is often unconscious, but it can better reflect his hidden true emotions, that is, to reflect people's true emotions. Existing experiments have shown that the ability to recognize a person's micro-expressions is positively correlated to the ability to recognize his lies. This indicates that micro-expressions can effectively help people identify lies.

Three types of mainstream methods for micro-expression recognition are (Zhang and He 2021): based on local binary pattern (LBP), based on optical flow, and based on convolutional neural networks (CNN).

8.5.2.1 Methods Based on Local Binary Pattern

In micro-expression recognition, the change of face texture indicates the micro-action on face. LBP can effectively capture the texture variation and has grayscale invariance and rotation invariance.

Basic LBP is defined for a 2-D image. Micro-expression recognition uses video, so some extensions are required. One suitable extension is local binary patterns from three orthogonal planes (LBP-TOP), in which three types of planes (*XY, XT, YT*) are considered (Zhao and Pietikäinen 2007). To take advantage of information other than appearance and motion information used by LBP-TOP, a spatiotemporal completed local quantization patterns (STCLQP) for facial micro-expression analysis is proposed (Huang, Zhao, et al. 2016). To fully use the discriminant information provided by integral projection for micro-expression recognition, a spatiotemporal local binary pattern with integral projection (STLBP-IP) is proposed (Huang et al. 2015).

To further consider the shape properties of face images and distinguish temporal and spatial micro-expression features, a spatiotemporal local binary pattern with improved integral projection (STLBP-IIP) is proposed (Huang, Wang, et al. 2016). These methods are listed in Table 8.4.

8.5.2.2 Methods Based on Optical Flow

Optical flow reflects the change of pixels in the video frame image in the time domain and the correlation and correspondence between adjacent frames, which can represent the motion of objects between adjacent frames. An assumption of using the optical flow method is that the object only has a small movement, that is, the change of time will not cause a sharp change of the gray value (appearance) of the object position. This is suitable for the micro-expressions recognition that has relatively small facial movements and is not easily detectable. In addition, the features extracted by optical flow techniques are mainly geometric features, so the feature dimension is not very high, which is more conducive to real-time recognition.

Micro-expressions are the result of facial muscle movements. From the perspective of determining facial muscle coordinates, a method for facial landmark localization using deep multi-task learning techniques is proposed (Li et al. 2016). This method computes histograms of oriented optical flow (HOOF) feature in region of interest (ROI). The result obtained by this method agrees with the principle of AU of FACS, which can be used to identify micro-expressions. This method has been further revised to consider the main direction of optical flow and to compensate the varying intensity by using enhance HOOF feature (Li et al. 2019). Another simple way to consider the main direction is to use the main direction average optical flow (MDMO) feature (a normalized statistical feature based on ROI) for micro-expression recognition (Liu et al. 2015). This method considers both local statistical motion information and spatial position, but its feature dimension is relatively small. These methods are listed in Table 8.5.

TABLE 8.4   Four typical methods based on LBP

Method	Working Principle	Applicable Scene
LBP-TOP	Given a video sequence, it can be viewed as three stacks of XY, XT, and YT planes along the temporal T-axis, spatial X-axis, and spatial Y-axis, respectively. Three histograms are derived from the three stacks of planes, respectively, and concatenated into one histogram as a dynamic video texture descriptor.	Natural directional light environment
STCLQP	It first extracts three interesting pieces of information including sign, magnitude, and direction components. Then, efficient vector quantization and codebook selection are performed on each component in the appearance and temporal domains to learn a compact and discriminative codebook for generalizing the classical mode types. Finally, based on the discriminative codebook, the spatiotemporal features of the sign, magnitude and direction components are extracted and connected into one feature using the subspace method.	More suitable for recognizing disgust and sadness expressions
STLBP-IP	It adopts the integral projection method based on differential images to obtain the horizontal and vertical projections and constructs a spatiotemporal local binary pattern based on integral projection to extract the appearance and motion features of the horizontal and vertical projections by using the local binary pattern operator	Un-occluded facial expressions
STLBPIIP	An improved integral projection method is proposed to maintain the shape attribute of micro expression. Then, the improved integral projection is combined with the local binary mode operator across time and space. Specifically, shape attributes are integrated into spatiotemporal texture features to extract new spatiotemporal features. Finally, a feature selection method based on Laplacian is used to improve the discrimination ability.	Un-occluded facial expressions

TABLE 8.5 Three typical methods based on optical flow

Method	Working Principle	Applicable Scene
ROI+HOOF	Firstly, the deep multitask convolution network is used to detect face landmarks, and these landmarks are used to segment face regions (ROI). Then, the optical flow features (HOOF) of micro expression are extracted from the facial region containing muscle changes by using the fusion convolution network. Finally, the feature information is refined by enhanced optical flow, and the features are classified and recognized by support vector machine classifier (SVM).	Places with stable lighting conditions
ROI+ Revised HOOF	Similar to ROI + hoof, but when calculating HOOF features, the maximum amplitude and direction of optical flow vector are used to represent the main part of muscle change in each region according to the proportion information of optical flow in the main direction.	Places with stable lighting conditions
MDMO	It applies a robust optical flow method to video clips containing micro-expressions, the facial regions is divided into regions of interest (ROIs) based on partial action units. An optical flow-driven approach is then used to align all frames of micro-expression video clips to reduce the effects of noise caused by head motion. Finally, a support vector machine classifier with MDMO features is used for micro-expression recognition.	Occasions that require fast speed but allow low precision

8.5.2.3 Methods Based on Convolutional Neural Networks

In recent years, convolutional neural networks (CNNs) have been used to extract the features required for micro-expression recognition, and the required recognition results can be obtained after analyzing the extracted features. Micro-expressions are characterized by relatively small facial movements. If a convolutional neural network is used, it is usually necessary to use other auxiliary methods to change the input of the network, or to change and optimize the network structure, so that the network can extract more useful features, thereby improving the recognition accuracy of micro-expressions (Zhang and Jia 2021).

Feature extraction with CNN for all frames of micro-expressions, from start to end, would be time-consuming. To solve this problem, a component for apex frame spotting (AFS) is added before the real micro-expression recognition (MER), in the (AFS+MER) system for micro-expressions recognition (Liong et al. 2018), as shown in Figure 8.22. The AFS component has five modules: (1) Using a landmark detector for annotating the facial landmark; (2) extracting the regions of interest (ROIs); (3) using LBP to obtain features of each frame; (4) computing the feature difference between the onset and the rest frames; (5) detecting the peak to find the apex frame. With AFS component, the system selects only the peak (apex) frame and the initial frame for using in the recognition, so the amount of computation would be well reduced.

A method based on the similar idea for selecting the apex frame using convolutional neural network (CNN), and combining *long-short-term memory (LSTM)* for micro-expression recognition is proposed (Kim et al. 2016). Taking advantage of the long-short-term memory module's ability to retain information from a long time ago for video detection, an *enriched long-term recurrent convolutional network (ELRCN)* is also proposed (Khor et al. 2018). The ELRCN model comprises a deep hierarchical spatial feature extractor and a temporal module that characterizes temporal dynamics. Two variants of the network are introduced: (1) ELRCN-SE: ELRCN with spatial dimension enrichment (SE), (2) ELRCN-TE: ELRCN with temporal dimension enrichment (TE). The above four methods are listed in Table 8.6.

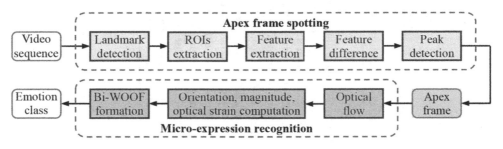

FIGURE 8.22 Framework of the micro-expression recognition system.

TABLE 8.6 Four typical methods based on optical flow

Method	Working Principle	Applicable Scene
AFS+MER	It uses temporal information to divide micro-expressions into different clips, then uses spatial information to detect intensity changes to extract peak video clips, and finally uses only peak (apex) frame and the initial frame to extract features for recognition.	Less computation
CNN+LSTM	It first uses a CNN to encode the spatial features of micro-expressions under different expression states (onset, start-to-apex, apex, apex-to-offset, and offset). The expression state is considered in the objective function to increase the separability of class expressions. Then, through feature learning, the learned spatial features with expression state constraints are transformed into temporal features for learning micro-expressions. LSTM recurrent neural network is then used to encode the temporal features of different states of micro-expressions.	Analyze post-acquisition images
ELRCN-SE	The network first encodes each micro-expression frame into a feature vector through a CNN module, and then makes predictions by passing the feature vector through LSTM. The spatial dimension enrichment is achieved by input channel stacking.	With a single database
ELRCN-TE	The network first encodes each micro-expression frame into a feature vector through a CNN module, and then makes predictions by passing the feature vector through LSTM. The temporal dimension enrichment is achieved by deep feature stacking.	With cross domain

REFERENCES

Abboud, B., and F. Davoine. 2004. Appearance factorization based facial expression recognition and synthesis. *Proceedings of the ICPR*, 4: 163–166.

Cheng, Z.D., Y.-J. Zhang, and X. Fan. 2009a. A generalized form of fisher linear discriminant function. *Pattern Recognition and Artificial Intelligence*, 22(2): 176–181.

Cheng, Z.D., Y.-J. Zhang, and X. Fan. 2009b. Criteria for 2DPCA superior to PCA in image feature extraction. *Chinese Journal of Engineering Mathematics*, 26(6): 951–961.

Cootes, T., et al. 1995. Active shape models-their training and applications. *Computer Vision and Image Understanding*, 61(1): 38–59.

Ekman, P., and W.V. Friesen. 1978. *Facial Action Coding System: A Technique for the Measurement of Facial Movement*. USA: Consulting Psychologists Press.

Ekundayo, O.S., and S. Viriri. 2021. Facial expression recognition: A review of trends and techniques. *IEEE Access*, 9: 136944–136972.

Friesen, W., and P. Ekman. 1984. *EMFACS-7: Emotional Facial Action Coding System*. Unpublished Manuscript, University of California at San Francisco.

Howe, N.R. 2003. A closer look at boosted image retrieval. *Proceedings of the CIVR*, 61–70.

Huang, X., S.J. Wang, X. Liu, et al. 2016. Spontaneous facial micro-expression recognition using discriminative spatiotemporal local binary pattern with an improved integral projection. *arXiv*: 1608.02255.

Huang, X., S.J. Wang, G. Zhao, et al. 2015. Facial micro-expression recognition using spatiotemporal local binary pattern with integral projection. *Proceedings of the IEEE International Conference on Computer Vision Workshops*, 1–9.

Huang, X., G. Zhao, X. Hong, et al. 2016. Spontaneous facial micro-expression analysis using spatiotemporal completed local quantized patterns. *Neurocomputing*, 175: 564–578.

Kanade, T., J.F. Cohn, and Y. Tian. 2000. Comprehensive database for facial expression analysis. *Proceedings of the Fourth International Conference of Face and Gesture Recognition*, 46–53.

Khor, H.Q., J. See, R.C.W. Phan, et al. 2018. Enriched longterm recurrent convolutional network for facial micro-expression recognition. *Proceedings of the 13th IEEE International Conference on Automatic Face & Gesture Recognition*, 667–674.

Kim, D.H., W.J. Baddar, and Y.M. Bo. 2016. Micro-expression recognition with expression-state constrained spatiotemporal feature representations. *Proceedings of the 24th ACM International Conference on Multimedia*, 382–386.

Li, Q., S. Zhan, and L. Xu. 2019. Facial micro-expression recognition based on the fusion of deep learning and enhanced optical flow. *Multimedia Tools and Applications*, 78(20): 29307–29322.

Li, X., J. Yu, S. Zhan. 2016. Spontaneous facial micro-expression detection based on deep learning. *IEEE 13th International Conference on Signal Processing (ICSP)*, 1130–1134.

Liong, S.T., J. See, K.S. Wong, et al. 2018. Less is more: Micro-expression recognition from video using apex frame. *Signal Processing: Image Communication*, 62: 82–92.

Liu, X.M., H.C. Tan, and Y.-J. Zhang. 2006. New research advances in facial expression recognition. *Journal of Image and Graphics*, 11(10): 1359–1368.

Liu, X.M., and Y.-J. Zhang. 2007. Facial expression recognition based on Gabor histogram feature and MVBoost. *Journal of Computer Research and Development*, 44(7): 1089–1096.

Liu, Y.J., J.K. Zhang, and W. Yan. 2015. A main directional mean optical flow feature for spontaneous micro-expression recognition. *IEEE Transactions on Affective Computing*, 7(4): 299–310.

Lyons, M., J. Budynek, and S. Akamastu. 1999. Automatic classification of single facial images. *IEEE-PAMI*, 21(12): 1357–1362.

Mehrabian, A. 1968. Communication without words. *Psychology Today*, 2: 53–56.

Mostafa M.K.A.E., and M.D. Levine. 2014. Fully automated recognition of spontaneous facial expressions in videos using random forest classifiers. *IEEE Transactions on Affective Computing*, 5(2): 141–154.

Pantic, M., and L. Rothkrantz. 2000a. Expert system for automatic analysis of facial expression. *Image and Vision Computing*, 18(11): 881–905.

Pantic, M., and L. Rothkrantz. 2000b. Automatic analysis of facial expressions: The state of the art. *IEEE Transactions on Pattern Analysis and Machine Intelligence*, 22(12): 1424–1445.

Pantic, M., and L. Rothkrantz. 2004. Facial action recognition for facial expression analysis from static face images. *IEEE Transactions on Systems, Man, and Cybernetics – Part B*, 34(3):1449–1461.

Rabi, G., and W. Si. 1997. Energy minimization for extracting mouth curves in a facial image. *Proceedings of the Intelligent Information Systems*, 381–385.

Tan, H.C., and Y.-J. Zhang. 2006a. An energy minimization process for extracting eye feature based on deformable template. *Lecture Notes in Computer Science*, 3852: 663–672.

Tan, H.C., and Y.-J. Zhang. 2006b. Detecting eye blink states by tracking iris and eyelids. *Pattern Recognition Letters*, 27(6): 667–675.

Tan, H.C., and Y.-J. Zhang. 2007a. Computing eigenface from edge images for face recognition based on Hausdorff distance. *Proceedings of the 4th ICIG*, 639–644.

Tan, H.C., and Y.-J. Zhang. 2007b. Person-independent facial expression recognition based on person-similarity weighted distance. *Journal of Electronics & Information Technology*, 29(2): 455–459.

Tan, H.C., and Y.-J. Zhang. 2009. An energy minimization process for extracting eye features based on deformable template. *Transactions of Beijing Institute of Technology*, 29(2): 128–132.

Tan, H.C., Y.-J. Zhang, and R. Li. 2003. Robust eye extraction using deformable template and feature tracking ability. *Proceedings of the 4th IEEE PCM*, 3: 1747–1751.

Tan, H.C., Y.-J. Zhang, and R. Li. 2007. Incorporating corner information for extraction of eye features. *Journal of Image and Graphics*, 12(7): 1224–1229.

Tan, H.C., Y.-J. Zhang, and Y.N. Zhao. 2009. Incorporating corner information for mouth feature extraction. *Journal of Beijing Jiaotong University*, 33(2): 30–33.

Tian, Y., T. Kanade, and J.F. Cohn. 2001. Recognizing action units for facial expression analysis. *IEEE Transactions on Pattern Analysis and Machine Intelligence*, 23(2): 97–115.

Tian, Y., T. Kanade, and J.F. Cohn. 2000. Dual-state parametric eye tracking. *Proceedings of the 4th International Conference on Automatic Face and Gesture Recognition*, 110–115.

Wei, W.M., F.X. Meng, Z. Cai, et al. 2021. Overview of facial expression recognition. *Journal of Shanghai University of Electric Power*, 37(6): 597–602.

Wen, Z., and T. Huang. 2003. Capturing subtle facial motions in 3d face tracking. *Proceedings of the ICCV*, 2: 1343–1350.

Xie, H.H., M. Li, Y. Wang, et al. 2021. Group sparse representation based on feature selection and dictionary optimization for expression recognition. *Pattern Recognition and Artificial Intelligence*, 34(5): 446–454.

Xu, J., and Y.-J. Zhang. 2011. Expression recognition based on variant sampling method and Gabor features. *Computer Engineering*, 37(18): 195–197.

Yan, Y., and Y.-J. Zhang. 2009. State-of-the-art on video-based face recognition. *Chinese Journal of Computers*, 32(5): 878–886.

Zhang, R., and N. He. 2021. A survey of micro-expression recognition methods. *Computer Engineering and Applications*, 57(1): 38–47.

Zhang, W.J., P. Song, D.L. Chen, et al. 2021. Cross-domain facial expression recognition based on sparse subspace transfer learning. *Journal of Data Acquisition and Processing*, 36(1): 113–121.

Zhang, X.S., and J.P. Jia. 2021. Micro-expression recognition algorithm based on 3D convolutional neural network and optical flow fields from neighboring frames of apex frame. *Pattern Recognition and Artificial Intelligence*, 34(5): 423–433.

Zhang, Y., and Q. Ji. 2005. Active and dynamic information fusion for facial expression understanding from image sequences. *IEEE Transactions on Pattern Analysis and Machine Intelligence*, 27(5):699–714.

Zhang, Y.-J. 2017. *Image Engineering, Vol.2: Image Analysis*. Germany: De Gruyter.

Zhang, Y.-J. (ed.). 2011. *Advances in Face Image Analysis: Techniques and Technologies*. USA: Medical Information Science Reference, IGI Global.

Zhao, G., and M. Pietikäinen. 2007. Dynamic texture recognition using local binary patterns with an application to facial expressions. *IEEE Transactions on Pattern Analysis and Machine Intelligence*, 29(6): 915–928.

Zhu, Y.F., F. Torre, and J.F. Cohn, et al. 2011. Dynamic cascades with bidirectional bootstrapping for action unit detection in spontaneous facial behavior. *IEEE Transactions on Affective Computing*, 2(2): 79–91.

Index